The Concept of the Foreign

The Concept of the Foreign

An Interdisciplinary Dialogue

Edited by Rebecca Saunders

LEXINGTON BOOKS
Lanham • Boulder • New York • Oxford

LEXINGTON BOOKS

Published in the United States of America
by Lexington Books
A Member of the Rowman & Littlefield Publishing Group
4720 Boston Way, Lanham, Maryland 20706

PO Box 317
Oxford
OX2 9RU, UK

British Library Cataloguing in Publication Information Available

Library of Congress Cataloging-in-Publication Data

The concept of the foreign : an interdisciplinary dialogue / edited by
    Rebecca Saunders.
        p. cm.
    Includes bibliographical references and index.
    ISBN 0-7391-0408-X (cloth : alk. paper) -- ISBN 0-7391-0409-8 (Pbk : alk. paper)
        1. Intercultural communication. 2. Strangers. 3. Philosophical
    anthropology. I. Saunders, Rebecca, 1961-

HM1211 .C657 2003
303.48'2—dc21   2002007291

Printed in the United States of America

⊖™ The paper used in this publication meets the minimum requirements of American
National Standard for Information Sciences—Permanence of Paper for Printed Library
Materials, ANSI/NISO Z39.48–1992.

This book is dedicated to those people—some close friends and some whom I will never see again—who have welcomed this foreigner into their cities and villages, their homes, their experiences, who have given me direction, explained what I didn't understand, made an effort to communicate with me, showed me how to see the world otherwise. You have been my greatest teachers.

Contents

Preface

Our title is perhaps already misleading, for it is questionable whether the *foreign* is a concept at all. What is more certain is that the notion of foreignness appears in a startlingly diverse number of roles: in history, as an insistent motif of historical records (many of which catalog contact between "foreigners") and as a figure for the past itself; in psychology, as a name for that which is repressed by, unknown to, or rejected from the self (indeed early psychologists were known as "alienists"); in philosophy, as a name for thought which cannot be epistemologically domesticated; in literature, both as a theme and as a formal characteristic of literariness; in everyday speech, as a name for the culturally different, for what, or who, does not belong. The foreign also plays a crucial role in current transdisciplinary debates on nationality, ethnicity, and culture; on gender and sexual difference; on relations of power and the regulation of deviance to elicit but a few. And if we can say with relative certainty that foreignness is in attendance at numerous theoretical gatherings, it is equally certain that when dressed up as a concept, foreignness bears dramatic social consequences: it may well govern where and in what manner one lives, why and how one dies. This fact became all the more pressingly evident in the final stages of editing this book, as the events of September 11 unleashed a scramble to identify foreignness as well as a torrent of fear, violence, and regulation directed toward foreigners.

But if the concept of the foreign is both widely invoked and consequential, it is by no means certain exactly what it means. Strutting around with all the impunity of self-evidence, it seems to scare off investigation, and, even when submitted to examination, proves distressingly ambiguous, intriguingly unstable, and possessed of a voracious semantic appetite. It is hopelessly entangled, as we shall see, with notions of belonging, distance, propriety, purity, presence, and mediation; truth and error; temporality and materiality—a web of entanglements that could be separated out and marshaled into a coherent argument only by the most ruthless metaphysical coercion. This violence we will attempt to resist. Hence, we cannot claim to proffer a *definition* of the foreign, to have packaged it into a useable, reproducible concept, nor to have cleaned up the ambiguous status it holds in numerous discourses, a status that is only partly the result of theoretical untidiness and as much a result of the obstreperous nature of foreignness itself. This book attempts, rather, to respect its complexity and inconsistencies, to bear witness to its discontents, to heed the significance of its perturbations. We will follow it, contemplatively, in its picaresque adventures, as it makes trouble, submits to discipline(s) but refuses to stay still; sometimes we will have to settle for indicating the direction it takes: we cannot keep up. We will let it make problems out of our finest solutions.

Among the finer of those solutions has been the theoretical discourse of the "other," under whose wing has transpired the majority of recent considerations of foreignness and which represents, in many instances, an admirable and compelling attempt to clean up its theoretical messiness. This term, which has been culled from critiques of the humanist subject and from a series of liberation movements, as well as from the work of Lacan, Levinas, Derrida, and numerous postcolonial and cultural theorists, has focused critical attention on identity categories such as "race," class, gender, ethnicity, sexual orientation, and physical ability; raised awareness of how certain groups are constructed as pathological or threatening to self-identity; and posed the crucial question of how to experience the other as other, rather than as a projection of the self. These have been exceedingly significant insights, and our work on the foreign is indebted to them. But the concept of the "other" remains primarily an academic one and is not, for the most part, deployed in everyday conversation. Indeed, to speak of the "other" is, in a sense, to decontextualize from everyday discourse in order to carry out our analysis in the clean, well-lit space of theory; it is to engage in that "cut out and turn over recipe" for theory so aptly laid out by de Certeau (see chapter 1). One sometimes finds the terms *foreign* and *other* used interchangeably in academic discourse; sometimes the term *foreign* appears only metaphorically or in scare quotes that indicate an author's ostensible refusal of its naiveté. But the foreign is a term alive and well, as much in the long corridors of history as in the overcrowded neighborhoods of daily discourse; it is one rarely analyzed and with more diverse and consequential nuances than often acknowledged in the shorthand of "otherness." Thus, while the two terms have much in common, they do not—cannot—have the same connotations or effects, for they belong to different discourse communities. This book thus wagers that there is something to be learned by muddling into places of theoretical imprecision, not so much to sanitize them as to investigate the ideological work that they do, to analyze what happens on the ground as much as in our own metaphors, to dialogue with whatever we "scared off" with our quotation marks.

Part I of this book draws together conceptions and images from the chapters which follow it and organizes them into another pattern; it maps out and analyzes the numerous and intriguing intersections between contributors' essays. In this endeavor, chapter 1 explores the instability of the concept of the foreign: its relative and negative nature, its ability to be simultaneously alluring and threatening, its variance in both degree and kind, its recidivistic metaphoricity, and its uncanny propensity for inhabiting its antonyms—such as nations, homes, and selves. It also examines how this instability is disciplined by laws, by context, and by academic disciplines and points to the dramatic social consequences of such discipline(s). Chapter 2 investigates how foreignness is constructed through notions of belonging and distance, its entanglement with family and kinship metaphors, with the nuances of *origin*, and with notions of (in)dependence. Chapter 3 charts both the ways in which foreigners are discursively imbricated with pathologized groups (the insane, the poor, the criminal) and the extent to which foreignness functions as an epistemological status—characterized, for example, by metaphysical impurity, unconsciousness, irrelevance, and error. Chapter 4 suggests that the foreign may be conceived as a particular relation to both temporal and material presence: as, for example, a fundamentally mediated or translated presence; as belated—external to modernity and the reach of globalization; or as especially encumbered with the concerns of the materially present.

Each essay in part II is authored by a scholar from a different discipline and investigates how that author's discipline engages and defines, implicitly or explicitly, the concept of the foreign.

In their chapter entitled "The Exile of Anthropology" Peter Redfield and Silvia Tomášková compare the tradition of ethnographic fieldwork (which incorporates foreignness into the essence of anthropology) with the condition of exile. Working with both anthropological texts and testimonies of Eastern European exiles, Redfield and Tomášková argue that while these two varieties of foreignness represent inverted patterns of experience—the ethnographer serving as a voluntary exile, the exile as an involuntary anthropologist—they both establish authority through *distance*: as the ethnographer is culturally distant, so too is the exile physically distant, from the object of his or her concern. A consequence of this construction of authority through distance is, they contend, a trivialization of the immediate and the everyday.

Women's Studies Scholar Margot Badran investigates gender as a species of foreignness in the context of modern Egypt in "Foreign Bodies: Engendering Them and Us." She explores linguistic markers of foreignness in Arabic, examines the role of Islam in mediating and constructing foreignness, and demonstrates the crucial role played by feminisms in reconceiving notions of nationalism, citizenship, and (thereby) foreignness. Drawing on her own fascinating experience as a woman who, in Egypt, holds an ambiguous status between foreigner and native, she also investigates the sometimes remarkable distance—the foreignness—between who one perceives oneself to be and how one is perceived by others.

My own chapter, "Expedition into the Zone of Error: Of Literal and Literary Foreignness and J. M. Coetzee's *Waiting for the Barbarians*" charts the relation between the "literary" foreignness postulated by formalist studies of literature (from the *defamiliarization* of Russian formalism to the *différance* of deconstruction), and the "literal" foreignness considered by, for example, postcolonial and cultural studies. I propose a description of the foreign as a *zone of error* and, through a comparative reading of Coetzee's novel and a series of contextual documents—including the 1978 Amnesty International *Report on Torture* in South Africa, the transcript of the inquest into the death of Stephen Biko, and a series of apartheid laws—argue for a significant and consequential homology between literary and literal foreignness.

Philosopher Michael Zimmerman explores the philosophical implications of reported encounters with extraterrestial life forms in his chapter, "Encountering Alien Otherness." This chapter calls into question the Western anthropocentrism which advocates a distinction between humankind and all other forms of life. Zimmerman investigates why the phenomenon known as "alien abduction" has been exiled from serious philosophical discussion and assesses the devastating effects of this paradigm-altering possibility on anthropocentric humanism. He argues that this phenomenon can be adequately understood neither by subjective/psychological nor by objective/physical explanations and that it requires conception of new ontological categories.

Psychologist Coco Owen, writing on "Xenotropism: Expatriatism in Theories of Depth Psychology and Artistic Vocation" demonstrates that for psychology, the foreign represents the subversive and pathological in psychic and cultural life. This chapter maps the figure of the foreign in depth psychology and describes artists as the foreign of their families and their nations, frightening the collective with their unimaginables. Owen further analyzes the role of the geographically foreign in the development of the artist's vocation; reading the testimony of writers in the "Writers at Work" series in the *Paris Review*, she investigates why artists often confirm their sense of self and their artistic vocation by xenotropism, a turn to the foreign.

In the chapter entitled "War to the Death: Nativism and Independence in Latin America," Historian John Charles Chasteen examines the role of foreignness in the rise of Latin American nationalisms and in the sweeping transformation of collective identities it entailed. Analyzing the struggle of American born Creoles to wrest political control from Spain and Portugal, Chasteen demonstrates that revolutionary rhetoric relied on a vituperation of foreigners at the same time that it constructed very diverse local populations into a homogenous "people." Drawing on newspapers, oaths, and public spectacles, this chapter elaborates the benefits that nativist leaders drew from their construction of, and confrontation with, foreign others.

Izumi Sakamoto, in her essay "Changing Images and Similar Dynamics: Historical Patterning of Foreignness in the Social Work Profession," examines the crucial role that foreignness has played in the development of social work in the United States. She assesses how foreignness has traditionally been viewed in the discipline and how that view is undergoing reassessment and contends that, although "multicultural social work" and "culturally competent practice" are increasingly integrated into mainstream disciplinary discourse, substantial residues remain of the discipline's historic image of foreigners. She demonstrates and contests these dynamics in a contemporary case study of Japanese immigrant women in America.

Although this volume has the appearance of being divided into discrete disciplines whose tidy edges are marked by chapter breaks, it will be immediately clear that the unruly crew of scholars participating in this project refuses to stay within disciplinary boundaries. This intractability results, in part, from our subject itself, because foreignness lurks *between* disciplines as often as it makes appearances in them: it loves to loiter in the shade of those institutionally uncharted spaces and, indeed, becomes increasingly *mise en évidence* as disciplinary borders dematerialize. If the essays in this book promptly expose as duplicitous our titular presumptions that the foreign is a *concept* and that distinct disciplines are maintainable, the remaining part of our title we stand by in good faith: this book is a *dialogue*. It began as a dialogue (in the dramatic, decaying indecorousness of the Columns Hotel in New Orleans, to be exact); it grew and got more complicated; we called out to others to join in, talk back. And if we have decided to translate this dialogue on the foreign into book form—accepting the ironies of standardizing English, of insisting on words the computer does not recognize, of referring to the self in the third person—it remains of the nature of an apostrophe, an attempt to initiate discussion: a dialogue that, we hope, will continue.

Rebecca Saunders

Acknowledgments

My primary debts in constructing this volume are due to its contributors, who agreed to embark on an unconventional and exploratory venture, none of us knowing quite where we might arrive. I am also grateful to Serena Leigh, Martin Hayward, and Lexington Books for wagering on a book that crosses multiple disciplinary borders and attempts to take seriously often disparaged kinds of evidentiary material, as well as some institutionally marginalized theoretical discourses. Several contributors, including Coco Owen and Michael Zimmerman, have also been readers, as have Vaheed Ramazani and Jen Travis. I am grateful to each of them for their insightful comments. My work in this volume has been further enriched by numerous dialogues, particularly at the conferences of the International Association for Philosophy and Literature (IAPL), and the American and International Comparative Literature Associations (ACLA and ICLA). It has been shaped by continuous conversation with Vaheed, whose profoundly meticulous thought is happily inextricable from my own. I have also been supported by several extraordinary research and production assistants at different stages of this project: Jason Hamel, Matt Felumlee, Betsy Koski, Greg Howard, and John Woolsey, each of whom I thank warmly. Much of the index is the handiwork of John Woolsey. For material support, I thank Illinois State University for a Summer Research Grant. Chapter 7 of this book appeared in somewhat different form in *Cultural Critique* 47 (Winter 2001) under the title "The Agony and the Allegory: The Concept of the Foreign, the Language of Apartheid, and the Fiction of J. M. Coetzee." I am grateful to the University of Minnesota Press for the right to reprint.

Part I

Theoretical Dialogue

Chapter One

Instability and Discipline(s)

However widespread and consequential, the concept of the foreign is perversely difficult to define. There are, as we shall see, reasons for this: its relativity, its equivocal valuation, the heterogeneity of the terms that constitute it, its recidivistic metaphoricity. Derived from a Latin term meaning "outside" (*foras*), the word *foreign* designates a quality or an entity conceived relatively: the foreign is always relative to the inside, the domestic, the familiar, a boundary. No entity is inherently foreign; s/he who is a foreigner in one place is at home in another; as the familiar is altered or a boundary redrawn, so too is the character of the foreign: it is a linguistic and conceptual container with infinitely variable contents. Symptomatic of the relative nature of the foreign is the necessity of defining the foreign negatively, a symptom exhibited by virtually any dictionary: to be foreign is *not* belonging to a group, *not* speaking a given language, *not* having the same customs; it is to be *un*familiar, *un*canny, *un*natural, *un*authorized, *in*comprehensible, *in*appropriate, *im*proper. As much the detritus of conceptualizing as a concept proper, foreignness must thus, at times, be approached *à rebours* (indeed one may be called on to *comprendre à rebours*: to misunderstand, engage in an anti-understanding).

This principle of negative relativity is borne out by numerous details in the essays which follow. Badran, for example, exploring how the foreign is gendered in Egypt and in Islam, demonstrates the way in which both foreigners and women are conceived as the *unnatural*. Similarly, Saunders lays out the way in which, in the context of South African apartheid, foreignness was discursively delineated in relation to the *proprius* or *proper*—in all the density of that overdetermined root—as the lack of identity, propriety, purity, literality, property.[1] Chasteen, in his chapter on Latin American nationalisms, demonstrates the way in which the parent states of Spain and Portugal became perceived as foreign powers through the nativist formula "America for the Americans"—a conceptual remapping that delineated domesticity in terms of native birth. If this domesticity (and the nations it prefigured) was composed of a motley assemblage of ethnicities, languages, and cultures, it was grounded in a shared negative relation: anti-Spanish and anti-Portuguese sentiment.

Already adumbrated by the conceptual negativity we have marked, already evident in our examples, is the hierarchical nature of such relations, the inability of oppositional terms to remain neutral, their tendency to condense into binaries, to enable the very power relations which condition them. This structure is perhaps most evident in Zimmerman's study of the philosophical import of reported encounters with extraterrestrial beings. The distinction between humanity and other life forms, he argues, operates as an assumption of human superiority over other life: the Enlightenment conception that man alone is endowed with reason and moral sensibility, interpreted as a right to domination, has, hence, resulted in violence against plants, animals, and entire ecosystems. What happens, Zimmerman asks, to anthropocentric humanism, which locates meaning, purpose, and value in humankind alone, if human beings find themselves bound by an opposition in which they are not at "the top of the cosmic heap?" (156). A more quiescent manifestation of this rule of hierarchy emerges in Owen's investigation of the way in which evocations of the foreign have served in psychological discourse to "define pathology as the not-us we say it is" (180). Owen's succinct formulation alerts us to the unspoken authorization of voice that subtends the delineation of the foreign: Who is the "we" that speaks in this phrase? By what right, or on what authority, does this "we" define the foreign? The assumption of that authority is itself a hierarchizing gesture; the very act of distinguishing places one on an upper tier in which the "us" is not only distinct from the foreign, but the bearer of authority, of the right to speak, of the ability to produce the distinction. The autobiographical inclusions in Badran's essay, which narrate her increasing and discomfiting awareness that the term *foreign* applied to herself, illustrate how this principle of authorization may be experienced.

A further recognition of the hierarchical structure that inheres in the concept of the foreign is embedded in Sakomoto's study of the foundations of social work in America, where the unspoken authority to define the foreign was assumed by the wealthy and educated, by industrialists and educators, reformers with leisure time, and the "friendly visitors" of social work whose assistance to foreigners necessitated, of course, first identifying them. This hierarchical structure is reiterated in the remarkable coincidence in nineteenth-century America of foreignness with other forms of social disempowerment: with poverty, lack of education, exclusion from socially cohesive communities. Another way of articulating this law of hierarchization would be to say that the foreigner and the national are produced by a distinction that inevitably renders one side of that distinction more distinguished—of greater value—than the other. The "undistinguished" side of that distinction is, further, customarily characterized by *indistinction*—that is, by the disorder, the confusion of categories, and the ambiguity of thought that constitute metaphysical impurity; that characterize the irrational, the unconscious, the barbarian, and the infantile; and that render one incapable of producing distinction.[2]

If the relative nature of foreignness means that it is defined negatively and thereby embedded in a hierarchy, it also means that the presence of the foreign simultaneously *thematizes* and *interrogates* the familiar, drags crepuscular familiarities into daylight and exposes them to inspection.

While that familiarity and that foreignness can and do take innumerable forms, the production of the foreign in the modern world is, as Chasteen points out, largely a result of nationalism; the most common meaning of the foreign is that conceived in opposition to state citizenship: a foreigner is a noncitizen. If the nation is clearly one of the most authoritative formulators of the meaning of foreignness, frenetically filling the category with contents, it also finds itself at once brought to consciousness and unsettled by the very entity it has had a hand in formulating. This double relation appears in Sakamoto's description of the era when social work emerged as a discipline: a moment when, on the one hand, social reform programs implied and necessitated a theorization of the nation as social unit and when, on the other hand, hostility towards immigrants was mounting. The two phenomena that characterize this moment are, to be sure, not unrelated; one bears the inverted imprint of the other.

But what is a nation? Such is the inescapable question posed by foreignness. If for a heady instant we allow ourselves a definition—a nation is a modern political principle of self-determination that holds that the state and the "people" (or "*ethnos*") should be coterminous—we are, despite the impressive theoretical genealogy of such a definition, immediately beset by problems. What, for example, does self-determination entail? Does it imply independence—and in what sense? How is such a volition identified? How are the people or *ethnos* delimited? In what manner, or to what degree, can it integrate diversity? How does one distinguish between insignificant heterogeneity and the foreign? And how are the phenomena of states and peoples to be translated into the calculable spatiality of the "co-terminous"? (It is also evident how, under the reign of such a definition, the naturalization of ethnic distinctions might cast the foreign itself as the unnatural—a phenomenon we have already encountered in Badran's work— or how rendering separation of ethnic groups desirable demands both production of a coherent ethnic identity and a protective process of purification. These topoi of the [un]natural, of *identity*, and of [im]purity will never be far from the concept of the foreign.)

Our provisional definition of the nation is, however, by no means the only one. The nation can be conceived in numerous ways—as, for example, contractual, voluntarist, organic, political, social, cultural, or economic—and each of these conceptions alters *who* the foreigner is, as well as the meaning of foreignness itself.[3] The specific aspect of the nation challenged by foreignness shifts along parallel lines: are those foreigners threatening the economy? The culture? The body politic? Such theoretical delineations bear significant social effects: while membership in a nation may secure rights for citizens, it also thereby limits to whom those rights are available.[4] In effect, they narrow the category of humanity—which Zimmerman argues is already itself too narrow—to that of the citizen or national.

Yet nations are not the only entities against which foreignness is defined, nor the only entities called into question by it. As Badran demonstrates, in the Middle East, foreignness is conceived as much in terms of religion as of ethnicity. Indeed, long before the categories of indigenous and foreign devised by modern states, Islam proffered the concept of the *umma*, the egalitarian community of believers which binds members, regardless of ethnicity or birthplace, by faith. If the *umma* has been politically appropriated as a model for nation states, pan-Arabism, and the United Nations (the Arabic term for which is *Ummum al-Muttahida* [community of nations]), it has also engendered its own array of foreigners, expressed, for example, in the evaluatively neutral term *ghair muslim/a* (non-Muslim) or the much more pejorative term *kafir/a* (unbeliever, infidel).

The foreign, moreover, can be much more personal. Such is the case with the foreignness that Julia Kristeva has elaborated psychoanalytically under the name of the *abject*.[5] Historically, such also was the case, Zimmerman reminds us, when native others were discovered in the "New World,"—a narcissistic trauma that shook not only religion, secular humanism, and political organization, but also personal identity. Indeed, as Badran relates, it is ultimately deceptive to believe that one can isolate the foreign as an object of knowledge; for it participates both conceptually and phenomenally in personal experience. Owen tenders us another perspective on the intimate reaches of foreignness, describing a process of identity formation that *turns to* the foreign. *Xenotropism*, she argues—a turn to the foreign that facilitates artistic development—is a very personal, subjective relation; not just a matter of nation states.[6]

If the relativity of foreignness appears irreducible—its very substance and not a mere attribute—Owen, following James Hillman, leads us to recognize that this relativity is not of necessity synonymous with opposition. Hillman, she writes, no longer "opposes the foreign to something"; rather, it is seen "as a perspective" (192): a refiguring that maintains the structure of relation in the concept of the foreign, but casts that relation as metonymic, as a relation of part to whole; and, imbedding foreignness in an (epistemologically familiar) metaphorics of space and sight, delivers it over to the fallibility of human senses, where panoptic pretensions are merely myopic. The binary and oppositional version of foreignness Hillman associates with the figure of Hercules, the heroic ego, for whom "it is a wrestle and a sweat to move in and out, to entertain differing alternatives, languages, customs—psychic realities and physical realities—at the same time" (cited in Owen, 192). The foreign in this sense "was always an artifact created by over-identification with the ego . . . what the ego construed as other when its own biases and perspectives were unexamined," and is a far cry from the concept of foreignness Hillman organizes around the figure of Hermes who, he writes: "inhabits the borderlines; his herms are erected there, and he makes possible an easy commerce between the familiar and the alien" (cited in Owen, 192). Conceiving the border as a country of its own, Hillman's schema enables us to think of the thematization and interrogation of the familiar we have outlined above less as a threatening indictment than as an instructive questioning; and it exposes as willful unknowing (an over-identification with the ego attendant on unexamined biases) what Redfield and Tomášková call "addiction [to] pure identity"(84).[7] Thus, if we follow Hillman, an unknowing that passes for the familiar functions as the ground of foreignness conceived as binary opposition; destabilized by its relativity, possessing no positive, substantial contents of its own, the concept of the foreign is also unsettled by the fact that unexamination logically precedes and conditions the oppositions through which it is routinely constituted.

If shifty relations render the concept of the foreign unstable, so too does the fact that foreignness may be either positively or negatively marked, may evoke, on the one hand, the exotic, artistic, or liberatory, or, on the other hand, the strange, improper, or threatening.[8] This evaluative equivocation appears in the "fear of, and attraction to, otherness" that characterizes the alien abduction phenomenon as described by Zimmerman, as well as in abductees' sense of being both hated and loved. It surfaces in the "Iberian experience" Chasteen studies "in which things foreign . . . excited both ridicule and imitation" (224) and in the situation of the foreign social worker who, Sakamoto notes, is sometimes viewed as a benign source of knowledge, sometimes as a detestable colonizer. And it resonates in Redfield's and Tomášková's depiction of the "tragic heroism of the vagabond of conscience" (73)—the exiled literati of Eastern Europe—a figure at once positive and negative, noble and debased, Orestes and Estragon.

This sense of foreignness as both threatening and alluring is rooted, it might be demonstrated, in a process of decontextualization, that is, of extracting objects, practices, or discourses from both material circumstances and cause/effect relationships. Foreigners, hence, appear irrational or improper because their acts and words are effects without cause, a principle evinced in the South African textbooks discussed by Saunders which, disregarding historical and material exigencies, as well as the motivations and decision-making processes of blacks, portray their actions as simply strange and incomprehensible. Operating under the same logic, the inverse trajectory of this process makes foreignness palatable, even exotic, by moving it outside (*exotikos*) of context, making of it a tastefully chosen accessory: the foreign term deployed as a sign of importance that Owen marks, or the affectation of foreign customs that, in Spanish, travels under the name *extranjerismo* (see Chasteen). It is this decontextualizing procedure, which, as Edward Said has demonstrated at length, subtends the Orient of

European invention, that "place of romance, exotic beings, haunting memories, and landscapes"[9] that necessarily dismisses consideration of the actual peoples living there. An equally important discussion of such decontextualization is James Clifford's critique of the 1984 Muesum of Modern Art (MOMA) exhibition, "Primitivism in Twentieth Century Art: Affinity of the Tribal and the Modern." He writes:

> At MOMA treating tribal objects as art means excluding the original cultural context. Consideration of context we are firmly told at the exhibition's entrance, is the business of anthropologists. Cultural background is not essential to correct aesthetic appreciation and analysis. . . . Indeed an ignorance of cultural context seems almost a precondition for artistic appreciation.[10]

We will have occasion to return to this issue of context below.

At least three conditions lend foreignness what we have called its evaluative equivocation. First, the contents of the *foreign* are, as we have seen, variable: if we can fill the category with tantalizing harems, we can also fill it with terrorists. Second, even when the category's content remains the same, it is subject to revaluation; the same entity may be reassessed in terms of political, social, economic, or psychic usefulness. This is the process Chasteen traces in which Spain and Portugal, once viewed as benign authorities and the very touchstone of political authenticity, became increasingly perceived as threatening, maleficent, the provocants of a "war to the death." It is also the principle at work in Redfield's and Tomášková's perception that the culture shock which is "purgatory for the exile [is] insight for the ethnographer" (77). Third, the very extraordinariness of the foreign, and particularly its hyperbolic reaches of exoticism and threat, partake of the structure of the sublime: beauty and terror become in it inseparable, two facets of the same intensity.

The more we expose ourselves to foreignness, the more evident it becomes that if the relativity and negativity of the foreign make it susceptible to a rigid "not-structure" like that dreamt of by apartheid (see Saunders), its equivocal valuation attests to the fact that matters are, outside the cleanly habitat of such systems, much more complex. The essays in this volume testify, moreover, to multiple shades and varieties of foreignness which we might, as a beginning gesture, organize in terms of *degree* and *kind*:

Degree. Foreignness varies in value, in part, because it varies in degree. Psychological discourse, for example, distinguishes (implicitly when not explicitly) between tolerable deviance (artists' eccentricities) and intolerable deviance (perversity). Thus "the image of the crazy artist has been fruitful for analysis" because perceived as the "familiar foreign" rather than the utterly barbaric other (Owen, 180). Along similar lines, Sakamoto marks the functional distinction between the "similar other" and the "dissimilar other" that, in the history of social work, determined who was or was not eligible for social services. Opportunities to alter one's degree of foreignness have also long presented themselves: the

Danaïdes in Argos, who will be granted asylum on the condition that they become suppliants, or the immigrants to America who will receive assistance in the form of Americanization programs (see Sakamoto).[11]

Kind. Redfield and Tomášková alert us to the differences in value between the exile—for whom key ingredients are a sense of homeland and of political significance, and who "must both define identity in terms of place, and be elite enough to have one's individual displacement be recognized, ordered, and enforced" (73)—and the common refugee, adventurous expatriate, or re-rooted émigré. The exile, unlike the refugee for example, "flees not simply to save a humble body, but also an exalted soul" (74).[12] Thus, while the most common colloquial and literal invocations of foreignness doubtless refer to ethnicity, a host of other attributes (a short list of which would include class, gender, age, sexual orientation, physical capacity, religion, "race," and profession) may be either the determinative ground of foreignness itself or may intensify or mitigate the *value* of foreignness. Such identity markers (themselves subject to much of the instability characteristic of the foreign) perform incessant and delicate titrations measuring exoticism and threat.[13]

Numerous alleys that open onto valuation are not, however, mapped by such a simple schema of degree and kind and, though confining ourselves to the barest sketch, we should acknowledge several. One we might call the *location of foreignness*. As Zimmerman points out, the foreigners one encounters when traveling present a different and more digestible degree of foreignness than those that immigrate to one's own country and, as Sakamoto demonstrates, being a "foreign" social worker can designate either one who goes to a less industrialized country and possesses great social capital or one who is foreign within a more industrialized country and thus has less social capital. In short, much depends on who is doing the moving (or who possesses the power of mobility), to whom a territory is perceived to belong, the relative economic statures of the places from which one comes and to which one goes, and the geographical and cultural distance between the two. Another such avenue we might call the *temporality of foreignness*: for the length of time one stays in a place also determines the degree, even the kind, of one's foreignness, though the relationships are by no means easily calculable. As Badran notes, a foreigner who has come to stay, despite the fact s/he becomes less exotic and less strange, poses a greater threat than the mere tourist. Finally, the equivocal valuation of foreignness is also abetted by its remarkable *semantic fluidity*; for the term *foreign* may refer to an experience, a state, an attribute, a concept, a metaphysical status, or a species. More often than not, it refers to some theoretically unholy mixture of such meanings. Hence, the degree to which one or another such meaning is privileged (e.g., foreignness is an attribute, foreignness is a state), combined with the value assigned to each of those conceptions (e.g., experiences bear more weight than concepts), will perform yet another delicate calibration of value.

If the character of the foreign is rendered unstable by the migrations and transformations of peoples, boundaries, and values, it is equally destabilized by the unsoundness of the opposition that produces it. For the entities in opposition to which foreignness is constituted—the self, the nation, the domestic, the familiar—are inevitably haunted by foreignness themselves: a principle developed psychoanalytically by Freud's theories of the unconscious, elaborated philosophically by Heidegger's *"unheimlichkeit* [uncanniness]"—*Dasein's* character as primordially "not-at-home" in the world—and evoked poetically by Rimbaud's *"Je est un autre* [I is an other]."[14] Foreignness, on this view, is precisely what is repressed in identity, in the proper, in signification: what is misrecognized as other.

We have already noted that among the most common meanings of the foreign is that conceived in opposition to the nation. Yet only a fraction of nations in the modern world possess even remotely homogenous populations, and in only half is there a single ethnic group that comprises 75 percent of the population.[15] Spanish colonizers recognized as much when they spoke of "the Spains," while native-born American nationalists, in their drive to transform Spain and Portugal into foreign powers, were obliged to disregard the fact that their own national populations were comprised of a staggeringly complex intermixture of indigenous peoples, natives of European descent, colonizers, *mestizos,* and enslaved Africans of the most diverse ethnic backgrounds (see Chasteen). Indeed, attempts to obliterate the heterogeneity of nations would comprise a by no means insignificant portion of any catalog of the atrocities of modernity.

A similar heterogeneity shadows personal identity. Badran's recognition that others can term one *foreign* is also the recognition that there exist components of one's identity over which one does not have control. Images of the foreign, as Owen shows, are deployed in psychology to figure the apparently contradictory principle that "we are simultaneously ourselves and not ourselves" (179), that what is foreign to us may *be* us, that becoming foreign may be becoming more truly the self.

Owen asks us to expand this recognition by examining another term in opposition to which foreignness is constituted: *home.* For if home is semantically coded as benign, this tenacious connotation (like those that trail after most modes of the familiar and the known) is both theoretically and existentially untenable. As Owen demonstrates, it is the domestic which, for many artists, is disenabling, which disrupts "creative adaptation," to borrow D. W. Winnicott's term; and many such artists find foreign places more nurturing than home. Imbedded in the reflexively benign image of home is, moreover, a double and potentially deleterious assumption: first, that what is familiar to one's culture is what is most familiar to the self. Creating such felicitous adequation of self and society may require a "false adaptation"—becoming foreign to one's sense of self in order to live comfortably within one's culture. Second, the benign image of home harbors the closely related assumption that it is both healthy and normal to conform to the social requirements of one's birthplace. From the perspective Owen offers us, this conformity may itself be pathological.[16] And if we were to transplant this conformity from theory into (for example) the social soil of South

African apartheid discussed by Saunders, it would be exposed, in addition, as ethically indefensible.

The entities that, through opposition, produce foreignness are, then, themselves fraught with foreignness both phenomenal and semantic. And if this heterogeneity contributes to the instability of the concept of the foreign, so too does the fact that the term is commonly used both literally and metaphorically. As we have already recognized, it functions in history both as a name for the noncitizen and as a metaphor for the past; in psychology, to designate both the culturally different and "the subversive in psychic and cultural life" (Owen, 180); in philosophy and literature, both as a term for those who speak a different language and as an image for the irrational, unrelated, errant, or strange. The overlapping images of this volume's contributors further evince this double duty: the metaphor of outer space employed by Owen's psychologists is the literality of Zimmerman's abductees; the *conquistadores* who function analogically for Zimmerman are the literal forebears of Chasteen's Latin American nationalists; the political process of estrangement and alienation that Chasteen traces functions, for Saunders, as a figure for literariness. It is indeed difficult, as Saunders argues, to determine at what point foreignness becomes metaphorical for "the originary denotation of words such as French *étranger*, Spanish *extranjero*, German *fremd*, and Greek ξένος is merely *strange* or *odd*."[17] In all these cases, "what we currently take to be the 'literal' or 'proper' meaning of the foreign—one who is from another country, one who is not a native or a citizen—is already a figurative meaning" (Saunders, 117). Dealing with "real" foreigners will always mean dealing, consciously or unconsciously, with the metaphors that produce them.

The concept of the foreign is thus rendered unstable by its relativity, by its equivocal valuation, by the heterogeneity of the terms that, through opposition, constitute it, and by an unctuous metaphoricity. The degree to which the foreign is conceived as instability is evinced in Sakamoto's discussion of the "settlement houses" offering services to immigrants—the precursors of social work in America that assumed, by their very name, that to be foreign is to be *unsettled*, an assumption that is also no doubt a projection of American apprehensions of foreigners as *unsettling*.

Yet the conceptual instability of foreignness would seem to be effectively obviated by the barbed wire that unmistakably demarcates the border or the green card that clearly designates who has rights and who does not. This stabilized meaning of the foreign has, in current usage, become primary; "It is precisely with respect to laws that foreigners *exist*," writes Kristeva.[18] This legal definition, in which *foreigner* means one who is not a citizen, "allows one to settle by means of laws the prickly passions aroused by the intrusion of the *other* in the homogeneity of a family or a group"; it renders "natural" and thus indisputable the idea that others do not have the same rights that I do (or, conversely, that I am not entitled to the rights that others are).[19] Not all of the "laws" by which foreignness and foreigners are defined and regulated, however, are of the sort formally inscribed by governments and judiciary systems; they range from the

severest of legalities to the most subtle of social sanctions: a glance askance, a
tone of voice, what Badran calls "invisible electric fences" (92). For however conceptually vague, foreignness is nonetheless both symbolically sharp and socially
consequential.

Disciplining the semantic profligacy of foreignness—a process that Saunders elaborates as the stabilization of signs by an allegorical code—accomplishes
at least three tasks:

1. It theoretically isolates foreignness, contains, and thereby masters, its disorder. It
reduces its protean forms to a single metaphysical concept, allows the term to
mean unstable without *being* unstable.[20]
2. It makes possible *accountability*, in the double sense of supervising ethical responsibilities and of implementing social regulation. It makes possible, for example, the quota laws to which Sakamoto refers, and it is the principle imbedded in the
inextricable relation between (the classificatory operations of) social work and social control that she signals.
3. It allows one to evade contaminating contact with foreignness or foreigners by
substituting for them a symbolic representation.[21]

Not only foreignness, but *foreigners* are, hence, routinely subjected to discipline, in all the density that Foucault has given to that term; subject, that is, to
a disciplinary mechanism that distributes individuals and fixes them in space,
manipulates their bodies, forms around them an apparatus of perpetual observation, registers and records their movements, classifies them, and constitutes on
them a useable body of knowledge. For example, one technique for organizing
the disconcerting variety of foreignness into a meaning-producing syntax is, as
Saunders contends, "rounding up threateningly heterogeneous phenomena and
detaining them within the confines of a stabilized name" (129), a name that, as
pioneering social worker Jane Addams recognized, can be deployed as a
weapon: "the Greeks," she writes, "are filled with amazed rage when their very
name is flung at them as an opprobrious epithet" (cited in Sakamoto, 242).

But what we have perhaps not captured is the subtlety of these processes of
stabilization, for they are often unthematized, even unconscious, and rarely as
mechanistic as Foucauldian language might lead one to believe. In more and less
explicit ways, a number of this volume's contributors suggest that *context* performs the double duty of stabilizing foreignness conceptually and designating
foreigners socially (the one task, of course, implying the other). On this view,
context governs foreignness in those shadowy corners of experience where the
department of justice or the bureau of immigration do not reach; indeed it often
lights the way, as it were, for institutionalized authorities to follow. According
to Sakamoto, for example, political, societal, cultural, and historical contexts
have determined how the discipline of social work defines foreignness and,
thereby, how it identifies foreigners. Context has thus regulated which groups
are eligible for the profession's concern. Saunders concentrates on the manner in

which context naturalizes and literalizes meanings. Elaborating context both in linguistic terms (as the series of syntagmatic relations that regulate the semantic relation between signifier and signified) and in hermeneutic terms (as an imperative of textual repatriation that regulates epistemological foreignness), she argues that a synonymy is established between foreignness and error, for just as taking a word or phrase "out of context" conditions semantic error, so too does being out of context condition and identify the foreigner—the one who is prone "to misinterpret, to be improper, to err" (Saunders, 119).

Indicting Heidegger's sharp distinction between *Dasein* and other entities, Zimmerman reminds us that context might also be conceived in Heideggarian terms as being-in-the-world, as a matter not only of social relations and of meaning, but of Being. In *Being and Time*, Heidegger writes:

> The everyday way in which things have been interpreted is one into which Dasein [literally, "being there"] has grown in the first instance, with never a possibility of extrication. In it, out of it, and against it, all genuine understanding, interpreting, and communicating, all re-discovering and appropriating anew, are performed. In no case is a Dasein untouched and unseduced by this way in which things have been interpreted, set before the open country of a "world-in-itself" so that it just beholds what it encounters. [22]

As Hubert Dreyfus paraphrases it, being-in-the-world is "a background of everyday practices into which we are socialized but that we do not represent in our minds."[23] It is a concerned involvement and absorption in the world that determines not only how we understand ourselves and others, but what we perceive, what shows up for us as something. Theoretical assertions (such as those posited about foreigners) are, in Heidegger's terms, a derivative form of understanding, drawn from a more primordial, and context-dependent, hermeneutics.[24] Dwelling in a context ratifies as obvious, natural, and literal a particular hermeneutic stance toward foreignness or foreigners; that stance is redoubtably protected, moreover, by its pre-theoretical status.

We are perhaps now in a better position to investigate that decontextualization that we have observed assisting at the procedure of valuing foreignness, better able to recognize that the extraction of objects, practices, or discourses from material and logical conditions that we have witnessed imbuing foreigners with the hue of the exotic or the taint of threat may also be a procedure that stabilizes, disciplines, and confines. But how can this be? How can that which contributes to the *instability* of the foreign function as a procedure for its *stabilization*? How can we say that both *context* and *decontextualizing* discipline? The most tenable response to this question is also the most apparent: when we speak of "taking something out of context," we nearly always mean not just decontextualizing but *recontextualizing*. It is not that we take a word or an entity out of *all* context— though, to be sure, both science and philosophy have aspired to do so—rather, that we transport it to a different context. Redfield and Tomášková, for example, mark the fact that "a hallmark trope of anthropological presentation is to incorporate fragmentary pieces of field languages, however incomprehensible they may be to a home audience" (181), a process that is a simultaneous decontextualization (from "the field") and recontextualization (within disciplinary discourse). Indeed returning to Clifford's critique of decontextualization, it becomes evident that if "history has been airbrushed out" of numerous museum collections such that "the actual ongoing life and 'impure' inventions of tribal peoples are erased in the name of cultural or artistic 'authenticity,'"[25] this process is not a matter just of subtracting, but of *replacing* context: in this case, with the museum exhibit—a context that establishes different relations between, and meanings for, objects. Hence, following Susan Stewart, Clifford contends that:

> Collections create the illusion of adequate representation of a world by first cutting objects out of specific contexts and making them "stand for" abstract wholes. Next a scheme of classification is elaborated for storing or displaying the objects so that the reality of the collection itself, its coherent order, overrides specific histories of the object's production and appropriation.[26]

This procedure of contextual substitution is familiar to readers of Michel de Certeau as the "cut-out and turn-over" recipe for theory, a formula that describes the regulation not only of the concept of the foreign, but of the foreignness of concepts or, more precisely, their epistemological domestication *qua* concept:

> Using the imperatives that punctuate the steps in a recipe, we could say that this theorizing operation consists of two moments: first, *cut out*; then *turn over*. First an "ethnological" isolation; then a logical inversion.
>
> The first move *cuts out* certain practices from an undefined fabric, in such a way as to treat them as *a separate population*, forming a *coherent whole* but *foreign* to the place in which the theory is produced. . . .
>
> The second move *turns over* the unit thus cut out. At first obscure, silent, and remote, the unit is inverted to become the element that illuminates theory and sustains discourse.[27]

We should not be so hasty, however, as to overlook the double inscription of authority in Redfield and Tomášková's example. For if, as we have suggested, the importation of field languages produces authority by recontextualizing phrases within a disciplinary context, this gesture also maintains the authenticity of the "original" context by insisting that some things are not translatable, that it would distort meaning to transport it out of its native tongue. Yet while the process of discursive recontextualization that Redfield and Tomášková evoke evinces one's mastery of a context (one speaks its language, understands its meanings), it does so in a thematized and theorized manner that is not that of the native population: Clifford Geertz's "being there" is not Heidegger's. Indeed such a gesture is, precisely, an attempt to finesse the rivalry of these two forms of authority: the authenticity of "original" context and the authority of disciplinary context.[28] Poised precariously between an epistemological nativism on the one hand (entities and discourses belong in their "original" context) and an imperialism on the other (they belong in the disciplined context of theories or museums), it is perhaps inevitable that we ask: is there, then, a context that produces proper meaning? Does one context yield more truth than another? The two questions, we should note, are not identical and the former, in particular, adroitly sidesteps the arguably more pressing inquiry of how proper meaning is produced; indeed, to determine which context produces proper meaning is to take both context and proper meaning as pre-existent, homogenous, and stable entities and to efface their genealogy. We would perhaps do well to shift our focus: to map and critique that process of production and examine how the literal is constituted, what it includes and excludes, rather than assigning proper contexts and fixing meaning, a gesture that simultaneously constructs epistemological foreignness and effaces the processes through which meanings accede to the sanctum of truth.

If the instability of foreignness is routinely regulated by context—put in order, rendered accountable, made (re)presentable—so too is it disciplined by academic disciplines; indeed foreignness seems necessary both to individual disciplinary content and to the structure of disciplinarity itself or, put otherwise, if numerous disciplines feed off of foreignness to sustain critical investigation or discourse, they also create their own foreigners. The particular kind of foreignness that Owen examines—the "idea of the crazy artist"—has, as she writes, "been fruitful for analysis": a structure in which the object of study is, not unlike the slave of Hegelian dialectic, at once devalued, but indispensable.[29] Similarly, Sakamoto argues that the discipline of social work embodies a fundamental dilemma in that it is constantly defining the foreign—that is, constructing it—while trying to eradicate it by breaking down the inequality between "foreigners" and "natives." Moreover, it is clear that the very act of distinguishing a discipline necessitates constructing disciplinary foreigners, that it is much like any other process of identity formation: the considerations shunned by the "better neighborhoods" of philosophy that Zimmerman marks (155); the informal social service systems developed by African Americans that, as Sakamoto notes, were neither legitimated by academia nor funded by business; the "internal exile of everyday moderns," the "impure present" or the "close to home" that, as Redfield and Tomášková note, have traditionally been exiled from the discipline of anthropology (84, 85, 81).

It is not without a particular significance to foreignness, then, that the contributors to this volume tend to draw on multiple disciplines and to explore the areas between disciplines, for acquainting oneself with disciplinary foreigners will (in a formation we have noted above) thematize and indict disciplinary assumptions and conventions. Just as Owen contends that evocations of foreignness inevitably "work against Western psychology's rationalist, objectivist fantasies of itself" (180), so too do invitations to disciplinary foreignness work to undo the rationalizations of disciplines.

Notes

1. The English root *proper* derives from medieval French and English *propre* and, ultimately, from Latin *proprius* (one's own, special, particular; a peculiar characteristic; lasting, permanent). The adverbial form [*proprie*] means "exclusively, particularly, characteristically, or in a proper sense."

2. Also pertinent here is Homi Bhabha's description of theories of cultural difference "where the Other text is forever the exegetical horizon of difference, never the active agent of articulation." In such formulations, he argues, "The Other loses its power to signify, to negate, to initiate its historic desire, to establish its own institutional and oppositional discourse," thus reproducing "a relation of domination." *The Location of Culture* (London: Routledge, 1994), 31.

3. For a comparison of approaches to the study of the nation, see John Breuilly, *Nationalism and the State*, 2nd ed. (Chicago: Chicago University Press, 1994), especially 404-424; for the voluntarist model of nationhood, see Ernest Renan, "What Is a Nation?" trans. Martin Thom, in *Nation and Narration,* ed. Homi K. Bhabha (New York: Routledge, 1990), 8-22; for the philosophical roots of the organic conception of nations, see Elie Kedourie, *Nationalism,* 4th exp. ed. (Oxford: Blackwell, 1993); for political models of nationhood, see John Breuilly and Ernest Gellner, *Nations and Nationalism* (Oxford: Blackwell, 1983); for social models of nationhood, see Ernest Gellner and Benedict Anderson, *Imagined Communities: Reflections on the Origin and Spread of Nationalism,* rev. ed. (New York: Verso, 1983); for a chronology of incarnations and permutations of the national principle, see E. J. Hobsbawm, *Nations and Nationalism since 1780: Programme, Myth, Reality,* 2nd ed. (Cambridge: Cambridge University Press, 1990); for an elaboration of nations as components of an interstate system, see Immanuel Wallerstein, *The Modern World-System,* 2 vols. (New York: Academic Press, 1974).

4. For a detailed analysis of these issues in European states, see Saskia Sassen, *Guests and Aliens* (New York: New Press, 1999).

5. See Julia Kristeva, *Powers of Horror: An Essay on Abjection,* trans. Leon S. Roudiez (New York: Columbia University Press, 1989). Judith Butler elaborates the abject in relation to the gendered body in *Bodies that Matter: On the Discursive Limits of "Sex"* (New York: Routledge, 1993). Also pertinent are both Sander Gilman's argument that the stereotype mimes processes of individuation and is rooted in subsequent anxieties about ego-disintegration and Frances Bartkowski's exploration of dislocations as restagings of the entry into language and subjectivity. See Sander L. Gilman, *Difference and Pathology: Stereotypes of Sexuality, Race and Madness* (Ithaca, N.Y.: Cornell University Press, 1985), 19-21; and Frances Bartkowski, *Travelers, Immigrants, Inmates: Essays in Estrangement* (Minneapolis: University of Minnesota Press, 1995).

6. For another example of xenotropically constructed identity, see Sidonie Smith, "Isabella Eberhardt Traveling 'Other'/wise: The 'European' Subject in 'Oriental' Identity," in *Encountering the Other(s): Studies in Literature History, and Culture,* ed. Gisela Brinker-Gabler (Albany, N.Y.: SUNY Press, 1995), 295-318.

7. Similar conceptions of the border as a country of its own have been elaborated theoretically by Walter D. Mignolo's pursuit of a complex "border gnoseology" which "rather than epistemology . . . is a new way of thinking that emerges from the sensibilities and conditions of everyday life created by colonial legacies and economic globalization." "Globalization, Civilization Processes, and the Relocation of Languages and Cultures," in

The Cultures of Globalization, ed. Fredric Jameson and Masao Miyoshi (Durham, N.C.: Duke University Press, 1998), 46; and institutionally by, for example, the *Colegio de la Frontera Norte* which maintains units along the U.S.-Mexico border, fosters research, and trains professionals dedicated to the border as a region of its own.

8. This double valuation is also central to Gilman's analysis of the stereotype. See *Difference and Pathology*. See also Bartkowski's analysis of the emotions of wonder and shame in *Travelers, Immigrants, Inmates*.

9. Edward Said, *Orientalism* (New York: Vintage, 1979), 1.

10. James Clifford, *The Predicament of Culture: Twentieth-Century Ethnography, Literature, and Art* (Cambridge, Mass.: Harvard University Press, 1988), 200.

11. On the Danaïdes in Argos, see Julia Kristeva, *Strangers to Ourselves*, trans. Leon S. Roudiez (New York: Columbia University Press, 1991), 42-49.

12. On the distinction between the traveler and the exile, see Caren Kaplan, *Questions of Travel: Postmodern Discourses of Displacement* (Durham, N.C.: Duke University Press, 1998). On the immigrant, refugee, and displaced person, see Sassen, *Guests and Aliens*.

13. Such variations in value are infinitely producible. Consider a single example: consider the difference in value between the foreigner who is a Christian, middle-aged professional and the one who is a young, underemployed Muslim; consider each residing in New York, Paris, Tehran, Buenos Aires.

14. Kristeva insists that recognition of this principle is key to ameliorating the everyday treatment of foreigners: "Strangely, the foreigner lives within us: he is the hidden face of our identity, the space that wrecks our abode, the time in which understanding and affinity founder. By recognizing him within ourselves, we are spared detesting him in himself." *Strangers to Ourselves*, 1. On the other as the uncannily familiar, see also Bernhard Waldenfels, "Response to the Other" and Angelika Bammer, "Xenophobia, Xenophilia, and No Place to Rest," in *Encountering the Other(s)*, 35-44, 45-62.

15. This figure is drawn from Benjamin Barber, *Jihad vs. McWorld: How Globalism & Tribalism are Re-Shaping the World* (New York: Ballantine Books, 1996), 9. Barber estimates the number of nations justly termed homogenous at less than 10 percent.

16. In *Being and Time*, Heidegger elaborates such conformity as an escape from the ontologically authentic recognition of our unsettledness. See Martin Heidegger, *Being and Time*, trans. John Macquarrie and Edward Robinson (San Francisco: Harper & Row, 1962).

17. On the nuances of German *fremdheit*, see Waldenfels, "Response to the Other," 35-36.

18. Kristeva, *Strangers to Ourselves*, 96.

19. Kristeva, *Strangers to Ourselves*, 41. In *Guests and Aliens*, Sassen documents the many ways Europe and the U.S. have disciplined migrants, refugees, and other foreigners.

20. An apt figure for this principle is the carnival which, while clearing a space and time for social disruption, also thereby contains and controls it. See M. M. Bakhtin, *Rabelais and His World*, trans. H. Iswolsky (Cambridge, Mass.: MIT Press, 1974) and Peter Stallybrass and Allon White, *The Politics and Poetics of Transgression* (Ithaca, N.Y.: Cornell University Press, 1986).

21. This process is homologous to the one Clifford describes in the MOMA exhibit, which naturalizes a process of selection in its construction of "tribalism." Relevant also are Gilman's analysis of the stereotype in *Difference and Pathology* and Sassen's analy-

sis, in *Guests and Aliens*, of the disjunction between social representations of immigrants and material fact.

22. Heidegger, *Being and Time*, 213.

23. Hubert L. Dreyfus, *Being-in-the-World: A Commentary on Heidegger's* Being and Time, *Division I* (Cambridge, Mass.: MIT Press, 1991), 3.

24. Accordingly, signs always indicate for Heidegger "primarily 'wherein' one lives, where one's concern dwells, what sort of involvement there is with something." *Being and Time*, 111. Before they refer to an object or signified, signs refer to context. As Dreyfus puts it, "A sign's signifying must take place *in a context,* and it signifies, i.e., it can *be* a sign, only for those who *dwell* in that context." *Being-in-the-World*, 102.

25. Clifford, *The Predicament of Culture*, 202.

26. Clifford, *The Predicament of Culture*, 220. For relevant passages in Stewart, see *On Longing: Narratives of the Miniature, the Gigantic, the Souvenir, the Collection* (Baltimore, Md.: John Hopkins University Press, 1984), 162-165.

27. Michel de Certeau, *The Practice of Everyday Life*, trans. Steven Rendall (Berkeley: University of California Press, 1984), 62-63. For an important and detailed illustration of this principle, see Mary Louise Pratt's analysis of the displacement of vernacular knowledges by the classifactory schemes of natural history in *Imperial Eyes: Travel Writing and Transculturation* (New York: Routledge, 1992), chap. 2.

28. A similar structure appears in those "delicate treasures"—jokes and poems—that "fade if exposed to the bright light of a foreign sun" (Redfield and Tomášková, 76), one that continues our previous discussion of value and points forward to our analysis of mediation. First, this transfer in context is at once a devaluation (the poem isn't as beautiful, the joke not as funny) and a hypervaluation (it's beyond your reach unless you have access to the requisite background; it is priceless, invaluable). Second, the fact that those jokes and poems are enfeebled by translation, sapped of their force, is because they require commentary, explanation. They are not direct, but overtly mediated; the context does not accommodate them without a certain metaphorical red tape.

29. An intriguing intertext for Owen's discussion of the artist as mad is Gilman's analysis of the mad as artists. See *Difference and Pathology*, chap. 10.

Chapter Two

Belonging, Distance

We have begun to locate the regions in which foreignness resides, how it comports itself, but we have barely begun to say what foreignness might *be*. It is no simple matter to be sure, but primary among the meanings of *foreign* is *not belonging*, a meaning that marks the negative, relative, and dependent nature of foreignness and forces us to approach it *à rebours*: to understand foreignness we must back up and investigate belonging.

The following essays adduce at least four nuances of belonging with which we must contend and which play havoc with the law of noncontradiction:

1. *To belong is to be bound by ties of affection, association, or membership*: This nuance figures a belonging comprised of multiple discrete components and a gesture of binding together. Not a matter of inherence, it bears the possibility of unbinding and rebinding; thus, in this scenario, a tie might be loosened and the foreigner come to belong.[1]

2. *To belong is to be a part of*: This organic meaning is one in which belonging is conceived of as being an integral portion of some "whole" without which that "whole" would be incomplete. It implies that being completes itself elsewhere—outside the self, in the nation, or a religious worldview, for example—and that one's place in that elsewhere is predetermined, necessary, and permanent. In this scenario, the foreigner has no part; s/he is constitutionally, essentially outside.

3. *To belong is to be classified with*: Belonging is determined by a metaphysical logic of genus and species, of ideal categories that subsume specific examples; it

works by establishing similarities and effacing differences and implies replacability. This scenario, which insists on a certain threshold of conformity, sets the stage for assimilation.

4. *To belong is to have a proper or usual place*: It is to be the proprietor of a place, in a relation governed by the vast semantic empire of the *proper*. This meaning also introduces an element of temporality into belonging—the usual; it thus makes the foreigner subject both to the peregrinations of the proper and to what we have called the "temporality of foreignness."

Belonging, moreover, implies a preposition: one belongs *to* or *in* or *with*; the notion of belonging always makes this synecdochic gesture. But what is the direction of this gesture, the *object* of the prepositions? It is hardly surprising (if we bear in mind that *not belonging* is a primary meaning of *foreign* and if we persist in our logic *á rebours*) that in answering this question we should find ourselves revisiting sites in opposition to which foreignness is constituted: home, nation, self.

If without a prepositional object, belonging is adrift, mooring it to *home* is by no means an immobilizing gesture. We have already noted the semantic heterogeneity of home and the problematic assumptions lodged in a reflexively benign image of it. In her introduction to a special issue of *new formations* on "The Question of 'Home,'" Angelika Bammer offers the following sketch of the meanings of home:

> Semantically, "home" has always occupied a particularly indeterminate space: it can mean, almost simultaneously, both the place I have left and the place I am going to, the place I have lost and the new place I have taken up, even if only temporarily. "Home" can refer to the place where you grew up (the place you perhaps threatened to run away from when you were five), the mythic homeland of your parents and ancestors that you yourself may never have actually seen, or the hostel where you are spending the night in transit. In other words, "home" may refer to a deeply familiar or a foreign place, or it may be no more than a passing point of reference.[2]

The fact that these very diverse conceptual and geographical locations are gathered into a single name not only alerts us to the delicate but fascinating thread of similarity that runs between them, but also issues a warning that the inspecificity of *home* may mask theoretical imprecision, overlook significant detail, or erase crucial differences.[3] Leaving aside a host of other nuances that merit more careful consideration—home as *habitus* in Bourdieu's sense, the association of home with conceptual clarity (bringing an idea home), and with ease (feeling at home), home as the place where something is invented or started, or as the direction of capital flow (the home office), to cite a precious few—let us turn, for the sake of specificity, to the instances where home appears in the chapters that follow.

Under the apartheid regime analyzed by Saunders, *homeland* designated "barren and essentially uninhabitable wastelands" to which black South Africans were forcibly removed in order to purify the "white areas" of the country in which blacks had been made statutory foreigners (127). The government, hence, counted on the term *homeland* to generate a sufficiently benign image in the minds of white South Africans (and the rest of the world) that the referent (the geographical space itself) was simply rendered irrelevant. Saunders elaborates this process, in which the discursive potency of *home* overrides material conditions and even determines perception, as a simultaneous reliance on, and denial of, the foreignness in language—of, in other words, the estrangement between signified (what *home* means) and referent (the material reality to which the word, in this instance, actually refers). The "homelands" of South Africa also put in evidence the privilege concealed within the customary notion of home, one that Doreen Massey, in another context, critiques as the erroneous "notion that everyone once had a place called home which they could look back on, a place not only where they belonged but which belonged to them, and where they could afford to locate their identities."[4]

Sakamoto's depiction of housing discrimination in America draws out the assumption that if you're not in your proper home, you don't merit the material entity of a house. Indeed, it is possible to measure the degree to which differing ethnic groups were perceived to *belong* in America by what it would cost them to establish a home: "While poor white immigrants had to endure inadequate housing conditions, African Americans of all income levels suffered housing problems. In Chicago, African Americans had to pay $12 to $12.50 on average for housing whereas Bohemians, Poles, and Lithuanians paid less than $8.50 and Jews in the ghetto less than $10.50" (Sophonisba Breckinridge, cited in Sakamoto, 242). Foreignness, in short, has its price. The inverse of this logic is identifiable in that herald of social work, the settlement house. For if the very idea of a settlement house assumes that foreignness is equivalent to being unsettled, it also suggests that to be a foreigner is not to have a home—or, that foreigners are in need of a house in order to be at home.[5]

Owen's work, as we have already seen, indicts the simplistically benign image of home and demonstrates that a "cathected site of expatriation" may correspond more closely to the connotations of home (site of nurturing, acceptance, growth) than does a literal home (201). Her typology of artistic expatriatism, moreover, exposes not only the complexity of homes, but the lacks and excesses that may be semantically sheltered by them: For the "hunger artists," she argues, neglect and insufficient attachment at home send them searching out of a longing to feel mirrored and more truly nurtured. "Escape artists are those pushed out by a sense of oppression, impingement, and intrusion who need to leave overpowering relationships" (203).

Redfield and Tomášková consider what home means for the exile. "A key ingredient of exile," they argue, "is a sense of homeland" (73). Home is thus a fundamental constituent of identity, a place one can leave, but not something one can leave behind. Yet home is also a point of no return: the exile, even when regimes collapse or borders open, cannot simply go home. It is thus that the exile functions not only as a figure for the inescapable plangeance of home, but as a deconstruction of home as an immutable entity "where there is imagined to be the security of a . . . stability and an apparently reassuring boundedness."[6] Home for the exile is, further, imagined space; it is "not simply removed, but constantly re-imagined" (Redfield and Tomášková, 73), a realm of possibility infused with more reality than present surroundings: a no place like home.

One measure of the degree to which foreignness is entangled with (not) belonging to home is the frequency with which discussions of the foreign invoke family and kinship metaphors.[7] Thus, turning to the foreign (xenotropism) is, in Owen's work, synonymous with leaving the father (expatriatism), while the artistic tradition and the creative work become for the artist the "true family." Family metaphors, in addition, conveniently bring with them connotations of a natural and benevolent hierarchy—that of parents over children—that has proven both highly useful, and the justification, for infantalizing and disempowering foreigners: colonizers represent non-Europeans as children, early social workers approach foreigners "as paternalistic Americanization agents" (Sakamoto, 253), home environments view artists as the "eternal child" (Owen, 209). Perhaps most intriguing, however, is the role played by kinship relations in the accounts of Zimmerman's abductees. On the one hand, abductees report that "they regress to infantile status, in which they ultimately experience the [alien] gaze as like the all-encompassing loving look of their mothers" (166). This scenario depicts abduction in terms of the mother-child dyad—the very archetype of belonging, where not even the foreignness produced by ego boundaries may intrude—and makes of abduction a kind of coming home. As we might predict, this image (grafted onto the long and venerable tradition associating foreigners, children, criminals, and the ill, which we will explore at greater length below) facilitates explanations of the coercive nature of alleged abductions: Whitley Strieber's book on abduction avers (in Zimmerman's paraphrase) that "people do use compulsion appropriately in some situations, e.g., in dealing with children, with people judged to be dangerous to themselves or society, and with patients who . . . resist treatment necessary to save their lives" (169). On the other hand, in a much less reassuring scenario, "Abductees report that the aliens remove sperm and egg samples, which are allegedly used to generate 'hybrid' babies, half-human, half-alien" (154). If not caught up with the fear of hybridity itself (which we will return to below), this programmatic breeding scene clearly presents a plot in which one's reproductive processes are out of one's control: a plot that not only denies that one's body and its capacities belong to the self, that not only usurps will and makes off with its weighty baggage of individualism, but that stages both a dispossession (not at all unlike the laborer's) in which what one produces can never be one's own and an ignorance that is also a knowledge: the knowledge that I have produced something outside of my knowledge.[8] Finally, in spite of the fact that some, like Strieber, have interpreted it as "a process of mutual exchange," this unhomely scene produces a doubled self-alienation (which might well be thought in its ambiguous relation to the one commonly coupled with modernity): for not only is one made into an instrument, de-humanized, and without agency, but the very material of the self—the body—becomes alien.[9]

Not only are home and family powerful loci of belonging, but they lend to that other crucial object of belonging—the nation—both a body of metaphors and a functional social structure. The nation, that is, is conceived in familial terms, as fraternity, *patria*, motherland, home. It also functions, to a considerable degree, through the heterosexual family unit which it relies on for economic, demographic, military, and moral sustenance. This intimate relationship between family and nation no doubt partially accounts for the experience of the artist (analyzed by Owen) for whom "two transferences, to family and country, have become fused into one arch-object" (205). Conceived both as place (where one lives or was born) and as the locus of kinship relationships (where the family is), modern nations combine those two legal principles that have historically defined the foreigner: *jus soli* and *jus sanguinis*, the law of birthplace and the law of blood.[10] And while the uncertain determination of nations we have sketched above would seem to make the nation a rather inconstant object of belonging, we should nonetheless not overlook the national education systems, shared symbols, museums, newspapers, and television—in short the *contexts*—that inculcate what Chasteen calls "feeling unity as mystical experience: unconditional, irrevocable belonging" (233).[11]

Zimmerman and Owen both disclose another object potentially at stake in belonging: the self. In the reported abduction experiences studied by Zimmerman, the self becomes a kind of transferable property and no longer one's own. This alienation effect is symptomatized by "being treated indifferently, like [a] lab animal" and by the sense that, as one woman put it, "[the alien's] eyes go inside you" (165). The invasion of private space that characterizes this experience, in which the very interior of the self no longer belongs to the self, is accompanied by what abductees call "mindscanning:" a process that allegedly involves an alien staring deeply into one's eyes while one is powerless to look away, during which one is either scanned for information or filled with specific emotions. Terrestrial analogies come readily to mind: enslavement, for example, torture, or false consciousness. Belonging to the self is also at issue in Henry Miller's description of his rebirth as a "spiritual being" in Paris: "Like it or not, I was obliged to create a new life for myself. And this new life I feel is mine, absolutely mine" (cited in Owen, 211). A condition of creative capability is, for Miller, possessing one's own life; and it is not without significance that the task of making this life required a realignment with both home and nation: a symbolic regression to a birthplace and a literal move to Paris.

Miller's narrative of reorigination leads us ineluctably back to a swamp of significance we have been sidestepping: the notion of origin. For both belonging and (thereby) foreignness are governed by myths of origin and by the closely related assumptions that one bears a particular and irreversible relationship to a place of origin, that where one came from is where one belongs. As we have already noted, that "origin" can be conceived either in terms of place of birth, or a more distal ethnic, "racial," or class heredity. Its most quotidian manifestation is no doubt the critical prohibition imposed on foreigners: "if you don't like it, go back to where you came from." One of its linguistic manifestations, to which Badran directs our attention, is the incommensurability in Arabic between *muwatin/a* (a citizen, a legal member of the nation) and adjectives such as *baladi* or *mahalli/yya* (used in reference to a native, or one who originates from the same region or village). But origin does not, of course, merely signify where one comes from, but a plethora of other things as well: first or earliest, conceptually new or unusual; the source or event from which something develops; not copied from, or based on, something prior; the genuine or pure form of something, not an imitation, authentic. Any reference to origin inevitably participates in these consequential meanings.

If personal origins are often conceived in terms of nationality, nations them-selves are at pains to authenticate their own origins, for they function as an ob-ject of belonging, in part, because they provide a shared origin. Indeed the word *nation* is derived from Latin *nasci*: to be born. As Ernest Renan famously put it in 1882, "Of all cults, that of the ancestors is the most legitimate, for the ances-tors have made us what we are. A heroic past, great men, glory (by which I un-derstand genuine glory), this is the social capital upon which one bases a na-tional idea."[12] That cult of origins, locating belonging in a putatively primary and authentic past and commonly deploying an imagery of rebirth or resurrec-tion (awakening, regeneration, *risorgimento*) occludes the messiness both of a nation's formation and of its motley makeup in the present.[13] Indeed, origins can be located wherever discontinuity or newness can be produced, as evinced by the Latin American nativisms studied by Chasteen which conceptually shifted origin from the archaic parent state to the new world and made the continent's new nations into the (genuine, uncopied, authentic) locus of belonging. Making the nation an origin also places it beneath an imperative of purity that prohibits mixing and merging and that has long been commensurate with the expurgation of foreignness: not only from languages, official narratives, and ethnological data, but also from populations.[14]

We are passing by at least two paths of inquiry that should certainly be pur-sued, but toward which we can here only gesture briefly. First, it is quite possi-ble that an articulable relation exists between (a) the meaning of *origin* as "source of development" and (b) the distinction commonly made between na-tions based on development (e.g., "developed," "developing," and "under-developed" nations). Second, Derrida's critique of origin as "a notion belonging essentially to the history of onto-theology"[15] and his positing of an arche-trace—a trace which is the origin of origin, which cannot be derived from a presence or an originary nontrace, and which remains "contradictory and not acceptable within the logic of identity"[16]—would, without doubt, be germane to interrogat-ing the efficacy and the effects of the identities, authenticities, and other signifi-cances grounded on origin that are implicated in the construction of foreignness.

Entangled in the semantic thicket of origin, belonging does not always work, nor does it stability make. Indeed we have already heard, in the conflicting meanings of belonging, in the shifting sands of home and nation, the murmurings of what we might call "belonging trouble." We will hear this murmur run, like a harbinger, throughout our discussions of foreignness, in the narratives of artists alienated by the very community to which they conceptually belong that Owen examines, or in Badran's recognition that being a "foreign citizen" is, while a statutory impossibility, quite possible for experience, or in Saunders's discussion of the egregious example in South Africa where black Africans have been made legal foreigners in their own home.[17] An ostensibly less dissonant murmur is heard from Redfield's and Tomášková's ethnographer who "is not native at either end of the translation" (82) and whose very vocation is a "flight from . . . where one doesn't feel at home": a variant of "belonging trouble" integral, they argue, to the production of anthropological knowledge (80). The political practice of colonization (analyzed here by Chasteen and Zimmerman) where peoples are, without their consent, coerced into a belonging structure where they are not at home, presents us with a further form of "belonging trouble," as do processes of migration and globalization, in which *jus soli* and *jus sanguinus* do not coincide, and may construct conflicting sites of belonging.

If numerous mutations of "belonging trouble" are readily imaginable, a significant swarm of such trouble can be witnessed coalescing around the notion of (in)dependence. Does belonging imply a dependence? Why do notions of dependence, independence, and autonomy appear so often in our examinations of the foreign? Before attempting a response, we should take note of the fundamental dissymmetry that inheres in dependence: to be *dependable* is a virtue, while to be *dependent* is a vice, an evaluation no doubt subtended by the logic of capitalism (the former implies a steadily productive source of work, the latter, a nonproductive drain on the economy). Depending, however, may be as much a matter of trust or loyalty as of money; it may be a matter of influence or logical support (to depend on), of politics (a dependent state), or of psychological or physiological reliance (dependency). These nuances, often conflated, create their own ruckus in meaning, and are carried over into the concept of *independence*. For if *independence* means acting or functioning free from the influence, control, or support of others, it is not, *qua* concept, independent: it is conceptually dependent, enclitic upon a notion of dependence however insistently signifying its absence.[18]

In Chasteen's work we encounter a set of familiar formulations: a nation is established through political independence; a foreigner is one who does not belong to the nation. What, in this triangulated structure, is the relation between independence and the foreigner? One response is immediately clear: claims to political independence are based on evidence of an autonomous identity (economic, cultural, linguistic, or ethnic) and depend on sorting out who does and does not belong. The process of establishing independence thus requires (in addition, usually, to a war) the conceptual or literal expulsion of the foreign (which, in turn, necessitates distinguishing between insignificant forms of difference and markers of foreignness).[19] Yet if, in the interstate system, nations are constitutively independent (of other nations), they are, to an equal extent, a formation of mutual dependence (between state and citizen). Belonging to a nation means depending on it for military protection, political organization, and social services; it also means that it can depend on me, as I can depend on fellow citizens, for loyal service, a vote, productive work, and tax revenue. What falls outside of, or disrupts, this circle of dependence is foreign; it is neither eligible to be dependent nor is it dependable. This is the strange logic behind what American politicians disparage as a "culture of dependency" (see Sakamoto)—a system that would provide social services to immigrants and foreigners, to those outside the legitimated circle of co-dependency.

Foreigners are both a byproduct of national independence and the remainder of its organized dependence. This figure of the internally dependent and the externally autonomous is the nation's way of resolving the difficult question of how much autonomy is a good thing—what degree of (in)dependence is desirable—a question that also appears on the more intimate terrain of psychology. Studying the transitional realm between infancy and autonomy, Winnicott, according to Owen, emphasizes the autonomy needs of the child: the need to break from parents and environment, to take independent creative control of one's own self. This autonomy is necessary, according to Owen, for creative adaptation to the (externally) foreign: capacity for authentic play and a refusal to be denatured by "pathological accommodation" (Winnicott, cited in Owen, 186). The question of personal autonomy is refocused by Zimmerman, who notes that some theorists view the alien abduction phenomenon as akin to a shamanistic initiation procedure that leads to a higher, more integrated, less ego-constricted mode of awareness. Such an initiation may be terrifying and depersonalizing, may indeed be experienced as a return to the absolute dependency of an infantile state, but may also disclose the finitude of the ego-structure in a manner that, according to Zimmerman, is not unlike that sought by the spiritual aspirant of Buddhism, a manner that urges that the world, nature, and environment not be made foreign to the self.

At least two other examples beckon us. In Sakamoto's work, the notions of independence and the foreign intersect in the narratives of women like Jane Addams, who established their independence through aiding foreigners. Women themselves were made foreign to self and society through their social and economic dependence on men, and it was the ability to act autonomously that granted them a sense of belonging. This incarnation of independence, conceived largely in terms of self-realization, rests on the assumption that dependence makes one both less a self and less a societal participant and, concomitantly, that meaningful belonging and authentic being necessitate independence. (Scholars of American culture could, I suspect, trace an influential history of this conception in the annals of national identity formation). It could be argued (though this would be only one, somewhat tendentious, reading of a complex narrative) that by constructing a system whereby the foreigner depended on them, these social work pioneers reenacted the patriarchal relation, as if having dependents verified one's independence. In this scenario, foreignness is measured by its degree of dependence and belonging by one's degree of independence.[20]

Saunders' essay examines what we might call hermeneutic (in)dependence: an (in)dependence of judgment or action that she analyzes both in the work of South African novelist J. M. Coetzee and in the context of apartheid. Dependence on a hermeneutic code, she argues, is a method for banishing the foreignness from signification; and that code most often takes the form of a context that domesticates, naturalizes, and literalizes determinate meanings and that is constructed through reiteration: through a dependence on what has repeatedly been signified, as well as on what has remained incessantly silent. In South Africa, this context was woven by government-controlled institutions and media, as well as by individuals (security police, bureaucrats, doctors, judges, voters). Acting independently in this scenario (as does, for example, Coetzee's main character, the magistrate) means creating "a disruptive and defamiliarizing lacuna in the empire's performative reiteration," a gesture that is synonymous with recuperating the foreignness in signs and venturing into what Saunders terms an epistemological "zone of error" (125). This zone of error also bears resemblance to the position of the social worker signaled by Sakamoto who, in the absence of a culturally differentiated national service policy, must make decisions independently, based on the changing needs of immigrants.

These examples suggest the degree to which notions of (in)dependence are, however desultorily, implicated in foreignness and (without, by any means, exhausting the possibilities of this relation) allow us to detect something of a pattern: a degree of independence may be necessary to adapt psychically to the foreign, to surmount one's own sense of foreignness, or to resist reiteration of a dominant discourse about the foreign. Yet insofar as it coincides with what we have called "identity addiction," processes of establishing independence may construct their own political, social, or environmental foreigners.

Foreignness, then, presupposes a conception of belonging, though belonging itself means multiple and contradictory things; though the objects to which belonging refers—home, family, nation, self—conceal a veritable epidemic of "belonging trouble"; though the semantically charged "origin" which frequently governs belonging is largely fictitious and, at any rate, irretrievable; and though its apparently intimate relations with (in)dependence remain unstable. But this is only half the equation: foreignness is *not* belonging, and, therefore, in order to understand it we must also investigate the nature of this "not." We must add to belonging (though it is an addition that subtracts) the concepts of distance, movement, separation, and loss that, with the logic of a privative, undo it. Let us concentrate on the concept that appears most frequently in the essays that follow—that is, *distance*. A comparative term, which requires a "from" as much as belonging demands a "to," distance implies both stability—the stable points that make it calculable—and movement. Indeed, movement itself seems at times to stand in for the "not" in the "not belonging" of foreignness, though it does not presuppose a directionality: one can move either toward or away from, or without going anywhere at all. Movement is often taken as tantamount to instability, as in opposition to, and undoing, entities presumed stable—home, nation, self; it is (hence) sometimes deemed synonymous with modernity.[21]

Redfield and Tomášková undertake to analyze two varieties of displacement: exile and anthropology, both of which represent culture at a distance, "be it the lost homeland (site of reinvented cosmopolitan high culture) or the 'field' (site of appropriately exotic others)" (72). It is not without significance that Redfield and Tomášková frequently describe distance in terms of "displacement" or "dislocation"—specific kinds of distance that presuppose a usual or proper location and that represent disruption of an order. Nor should it be overlooked that both the condition of exile they describe ("a status attained between place and loss") and the word itself (from *ex-salire*, to leap out of—a movement which "implies a site of departure, a ground below the flight") adjoin, in exemplary fashion, the distance or movement with the ostensibly stable site of belonging that we have argued is the framework of the foreign (73). They contend, moreover, that distance comes "built in" to the discipline of anthropology; it both defines its subject matter and founds its central method—ethnography. Ethnographic practice, that is, begins with a dislocating movement, which is also a separation from the perceived cultural center: from what a previous age did not hesitate to call "civilization." Distance functions both to establish disciplinary authority and to distill culture—purify it, reveal its essential truth: a formula which has customarily equated greater distance with greater authenticity and that the despondent Lévi-Strauss, for whom cultural authenticity remained forever beyond the horizon, inadvertently exposed as "the addiction of pure identity" (Redfield and Tomášková, 84).[22] If, in the years since Lévi-Strauss, global circumstances have increasingly diluted the putatively purgative effects of distance, so too, according to Redfield and Tomášková, have disciplinary realignments shifted distance from its previously central position in the discipline. Many an anthropologist has thus, they contend, experienced a disorientation like that of an exile free to return, a simultaneously beneficial and painful loss of estrangement that is also the disquieting recognition that nothing is more foreign than home.[23]

If in the figure of the anthropologist we witness the way in which distance has traditionally functioned to establish authority and purify culture, we learn from the exile that distance is not merely spatial, but also conceptual and emotive—a principle theorized by Heidegger, for whom disinterested physical space is merely a privative, deworlded mode of the space of everyday involvement. The exile, indeed, might be defined as one whose ideological distance from home has been literalized, in a spatial ratification of thought. What follows from this interested, conceptual, and affective experience of space? First, the lost world of the exile is not simply removed, but constantly reimagined; distance conditions the free, imaginative play of possibility. Second, the spatially distant may be far more cognitively present than immediate surroundings, the distant becomes the proximal, or as Marcel Proust inimitably puts it, "Even from the simplest, the most realistic point of view, the countries for which we long occupy, at any given moment, a far larger place in our true life than the country in which we may happen to be" (cited in Redfield and Tomášková, 71). Third, a return in geographical space is by no means commensurate with "going home." Sylvie Richterová, responding to Milan Kundera, articulates the point this way: "An artist cannot return, cannot cancel the distance that he overcame, neither in the geographic nor in the social sense; he does not have to, maybe cannot, separate the spiritual journey from the earthly one" (cited in Redfield and Tomášková, 83).

Saunders focuses on the distance that inheres in the structure of language, in what Saussure calls the arbitrary and differential nature of the linguistic sign. While the distance between signifier and signified, which allows for movement and even instability, has often been denounced as a harrowing threat to stable meaning, Saunders contends that this distance—or what she calls "the foreignness in signification"—is an epistemologically and ethically crucial space of possibility. Analyzing the language of Coetzee's allegorical empire (which bears an unmistakable resemblance to the language of apartheid), Saunders marks the degree to which it attempts to eradicate the foreignness from signs, to collapse the distance in signification in a manner that immobilizes meaning and wards off interpretation. By contrast, the novel's magistrate (whose hermeneutic independence we have already noted) insists on exploring the distances between signs, meanings, and referents. Venturing into this "zone of error," he "recuperates the foreignness in signification that the empire has attempted to banish, introduces uncertainty into the knowledge it produces about itself, and simultaneously renders interpretation possible and determination impossible" (Saunders, 122). The magistrate's recuperation of linguistic foreignness, moreover, has a direct impact on "literal" foreigners—the "barbarians" of the novel's title; this is no coincidence, Saunders argues, for "patrolling and suppressing linguistic foreignness is a standard procedure for disciplining 'literal' foreigners" (139).

Sakamoto alights on a tantalizing narrative moment, an emergence of distance that should not be passed by as irrelevant detail: *it was on a trip to Europe* that founding social workers Addams and Starr:

> shared with each other their concern with the lack of meaningful options for women, particularly educated women. Although they were influenced by the social and cultural goals of Toynbee Hall in England, the goal of both women in starting Hull-House was to provide for themselves and for other women a new avenue for living independently and giving meaning to life. (Susan Donner, cited in Sakamoto, 248)

It is this distance from home—a coinciding of literal and perceptual separation from the familiar and a spatial enactment of their sense of "not-belonging"—that, arguably, renders possible (and here we encounter again the play of possibility conditioned by distance) the translation of a previously unarticulated "concern" into an object of reflection (one which, it should not be overlooked, links meaning and belonging to independence). Recognizing their own distance from American society, Addams and Starr conceptualize an advantageous middle distance: a kind of work between the public and the private, a mediation between foreign and domestic.[24] This vocation, a calling from elsewhere to a profession that does not yet exist—to "options," possibility, the unknown—holds out the promise of meaningful work (as opposed to *alienating* labor) and effects a double displacement: of the women's own sense of foreignness onto the ethnic foreignness of immigrants and of the threat educated women posed to patriarchy onto a contained and localized sphere of work deemed appropriate for women.

Zimmerman directs our attention to another phenomenon reliant on distance: the gaze. For Sartre, he shows, the distance of the gaze is agonistic, less a space of possibility than of a struggle for power; it is a distance through which one can be reduced to a (foreign) object, a place where "one of the contesting parties becomes a free subject, while the other is reduced to an object held captive in the gaze of the victorious other" (164). For these reasons, Sartre's elaboration of the gaze helps explicate reports of an ostensibly even more foreign gaze—the alien's. While Zimmerman identifies at least four variants of the gaze in reports of alien abduction—the indifferent gaze of a researcher, the malevolent gaze that seeks to dominate, a loving gaze, and a challenging gaze—perhaps the most commonly reported experience is one in which "abductees" are both intensely gazed at by, and forced to look into, the large, black, almond-shaped, and apparently impenetrable eyes of the aliens, a process which drains them of both subjectivity and agency and, as we have seen, is accompanied by the procedure dubbed "mindscanning," in which "abductees commonly feel that data of some sort is being extracted from their minds" (David Jacobs, cited in Zimmerman, 166). Particularly striking here is the dissymmetry of this gaze: it is experienced both as an absolute distance and as an eradication of distance. On the one hand, the impenetrable eyes of the aliens place them at an infinite distance; though only inches away, they are too distant to perceive, they are absolutely foreign. On the other hand, their panoptic and invasive gaze, that penetrates the inward, private space of mind and soul, seems to collapse distance; nothing remains foreign to it. Perhaps an ironic version of Cartesianism—of the desire for a universal and godlike gaze that eliminates all distance and perspective, this latter gaze is both homologous to the collapse of distance in signification that Saunders has marked in imperial discourse and reminiscent of a principle we have encountered in Redfield and Tomášková: while the distance that inheres in foreignness may be experienced as loss, *loss of distance* may be the ultimate form of foreignness.

There are, to be sure, many loose ends that remain to be tied together in this brief analysis of distance; and while the examples on which we have relied suggest inquiries that we cannot undertake here, we will attempt, at least, to formulate three of them. First, we might profitably return to Heideggerean distance to

which we have made brief reference above and examine how the spatiality specific to *Dasein* (formulated in chapter 3 of *Being of Time*), which is characterized by dis-stancing and directionality (*Ent-fernung* and *Ausrichtung*), might
elaborate, revise, or be challenged by the kinds of distance we have found to in-
here in the concept of the foreign.[25] Second, we might interrogate the relation of
the dislocations within foreignness as sketched above to *displacement* in the
psychoanalytic sense, to "the fact that an idea's emphasis, interest, or intensity is
liable to be detached from it and to pass on to other ideas, which were originally
of little intensity but which are related to the first idea by a chain of associations."[26] We might, for example, explore the significance of this spatial conception of symptom formation both to the distance of foreignness and the processes
of pathologizing we discuss below; the degree to which the stable points that determine distance might be read in terms of manifest and latent content; or the
processes of condensation involved in constructing those stable points. Third,
we might investigate the relation this distance bears to the distance marked by
Derrida in the concept of friendship. We might begin by inquiring into the ways
that the friend functions as the inverse of the foreigner, then turn to Derrida's
readings of Nietzsche, who "dares to recommend separation . . . to prescribe distancing in the code excluding distance"; of Kant, whose imperative of distance,
formulated through the law of attraction and repulsion, introduces into the tradition "a principle of *rupture* or *interruption* that can no longer be easily reconciled with the values of proximity, presence, gathering together, and communal
familiarity which dominate the traditional culture of friendship"; and of Blan-
chot, who writes that friends "reserve, even in the greatest familiarity, an infinite
distance" and that "it is the interval, the pure interval which, from me to this
other who is a friend, measures everything there is between us, the interruption
of being which never authorizes me to have him at my disposition."[27]

Notes

1. This act of binding, which necessitates a foreign presence (an entity or power beyond the components themselves), is manifested in multiple forms: it is a decision, coercion, seduction, "fact of nature."

2. Angelika Bammer, introduction to "Questions of 'Home,'" *new formations*, no.
17 (Summer 1992), vii.

3. We must also be wary of settling down, as it were, in the instability of home, in
such a way that that instability itself might be used either to dismiss the significance of,
or to essentialize, home—to confuse instability for irreality or to confuse one of its attributes for its very being. Rather, such a recognition of instability should, I would argue,
initiate the much more complex tasks of identifying the diverse ways in which home
bears both significance and consequences, of examining the different modes of belonging
through which one is tied to home, and of (thereby) investigating the very diverse, sometimes bothersomely minute, processes that produce foreignness. This principle holds true
for the other entities whose instability we mark: foreigners, nations, families, selves.

4. Doreen Massey, "A Place Called Home?" *new formations*, no. 17 (Summer 1992), 10.

5. Largely designed to imitate through social engineering what would "naturally" be supplied at home, these settlement houses were also the home—the birthplace of, and site of development for—the discipline of social work. Indeed the many critical functions that current social work inherited from the settlement house movement have constructed a kind of *disciplinary* home, a body of practices in opposition to which disciplinary foreignness can be identified.

6. Massey, "A Place Called Home?" 13.

7. Such discussions extend to immigration policy which, in many nations, functions largely around the principle of family reunification.

8. This scenario insists, moreover, on a reconceptualization of both *belonging* and *family*, makes them foreign to their own meaning. For one's family would be alien (rather than opposed to the alien) and relations would not belong to the *familia* (the familiar, the family).

9. This alienation of the body is also, significantly, a way of describing physical pain, as we shall explore at greater length in chap. 4. See Elaine Scarry, *The Body in Pain: The Making and Unmaking of the World* (New York: Oxford University Press, 1985).

10. On the legal deployment of these principles within European states, see Saskia Sassen, *Guests and Aliens* (New York: New Press, 1999), particularly chaps. 4-6. See also Julia Kristeva, *Strangers to Ourselves*, trans. Leon S. Roudiez (New York: Columbia University Press, 1991), 95.

11. See, for example, Ernest Gellner, *Nations and Nationalism* (Oxford: Blackwell, 1983) and Benedict Anderson *Imagined Communities: Reflections on the Origin and Spread of Nationalism*, rev. ed. (New York: Verso, 1983).

12. Ernest Renan, "What is a Nation?" in *Nation and Narration*, ed. Homi K. Bhabha (New York: Routledge, 1990), 19.

13. Anderson notes the way in which "the new [European] nationalisms almost immediately began to imagine themselves as 'awakening from sleep'"(195)—a metaphor that allowed the intelligentsia "who were becoming conscious of themselves as Czechs, Hungarians, or Finns to figure their study of Czech, Magyar, or Finnish languages, folklores, and music as 'rediscovering' something deep-down always known" (196). On *risorgimento* nationalism, see also Peter Alter, *Nationalism*, 2nd ed. (New York: Edward Arnold, 1994), 19-23. Bhabha argues that it is politically urgent to "think beyond narratives of original and initial subjectivities and to focus on those moments or processes that are produced in the articulation of cultural differences." Homi Bhabha, *The Location of Culture* (London: Routledge, 1994), 1.

14. For a fascinating case study of this process, see Michael Herzfeld, *Ours Once More: Folklore, Ideology, and the Making of Modern Greece* (Austin: University of Texas Press, 1982).

15. Jacques Derrida, *Of Grammatology*, trans. Gayatri Chakravorty Spivak (Baltimore, Md.: Johns Hopkins University Press, 1974), 23.

16. Derrida, *Of Grammatology*, 61.

17. This strangely antonymous relation between origin and belonging is not, however, without a venerable history that reaches back at least as far as the anti-heretic legislation discussed by Kristeva, that, up until the fifth century, transformed heretics into foreigners in their own country, rendered them ineligible for administrative or military service, incapable of bearing witness, inheriting property, or, sometimes, engaging in

commercial transactions. See *Strangers to Ourselves*, 88-90.

18. For an analysis of cultural (in)dependence and the African university, see Ali A. Mazrui, "The 'Other' as the 'Self' under Cultural Dependency: The Impact of the Post-colonial University," in *Encountering the Other(s): Studies in Literature History, and Culture*, ed. Gisela Brinker-Gabler (Albany, N.Y.: SUNY Press, 1995), 333-362.

19. Indeed the difficulties of such processes of sorting, distinguishing, and expulsing can be finessed by designating a shared enemy: *our* identity consists of being *their* antagonists. As Chasteen argues of Latin American nationalisms, "focus on a common enemy had tremendous political utility in the creation of broad political alliances because, unlike problematical aspirations of national solidarity, anti-Spanish and anti-Portuguese sentiments were something Americans of all social classes did indeed share" (230). If national independence ideologically dismantles the hierarchy of dominator and dominated (that inheres in both imperialism and the concept of the foreign), it nonetheless involves a material struggle for power and resources that may, to a large degree, reinforce structures of dominance. As Chasteen contends, leaders of independence movements in Latin America were, with rare exception, members of an elite, white minority "who sought not to remake colonial society but to assume control of it themselves. Independence promised them above all the opportunity to wrest political and economic privileges away from those born in Spain or Portugal" (230). On changing conceptions of national sovereignty and the foreigners they produce, see Sassen, *Guests and Aliens*.

20. We cannot overlook the fact, however, that the kind of independence pursued by Addams was not merely a matter of volition, but of membership in a privileged class; she came from one of the richest families in Illinois. In a figure we have glimpsed in our discussion of *kinds* of foreignness, that aspect of identity endowed with less social capital (gender) borrowed, as it were, from that aspect of identity with more (class).

21. Distance may indicate either the space between two points or the state of being apart, the space itself or the experience of it, and it drags in tow a number of meanings for which space is only a metaphor, as in a distant manner or concept. The related concept *separation* may designate a barrier between spaces, the act of parting, or the state of being parted from, division into component parts, or, more figuratively, distinction or independent consideration; it always implies a previous (or prospective) unity. The negation of belonging is, further, frequently temporalized in terms of loss, of a former possession and subsequent dispossession; and it almost always entails conceptual as well as physical property: a lost homeland is more than geographical space. A measure of the affective potency of loss can be read in the fact that the term can be used to stand for death. The concepts that inhabit this "not" all carry weighty baggage; the possibilities of their combination with forms of belonging are, moreover, infinite: distance from family, loss of origin, separation from nation, movement from home. Any attempt at an exhaustive typology of "not belonging" would thus be doomed from the outset or condemned to the silliness of making foreigners to foreignness, who would not be foreign. For a critique of the notions of travel and displacement in contemporary Euro-American criticism, particularly in the discourses of "modernism" and "postmodernism," see Caren Kaplan, *Questions of Travel: Postmodern Discourses of Displacement* (Durham, N.C.: Duke University Press, 1998).

22. See Claude Lévi-Strauss, *Tristes Tropiques*, trans. John and Doreen Weightman (New York: Penguin, 1973).

23. Another intriguing notion of distance woven into Redfield and Tomášková's work is what we might term the "middle distance," a site descried in three, by no means unrelated, contexts: in the thought of those early and influential ethnographers with "off-

center" profiles who find themselves "not native at either end of the translation" (81, 82)—the Malinowskis whose "uncertain status in the civilized center makes [them] closer to the savage margin" (76); in the epistemological stance of the "participant observer" who must hover between the proximal and the distant; and in the discipline's recent inter- rogations of the significance of distance and of the cultural authenticity it is supposed to deliver, its awakening to "partial homecomings, [and] motions of uncertain distance" (85). It is quite possible that one might trace a causal chain between these manifestations of a "middle distance" in the discipline.

24. It would no doubt be profitable to pursue the relations between this "middle dis- tance," the "middle distance" noted by Redfield and Tomášková (see note 23) and the *metaxy* or "middle realm" between childhood and adulthood analyzed by Owen (see 208).

25. *Ent-fernung* is a Heideggerean neologism, translated in the standard edition as "de-severance," but more plausibly by Dreyfus as "dis-stancing."

26. J. LaPlanche and J.-B. Pontalis, *The Language of Psycho-analysis*, trans. Donald Nicholson-Smith (New York: Norton, 1973), 121.

27. Jacques Derrida, *Politics of Friendship*, trans. George Collins (New York: Verso, 1997), 55, 255, 294. I have attempted to theorize the distances elaborated by Hei- degger and Derrida in "Keeping a Distance: Heidegger and Derrida on Foreigners and Friends," *Crossing Borders: Nations/Bodies/Disciplines*, ed. Hugh Silverman and Mi- chael Sanders (New York: Continuum Books, forthcoming).

Chapter Three

The Pathologized, the Improper, and the Impure

Structurally, then, the foreign would appear to be a relation between a certain belonging and a certain distance. Although these notions configure foreignness primarily in quantitative terms, they have also provided ample evidence not only of the ways in which the foreign is conceived qualitatively, but of the degree to which the foreign is discursively imbricated with (figurally related to and conceptually undifferentiated from) other pathologized groups; the degree, that is, to which the foreign is perceived to share properties with insanity, poverty, illness, physical disability, homelessness, femininity, criminality, and childhood.[1]

The component of movement that we have marked in foreignness, for example, makes conspicuous appearances in the history of madness: in the itinerant Ship of Fools or the medieval madman who wandered the countryside; in descriptions of madness as a disorderly, irregular movement of the spirits; or in the treatment of insanity through the regulation of bodily movements.[2] Classical descriptions of mental illness, moreover, rely on a language of climatic, geographic difference—"The world of melancholia was humid, heavy, and cold; that of mania parched, dry," arid and desertlike—such that being insane, like being foreign, means coming from a different geographical space.[3] Foreignness and insanity both participate in a constellation of images surrounding childhood and the family. For just as being foreign is frequently conceived as not belonging to the family, or as commensurate with an infantalized status and a need for parental guidance, so too are the insane, at identifiable moments of clinical history, "transformed into minors" and treated by institutions that symbolically re-constitute "the social structure of the bourgeois family."[4] Madness bears the structural negativity of the foreign and, like it, thematizes and indicts the famil-iar: it is "a manifestation of non-being," the *déjà-là* of death, the mirror in which "civilized man" observes the hinterland of his own nature.[5] Both insanity and foreignness, it could be shown, have been elaborated as an excessive prolifera-tion of meaning, as a mediated (and therefore distorted) relation to truth, as er-ror, as an unwholesome relationship with the imaginary, and as nonreason. Eas-ily recognizable in Foucault's description of madness and its cures in the classical period are the negativity and the lack of context we have associated with foreignness, as well as the error and the impurity that we will elaborate at greater length below:

> Being both error and sin, madness is simultaneously impurity and solitude; it is withdrawn from the world, and from truth; but it is by that very fact imprisoned in evil. Its double nothingness is to be the visible form of that non-being which is evil, and to utter, in the void and in the sensational appearances of its delir-ium, the non-being of error. . . . Cure is organized around these two fundamen-tal themes: the subject must be restored to his initial purity, and must be wrested from his pure subjectivity in order to be initiated into the world.[6]

If, like madness, the foreign is pathologized in terms of mobility, childish-ness, negativity, unreason, and impurity, it also signifies the socially improper; it is perceived, as Foucault writes of insanity, "on the social horizon of poverty, of incapacity for work, of inability to integrate with the group."[7] Indeed (announc-ing again the negative relativity of foreignness to the *proper*), the word denoting *foreign* can, in numerous languages, be used synonymously for *inappropriate*. In this sense, foreignness not only bears a resemblance to madness, but attaches to criminals, the poor, the physically disabled, children, and (as Owen evinces) to artists (hence, "the writer as secret criminal"). This infectious strain of nuance begins to explain why early social workers, as Sakamoto shows, "treated" for-eignness by addressing such issues as poverty, labor rights, and the protection of women and children.[8]

But pathology is more than the sum of its parts; more, that is, than a string of improper acts. For "to pathologize" is precisely to submit such acts to a struc-tural extrapolation that makes of them signs of a condition, such that foreignness (like other pathologies) exists prior to and outside of the improper acts that iden-tify it, such that foreignness is not what one does, but what one is. It is a pattern that Paul Ricoeur in his study of the language of fault has identified in Greek penal thought as the "mystery of iniquity" through which the city "reconstructs in the criminal, but beyond his acts, a will to evil for the sake of evil."[9] It is also the process that Foucault has marked in the establishment of the delinquent who "is to be distinguished from the offender by the fact that it is not so much his act as his life that is relevant in criticizing him."[10] This diffusion from specific act to essential character appears, as Sakamoto notes, in the history of social work, in which foreigners with different cultural practices were suspected of lacking "values, standards, and character" (253). It is also manifested in the expectation, marked by Owen, that artists will invariably be characterized by "'deviant' sexuality or untoward passions" (181). It is detectable in the process signaled by Chasteen through which "clothes, accent, music, dance, and food gained salience as markers of native identity," as well as in the fact that failure to exhibit such markers identified "lack of patriotism or even suspicious foreign influence" (231).[11] It is perhaps not surprising, therefore, that foreigners are frequently subjected to the kinds of discipline imposed on the pathologized; they are restrained, contained, isolated, regularized, observed, recorded, punished, rehabilitated. They are regulated—to borrow once again from Foucault's discourse on madness—through the consolidated forces of "Family-Child relations, centered on the theme of paternal authority; Transgression-Punishment relations, centered on the theme of immediate justice; [and] Madness-Disorder relations, centered on the theme of social and moral order."[12]

The radiating movement from act to essence that characterizes pathology is abetted by the logic of purity and defilement that follows from the foreigner's lack of the *proprius*: by the conception of an uncleanliness that is simultaneously physical and moral—both literal dirtiness and a symbol for fault; that is contagious—spread by contact with, for example, a corpse, a menstruating woman, a leper, a madman, a foreigner; and that is thus avoided or eliminated by separation—by burying the dead outside city walls, separating the sexes, marginalizing the ill, confining the insane, evicting the foreign.[13] While we have arrived at this border between purity and defilement by following the path of pathology—by signaling the conceptual similarities between madness, criminality, and the foreign, in particular—we could also have arrived by merely following the signposts in this volume's essays, for (im)purity is a concept that appears in them with a clearly significant regularity. Indeed we have already taken note of the way in which *belonging* requires conceptual ablutions, the notion of *origin* functions as a cleansing agent, nations perform purification rites, distance filters out the silt of the "impure present," and a museum exhibit cleans up the annoying modernity of "tribal peoples."

The affinity that emerges between figures of defilement and the concept of the foreign is ratified by Mary Douglas's famous definition of defilement that, it should not be overlooked, might equally describe the foreigner: defilement is, she writes, "matter out of place."[14] Perhaps this affinity begins to explain why contact with the foreign has long been considered a primary source of defilement. Theologian W. Eichrodt, for example, notes that in the purity laws contained in the Hebrew Bible, "everything which has to do with alien gods or their *cultus* is condemned as unclean. . . . Foreign land and foreign food are therefore unclean. The use of many animals for food is forbidden for the reason that they figure in alien cults or magic rites."[15] The linguistic root, moreover, of the Hebrew word for defilement (*tame*) is used as a simple synonym for *alien* and *strange*. It is a perception that, Sakamoto makes clear, is still alive and well in nineteenth-century America where foreigners were perceived to be in need of "cleansing," and where social work, in response, developed programs to teach immigrants the "proper" way of living in America.

Mixture is also a form of defilement, a violation of the logic of purity which requires that individuals "conform to the class to which they belong" and that "different classes of things . . . not be confused."[16] Put otherwise, mixture is always a contact with the foreign. The purity—of a nation, an identity, a self— entails not only separation and distinction, but avoidance of admixture. In his sociological critique of Kantian (and other) "pure" critique(s), Bourdieu puts the matter this way:

> The sense of distinction, the *discretio* (discrimination) which demands that certain things be brought together and others kept apart, which excludes all misalliances and all unnatural unions—i.e., all unions contrary to the common classification, to the *diacrisis* (separation) which is the basis of collective and individual identity— responds with visceral, murderous horror, absolute disgust, metaphysical fury, to everything which lies in Plato's "hybrid zone."[17]

The ideology of apartheid South Africa, analyzed by Saunders, illustrates this principle. For it is an ideology grounded in the "white nation's" apprehensions of contagious defilement produced by contact and admixture, of physical fusion that is simultaneously metaphysical confusion. Allowing racial groups to mix in urban areas, for example, evoked on the part of apartheid authorities precisely that "horror," "disgust," and "fury" marked by Bourdieu:

> Mass urbanisation has to a certain extent had a deleterious effect on the psycho-social development of the blacks, resulting in a disturbing measure of emotional and social maladjustment to the complex urban-industrial way of life; a proliferation of crime; increased family disorganization and slum conditions; a disquieting collapse of those ethnic values basic to the maintenance of social stability; considerable artificial deculturisation and a host of social diseases normally attendant upon population processes of this nature.[18]

That threat of impurity is, hence, counteracted by separation: by an "apartness" that in South Africa is manufactured by, and named, apartheid.

But the horror elicited by defilement conceals an underside of fascination; it participates in what we have called the equivocal valuation of foreignness. This dynamic, the capacity of defilement to be simultaneously threatening and liberating, will reveal itself if we follow the impurity with which Redfield and Tomášková begin their essay:

> When published in 1967, well after his death, Bronislaw Malinowski's *A Diary in the Strict Sense of the Term* caused quite a scandal. Its pages, laboriously translated from a scribbled Polish sprinkled with other tongues, revealed that a master figure of anthropology, the mythic father of ethnography, had had impure thoughts. Amid his recounting of daily routine in his field in the Trobriand

Islands, Malinowski recorded his memories of the lives he had left behind in Poland, England, and Australia, his shifting tides of passion and lust, his longings for civilization, his indulgences in novel reading and other signs of laziness, his anxieties about his work, his petty irritations, and his occasional revulsion for the people he was studying. (71)

This covert mixture of other presences with disinterested anthropological judgment is, it turns out, a harbinger of defilements that will spread across the entire discipline. For "as the political, economic, and ethical basis for neutral observation at a distance erodes," the ostensible purity of the ethnographic stance "has grown increasingly difficult to sustain" (84). But through its very effect of disorientation, this impurity "offers the possibility of . . . [new] engagements with the world" (72), allows (in)sight to happen in "the colder light of immediate reality" (84), and opens up to significance those "partial exiles and homecomings, [those] less comfortable motions of uncertain distance" that seem to characterize modernity (85).

The disorienting, liberatory power that inheres in defilement has, according to Douglas, long been recognized by ritual, which actively opposes order, engages irrationality, and pursues altered forms of consciousness:

Ritual recognizes the potency of disorder. In the disorder of the mind, in dreams, faints, and frenzies, ritual expects to find powers and truths which cannot be reached by conscious effort. Energy to command and special powers of healing come to those who can abandon rational control for a time. . . .

In these beliefs there is a double play on inarticulateness. First there is a venture into the disordered regions of the mind. Second there is the venture beyond the confines of society. The man who comes back from these inaccessible regions brings with him a power not available to those who have stayed in the control of themselves and of society.[19]

This liberatory and disordering power is the source on which Homi Bhabha draws to think the tenor of hybridity. He aims to theorize cultural "identity" from a scene of impurity, from an "interstitial passage between fixed identifications [that] opens up the possibility of a cultural hybridity [and] that entertains difference without an assumed or imposed hierarchy."[20] This project bears clear relevance to what we have elaborated as the negativity of foreignness; it overtly aspires to "destroy those negative polarities between knowledge and its objects, and between theory and practical-political reason."[21] If the term *hybridity* itself by no means extricates us from the logic of typology (and, perhaps tellingly, bears the nuance of an exotic, hothouse orchid-like creation), as Bhabha theorizes it in the colonial and postcolonial context, hybridity "is not a *problem* of genealogy or identity between two *different* cultures which can then be resolved as an issue of cultural relativism. . . . What is irremediably estranging in the presence of the hybrid," he contends, "is that the difference of cultures can no longer be identified or evaluated as objects of epistemological or moral contemplation: cultural differences are not simply *there* to be seen or appropriated."[22] It is evident from this passage that thinking from the impure site of hybridity is simultaneously a shift in focus from ostensibly stable objects of knowledge to the processes of their production, "from the cultural as an epistemological object to culture as an enactive, enunciatory site."[23] This is a turn homologous to that made by Saunders's work, which, as we have noted, both resists the fixed meanings whose byproduct is epistemological foreignness and investigates how such proper meanings are produced. It is a turn that Bhabha elsewhere describes as a distinction between cultural diversity and cultural difference:

> Cultural diversity is an epistemological object—culture as an object of empirical knowledge—whereas cultural difference is the process of the *enunciation* of culture as "knowledge*able*," authoritative, adequate to the construction of systems of cultural identification. If cultural diversity is a category of comparative ethics, aesthetics, or ethnology, cultural difference is a process of signification through which statements *of* culture or *on* culture differentiate, discriminate, and authorize the production of fields of force, reference, applicability, and capacity.[24]

This refocus introduces into thought a metaphysical impurity: ambivalence. But this ambivalence, according to Bhabha, has its possibilities: it is a space of negotiation and a time of modulation, a "temporal caesura, which is also the historically transformative moment."[25]

By now, the point is heavily overdetermined, but we will state it nonetheless: foreignness is an epistemological status. It is the inverse of order, logic, and reason, a menacing defilement of philosophical purity. This congeries of meanings might be mapped historically, as Kristeva has proposed:

> The Median wars intensified the rejection of the barbarian, but this can also be understood as a counterpart to the remarkable development of Greek philosophy, founded on the logos seen both as the Greeks' idiom and as the intelligible principle in the order of things. The barbarians are outside this universe on account of their outlandish speech and dress, their political and social peculiarities.[26]

We have already witnessed this principle in operation. We have seen it, for example, in the fact that the foreign is as much the residue of conceptualizing as a concept proper and in its position of *indistinction*—a position characterized by disorder, confusion of categories, and ambiguity of thought. We have seen it in the impropriety and incomprehensiblity produced by decontextualization and in the association of foreignness with movement and instability, in the zone of error residing in language, and in the figural resemblances between foreignness and madness. We have seen it in the hybridity that Bhabha describes and in the ambivalence that he suggests it introduces into social relations.

These glimpses into the foreign as an epistemological status are cryptic signposts to a vast territory that we can by no means submit to an exhaustive theoretical geography, but about which we might risk the following observations:

The foreign is tantamount to philosophical impurity. Purity designates ordered thought; the terms *katharos* and *katharsis,* for example, as Ricoeur has laid out, came increasingly in the ancient world "to express intellectual limpidity, clarity of style, orderliness, absence of ambiguity in an oracle . . . absence of moral blemish or stigma," as well as "the essential purification, that of wisdom and philosophy."[27] If defilement, by logical extension, attaches to disordered thought, the foreign is both defiled and defiling "for it simultaneously is characterized by, and refers to, the irrational, the ambiguous, the confused, the anomalous, the uncertain, the mysterious, the imaginative, the erroneous: what cleanly thought sweeps hurriedly under the rug of untruth" (Saunders, 118). The foreign, that is, both *designates* ambiguous cognitions, strange experiences, anomalous persons, confusing behaviors or practices, and *is* itself conceptually confused: exhibiting, for example, the telltale symptoms of semantic profligacy, relativity, equivocal valuation, heterogeneity, and metaphoricity we have sketched above. This doubled defilement accounts for why the hermeneutic tradition, as Saunders shows, commonly describes, "error, uncertainty, or absence of understanding" in terms of foreignness (116). And it also no doubt explains, at least partially, why respectable philosophy should turn its back on an uncertain "phenomenon" like contact with extraterrestrial life, for it requires granting significance to those "dimensions of consciousness" devalued by modern Western society (Zimmerman, 155); it demands, as Zimmerman argues, that one venture into precisely those defiled regions of reality and consciousness sloughed off by natural science. In its affront to philosophy, in its unseemly collusion with unreason, uncertainty and error, the foreign is, moreover, easily translated into the *inhuman*; for if humans are ζοὄν λόγον ἔχον [animals possessing language and reason], then those like the "commoners, women, and New World natives" of whom Zimmerman speaks, who do not possess *logos*, lack the "rationality necessary for inclusion in the class of fully human" (157-158). It is thus a relatively simple step from the foreign conceived as philosophical impurity to the foreign as a monstrosity to be feared, a contagion to be contained and controlled, a stain to be eliminated.

Two moments in the history of Western philosophy are adduced in the following essays that display with particular cogency the association of the foreign with philosophical impurity. The first is Descartes's systematic erasure of the defilement of doubt, which engages the "epistemologically foreign" in an intimate *agon* in order, precisely, to master it: it strives to know enough of uncertainty (personified in the *Meditations* as the demon of doubt) to make it submit, but not so much as to allow it significance on its own terms. This philosophical clean-up crusade is perhaps not unrelated, Zimmerman suggests, to the moment in which it transpires: when encounters with foreigners, particularly New World peoples, threatened the purity of European identity. Foreigners, it would seem, bear dangerous philosophical impurities. The second is Nietzsche's analysis of the uncanny guest that stands at the door of philosophy: nihilism. This uncanny guest appears in the foreignness in language described by Saunders and evokes "an unstable and transitional moment characterized by an incipient denaturaliza- tion of the highest values, by a radical reassessment of such metaphysical cate- gories as knowledge, goodness, and humanity, and by an indictment of that 'in- finitely superior whole' that works through subjects, imbeds them in a meaningful context, and guarantees their value" (Saunders, 125). Nihilism is, then, a foreignness that thematizes and interrogates philosophy itself and from which philosophy has feared the ultimate defilement: its own death. Hence, much as one protects home by ignoring the stranger at the door, one ratifies the scrupulous conscience by shuddering at the very thought of nihilism.[28] But this is to overlook the fact that, for Nietzsche, nihilism is a point of departure for a thinking that is first, genealogical, that investigates the conditions that enable in- terpretations and values, and that shifts focus, as Saunders and Bhabha have proposed, from ostensibly stable objects of knowledge to the processes of their production; and second, a form of literary exploration and artistic play, capable of nothing less than the creative transformation of the world.

   The foreign disrupts metaphysical categories. Or, conversely, what disrupts metaphysical categories is *considered* foreign. This principle is adumbrated by three recognitions we have made above: that the instability of foreignness is regulated by systems of (metaphysical) law that are not one hundred percent ef- ficient; that the presence of the foreign simultaneously thematizes and interro- gates the opposing term that constitutes it—the nation, the self, the normal, the logical; that mixture or hybridity are simultaneously a kind of foreignness and anathema to the process of metaphysical distinction. One empirical sign of this disturbance is the frantic proliferation of categories intended to bring those who fall between or outside them within the sphere of regulation. Chasteen, for ex- ample, notes that because mestizos in the New World confounded the Iberian system of law, more categories were promptly created to include them. Simi- larly, the Population Registration Act enacted by apartheid officials established a grid for classifying the population by "race," divided "Coloureds" into seven sub- groups and created a board to make determinations on ambiguous cases; the board was charged with examining hair, cuticles, and eyes and with considering the anomalous one's habits, education, speech, and deportment. An alternative to this categorizing frenzy would seem to be simply denying the existence or significance of what falls between categories. Sakamoto, for example, shows how in the early years of social work African Americans, who were considered foreign less be- cause they conformed to a notion of foreignness than because they did not fit into the category either of "domestic" or "foreign", were simply ignored by so- cial service plans.

   Foreign phenomena or experiences also effect this metaphysical distur- bance; indeed, they cannot be contained or understood within metaphysical categories because they are a disturbance in them. It is precisely these "disturbances"—the unconscious or pathological, images, and dreams—that Hillman, in psychological practice, attempts to recuperate and "honor," rather than translate and cure. This process—which we have approached figurally in his valorization of the border realms of Hermes over the oppositional world of Hercules—necessitates defying the metaphysical distinctions that have long organized both psychological theory and therapeutic practice: between interior and exterior, for example, the individual and society, imagination and reality. Running the metaphysically precarious border between therapeutic psychology and cultural analysis, Hillman has sought to relax "the artificial tension between soul and world, private and public, interior and exterior" that, he argues, "disappears when the soul as *anima mundi*, and its making, is located in the world" (cited in Owen, 193). Moreover, as Owen shows us, Hillman "hails images as real, as complementary, Dionysian rites through which Eros (the unconscious) gestures at Logos (the ego), seducing its attention and attempting its correction." In therapeutic practice, then, "the archetypal analyst would be 'giving support to the counter-ego forces, the personified figures who are ego-alien' and encouraging a patient to consider experience as broad as the imagination" (Hillman, cited in Owen, 194). A similar challenge to the categories of, and distinction between, the real and imaginary is mounted by Zimmerman; he indicts the "exclusionary either/or that prevails in modern Western science" and that insists that "the abduction phenomenon must either be psychological in nature, and thus subjective, or physical in nature, and thus objective" (154). Zimmerman (among others) seeks out a position that would inhabit, rather than eradicate, the foreignness of this phenomenon, that would accept that abductees are encountering an otherness that resists being explained as either mental or physical, and that would allow a more "nuanced stance toward the ontological status of the 'aliens'" (168).

The foreign is an agent of defamiliarization. We borrow the term from literary theory, from the Russian formalists who, "attempting to designate the distinguishing feature of literariness, defined literature as *ostranenie* [defamiliarization]" (Saunders, 116). Defamiliarization combats the automatic and habitual nature of perception and dispels the ideologies that separate us from "genuine existential contact with things and the world" (Viktor Shklovksy, cited in Saunders, 116). In other words, if the foreign disturbs metaphysical categories, so too does it unsettle ideological or cultural assumptions.[29] Hence, Zimmerman argues that "aliens" (whoever or whatever they may be) are "ultraterrestrial agents of cultural deconstruction" that have a devastating effect on anthropocentric humanism in particular (Carl Raschke, cited in Zimmerman, 172). Tracing this ideological shaking in Coetzee's novel, Saunders contends that the magistrate's reading practices are contrasted with "wisdom" because they grant asylum to linguistic foreignness: "they recuperate what the empire has relegated to meaninglessness; they defamiliarize and contest the discursive 'wisdom' through which the empire maintains power" (123). Defamiliarization may also be deployed on a disciplinary, as well as on a cultural, level; drawing on "foreign" disciplines and exploring the spaces between disciplines emerge, here and elsewhere, as methods for challenging disciplinary assumptions and conventions. We should not overlook, moreover, that to describe the foreign as "an agent of defamiliarization" is to contend that the foreign not only resists reflection, but disturbs perception, transforms not merely how we think, but what we see and hear. Two examples present themselves: the disruption presented by the foreignness in language that, Saunders contends, is a tool for seeing beyond the literality of language, for stepping outside the discursive hegemony deployed by ideology that renders circumstances and images natural and that determines perception. The foreign, for Freud, as Owen shows, is the means by which unconscious ideations, desires, cognitions become conscious; it is the parapraxes, symptoms, and dreams—"the 'alien' symptom telling out the neurosis"—that makes them perceptible (184).

The foreign both is and is like the unconscious. It would require an act of the utmost arbitrariness to designate a point at which the literality of this copula becomes metaphorical (or, for that matter, to establish in which direction this becoming logically or chronologically unfolds). We may say that the foreign is like the unconscious in its negative relativity and its alogicality, by virtue of being the object of repression, and because it is perceived as disclosing itself in obscure signs that must be submitted to a translation. "In elaborating the concept of the unconscious inductively," writes Owen, "from its manifestations in the irrationalities of dreams and parapraxes, Freud, like so many artists and innovators, worked by xenotropism"—a turn to the foreign, which in this case is the nonrational (183). Freud's personification of the repression barrier as a border guard, as well as the cartographic metaphors of his early work and his later imagery of movement, drives, displacement, and transference, also argue for this affinity between the foreign and the unconscious. But to speak in terms of metaphor is to suggest a nonidentity between the foreign and the unconscious that is potentially misleading, for, in many instances, insofar as concepts bear literal relationships, the foreign *is* (the) unconscious; it *is* the unknown: *das Unbewusste*.[30] It is that which remains unacknowledged in, for example, the nightly news, the national curriculum, or "public opinion." To describe the foreign as the cultural unconscious is to recognize that a society is governed, in part, by relationships, activities, and drives of which it is itself unaware. It is also another way of articulating the simultaneously exotic and threatening nature of foreignness: of acknowledging the *foreign* as a repository of a culture's hidden fears and desires, as what or who a culture cannot recognize in itself. These are among the many complex indices that lead Lacan to declare that "the unconscious of the subject is the discourse of the Other."[31]

Foreigners are, moreover, quite literal objects of repression: of forgetting, public erasure, disenfranchisement, dismissive stereotyping, economic marginalization. In her analysis of the inquest into the death of Stephen Biko, Saunders, for example, lays out the methods by which the black leader was repressed into obscurity, particularly within the white community: he "was banned; it was illegal for him to publish anything, to speak publicly, or to be quoted in any form and thus whites knew little or nothing about him or his views" (134). When such repressive mechanisms proved inadequate to eradicate him from national consciousness, he was detained, tortured, and killed; those who worked with him were incarcerated, the organizations he supported were banned, and newspapers sympathetic to him were shut down. While many societies, to be sure, exercise more subtle mechanisms of repression, the conscious/unconscious system, as Lacan's work has taught us, conforms remarkably to the Hegelian master/slave dialectic:

> the term "consciousness" can easily replace that of "master"; and that of "unconscious" can stand in for "slave." The unconscious, like the slave, is repressed. But the unconscious works, while consciousness sleeps and catches the latter unawares. The unconscious, further, will produce the materials which allow for the very existence and shape of consciousness. . . . Without the material "goods" supplied to consciousness by the unconscious, the first has nothing by which—or with which—to function.[32]

This depiction is particularly resonant in the context of West/East relationships, in which, as we shall argue below, the "belated" nations of the so-called "third" or "developing" world remain both foreigners to modernity and the (unacknowledged) producers of goods for Western masters.

The foreign is errant. It is embedded in the semantic field circumscribed by the Latin term *erre*, to lead astray, which bequeaths to English such words as *err, error, erroneous, errability, errancy, erratic,* and *erratum.* These children of *erre* always signify both fault and wandering: two notions that we have, on repeated occasions, found associated with the foreign. We have noted, for example, the relationship that hermeneutics draws between foreignness and error and the manner in which foreigners may be identified by linguistic or social errors, as well as the component of (potentially random) movement within foreignness, the errancy presupposed by the conception of the "settlement house," and the way foreignness shares with madness the characteristics of both wandering and untruth. It is perhaps not surprising that this wandering should characterize the methods of an excavator of the unconscious. For as Owen contends (furrowing into the etymological association of *expatriare* with *exspatiare* [to wander, digress, move about freely or at will]), "Freud's intellectual expatriatism and wandering, his errancy, began in his first psychological work on the 'talking cure' with Breuer and 'Anna O,' and with his experiments in hypnosis" (183). And then, he followed the wanderings of free association, the error of symptoms, the digression of dreams. This willingness to wander, even to err, also characterizes the kind of reading practice that, according to Saunders, recuperates the foreignness in signification. It is a practice, illustrated by Coetzee's magistrate, that "follows meandering and unmarked trails through the semantic," (130) that embarks on the kind of "strategic and adventurous" journey that Derrida associates with (the delineation of) *différance*:

Strategic because no transcendent truth present outside the field of writing can govern theologically the totality of the field. Adventurous because this strategy is not a simple strategy in the sense that strategy orients tactics according to a final goal, a *telos* or theme of domination, a mastery and ultimate reappropriation of the development of the field. (Cited in Saunders, 118)

That absence of mastery, the trial and error, digression, indirection that conceptually attaches to foreignness might also describe the quotidian experience of being a foreigner: those who, as Sakamoto shows, rate high on the "Daily Hassles Scale"; or those for whom living under apartheid means taking detours around the law, circumventing the legitimate economy, diverting meaning and power from others' literality.

The foreign is inessential. It falls outside the borders of significance; it is supplemental, excessive, extraneous, irrelevant. It is what spills over the container of essence, what medieval thought called *accidentia*. A striking example of this tenet and its consequences, Saunders argues, is evinced in the Biko inquest, in which doctors and security police justified their dismissal of Biko's (torture-induced) physical symptoms on the grounds that they were odd and uncertain—that is, foreign and therefore insignificant, though ignoring those symptoms clearly led to Biko's death. They deployed a similar relegation of the uncertain to irrelevance in order to dismiss the import of errors in their own testimony.

This volume's essays allow us to name at least two more particularized forms of this inessentiality: one is imagination, the other is figurality. Connoisseurs of imagination—artists, writers, musicians—guilty of falling for Reason's decorative sister (who, however captivating, should not be taken too seriously) are, as Hélène Cixous suggests, perpetual foreigners: "The author writes as if he or she were in a foreign country, as if he or she were a foreigner in his or her own family" (cited in Owen, 196). It is not without precedent, then, that "depth psychology," as Owen remarks, "has made art and artists, along with the symptom, a chief *topos* of the foreign" (180). Indeed, while psychology must make frequent business trips to the outlandish land of imagination, it does not, to be sure, confuse it with home. "Because of psychology's manifest wish to establish itself as an empirical science," Owen writes, "however phenomenological its early emphasis, most analytical theorists, whether of the Freudian or Jungian schools, have felt that rationality rather than imagination was their genre" (180). If the creative imagination is deemed an expendable ornament on the staid cloak of reason, so too are figures a frivolous decoration on the literality of language. And we have already acknowledged that the concept of the foreign is characterized by an errant figurality, that it is difficult, if not impossible, to determine at what point foreignness becomes metaphorical, and that to be foreign is, in many senses, to become a figure, to fall outside of proper meaning. Indeed, in the *Rhetoric*, Aristotle's terms for *literal* and *figural* are, respectively, the κύριος (*kurios*: authoritative or, substantively, an owner, possessor) and the ξένος (*xenos*: foreign). According to Saunders, this association of the foreign with an extraneous figurality can be descried in the social relations of apartheid South Africa, where blacks' words and actions are consistently interpreted through the detour of figurality: not taken at face value, but assumed to be allegorical, to say something other than what they seem to say or, more simply, to be extraneous to significance. When Redfield and Tomášková vow to "take metaphorical allusions to exile seriously" they move to recuperate what has been seen as inessential to the discipline of anthropology: decorative, but irrelevant to the essence of its truth (72). And when Owen describes artistic expatriatism as *xenotropism*, she reconceives it in terms of a figure: a trope, a turn, a swerve, an existential ornamentation that is anything but insignificant.

The foreign is possibility. Let us retrace the steps that might lead us to such a proposition. Thematizing and indicting the familiar, the foreign introduces possibility into it: into the assumptions and conventions of a discipline, a discourse, a culture. Both the lure of the exotic and the threat of the unknown are symptoms of this possibility. The movement that belongs to foreignness is a figure for possibility; distance is its open field: the distance that, for the exile, makes home reconceivable, or the distance in signification that makes other meanings imaginable. The independence entangled with foreignness is, in at least two instances, clearly linked to possibility: the independence sought by women like Addams and Starr that would open up possibilities for them, and the hermeneutic independence illustrated by Coetzee that brings into the conceivable meanings not authorized by the hermeneutic code. We have seen that the impurity that attaches to the foreign has the capacity to offer the possibility of new engagements with the world (Redfield and Tomášková), to evoke "powers and truths" not available to those who remain within the confines of society (Douglas, 94), and to "open up the possibility of a cultural hybridity," a time of negotiation "which is also the historically transformative moment" (Bhabha, 242). We have witnessed forms of this possibility emerge: dimensions of consciousness denigrated by Western culture, artistic and imaginative work, a thinking contrary to the dictates of metaphysics.

It would be worthwhile to explore whether this description of foreignness as possibility might not arrive at the freedom that Heidegger formulates as the essence of truth: that freedom that "reveals itself as letting beings be," that (far from indifference) consists in "engag[ing] oneself with the open region and its openness into which every being comes to stand," and which, most importantly, "is intrinsically exposing, ek-sistent."[33] Is there a relation between this ecstatic standing outside of itself that characterizes freedom and the standing outside that is at the root of foreignness (*foras*)? Would freedom and, hence, truth necessitate a certain foreignness? It would also be prudent to heed Kierkegaard, whose formulation of anxiety as "the dizziness of freedom which emerges when . . . freedom looks down into its own possibility" bears a suggestive relation to the anxiety we have seen evoked by foreignness.[34] But perhaps the most crucial recognition to which Kierkegaard leads us is that "[t]he possible corresponds exactly to the future. For freedom, the possible is the future, and the future is for time the possible."[35] Would it be tenable to translate this statement—and what would be the consequences if we dared?—by substituting the *foreign* for the *possible*? Moreover, if the foreign is possibility, then (following a conversation that runs from Kierkegaard to Heidegger to Derrida) the act of "addressing one-self to the possible"[36] that conditions *decision*—that would be involved in any social or political change—would, accordingly, mean addressing the foreign in all the unstable density we have found to characterize it. "[L]et us not be blind," writes Derrida, "to the aporia that all change must endure. It is the aporia of the *perhaps*, its historical and political aporia. Without the opening of an absolutely undetermined possible, without the radical abeyance and suspense marking a *perhaps*, there would never be either event or decision."[37] Although decision also demands "suspending the *perhaps*," no decision (ethical, juridical, or political) is possible without interrupting determination by engaging oneself with the perhaps. This aporia, this absolutely undetermined possible, this foreignness, is simultaneously a crucial constituent of responsibility and (as our foregoing discussion might lead us to predict) a leap out of knowledge: out of what we have delineated as philosophical purity, metaphysical categorization, the familiar, the conscious, the correct and stable, the essential. Derrida puts the matter this way:

> [K]nowledge is necessary if one is to assume responsibility, but the decisive or deciding moment of responsibility supposes a leap by which an act takes off, ceasing in that instant to follow the consequence of what is—that is, of that which can be determined by science or consciousness—and thereby *frees itself* (this is what is called freedom), by the act of its act, of what is therefore heterogeneous to it, that is, knowledge. *In sum a decision is unconscious*—insane as that may seem, it involves the unconscious and nevertheless remains responsible.[38]

Notes

1. For a more detailed discussion of the imbrications of "race," sexuality, and pathology in nineteenth-century Europe, see the important work of Sander L. Gilman, *Difference and Pathology: Stereotypes of Sexuality, Race, and Madness* (Ithaca, NY: Cornell University Press, 1985), 19-21.

2. See Michel Foucault, *Madness and Civilization: A History of Insanity in the Age of Reason*, trans. Richard Howard (New York: Vintage, 1965). Note also Gilman's description of pathology as "disorder and the loss of control, the giving over of the self to the forces that lie beyond the self." Gilman, *Difference and Pathology*, 24.

3. Foucault, *Madness and Civilization*, 129.

4. Foucault, *Madness and Civilization*, 252, 254.

5. Foucault, *Madness and Civilization*, 115.

6. Foucault, *Madness and Civilization*, 175-176.

7. Foucault, *Madness and Civilization*, 64.

8. It also shows up the logic operating in South African school textbooks, which

rendered the legal alienation of blacks "logical" by depicting their social and political activities as inherently improper. See Elizabeth Dean, Paul Hartmann, and Mary Katzen, *History in Black and White: An Analysis of South African School History Textbooks* (Paris: Unesco, 1983). And it illuminates why the improprieties that reputedly characterized black South Africans—"desertion, failure to commence work on time, insolence, drunkenness, negligence, and similar misconduct"—should be made into criminal offenses. John Dugard, *Human Rights and the South African Legal Order* (Princeton: Princeton University Press, 1978), 85.

9. Paul Ricoeur, *The Symbolism of Evil* (Boston: Beacon Press, 1967), 117.

10. Michel Foucault, *Discipline and Punish: The Birth of the Prison*, trans. Alan Sheridan (New York: Vintage, 1979), 251.

11. It seems to me that to a certain degree, this conception is continued by Kristeva's symptomology of foreignness in *Strangers to Ourselves*, which implicitly takes the foreign as a coherent pathological category with identifiable symptoms: the foreigner is, for example "a devotee of solitude, even in the midst of a crowd, because he is faithful to a shadow"; "he readily bears a kind of admiration for those who have welcomed him, for he rates them more often than not above himself, be it financially, politically, or socially"; "he is never simply torn between here and elsewhere, now and before. Those who believe they are crucified in such a fashion forget that nothing ties them there anymore, and, so far, nothing binds them here"; "the foreigner . . . remains that insolent person who, secretly or openly, first challenges the morality of his own country and then causes scandalous excesses in the host country" etc. Julia Kristeva, *Strangers to Ourselves*, Trans. Leon S. Roudiez (New York: Columbia University Press, 1991), 5, 6, 10, 30.

12. Foucault, *Madness and Civilization*, 274.

13. These processes overlap to a striking degree with the deployment of disgust as a basis for social discipline and law, cogently critiqued by Martha Nussbaum; she argues that disgust "expresses a refusal to ingest and thus be contaminated by a potent reminder of one's own mortality and animality" and "has throughout history been used as a powerful weapon in social efforts to exclude certain groups and persons" such as Jews, women, homosexuals, untouchables, lower-class people, and, I would add, foreigners. See "'Secret Sewers of Vice': Disgust, Bodies, and the Law," in *The Passions of Law*, ed. Susan Bandes (New York: New York University Press, 2000), 25, 29.

14. Mary Douglas, *Purity and Danger: An Analysis of Concepts of Pollution and Taboo* (New York: Praeger, 1966), 35.

15. W. Eichrodt, *Theology of the Old Testament* (Philadelphia: Westminster Press, 1967), 134.

16. Douglas, *Purity and Danger*, 53.

17. Pierre Bourdieu, *Distinction: A Social Critique of the Judgement of Taste*, trans. Richard Nice (Cambridge, Mass.: Harvard University Press, 1984), 474-475.

18. *1978 South African Yearbook* (Johannesburg: South African Department of Information, 1979), 226.

19. Douglas, *Purity and Danger*, 94-95.

20. Homi Bhabha, *The Location of Culture* (London: Routledge, 1994), 4. For a history of theories of cultural and "racial" hybridity, see Robert J.C. Young, *Colonial Desire: Hybridity in Theory, Culture, and Race* (New York: Routledge, 1995); for a comparison of Bhabha's "conflictual" model with Todorov's and Kristeva's universalizing ones, see Angelika Bammer, "Xenophobia, Xenophilia, and No Place to Rest," in *Encountering the Other(s): Studies in Literature History, and Culture*, ed. Gisela Brinker-Gabler (Albany, N.Y.: SUNY Press, 1995), 45-62; for a grammatical analysis of

Bhabha's uses of the terms *hybrid, hybridization,* and *hybridity,* see Monika Fludernik, "The Constitution of Hybridity: Postcolonial Interventions," in *Hybridity and Postcolonialism: Twentieth-Century Indian Literature,* ed. Monika Fludernik (Tübingen: Stauffenburg Verlag, 1998), 19-53.

21. Bhabha, *The Location of Culture,* 25.

22. Bhabha, *The Location of Culture,* 114.

23. Bhabha, *The Location of Culture,* 178.

24. Bhabha, *The Location of Culture,* 34.

25. Bhabha, *The Location of Culture,* 242.

26. Kristeva, *Strangers to Ourselves,* 51.

27. Ricoeur, *The Symbolism of Evil,* 38.

28. Gilman analyzes several notorious instances of this shuddering, as well as the figure of Nietzsche as pathogen, in *Difference and Pathology,* chap. 2.

29. In another context, Clifford has noted the degree to which the "exotic" has functioned "as a primary court of appeal against the rational, the beautiful, the normal of the West." *The Predicament of Culture: Twentieth-Century Ethnography, Literature, and Art* (Cambridge, Mass.: Harvard University Press, 1988), 127.

30. Freud's word for the unconscious, *das Unbewusste,* is also the German word for *unknown.* Pertinent here also is Gayatri Spivak's analysis of the purifying foreclosure of the "native informant" and his/her perspective from (the Symbolic of) the discursive mainstream. See *A Critique of Postcolonial Reason: Toward a History of the Vanishing Present* (Cambridge, Mass.: Harvard University Press, 1999).

31. Jacques Lacan, *Ecrits: A Selection,* trans. Alan Sheridan (New York: Norton, 1977), 55.

32. Françoise Meltzer, "Unconscious," in *Critical Terms for Literary Study,* ed. Frank Lentricchia and Thomas McLaughlin (Chicago: University of Chicago Press, 1990), 158.

33. Martin Heidegger, "On the Essence of Truth," *Basic Writings,* rev. and exp. ed., ed. David Farrell Krell (San Francisco: Harper, 1977), 125.

34. Søren Kierkegaard, *The Concept of Anxiety: A Simple Psychologically Orienting Deliberation on the Dogmatic Issue of Hereditary Sin,* trans. and ed. Reidar Thomte in collaboration with Albert B. Anderson (Princeton: Princeton University Press, 1980), 61. According to Kierkegaard, the mood that attaches to possibility is *anxiety*: "In a logical system," he writes, "it is convenient to say that possibility passes over into actuality. However, in actuality it is not so convenient, and an intermediate term is required. The intermediate term is anxiety." *The Concept of Anxiety,* 49.

35. Kierkegaard, *The Concept of Anxiety,* 91.

36. Jacques Derrida, *Politics of Friendship,* trans. George Collins (New York: Verso, 1997), 67.

37. Derrida, *Politics of Friendship,* 67. Derrida's "perhaps" is an elaboration of the Nietzschean *vielleicht* in *Human all too Human* and elsewhere.

38. Derrida, *Politics of Friendship,* 69.

Chapter Four

The Present: Temporality and Materiality

If we piece these fragments together into another pattern, we begin to detect the complex relation of foreignness to *presence*. The relativity of foreignness, for example, its variable and shifting contents, the term's penchant for indiscriminately signifying experiences, concepts, and attributes, make it difficult to determine precisely when and where the foreign is present. The position of the foreign on the "undistinguished" side of customary distinctions, as well as the ways in which foreignness is pathologized, rendered unconscious, or relegated to irrelevance signal, moreover, the extent to which the foreign coincides with a lack of social presence, with the politically unapparent. And if the experience of being a foreigner—an exile, for example—teaches us the untenability of a simple equation of distance with nonpresence, it also shows us, inversely, the inadequacy of conceiving presence in terms of a binary opposition with absence. Indeed, we might say that to sense the presence of the distant—a feeling which might surface in times of loss, mourning, desire, or religious experience, for example—is to experience the foreign. As we have witnessed in the juxtaposition of Geertz's with Heidegger's "being there," moreover, presence can mean more than one thing: when one is a foreigner (like Geertz's anthropologist) "being there" means something different from when one is at home (like Heidegger's *Dasein*). What is at stake in placing the anthropological "participant observer" (which Clifford astutely terms "existential shorthand for the hermeneutical circle") alongside the fully immersed *Dasein* of absorbed coping is the degree of reflection constitutive of presence.[1] It is, in a sense, to rephrase the great

Proustian dilemma: where exactly *is* presence bred—in immediate experience or in the (reflecting) head?

Following other lines might lead us to interpret the picture this way: foreignness is the impossibility of immediacy; it is to bear a mediated relation to the present. This principle is adduced in Sakamoto's descriptions of immigrants in America, who, in order to access the present, must take a detour through the settlement house or social work agency. What natives do in unmediated fashion—speak, work, shop, set up homes, raise children, socialize—must be mediated for the foreigner by an "in-between" figure capable of translating and negotiating with the dominant culture and its institutions.[2] Similarly, pursuing the proposition that to be foreign is to become a figure, Saunders contends that if being at home means "having access to (ostensibly) immediate meaning," to be foreign is "to be encumbered by an awareness of mediation, to be detained by language itself" (120). Presence, for the foreigner, is, hence, occluded by practices and speech that must be thematized, reflected upon, interpreted. Another way of describing this process of mediation, this encumbrance of reflection, would be as translation: speaking to or about another culture, Badran suggests, is always a translation because it "involves shuttling between two languages without fully parallel words" (96).

We would do well to linger on this notion of translation, for it is arguably the method through which a foreigner attains to the present, as well as a necessary skill for engaging with the foreign when it is present. Moreover, translation, like foreignness, bears both the nuance of movement and the structure of figurality: to read a figure requires a kind of translation; to translate is to read figurally.[3] Translation has (like truth) been largely conceived in terms of adequation (or, more intimately, as *fidelity*), a conception that not only assumes that culture is a stable, portable object of knowledge, but that follows the logic of metaphor—another manner of "carrying across" and the trope that has traditionally governed translation. If Bhabha's notion of hybridity has taught us to question the former of these assumptions, it is Walter Benjamin's image of a broken vessel that most famously shatters the latter:

> Fragments of a vessel which are to be glued together must match one another in the smallest details, although they need not be like one another. In the same way a translation, instead of resembling the meaning of the original must lovingly and in detail incorporate the original's mode of signification, thus making both the original and the translation recognizable as fragments of a greater language, just as fragments are part of a vessel.[4]

What Benjamin proposes is thus a translation that is no longer metaphor, but metonymy, "a metonymic, successive pattern," as Paul de Man puts it, "in which things follow, rather than a metaphorical unifying pattern in which things become one by resemblance . . . [Benjamin] is not saying that the fragments constitute a totality, he says the fragments are fragments, and that they remain essentially fragmentary."[5] While no less figural (and nonetheless mediated), translation from this perspective is less a matter of adequation and similitude, than of contiguity and contact: a perspective that, by extension, conceives the foreign not in terms of fidelity to an original or a mastertext, but as an adjacence similar (only) in its fragmentariness.[6] Equally germane in Benjamin's theory of translation is his insistence that "a real translation is transparent; it does not cover the original," that translation should not strive to turn the language of the original into the language of the translation, but rather to allow the new language to be powerfully transformed by the foreign tongue, to give "voice to the intention of the original not as reproduction but as harmony."[7] A translation that is neither assimilation nor travelogue, which resists adapting cultures to accommodate consumer demands, Benjamin evokes a contact with the foreign that is powerfully transformative, an opening to foreignness that intricately rearticulates being. Finally, following the pattern we have adduced above in which the presence of the foreign thematizes and interrogates the familiar, Benjamin's essay not only reconceives the status of translation—traditionally viewed as derived, secondary, unoriginal—but contests those slippery nuances of *origin* we have marked above. For translation, in Benjamin's terms, illuminates and destabilizes the original; it shows in the original, according to de Man's reading of Benjamin, "a mobility, an instability, which at first one did not notice." Translations thus "disarticulate [and] undo the original, they reveal that the original was always already disarticulated."[8] De Man, significantly, describes this movement of disintegration and fragmentation of the original as a kind of absolutized foreignness: it "is a wandering, an *errance*, a kind of permanent exile if you wish, but it is not really an exile, for there is no homeland, nothing from which one has been exiled."[9] Benjamin and de Man thus lead us to see that the principle of heterogeneity we have sketched above falls over the vast semantic field of origin: the original is foreign.

Two further, and intriguingly conflicting, relations of foreignness to presence beckon for our attention. On the one hand, Redfield and Tomášková argue that a valorization of the foreign, like that which inheres in anthropology, risks being a *denigration* of the present: "a trivialization of immediacy, and a relegation of meaning to everyday experience that lies over a horizon" (72). This divestment of presence coincides with a nostalgia for cultural purity in which the remote, perceived to be less tainted by hybridity, is equated with the authentic: the pure is never (the) present. It also coincides with the inability to recognize "more common displacements, the partial travels of daily life across small divides, and our own active, imperfect sensibilities"; it has thus "deferred anthropology's engagement with more immediate milieux" (72), with modern life, with "partial natives and strangers inhabiting different, but imperfectly artificial worlds" (85). For the other figure studied by Redfield and Tomášková—the exile—the present, similarly denigrated, takes on the mien of menace: it is a threat to purity; it bears a perpetual warning label that meaningful being can only be achieved elsewhere. On the other hand, the perspective from which Saunders begins her essay—the literary theory of defamiliarization we have introduced above—suggests that foreignness is a prerequisite for entry into the present. The argument made by Viktor Shklovsky and, differently, by Berthold Brecht, stipulates that in order to be fully present to our own world—inevitably obscured by its very familiarity—we need a foreign agent: an alienation effect that renders the world foreign, that dissolves the ideologies that separate us from "genuine existential contact with things and the world," and that makes visible (like a smudge on glass) the ordinarily transparent structure of mediation that conditions the obvious, the literal, the "apparently uninterpreted meaning" of words, acts, and persons.[10]

Presence, it behooves us to recognize, is a matter of both time and space; it bears meaning both to temporality and to materiality.

Chasteen's evocation of the past as a foreign country is testimony to the fact that the foreign is routinely associated with what is not temporally present. So too is the coupling of foreignness with the archaic in analyses of the psychological symptom (see Owen). Subtending these semantic alliances and their inverted image—the stability (that is, the *timelessness*) nostalgically attributed to homes, nations, and personal identity—is the principle that the passage of time leaves behind foreignness: a forgotten self, an inscrutable ancestor, a strange way of doing things, death.[11] By the same logic, any recognition of temporality is an apparition of foreignness; and the foreigner, uncannily, an announcement that time passes, a *memento mori*. This corroborates Zimmerman's position that hostility towards foreigners, as well as attempts to dominate nature and other human beings, is a way of masking one's own mortality. It also explains why the alienation effect for Brecht is a matter of temporality, of scratching the mirage-like veneer of permanence and stability coating the present (see Saunders).

As much in the foregoing discussion indicates, foreignness might be described as a relation to that particular formulation of temporality we call "modernity": a term which functions as a common synonym for the present. When Redfield and Tomášková depict the ethnological vocation (via Malinowski) not only as seeking out the foreign but as "fleeing the modern," they adumbrate the equation of foreignness with the opposite of modernity (89). It is, in large part, the collusion of modernity with *nation states* that produces this foreignness. For if the foreign is, as we have noted, largely defined in opposition to the nation, and if the nation is a specifically modern political formation, then not to be a nation is to be foreign to modernity (and the negative relativity of the foreign is as much temporal as cultural).[12] As Benedict Anderson famously contends, the nation state is not only predicated on a distinctly modern conception of time—a simultaneity measured by clock and calendar, expressed in novel and newspaper—but is structured "modularly": because it became "a known model, it imposed certain 'standards' from which too-marked deviations were impermissible."[13] If, moreover, the rise of the nation state can be located at the moment of transition from agrarian to industrial society as Ernest Gellner argues, this etiology establishes a tacit equation between nation, modernity, and industrial development; an equation that ensures that peoples who form nations in the absence of industrialization (and the social conditions productive of, and attendant upon, it) will remain foreign to "developed" nations and, hence, to the culture of modernity.[14] We might rephrase this recognition, recalling our discussion of origin, by describing these circumstances as an alienation both from the original conception of nation and from the nation conceived as origin. If *origin*, as we have noted, signifies "source of development," then "less developed" nations, accordingly, are *not* an origin, not authentic; they are derived, a translation in the traditional sense—a status that extends to their cultural productions: "In this temporal setup," writes Clifford, "a great many twentieth-century creations can only appear as imitations of more 'developed' models."[15] This conceptual alienation also often entails a literal alienation of a country's work force, in the form of migration to industrial centers. The geography of foreignness characteristic of modernity is thus routinely conceived as an opposition between "the West" and "the rest" (referred to alternately as the "non-West," the "Third World," the "underdeveloped," or "developing world"), not least because "excluding oil and mining concerns, there is not a single African, South American, Middle Eastern, or Indian company among the top five hundred corporations" in the world.[16] In this temporalized geography of modernity, to be foreign means to be backward, dependent, immobilized in time past.

Modernity is also customarily conceived in opposition to "tradition." Clifford notes, for example, that "anthropological culture collectors have typically gathered what seems 'traditional'—what by definition is opposed to modernity."[17] The term *traditional*, moreover, has been known to function as a synonym for "non-Western" and this schema, this dense connotative impasto, entails two effects: first, that "what is different" about peoples in modernity "remains tied to traditional pasts, inherited structures that either resist or yield to the new but cannot produce it";[18] and, second, that the "traditional" is relegated to an irrelevant past, rendered trebly foreign: "non-Western," temporally nonpresent, inessential. Perhaps never have these layers of connotation been brushed with thicker intensity than on the canvas of Islam, where (in an inverse formulation to that described above) *modernity* is the threatening foreigner and where, as Badran shows us, feminists encounter the widespread conception that if feminism means becoming modern, it must also mean abandoning tradition and becoming "Western."[19] In other words, feminists have found themselves confronted with the clearly unacceptable ultimatum that in order to participate in the temporal present, they must become radically foreign to their geographical and cultural present. Yet it is from this very position that non-Western feminisms have descried new possibilities and have assumed the crucial task of forging new conceptions of tradition, modernity, and feminism. For if feminism is a species of foreignness in that it challenges practices and traditions that subtend the domesticity of patriarchal privilege, if it is "modern" because, to some degree, it attempts to break with the past, feminists in the context of Islam have demonstrated that there can exist other modernities aside from that prescribed by the

West; that *modern* need not be defined in opposition to tradition; and that Islamic traditions—its egalitarianism, its respect for women, for example—may not only be incorporated into both modernity and feminism, but function as a sound foundation for them.[20] From them, Western feminists have learned that theirs is not the only present.

While "modern," "non-traditional," and "Western" signify a greater temporal presence than, and make foreigners of, the archaic, "traditional," or "non-Western," the present is increasingly characterized by processes of globalization that would seem to make the concept of the foreign obsolete.[21] "Modern transnational corporations in quest of global markets cannot really comprehend 'foreign policy,'" writes Benjamin Barber, "because the word *foreign* has no meaning to the ambitious global businessperson."[22] The dramatic growth of global markets and finance since the late 1970s; a decrease in governmental regulation of, and increase in privatized apparatuses for, cross-border transactions; the greater mobility of capital; interaction and transactions in cyberspace; the decline of national sovereignty and transfer of economic and legal authority to transnational entities: these circumstances (customarily gathered under the rubric of *globalization*) have, to be sure, conditioned a significant reformulation of the concepts of nation, citizenship, and belonging around which the foreigner is constituted.[23] The nation no longer bears exclusive sovereignty over its people or their transactions with those of other nations; it is superseded in certain economic and legal arenas, for example, by the World Trade Organization, the International Monetary Fund, and the World Bank, and challenged by human rights covenants and environmental mandates.[24] Processes of globalization, like a translation that disarticulates the original, have, moreover, exposed the fact that nations have never been unitary institutions and that a good many of their own citizens (women and ethnic minorities, for example) have remained alien to nations' singularized identities and "will." Citizenship has been revalued accordingly; in the age of globalization, it is neither the only foundation for rights (many of which have been reformulated as "human" rather than "civil"), nor is it the sole guarantor of political viability: individuals and organizations increasingly pursue political engagements independently of nation states.[25]

Globalization shuffles traditional constituents of identity and realigns the borders of belonging: the American businessperson may well be more at home in Tokyo than in Tupelo; one's sense of belonging may well be organized around a mobile and cosmopolitan society—what Leslie Sklair has named "the transnational capitalist class"[26]—rather than a geographical place, a home, or a nation. While globalization alters the aspect of foreignness, it also readily absorbs, co-opts, and commodifies it, aggressively marketing exotic fashions, objects for the home, music, food, and other "ethnic" artifacts. Indeed one's membership in the transnational capitalist class is, to a large degree, certified by appreciating and possessing such foreign goods. But these lifestyle accessories are neither the only, nor the most consequential, survival of foreignness in the era of globalization, for globalization is also responsible for provoking resurgent nationalisms, for delineating its own body of foreigners, and for contributing directly to processes of immigration.

First, virulent nationalisms are a significant by-product of globalization, an effort to ward off the perceived homogenization of culture associated with globalization, often quite rightly equated with American cultural imperialism, secularism, and consumerism. Barber contends that a deeply dialectical relation exists between what, on the one hand, he calls "McWorld"—a secular, uniform, and universalizing mass culture that, spread through the "infotainment telesector," displaces diverse indigenous traditions, "forges global markets," and insists with apparent impunity that "the laws of production and consumption are sovereign, trumping the laws of legislatures and courts"—and what, on the other hand, he calls "Jihad"—the reinvigoration of local cultures, ethnic, and religious identities, tribalisms, and nationalisms, a frenzied "preservation" of culture threatened by outside influences and, above all, by modernity.[27] In other words, a causal relation can be readily identified (though it is imbedded in a complex system of polyvalent causes and effects) between globalization and the jingoism that manufactures foreigners.

Second, globalization creates its own foreigners—alien to (and alienated from, in a fashion not unlike that described by Marx) the economic class, work culture, and lifestyle inhabited by the "global citizen." It has created vast numbers of low-wage jobs, not only in production and assembly, but "through the demand for workers to service the lifestyle and consumption requirements of the growing high-income professional and managerial class."[28] The "new" foreigners produced by these circumstances bear a clear family resemblance to the ones we have been following all along, not only in their position on a disadvantageous rung of a simultaneously conceptual and social hierarchy, but in their status as societal unconscious, for the noncorporate actors crucial to the functioning of global industry and finance remain largely overlooked by economic and political discourse on globalization; they are that which globalization does not recognize in and as itself. Falling outside the economy of the proper, these global foreigners, moreover, increasingly resort to circumventing the "proper" economy, that is, to operating in the informal economy, informalizing work space and relations, subcontracting, shifting market functions to the community or household, engaging in "income-generating activities occurring outside the state's regulatory framework."[29] These practices—pathologized, criminalized, disciplined—are, tellingly, suspected of being foreign imports. Saskia Sassen writes:

> Until recently, theorization about the informal economy has focused on the shortcomings of less developed economies: their inability to attain full modernization, to stop excess migration to the cities, and to implement universal education and literacy programs. The growth of an informal economy in highly developed countries has been explained as the result of immigration from the Third World and the replication here of survival strategies typical of the home countries of migrant workers.[30]

Third, globalization not only creates new forms of foreignness, but contributes to processes of immigration that produce foreigners in the most traditional sense. In the sort of wry irony that makes silt of social policy, foreign investment seeks to keep "Third World" low-wage workers—the prototypical foreigners to modernity—in their place, but in fact produces circumstances that condition migration: it displaces people to industrial zones, disrupting traditional work structures and making it difficult for them to return to rural communities; it simultaneously accustoms individuals to uprooting, making them subjectively open to moving again, and exposes them to "Westernization"; and it creates a reserve of unemployed wage laborers. Thus, Sassen writes, "the very measures commonly thought to deter immigration—foreign investment and the promotion of export-oriented growth in developing countries—seem to have had precisely the opposite effect."[31] The transnationalization of labor has not only dramatically increased global migration, but solidified the association of the foreigner with poverty, and with particular ethnic groups. For example, whereas at mid-century, more than two-thirds of immigrants to the United States came from Europe, today the vast majority come from Latin America, Asia, and the Caribbean Basin. As Sakamoto points out, the word *immigrant* in America has come largely to signify "one who comes to the United States from a 'less industrialized' or 'poor' country supposedly in order to receive social benefits such as a job and income security" (259). This deeply engraved, negative image of immigration contains, as Sassen argues, "an implicit valorization of the receiving country and a devalorization of the sending country."[32] Moreover, "because immigration is thought to result from unfavorable socioeconomic conditions in other countries, it is assumed to be unrelated to U.S. economic needs or broader international economic conditions. In this context, the decision becomes a humanitarian matter; we admit immigrants by choice and out of generosity, not because we have any economic motive or political responsibility to do so."[33]

This interested misrecognition has no doubt fed the anti-immigrant sentiment that has swept across "First World" countries and functioned as the alibi for a veritable panic of regulation and discipline, reinforced borders, pageants of criminalization, and laws that very considerably erode immigrant's rights. In the late 1970s and early 1980s, although Western European countries made efforts to integrate permanent second generation immigrants, they also closed legal labor immigration, actively encouraged voluntary return migration, instituted punitive measures to control immigrants (such as deportation and penalties for those who employed illegal immigrants), witnessed increasing public outcry over *Überfremdung* [Overforeignization], and saw the rise of anti-immigrant parties such as the National Action Against Overforeignization of People and Fatherland in Switzerland and Jean-Marie Le Pen's *Front National* in France. In the later 1980s, dramatic increases in the number of those seeking political asylum raised the thorny issue of who has the right to claim such status, while, in Europe, both the Schengen Treaty and the Dublin Convention set out procedures for restricting an influx of asylum seekers and refugees. In 1993, The E.U. Working Group on Immigration began preparing a common list of undesirable aliens to be circulated among law enforcement agencies, initiated common training of officials and a center for information exchange on border crossings and immigration, Germany reinforced its borders vulnerable to Eastern European immigration, and France, implementing harsher naturalization restrictions, revoked its policy of automatic citizenship for second generation immigrants.[34] A core of E.U. states is currently discussing the creation of a common European border guard. In the United States, the "Illegal Immigration Reform and Immigrant Responsibility Act of 1996" provided for, among other things, an increase in border patrol agents, improved technology, harsher penalties for illegal entry, wiretap authorization for investigating alien smuggling or document fraud, expedited removal of inadmissible arriving aliens, a broadened range of offenses for which one can be deported, further exclusions from the family unity program, increased funds for removal of aliens, limitations on public assistance and benefits, greater surveillance of non-immigrant foreign students, and, creatively, a border patrol museum.[35]

Another ingredient at work in the reconfigurations of identity produced by globalization is gender. Increasingly incorporating women into the work force, globalizing processes have also made many women into migrants. While this means that women have ventured into the multiply foreign territory of the masculine work sphere, of paid labor, and of urban space (and thereby dismantled the armature of work in traditional communities), it has also, in many instances, been an investment in, and reinforcement of, patriarchal society. For as Sassen notes, "young women in patriarchal societies are seen by foreign employers as obedient and disciplined workers, willing to do tedious, high-precision work and to submit themselves to work conditions that would not be tolerated in the highly developed countries."[36] Yet women's international migrations, their work experiences and income, have also served as sources of empowerment—increasing women's autonomy, giving them greater control over domestic decisions and budgeting, positioning them as families' liaisons with the dominant culture—and thereby have assisted in redrawing the lines that define gender-proper and "foreign" behavior and had a significant impact on the way gender is constructed and performed.[37]

We have been speaking of globalization in temporal terms, but its presence is also physical; it extends in space, is built of, and recognizable by, particular material configurations. Although the glossy cover of globalization promises a physically deterritorialized cyberspace devoid of material presence, the phenomenon itself is more place-bound than such representations suggest: globalizing information systems require an extensive infrastructure, the material presence of buildings, machines, and workers that are (as a matter of fact and a fact of matter) located within particular national boundaries (and *not* within others). Indeed, the new forms of inclusion and exclusion created by globalizing processes can, to a large degree, be spatially mapped in terms of urban centers and their tuberous peripheries of foreignness. Thus the conceptual spectrality of foreignness, the logical difficulties of pinning down its presence, are, in practice, harnessed to the presence (or absence) of specifiable material objects. If, in an earlier era, this was a matter of the typewriter without diacritical marks evoked by Redfield and Tomášková, or the clothes, music, and cuisine that, as Chasteen observes, became the markers of native identity, it has become, in the era of globalization, a matter of possessing "relatively expensive global brands in order to forge some sense of identity with what we can only call, in a rather crude sense, 'symbols of modernity.'"[38] What remains constant is that material objects function as the chalk that, with the insolently thick insistence of compressed dust, draws the line between the foreigner and the native.

Foreigners, moreover, are often perceived as material objects: they are the subjects of reification, their value assessed in terms of capacity for physical labor, their presence (perhaps because it seems otherwise so difficult to grasp) confined to the body. This association of the foreigner with materiality bears two consequences that are, incestuously, also its causes. First is the assumption that foreigners cannot (or should not) transcend the material body, a conception that positions the foreigner in the lower social classes and nourishes the simultaneously repelling and alluring nature of foreignness: the foreigner is tainted by the debased social status of physical labor, while exoticized by an association with carnal pleasures—and closer to the animalistic in either case. Bourdieu's depiction of the customary equivalence between the bourgeoisie, "culture," and transcendence of the body on the one hand, and the lower classes, nature, and embodiment on the other, translates, in many contexts, into a distinction between the native to modernity and the foreigner: "The antithesis between culture and bodily pleasure (or nature) is rooted in the opposition between the cultivated bourgeoisie and the people, the imaginary site of uncultivated nature, barbarously wallowing in pure enjoyment."[39] Second, the semantic association of foreigners with materiality intensifies the foreigner's impurity. For defilement *is* material; it is dirt, stain, blood, "*matter* out of place."[40] And in a long tradition that extends from Plato's *Phaedo* to Descartes's distinction between *res extensa* and *res cogitans* to Kant's pure reason, philosophy expels the material as impurity. Hence, foreignness represents a defilement of philosophy not only because of its association with disordered thought (as we have sketched above), but by virtue of the foreigner's exaggerated materiality.[41]

This logic also works in reverse. If foreigners are essentially material, one can be made foreign by being reduced to the materiality of the body. Indeed, the evidence is all too clear that the presence of foreignness is routinely verified on the body: by the riots and hangings that Sakamoto recalls in America, or the torture evinced in the Biko trial that Saunders analyzes, events that at once concretize the intangibility of foreignness, degrade the foreigner into nothing but the material of the body, and ensure that the foreigner is made sensibly to experience his/her foreignness.[42] For as Elaine Scarry has taught us, physical pain has the capacity to make one's own body adversarial: "the person in great pain experiences his own body as the agent of his agony," she writes. The signal of the body in pain "contains not only the feeling 'my body hurts' but the feeling 'my body hurts me.'"[43] Indeed, the negation that we have located at the foundation of foreignness is also the primary attribute of physical pain:

> The first, the most essential, aspect of pain is its sheer aversiveness. While other sensations have content that may be positive, neutral, or negative, the very content of pain is itself negation. Pain is a pure physical experience of negation, an immediate sensory rendering of "against," of something being against one, and of something one must be against. Even though it occurs within oneself, it is at once identified as "not oneself," "not me," as something so alien that it must right now be gotten rid of.[44]

Pain is thus a form of foreignness; but even more relevant to our present discussion of the foreign as a particular kind of *presence* is the fact that intense pain, as Scarry contends, robs one of the presence of the world. It is, she writes,

> a destruction experienced spatially as either the contraction of the universe down to the immediate vicinity of the body or as the body swelling to fill the entire universe. Intense pain is also language-destroying: as the content of one's world disintegrates, so the content of one's language disintegrates; as the self disintegrates, so that which would express and project the self is robbed of its source and its subject.[45]

In this scenario, the foreigner's body is hyperbolically present, while his or her world (in a manner that recalls the decontextualization we have examined above) is effectively eradicated: "the absence of pain is a presence of world; the presence of pain is the absence of world."[46] Further, because pain is language destroying, it has the effect of rendering people foreign by likening them to animals, infants (*infans* = without language), and barbarians, by making them, as literally as possible, ζοὄν λόγον οὐκ ἔχον [animals not possessing language/reason].

Yet we seem to be faced with something of a contradiction here, for we have argued above that to be foreign is to be *de-materialized,* to become a figure. These positions, however, may not be so divergent as they at first seem, for figures regularly lend themselves to material effects. In the most traditional manifestation of metaphor—the exchange of an abstract noun for a concrete one, of value for a commodity—to be a figure is to be compared to a material object; and this is a comparison that slips easily and frequently into an identity with *insentient matter*. By an alternate logic, the metaphors deployed in wartime (which, for example, depict bodily injury as a by-product of another pursuit or as the purchase price of an *abstract principle* like freedom) render the destruction of material (such as bodies, buildings, or infrastructures) cognitively acceptable precisely through their ability to de-materialize. In everyday practice, this covert substitution of insentient matter or abstract principle for human bodies translates into: (a) the formula that the more *immaterial* one's presence is to society, the more subject one is likely to be to *material* concerns[47] and (b) a structure in which natives hold the middle ground of material well-being that frees them to pursue less embodied concerns—business, social life, aesthetics, philosophy[48]—while foreigners are shunted into theoretically opposing, yet surprisingly interchangeable, margins: the purely figural (in which one is without substance) and the intensely embodied (where one is nothing but a substance). In other words, the necessary condition for bringing to presence matters beyond bodily needs is access to material objects (as, for example, a room with heat, light, and a chair allow one to concentrate on reading a book) and being foreign, in many instances, means having diminished access to material privileges: a principle we have witnessed in, for example, the housing discrimination analyzed by Sakamoto, the dramatic material discrepancies that, as Saunders evinces, characterize apartheid society, or the new foreigners produced by globalization. It is a place we have also already arrived at theoretically by recognizing the foreigner's exclusion from (the) proper(ty).

Notes

1. James Clifford, *The Predicament of Culture: Twentieth-Century Ethnography, Literature, and Art* (Cambridge, Mass.: Harvard University Press, 1988), 263.
2. Kristeva describes the way such mediation was institutionalized in ancient Athens in the person of the *proxenus*, who functioned "as the *middleman* between the polis and those belonging to a foreign community, providing a remedy to their statutory incapacity." Julia Kristeva, *Strangers to Ourselves*, trans. Leon S. Roudiez (New York: Columbia University Press, 1991), 49.
3. Indeed the German word for translation—*unbersetzen*—which appears in the title of Walter Benjamin's "The Task of the Translator" also means metaphor. This essay is discussed below and is found in *Illuminations*, ed. and with an introduction by Hannah Arendt, trans. Harry Zohn (New York: Schocken Books, 1968), 69-82.
4. Benjamin, "The Task of the Translator," 78.
5. Paul de Man, "Conclusions: Walter Benjamin's 'The Task of the Translator,'" in *The Resistance to Theory*, foreword Wlad Godzich, Theory and History of Literature, Volume 33 (Minneapolis: University of Minnesota Press, 1986), 90-91. This distinction between metaphorical and metonymic conceptions of translation would bear interesting comparison to Hillman's contrast between the figures of Hercules and Hermes, which we have explored above.
6. We should not, however, overlook the problems that remain with taking this conception of translation as an ideal for conceiving foreignness; at issue, certainly, would be the inequality of fragments and who or what stands for the whole. Benjamin further argues that the "essential quality [of translation] is not statement or the imparting of information" and that "any translation which intends to perform a transmitting function cannot transmit anything but information—hence, something inessential." Though it is no doubt perilous to equate Benjamin's conception of the literary work with culture, his contention nonetheless seems curiously relevant to multiple forms of mediating foreignness and

points to the fact that culture is not only highly textualized, but, like a literary text, consists largely of "what it contains in addition to information"—a principle we have analyzed under the sign of *context*. Benjamin, "The Task of the Translator," 69, 70. On translation, see the essays in *Public Culture* 13, no.1 (Summer 2001); on translation and the degree to which culture is textualized, see Françoise Massardier-Kenney, "Translation Theory and Practice," in *Translating Slavery: Gender and Race in French Women's Writing, 1783-1823*, ed. Doris Y. Kadish and Françoise Massardier-Kenney (Kent, Ohio: Kent State University Press, 1994), 11- 25.

7. Benjamin, "The Task of the Translator," 80.

8. De Man, "Conclusions," 84.

9. De Man, "Conclusions," 92.

10. The former phrase is Shklovsky's, cited by Saunders, 116; the latter is a paraphrase of Stanley Fish. See Saunders, 142, note 27.

11. Hence, the exile examined by Redfield and Tomášková casts a government as foreign by appealing to a stability beyond "temporary governments," an ostensible permanence like "civilization."

12. Chasteen reminds us that the nation became the standard for decolonization. Bhahba signals the irony inherent in the fact that "the political unity of the nation consists in a continual displacement of its irredeemably plural modern space . . . into a signifying space that is archaic and mythical, paradoxically representing the nation's modern territoriality, in the patriotic, atavistic temporality of Traditionalism." Homi K. Bhabha, "DissemiNation," in *Nation and Narration*, ed. Homi K. Bhabha (New York: Routledge, 1990), 300.

13. Benedict Anderson, *Imagined Communities: Reflections on the Origin and Spread of Nationalism*, rev. ed. (New York: Verso, 1983), 81. This imperative, and the destabilizing effect it has had on indigenous political systems, has, particularly on the continent of Africa, contributed to the rise of authoritarian regimes, single-party systems, and ethnic conflict. A good introduction to these issues can be found in Peter J. Schraeder, *African Politics and Society: A Mosaic in Transformation* (New York: Bedford, 2000).

14. See Ernest Gellner, *Nations and Nationalism* (Oxford: Blackwell, 1983). Sakamoto thus insists on quotation marks of protest around the term "underdeveloped," which is both prescriptive—suggesting that the ultimate goal of societies *should* be industrial development—and evaluative: it positions those nations on the negative side of a binary opposition, in the region of lack. See also Walter Mignolo: "Toward the end of the nineteenth century, however, spatial boundaries were transformed into chronological ones. In the early modern period, a transformation took place between geographical and human boundaries; at the end of the nineteenth century, savages and cannibals in space were converted into primitives and exotic Orientals in time." "Globalization, Civilization, and Languages," in *The Cultures of Globalization*, ed. Fredric Jameson and Masao Miyoshi (Durham, N.C.: Duke University Press, 1998), 35.

15. Clifford, *The Predicament of Culture*, 16.

16. Benjamin Barber, *Jihad vs. McWorld: How Globalism and Tribalism are Reshaping the World* (New York: Ballantine Books, 1995), 54. As Clifford notes, "When we speak today of the West, we are usually referring to a force—technological, economic, political—no longer radiating in any simple way from a discrete geographical or cultural center." Clifford, *Predicament of Culture*, 272. Stuart Hall has written perceptively on this distinction in *Modernity: An Introduction to Modern Societies*, ed. Stuart Hall, David Held, Don Hubert, and Kenneth Thompson (Cambridge Mass.: Blackwell,

1996), chap. 6. On the role of travel and exploration writing in producing this distinction, see Mary Louise Pratt, *Imperial Eyes: Travel Writing and Transculturation* (New York: Routledge, 1992).

17. Clifford, *The Predicament of Culture*, 231.

18. Clifford, *The Predicament of Culture*, 5.

19. I do not mean to suggest that Islam can be treated monolithically. On the contrary, this dynamic appears in multiple and varied forms, nuanced both by the very diverse Islamic beliefs, practices, and communities found in the modern world and by differing varieties of feminism. This phenomenon, moreover, is not unique to Islam; very similar issues have been confronted by women in other "non-Western" societies.

20. See, for example, Fatima Mernissi, *The Veil and the Male Elite: A Feminist Interpretation of Women's Rights in Islam* (New York: Addison-Wesley, 1991) and Leila Ahmed, *Women and Gender in Islam* (New Haven, Conn.: Yale University Press, 1992).

21. Frederic Jameson and others identify this stage of late capitalism as *postmodernity*, though time and circumstances are, of course, incorrigibly truant to such containers. See Frederic Jameson, *Postmodernism, or, the Cultural Logic of Late Capitalism*, Post-Contemporary Interventions Series (Durham, N.C.: Duke University Press, 1992) and Jameson and Miyoshi, *The Cultures of Globalization*. I tend to resist this designation both because constructing an identity for the postmodern has relied so heavily on a vastly oversimplified caricature of modernity and because it has tended to construct an exceedingly Eurocentric version of modernity which, in effect, denies the possibility of modernist practices appearing in different contexts at differing times. I discuss these issues further in *At God's Funeral: Lamentation and the Culture of Modernity* (forthcoming).

22. Barber, *Jihad vs. McWorld*, 29.

23. I have developed this argument at length in "Uncanny Presence: The Foreigner at the Gate of Globalization," *Comparative Studies of South Asia, Africa, and the Middle East* 21, no. 1 (Summer 2002). I have drawn heavily in my discussion of globalization on Saskia Sassen, *Globalization and Its Discontents: Essays on the New Mobility of People and Money*, foreword by K. Anthony Appiah (New York: New Press, 1998) and on the essays in Jameson and Miyoshi, *The Cultures of Globalization*. In both *Globalization and its Discontents* and *Guests and Aliens* (New York: New Press, 1999), Sassen marks the discrepancy between a global economic regime aimed at neutralizing borders and national immigration policies that seek to reinforce them. On processes of globalization, see also Barber, *Jihad vs. McWorld*; Arjun Appadurai, ed., *Globalization* (Durham, N.C.: Duke University Press, 2001); and Anthony D. King, ed., *Culture, Globalization, and the World-System: Contemporary Conditions for the Representation of Identity*, Current Debates in Art History 3 (Binghamton, NY: Department of Art and Art History, State University of New York at Binghamton, 1991). For historicizing perspectives on globalization (including arguments for and against globalization as a new phenomenon), see Enrique Dussel, "Beyond Eurocentrism: The World System and the Limits of Modernity"; Walter Mignolo, "Globalization, Civilization, and Languages"; and Masao Miyoshi, "'Globalization,' Culture, and the University" in Jameson and Miyoshi, *The Cultures of Globalization*, 3-31, 32-53, 247-270.

24. The WTO, for example, has the authority to override decisions of, and discipline, individual nations; and international human rights covenants have successfully challenged the legislatures and judiciary systems of nation states and, in Europe, had a significant impact on national policy formation. On the role of human rights organizations in globalization, see Sassen, *Globalization and Its Discontents*; on environmental

movements, see Joan Martinez-Alier, "'Environmental Justice' (Local and Global)" and David Harvey, "What's Green and Makes the Environment Go Round?" in Jameson and Miyoshi, *The Cultures of Globalization,* 312-326, 327-355.

25. Both Paul Gilroy and Michael Hanchard have located important precedents for this trend in the political engagements of peoples of the African Diaspora. See Paul Gilroy, *The Black Atlantic: Modernity and Double Consciousness* (Cambridge, Mass.: Harvard University Press, 1993) and Michael Hanchard, "Afro-Modernity: Temporality, Politics, and the African Diaspora," *Public Culture* 27 (1999): 245-268.

26. Leslie Sklair, "Social Movements and Global Capitalism," in Jameson and Miyoshi, *The Cultures of Globalization,* 299.

27. Barber, *Jihad vs. McWorld,* 13. Stuart Hall has made a similar point, arguing that the nation does not just "bow off the stage of history," but "goes into an even deeper trough of defensive exclusivism" marked by "a regression to a very defensive and highly dangerous form of national identity which is driven by a very aggressive form of racism." "The Local and the Global: Globalization and Ethnicity," in King, *Culture, Globalization, and The World-System,* 25-26. Elie Kedourie identified the beginnings of this dynamic even before the advent of those processes we now call globalization:

The relentless developments of modernity have also worked to debilitate and destroy tribalism and its social and political traditions. The consequence is an atomized society which seeks in nationalism a substitute for the old order, now irrevocably lost. Its members find for themselves a link with obscure and mysterious kingdoms, seeking solace in archaeological speculations; or else, in search of the fulfillment which reality denies them, they re-enact with conscious and deliberate frenzy tribal practices which anthropologists had surveyed and recorded and which Western rule, by destroying their social context, had robbed of significance. Elie Kedourie, *Nationalism,* 4th exp. ed. (Oxford: Blackwell, 1993), 107.

Jameson articulates this principle (of globalization's role in producing nationalisms) in terms of the negative relativity which we have identified as productive of foreignness; he describes globalization "as an untotalizable totality which intensifies binary relations between its parts—mostly nations, but also regions and groups." Such relations are, he argues, "first and foremost ones of tension or antagonism, when not outright exclusion: in them each term struggles to define itself against the binary other." Jameson and Miyoshi, *The Cultures of Globalization,* xii.

28. Sassen, *Globalization and Its Discontents,* 48. Currently, the gap in wages between corporate CEOs and line workers is 531 to 1. See Sarah Anderson, John Cavanagh, Chris Harman, and Betsy Leondar-Wright, "Executive Excess 2001: Layoffs, Tax Rebates, the Gender Gap, Eighth Annual CEO Compensation Survey" (Washington, D.C.: Institute for Policy Studies and United for a Fair Economy, 2001): http://www.ufenet.org/press/2001/EE2001.pdf, Oct., 2001. I am indebted to Dale Fitzgibbons for his assistance in locating this information.

29. Sassen, *Globalization and Its Discontents,* 153. Like the not-structure of foreignness itself, these "improper" practices are defined by the very regulatory framework they evade. Manthia Diawara describes a similar dynamic in West Africa between, on the one hand, traditional markets and merchants and, on the other hand, nation states and their multinational allies. See Diawara, "Toward a Regional Imaginary in Africa," in *The Cultures of Globalization,* 103-124.

30. Sassen, *Globalization and Its Discontents*, 153.

31. Sassen, *Globalization and Its Discontents*, 34.

32. Sassen, *Globalization and Its Discontents*, 31.

33. Sassen, *Globalization and Its Discontents*, 31.

34. For further discussion of these regulations, see Sassen, *Guests and Aliens*, chap. 6. On the refugee claim process in Canada, see Robert F. Barsky, "The Construction of the Other and the Destruction of the Self: The Case of the Convention Hearings," in *Encountering the Other(s): Studies in Literature History, and Culture*, ed. Gisela Brinker-Gabler (Albany: SUNY Press, 1995), 79-100.

35. The document is available at http://www.telalink.net/~gsiskind/docs/IIIRA.html Sept., 2001.

36. Sassen, *Guests and Aliens*, 42.

37. A good introduction to these issues can be found in Susan Bullock, *Women and Work* (Atlantic Highlands, N.J.: Zed Books, 1994).

38. Sklair, "Social Movements and Global Capitalism," 303.

39. Pierre Bourdieu, *Distinction: A Social Critique of the Judgement of Taste*, trans. Richard Nice (Cambridge, Mass.: Harvard University Press, 1984), 490. Also relevant here is Nussbaum's analysis of disgust as a method for policing the boundaries between ourselves and our own materiality. See Martha Nussbaum, "'Secret Sewers of Vice': Disgust, Bodies, and the Law," in *The Passions of Law*, ed. Susan Bandes (New York: New York University Press, 2000), 19-62.

40. The phrase is Mary Douglas's. See *Purity and Danger: An Analysis of Concepts of Pollution and Taboo* (New York: Praeger, 1966) and chap. 3.

41. This conceit can also be located in Hebrew thought, in the idolatry that contaminates YHWH, and, in psychoanalytic theory, as the maternal that contaminates signification. On the latter, see Julia Kristeva, *Powers of Horror: An Essay on Abjection*, Trans. Leon S. Roudiez (New York: Columbia University Press, 1982). Bourdieu's paraphrase of Kant is also helpful: "'pure' taste and the aesthetics which provides its theory are founded on a refusal of 'impure' taste and of *aisthesis* (sensation), the simple, primitive form of pleasure reduced to a pleasure of the senses." Bourdieu, *Distinction*, 486. I have developed this concept at greater length in "Shaking Down the Pillars: Lamentation, Purity, and Mallarmé's 'Hommage' to Wagner," *PMLA*, vol. 111, no. 5 (1996): 1106-1120.

42. There is a distinct resemblance between this certification of foreignness and the process Elaine Scarry identifies in the Old Testament, where "the Word is never self-substantiating; it seeks confirmation in a visible change in the realm of matter" and in which "hurt becomes the vehicle of verification; doubt is eliminated through the incontestable reality of the material world." Scarry, *The Body in Pain: The Making and Unmaking of the World* (New York: Oxford University Press, 1985), 202.

43. Scarry, *The Body in Pain*, 47.

44. Scarry, *The Body in Pain*, 52.

45. Scarry, *The Body in Pain*, 35.

46. Scarry, *The Body in Pain*, 37.

47. This concurs with the principle Scarry develops in her discussion of the Hebrew scriptures: "[T]o have no body is to have no limits on one's extension out into the world; conversely, to have a body, a body made emphatic by being continually altered . . . is to have one's sphere of extension contracted down to the small circle of one's immediate physical presence. Consequently, to be intensely embodied is the equivalent of being unrepresented and (here as in many secular contexts) is almost always the condition of those

without power." Scarry, *The Body in Pain*, 207.

48. This native middle-ground is commensurate with Bourdieu's depiction of the aesthetic disposition: "a generalized capacity to neutralize ordinary urgencies and to bracket off practical ends, a durable inclination and aptitude for practice without a practical function, can only be constituted within an experience of the world freed from urgency and through the practice of activities which are an end in themselves." Bourdieu, *Distinction*, 54.

Part II

Local Manifestations

Chapter Five

The Exile of Anthropology

Peter Redfield and Silvia Tomášková

Even from the simplest, the most realistic point of view, the countries for which we long occupy, at any given moment, a far larger place in our true life than the country in which we may happen to be.

— Marcel Proust, *Remembrance of Things Past*

When published in 1967, well after his death, Bronislaw Malinowski's *A Diary in the Strict Sense of the Term* caused quite a scandal. Its pages, laboriously translated from a scribbled Polish sprinkled with other tongues, revealed that a master figure of anthropology, the mythic father of ethnography, had had impure thoughts. Amid his recounting of daily routine in his field site in the Trobriand Islands, Malinowski recorded his memories of the lives he had left behind in Poland, England, and Australia, his shifting tides of passion and lust, his longings for civilization, his indulgences in novel reading and other signs of laziness, his anxieties about his work, his petty irritations, and his occasional revulsion for the people he was studying. While this last feature provoked the most controversy, the general lapse from the austere life he sought to lead and the multiple signs of his active struggle all contrasted sharply with his received legacy.[1] Had Malinowski really "been there" when he was in the field, the first of a new breed of engaged explorer, or had he only lived like any other expatriated exile?

The following essay will focus on the tradition of ethnography in anthropology, comparing it to the condition of exile, particularly as represented in Eastern European literature. The comparison is intended as a heuristic exercise engaging abstracted conditions, but one which retains a foothold in historical particularity in its effort to understand intersections between place, politics, and cultural representation. Taken broadly, these two varieties of displacement—ethnography and exile—present inverted patterns of experience; opposite ends of a common condition of displacement. Both have created traditions of representing culture at a distance, be it the lost homeland (site of reinvented cosmopolitan high Culture) or the "field" (site of appropriately exotic others). In each case, authority depends on a trivialization of immediacy and a relegation of meaning to everyday experience that lies over a horizon. It is precisely this motion—from the familiar to the foreign, from the present to the past—that has distilled concepts of culture derived from the writings of exiles and anthropologists, purifying them with an effect of distance. In remaining attached to such purity, we forget more common displacements, the partial travels of daily life across small divides, and our own active, imperfect sensibilities. Thus, while a condition of foreignness reveals the outlines of cultural forms most acutely, it also removes them from the foreground of experience.

Our purpose in pursuing this heuristic comparison between ethnography and literary exile is not to reiterate two decades of criticism of the authorial strategies of anthropologists (although, in the curious circularity of interdisciplinary influences, reiteration might benefit some ends of cultural studies).[2] Rather, our point is to take metaphorical allusions to exile seriously, furthering an interrogation of anthropology's long romance with the foreign and the manner in which writing about elsewhere in space and time deferred the discipline's engagement with more immediate milieux. Recent shifts in global circumstances and academic frontiers present anthropology with suddenly foreshortened horizons, something not unlike the excitement and pathos of an exile suddenly free to return. It is our contention that this loss of sure estrangement—the certainty of measured distance—can be beneficial as well as painful, and that the resulting disorientation offers the possibility of recalibrating scholarship around less perfect placements and engagements in the world.

Displacement and the Literary Hero

To begin the discussion, let us sketch the figures before us, starting with the elder, that of exile. We could propose a number of genealogies for the condition we call "exile." One account would track it to ancient Israel and Greece,[3] where another would locate a point of origin in the banishment of Ovid to the Danube in A.D. 18, outside the magic circle of literate Rome.[4] A generalizing anthropologist, unwilling to anchor origin so comfortably to the narrow band of classical history, might describe exile as a condition of expulsion, of enforced foreignness, and suggest a probable, sporadic pattern of this practice since the emergence of complex polities, if not earlier. A critically minded historian might caution against projecting conditions common to modern nation states back before industrialization. Nevertheless, we can identify certain principles for the purposes of our analysis, and distinguish the condition from a number of close relatives. The key ingredients of exile are a sense of homeland and of political significance; one must both define identity in terms of place and be elite enough to have one's individual displacement be recognized, ordered, and enforced. The "refugee," the "expatriate," and the "émigré" experience related conditions, but do so in ways distinct from the "exile." For the refugee is a mass object, the expatriate a free adventurer, and the émigré a permanent graft. Between them we find the exile, like the refugee a figure of temporary suffering, like the expatriate and the émigré a solitary being. As Joseph Brodsky bluntly reminds us, Turkish *Gastarbeiters*, Vietnamese boat people, and Pakistanis in Kuwait are never invited to conferences on the exiled writer.[5] Rather, in the twentieth century, the political flight of those without aesthetic stature has become a staple of bureaucratic calculation and photojournalism.[6]

Dislocation marks the essential condition of exile, a status attained between place and loss. Randolph Starn points out at the beginning of his study of exile in medieval and Renaissance Italy that the issue is "fundamentally a matter of location and defined positions in space."[7] While the word *exile* may derive from the Latin *ex* and *salire* (to leap out of), the movement itself implies a site of departure, a ground below the flight.[8] An alternative seventh-century etymology connects the Latin *exsilium* to *extra solum* (outside the soil) or, in Starn's case, beyond the city-state.[9] Starn follows these connections to urban life, crucial to so much of our political vocabulary (e.g., *citizen*, *politics*), to suggest the figure of the exile as an inverse of the citizen, and to describe the shadowy world of the refugees of politics as a "contrary commonwealth." Thus, the lost world of the exile is not simply removed, but constantly reimagined, a realm of possible pasts and futures, and of justice literally defined in geography. Exiles are irritable, potentially dangerous, and usually left with plenty of time on their hands (in the twentieth-century landscape one usually imagines them in a café); as they begin to write, they become difficult to ignore for those in power and for chroniclers alike. Their revenge is to wander in visible righteousness, appearing across the historical record.[10]

The link between exile, political romanticism, and writing in European history becomes all the more clear as we move closer to the present. The tumultuous upheaval of the late eighteenth and early nineteenth centuries in Europe produced a range of displaced writers, Rousseau on. The figure of the gloomy exile invaded literature, even as failed revolutionaries and defeated nationalists began to flee across borders and regroup in foreign cities, usually London or Paris. In the twentieth century, the tragic heroism of the vagabond of conscience still stood out against the ever increasing blur of migrants and refugees, coalescing around intellectual culture bearers, the repositories of refinement, fleeing the implosion of European political extremism. One such group, only recently vanished, was comprised of the *literati* of Eastern Europe. Here we will focus on this last group of exiles, near enough in memory to be familiar, while prominent enough in Cold War politics to provide a particularly telling illustration for our comparison.[11]

In an article that presciently appeared in the crucial political divide of 1989, Ewa Thompson examines cracks in the facade of the pure victims of crude and corrupt regimes of the former communist bloc. She assures us that the writer in exile has fared far better of late than in times past, noting that "[t]oday, it seems to be a rule that writers from the smaller or less developed countries go to the larger or more advanced ones, rather than, as in antiquity, abandoning the circle of civilization and going to an unlettered region of the world."[12] Exile these days can actually represent an increase in visibility. In the case of Eastern Europe, the very displacement of intellectuals (whether physical or psychological) allowed them to reimagine the European map, expanding a world of lost civic virtue eastward. To a certain body of intellectuals East and West, dissident culture represented high Culture, the possibility of civilization and a virtuous opposition to evil. In the stark light of crude oppression, noble forms emerged, all the more noble when viewed from afar.

The figure of the exile, then, gives us the displacement of high culture and the most pure of literary heroes: authors who live as characters in their own transplanted epic. For unlike the common refugee, the exiled writer flees not simply to save a humble body, but also an exalted soul, and the very possibility of moral life. Named enemies of corrupt regimes can claim the mantle of Zola when deported for speaking something feared as truth. Where women and children arrive *en masse* at the border with hastily packed bags and their small hopes of everyday pleasures, the exiled writer carries the weight of a language on his back, as well as the lonely consciousness of grand responsibilities.[13] The frequency of masculine pronouns in writings on exile should not surprise us; gendered expectations of public life (especially in Eastern Europe) as well as greater male mobility across social boundaries and away from social ties produce a stream of great men in poor suits, forever writing letters of protest. Leaving the literary hero in some shabby hotel room surrounded by empty bottles and the stale odor of cigarettes, let us now turn to the anthropologist, the author of exotic common culture and scientific travel.

Exotic Culture and Scientific Travel

Of all academic disciplines, anthropology is the most intimately associated with elsewhere. A sense of the foreign pervades the formal study of humanity; every direction one looks lies a horizon. The unlikely sprawl of the classic American tradition of the discipline (mixing primate teeth with polygyny) frames itself with distances traveled in space and time. To trace the outline of *homo sapiens*

sapiens, one heads for every border and the limits of human existence, recording distant cousins, forgotten ancestors, and the country of first and last things. The key methodological tradition of social and cultural anthropology, the research experience known as "ethnographic fieldwork," incorporates foreignness into the essence of the discipline, institutionalizing travel as the basis for knowledge of humanity. The authority to write about another culture rests on an extended stay, knowledge of the vernacular, and engagement with everyday practice—on the elusive experience of "being there."[14] Anything less risks superficiality, the contamination of unreliable witnesses citing mere travel or journalism; anything more risks a loss of perspective, the taint of unreflective natives deceived by familiarity.

In internal myths of anthropology's legacy, the totemic figures of Bronislaw Malinowski and Franz Boas serve to mark the turning point whereby the practice of the discipline shifted from gentlemanly rummaging through reports gathered from all manner of travelers past and present (in the manner of James Frazer or E. B. Tylor) to the direct collection of information "in the field." While the historical record may indicate a more complex heritage, Malinowski's name in particular remains attached to the adoption of an adventurous foray into the lives of distant people as the hallmark of ethnographic method.[15] In the introduction to his 1922 classic, *Argonauts of the Western Pacific*, Malinowski lays forth the criteria under which a proper study can be conducted. One is exhorted to work directly with the people in question, without intermediaries and in their native language, and cautioned against associating too freely with other expatriates. To function as an observer of the sort that Malinowski deems superior to traders, missionaries, and other potential rivals, one must go further than they have, displacing oneself more violently from ties to home while simultaneously maintaining purity of purpose. In essence, one must become a more distant exile, and yet an exile whose gaze focuses ahead rather than behind. For an ethnographer travels into foreignness to interrogate foreign life, not to lament home.

At times, Malinowski's scientific traveler may even play native, trying on strange habits in the hope of understanding them. In one of the most famous passages from *Argonauts*, the author calls for a degree of participation on the part of the observer, for an engagement with the flow of life sweeping by:

> Again, in this type of work, it is good for the Ethnographer sometimes to put aside camera, notebook, and pencil, and to join in himself in what is going on. He can take part in the natives' games, he can follow them on their visits and walks, sit down and listen and share in their conversations. I am not certain if this is equally easy for everyone—perhaps the Slavonic nature is more plastic and more naturally savage than that of Western Europeans—but though the degree of success varies, the attempt is possible for everyone.[16]

The passage is doubly interesting to us in that at the very moment Malinowski self-consciously announces the birth of the participant observer, he acknowledges his own displacement as a Slav amid Western Europeans in an ironic aside. For him, the British academy represents exile and emigration, not home. But he will turn that condition—in both humor and practice—to his advantage; if uncertain of his status in the civilized center, he is one step closer to the savage margin, and hence a more natural ethnographer. The "plastic" nature of a Pole, properly educated and positioned, can bridge the gap between the high culture of science and the low culture of the primitive.

Since the era of Malinowski, the practice of social and cultural anthropology has consciously centered on fieldwork and the production of ethnographies, monographs written on the basis of direct experience with a particular group of people. The slow dissolution of ties to other subfields in the American variant of the discipline, a series of crises in response to decolonization, social turmoil, feminist and textual criticism, as well as the emergence of new interdisciplinary domains and exchanges within the academy, have only heightened the identification of anthropology with ethnographic fieldwork. Anthropologists sought to solve methodological issues of boundary definitions through the study of sharply defined communities, anchoring general assertions about humanity with specific knowledge of a people in place, by choosing a site and "being there." To know a community, went the logic, is to know its language and customs. In practice this principle translated into knowledge of a community in geographic terms, the ability to locate it and map its boundaries within a larger area. Particularly with the vast expansion and increasing degree of specialization within anthropology following the Second World War, and the rise of area studies, one was expected to master one's village and report back from it into a greater surrounding literature, becoming an Africanist or a Latin Americanist as the case might be, amid a community of scholars. Despite historical and political questions one might well begin to raise about the structure of such a system as a whole, and about the effects of scholarly knowledge in relations of power, from a technical and methodological standpoint, the move was a strong one.[17] Detail makes the everyday convincing, and localized knowledge comes from the ground. As its increasing diffusion into other domains suggests, the practice of ethnography retains a vital allure, that promise that, if well done, it will offer rich rewards: moments of experience, an echo of different voices, and that crucial reminder that things could be otherwise.

Inverted Patterns, Temporary Distances

Before us then, we have two figures: the exile attached to a homeland and the ethnographer attached to the field. Identity in the first case is ever removed, a distant familiarity presented in foreign surroundings. Identity in the second case is also ever removed, a foreign familiarity presented in familiar surroundings. These two figures form an inverted pair, with the ethnographer serving as a kind of voluntary exile and the exile as an involuntary anthropologist. Beyond intentionality, they differ with regard to motives and audience. Culture shock constitutes a purifying fire of purgatory for the exile and the basis of insight for the ethnographer. Yet both ends of this inverted pair derive their status from displacement, and their authority remains a function of distance. The space of exile and the space of ethnography both involve mobility, the masculine freedom to travel at will. The place, the people, the ways of life they represent are over the horizon, not immediately available. "Culture," a key term for each of these figures, is culture at a distance. Whether high or low, it lies tantalizingly beyond grasp. In both cases, the author depends on notes and memory, the audience on the author's knowledge of an impenetrable regime or inaccessible people.

The sense of culture involved in what we are calling "culture at a distance" may be fixed, but it simultaneously remains subject to constant tension. For both exile and ethnographer are temporary foreigners, their status liminal. Whether or not an end is in sight, the very condition denotes transience, and the possibility of other states. To resign oneself to life in another land means a loss of virtuous exile; to settle in a field site means a loss of ethnographic authority.[18] Neither figure can "go native," even as neither can simply "go home." To better illustrate the significance of these points, we review a few examples drawn from Eastern European exile and anthropology.

Culture at a Distance

Part way through Milan Kundera's work, *The Book of Laughter and Forgetting*, the narrator introduces a central character, a woman who will represent exile in the form of a café waitress, mourning love lost at a distance. He calls her Tamina, a name no other woman has ever borne, in order to make her more perfectly his own creation.[19] She, we are told, means more to him "than anyone ever has," and he pictures her as "tall and beautiful, thirty-three and a native of Prague."

> I can see her now, walking down a street in a provincial town in the West of Europe. Yes, you're right. Prague, which is far away, I call by its name, while the town my story takes place in I leave anonymous. It goes against all rules of perspective, but you'll just have to put up with it.[20]

We do indeed have to put up with it, for Tamina is exile embodied, a figure living her life in relation to elsewhere past. She cannot help herself; all her energy is displaced. Her schemes and actions constitute efforts to connect with remnants of her vanished happiness (a packet of love letters) or to escape her increasingly alien surroundings. The coherence of her being comes into focus in the distance, in Prague, in the past, not in the nameless, provincial present. As the work progresses, her ties to everyday life unravel and by the end of the novel she voyages to an allegorical island populated by children. Reality lies both spatially and temporally elsewhere for the exile, whose present experience constantly dissolves into the lost past or defers into an imagined future. The point becomes even clearer in a self-parodying passage taken from Vladimir Nabokov's memoir, *Speak, Memory*:

> As I look back at those years of exile, I see myself, and thousands of other Russians, leading an odd but by no means unpleasant existence, in material indigence and intellectual luxury, among perfectly unimportant strangers, spectral Germans and Frenchmen in whose more or less illusory cities we, émigrés, happened to dwell. These aborigines were to the mind's eye as flat and transparent as figures cut out of cellophane, and although we used their gadgets, applauded their clowns, picked their roadside plums and apples, no real communication, of the rich human sort so widespread in our midst, existed between us and them. It seemed at times that we ignored them the way an arrogant or very stupid invader ignores a formless and faceless mass of natives; but occasionally, quite often in fact, the spectral world through which we serenely paraded our sores and our arts would produce a kind of awful convulsion and show us who was the discarnate captive and who the true lord.[21]

The exile clings to elsewhere, for without it, significance vanishes. The present, and its reminders of immediate context, are consequently dangerous. For in the present, all the exile holds near and dear is of little consequence. Nabokov's émigré circles would have to admit that the Russian revolution fails to preoccupy the surrounding French and German citizens, that it is fading into history, and patience for its refugees grows thin. Furthermore, they would have to admit that they are powerless refugees, in the midst of other systems of documentation and rule, not to mention languages and histories.

Beyond painfully small suitcases, new exiles carry with them the habits of their lives, and it is this heavier cultural baggage that marks the most precious tie to former identity. Politics, language, customs, delicate treasures made of fierce conviction and wry humor fade if exposed to the bright light of a foreign sun. Jokes and poems pose the most difficult problems to translation, Stanislaw Baranczak reminds us, and the subtleties of style crucial to eloquence the least likely elements to be mastered in a foreign tongue. In exile, a writer's gag may be loosened, but his tongue is tied. The retention of identity demands a retention of the past, a careful conservation of experience slowly growing obsolete.[22]

In the case of the former Eastern Europe, the object of loss was not so simply a nation or native tongue. Rather, in a region composed of complicated, conflicting, and overlapping ethnic histories, artificially clarified by the authoritarian rule of Communist regimes, the loss was filtered by an educated elite mourning the absence of civic freedom and yearning, as Ewa Thompson reminded us earlier, to assert their identity as Europeans. Thus, the focus shifts to cities and cultivated language rather than a country. Witness the following two quotations from a Czech collection on exile:

I don't miss Czechoslovakia, it's a chimera, unfortunately I don't miss Bohemia either; the spine of this country has been broken several times virtually topographically; but what I will always miss is Prague, the irreplaceable city. My library has numerous volumes about Prague that I don't dare to open; recently I received a heartbreaking present—Soudek's *Panorama of Prague*; I started to leaf through it, became faint, and shut the book. Prague is even in my dreams, entirely non-émigré dreams, since I am always happy in them that I can walk around the city, and even in the dream I realize that it is merely a dream but I am grateful even for that.[23]

The territory of literature is different than the territory of any government. The territory of Czech literature extends for a thousand years on the map of Europe. Its border stones are legends and songs, chronicles and royal decrees, names of villages, towns, rivers, and names of lineages. But also stakes at which people and books were burnt. Our law is old and independent. While temporary governments here came and went in various ways, the rule of the Czech thought and word persists.[24]

In the first case, Prague constitutes the site of dreams and desires, a national capital to be sure, but rather more as the writer indicates: an ancient city of books and cultivation, less ephemeral than a country or a region. In the second case, literature represents the essence of Czech virtue, the accumulated thought and word of a thousand years whose wisdom endures the rise and fall of "temporary governments." The object of loss here is the seductive combination of urbanization and literacy once commonly described by the term "civilization." Beset by oppressive regimes, driven from familiar landscapes, Eastern European exiles claimed their birthright in the Enlightenment by lamenting its loss.

Turning away from the city to the country, we observe parallel patterns in the inverse figure of the ethnographer. Anthropological authority lies in explicating otherness, humanness at the far end of the spectrum from the immediate. Michel-Rolph Trouillot suggests that anthropology grew to occupy a "savage slot" in Western imagination, explicating a previously defined form (the savage) that had already been carefully separated from denizens of the civilized West.[25] It was only natural, then, that anthropology sought the savage in out-of-the-way places. The social life of interest, "real" culture, lay as far from the center as possible, for, from the perspective of anthropology, the center represented the contamination of civilization, and hence the corruption of the primitive. When our mythic protagonist, Malinowski, set forth to gather data on the human condition, he, like his forebears and successors, sought the margin. The Trobriand Islands, a minor archipelago off New Guinea, offered our London-based Pole an appropriate tableau of qualities then understood straightforwardly as "primitive." His work subsequently lent a limited measure of fame to the area (destined to be far more familiar to a small circle of anthropologists than to colonial administrators or historians of world events). Moreover, it reinforced a set of prescribed methods for proper fieldwork with an implied setting for their enactment. Anything less remote was less authentic. Thus the central method of the discipline came with a measure of distance built in, as did the concept of culture it produced.

A less comfortable landmark in the anthropological canon, Claude Lévi-Strauss's unconventional travel memoir, *Tristes Tropiques*, illustrates the intersection between distance and culture in its narrative trajectory. Here the anthropologist reluctantly sets himself in motion to seek knowledge of otherness, across the cultural cauldron of coastal Brazil, through disappointing encounters with partly assimilated Amerindians. The pure savage remains always over the horizon, appearing only to vanish in twilight, leaving a deep sense of loss behind. In comparison, modern reality (Brazil, circa 1930s) appears pale and empty. *Tristes Tropiques* is a famously despondent work, a vision of loss and regret in the wake of modernization that inspired Susan Sontag to portray Lévi-Strauss as a kind of literary hero, and describe his profession as a "total occupation," an all-consuming spiritual commitment similar to the work of an artist. She concludes her essay with a description of alienated scholarship deep in the museum of reason:

> The anthropologist is thus not only the mourner of the cold world of the primitives, but its custodian as well. Lamenting among the shadows, struggling to distinguish the archaic from the pseudoarchaic, he acts out a heroic, diligent, and complex modern pessimism.[26]

Lévi-Strauss himself portrays the matter even more starkly, suggesting that the voyage to the primitive is most often made by those fleeing the modern:

> For many anthropologists, perhaps, not just myself, the ethnological vocation is a flight from civilization, from a century in which one doesn't feel at home. That is not the case for everyone. Margaret Mead, for example, felt a part of her society and her time. She wanted to serve her contemporaries. If I have occasionally made similar statements I was not speaking from the heart.[27]

This anthropologist, at least, would speak as a metaphorical exile, passing judgment on the current century from a vantage point elsewhere in time, finding vision in a view "from afar."[28] The infamously self-proclaimed reluctant traveler of *Tristes Tropiques* finds comfort ever at a remove.

Lévi-Strauss's caveat about Margaret Mead notwithstanding, distance has permeated the defining image of the discipline and its subject matter. Despite the efforts of a number of significant early practitioners (Boas and Malinowski among them, and not forgetting Benedict in addition to Mead), modern life eluded anthropology to the extent that, in the postwar era, conducting research in the United States became nearly unthinkable within American anthropology, and the thought of "studying up" (examining home elites and institutions along with less privileged foreign groups) a radical act of re-engagement.[29] The map of social science represented outlines of old and new empires, with anthropology in charge of outlying districts.

For all that the monograph form may have grown to be an anachronism, the essence of ethnography has remained the same: in order to understand, one must first displace oneself, and then engage. The method requires motion and alienation. While increasing numbers of anthropologists work on topics near at hand (as some national traditions have since their inception), the dominant American field retains a bias against working too close to home in favor of exotic distance.[30] While one may shift interest later in a career, fieldwork remains the essential rite of passage, invoked constantly in the maintenance of disciplinary identity.

Yet as the author of *Tristes Tropiques* himself reminds us, travel is not only a displacement from here and now, but also a matter of social rearrangement: "A journey occurs simultaneously in space, in time, and in social hierarchy."[31] We should therefore also read his metaphor of exile in reverse, and not forget that quite a few of the prominent early figures in anthropology were displaced or marginal characters in their own right. Women, Jews, and immigrants take their place beside more conventional male authors well back in the lineage. Such ethnographers achieve their professional detachment naturally, for they are, in Malinowski's sardonic terms, more "plastic" and "savage." Both canonical authors we have briefly examined exhibit slightly off-center profiles. In addition to his tour of duty as a sociology professor in Brazil and as lonely fieldworker (wife and entourage notwithstanding), Lévi-Strauss experienced literal exile during the Second World War, as a Jewish refugee in the United States. And of course the figure with whom we began, Bronislaw Malinowski, illustrates the complexity involved quite well. The son of an eminent linguist, he left Krakow at the age of twenty-six after training in physical science and moved to England. He conducted his definitive fieldwork in Melanesia as a foreigner within the very empire his presence represented. He cursed in English and counted in Polish, all the while defining a neutral scientific method for examining distant societies.[32] The real shock of the publication of his diary then, was that it revealed a different stylist: the erratic voice of a frustrated exile within the steady, dispassionate tones of anthropology.

Style matters in cultural terms, particularly when calculating distance. The concerns of exiled writers over language and translation echo through ethnography, where a command of the vernacular has constituted an accepted precondition of serious work since Malinowski's day. Our cosmopolitan son of a linguist was at least as clear about this point as he was fond of laboratory metaphors as a onetime science student, and he dismissed his hired translator to struggle forward on his own. Rather than seeking to preserve a transported heritage as a key to identity, here the obverse prevails in an effort to mine another tongue for trade goods. A hallmark trope of anthropological presentation is to incorporate fragmentary pieces of field languages, however incomprehensible they may be to a home audience. Translation here is a double game, from foreign to familiar and then to familiar foreign, in an effort to represent another cultural code while establishing the authority to explain it. The further the language from the researcher's own, the greater the status in mastering it, although in the case of classically remote field sites, any test of mastery itself remains comfortably distant. And yet, under scrutiny, the fluid ease of movement between worlds breaks down. Not only are many ethnographers imperfect linguists, but they cannot reveal themselves as native at either end of the translation. Lévi-Strauss's admission to linguistic limits is matched by Malinowski's revealing diary; where the latter may have achieved fluidity in English rivaling his fellow émigré Conrad (if not the equivalent in the Kiriwinian of his Trobriand informants), he could never expose the imperfections of his historical position without threatening his authority as the archetype of a purely scientific traveler.[33] Alone in his tent, beset by anxiety and depression, the tone of his private writing in the field often echoes that of an earlier letter to Poland from his first days in England: "Today I am suffering from a fit of deep nostalgia, which I never knew before but which now occurs frequently. . . . I am completely alone here and especially on account of the great stiffness of the Englishmen I feel lonely, and rather abandoned."[34] Such common discomfort deflates the anthropologist as hero; he becomes an exile, and, hence, a displaced native. In Baranczak's exile metaphor, an ethnographer at home is neither gagged nor tongue-tied, but only ordinary, and as such not foreign at all.

The End of Exile, the Return of the Present

The introduction of *Argonauts* recasts Malinowski's exile, transforming the strictures of quasi-internment as a foreign national during wartime into the virtues of a research method.[35] By largely evacuating his biography from his narration and appealing to his background training in natural science, its author repositions himself as an authoritative witness of the distantly foreign. However questionable in absolute terms, we should not forget that the immediate, situational effects of this move were liberatory. Just as the title of his work imbues his non-European subjects with the reflected nobility of Greek myth, Malinowski's appeals to the rigor of neutral method allowed him to sufficiently overcome his own foreignness (relative to both England and the Trobriands) to translate and testify about Kiriwinian humanity. Combining crafted style with a faith in objectivity, he was indeed able, as he once reportedly boasted, to become the Joseph Conrad of anthropology, the native ancestor of a discipline.[36] This achievement came at a personal price, as the anguish of the diary attests. But the real mistake would be made by his followers, particularly those who felt no tension of a double displacement, and who left no diaries. Among them, objective observation would become a project of purification, detached from all contingencies and institutionalized as a method for mapping alterity. They would forget its origins, even while venerating its early prophet and his call for studied participation. How else could they be shocked by the revelation of his private turmoil, the scope of his distractions, and his irritated sense of a "surfeit of native"?[37]

"Critical substance," argues Joan Vincent, "requires that Malinowski be restored to the cosmopolitan European intellectual tradition in which he was raised, and to Cracow and Leipzig in which he lived, once sitting across a café table from the exiled V. I. Lenin."[38] Reuniting the figures of the ethnographer and the exile, however, is not simply a matter of history; it is the only way to acknowledge the nostalgia embedded in their mutual, if inverted, displacements and the instability of their identities. For banishment can come to an end and the gap between "field" and "home" grow perilously thin. At such points purity becomes impossible to sustain; one must move in the uncertainty of an ever-reconfiguring present. Malinowski the ethnographer is also Malinowski the displaced Pole; the ambitious scholar is also the tormented lover, reading novels, sleeping badly, and practicing Swedish gymnastics on the beach. It is only when dressed in stark white, head crowned by a pith helmet as he surveys a native village, that such a complicated figure could translate simply into a model European facing the foreign.[39] Lacking such accessories, along with the confidence in civilization that they signify, his disciplinary descendents are at the mercy of their own complications.

In 1989, the harsh certainty of "Eastern" Europe ended. Beyond transforming the conditions of everyday life for citizens of former Soviet satellite regimes, the fall of the Berlin wall and associated events marked the end of the political clarity that had sustained political exiles abroad. Suddenly, they were free to return. To stay away was now a choice, no longer an act of enforced virtue. Moreover, authority derived from virtuous resistance faded with the power of the collapsed regimes, even as the thin facade of Enlightenment heritage eroded with the triumph of mass consumption. In the face of emerging markets and reinvented nationalisms, the gas lamp of civilization grew harder to imagine (from the West as well as from the East). After the first flush of revolution, intellectual political parties tended not to do well, and new sufferings replaced the old, together with new nostalgias. The confused ethical terrain demanded other stories. One that emerged now privileged artistic integrity over political commitment:

> In his article "Liberating exile," Milan Kundera asks why not one of the great émigrés returned to his homeland after the fall of communism. . . . An artist cannot return, cannot cancel the distance that he overcame, neither in the geographic nor in the social sense; he does not have to, maybe he cannot, separate the spiritual journey from the earthly one: he is going somewhere and reaching for a destination; and the meaning of this direction can be seen only through his work.[40]

The creator of Tamina, exile embodied, tells us that he and his brethren no longer yearn with her for Prague. The Prague perfected in memory was but a way station; it has vanished along with the border controls from Paris and he cannot return, for to do so would be to betray what he has become. In the very moment of political triumph, the act of return loses its personal meaning. An exile cannot simply "go home."

Nor can anthropology ignore the collapse of its former boundaries. In the disruptions of discipline in the contemporary academy, it has perhaps gained and lost the most; not only have marginal heritages lost the certain protection of obscurity, but low culture of all provenances has infiltrated the high. Moreover, the practical geography of the world is in flux; amid global configurations of high speed cultural exchange done in light wash, both the ethnographer's tent and the exile's café table become increasingly difficult to isolate in pure form. "Anthropology begins at home," Malinowski reiterates in his introduction to Jomo Kenyatta's 1938 monograph, *Facing Mount Kenya*, noting that the phrase should be as obviously true in Africa as in Europe.[41] Home, of course, may not be a fixed location; Kenyatta, Malinowski's onetime student in London, would not only function as an ethnographer of his own people, but later play a significant role in the decolonization of Kenya and emerge as its leading political figure. As the political, economic, and ethical basis for neutral observation at a distance erodes, the continued exile of anthropology has grown increasingly difficult to sustain.[42] This is not to claim the end of the foreign, but rather its opposite. Late and modern, exiles and ethnographers, we are no longer sure of what we have lost or where we stand, surrounded by qualifications. As the quintessential agonized voice of modern literature, Franz Kafka, wrote to his closest friend, "I am away from home and must always write home, even if any home of mine has long since floated away into eternity. All this writing is nothing but Robinson Crusoe's flag hoisted at the highest point of the island."[43] In the end, the internal exile of everyday moderns may prove the most uncomfortable anthropology of all. How might one proceed, when faced with such a challenge? The dream of elsewhere, of culture at a distance, is the addiction of pure identity. It's an old habit. And habits die hard. The slow withdrawal to the colder light of immediate reality is as painful and messy as any withdrawal must be, yet it remains the only tangible acknowledgment of our condition, of what it means to live both in awareness—and in partial, nagging uncertainty.

This generation of scholars now has the benefit of quite a few works to assist in decentering visions of culture and identity. Circulating through regions of anthropology, Arjun Appadurai's *Modernity at Large* notes discontinuities between people, land, and ethnos, revealing processes of localization with globalization, while Homi Bhabha's *The Location of Culture* suggests to cultural and postcolonial studies that complex figures of difference and identity unfold from boundaries, and not within them.[44] The legacy of feminism inflects gender as a crosscutting tension within any geography of subject positions, only further destabilized by queer theory. In place of Malinowski's prescriptions for objective vision stands Donna Haraway's injunction to present "situated knowledges" and a heterogeneous gesture towards reflexivity in ethnography.[45] Against the background of such work we have focused this short sketch at a more particular level around the legacy of ethnography within anthropology. Our aim has been to highlight the way in which an algorithm of distance has been inscribed into the historical object of the discipline, and lingers in the intellectual and emotional sensibilities of practitioners as their particular weaknesses for something far away.

Near the end of his essay "Reflections on Exile," Edward Said quotes a twelfth-century monk named Hugo of St. Victor: "The man who finds his homeland sweet is still a tender beginner; he to whom every soil is as his native one is already strong; but he is perfect to whom every soil is as a foreign land."[46] If we take the multiple legacy of Malinowski seriously, this stern monastic path to cosmopolitan virtue is not unfamiliar to the anthropology of a circular world. One travels the farthest only to return, having lost both "home" and the "foreign." Beyond exile, beyond ethnography, lies the impure present, and it is there we are condemned to live, aware or not, with our inherited forms and imagined futures. Abandoning the purity of culture requires accepting partial exiles and homecomings, less comfortable motions of uncertain distance. To study other restless moderns, partial natives and strangers inhabiting different, but imperfectly artificial worlds, anthropologists must relinquish the certainties of field and home, accepting every soil as foreign land. In doing so they actually recall the older promise of anthropology behind the tradition of ethnography, the legacy of estrangement that shifts horizons of habit, wherever they may lie, in order to glimpse that which has been, and that which is. To echo our onetime displaced Pole: "though the degree of success varies, the attempt is possible for everyone."

Notes

This essay itself has been displaced by our other work for many years since we first produced a sketch of it for a conference on "Culture and Addiction" held at Claremont Graduate School in 1996. During that time we have received helpful readings from a number of people, including Judy Farquhar, Mike Fischer, Richard and Sally Price, Marc Redfield, Rebecca Saunders, Patricia Sawin, Dan Segal, Katie Stewart, and Kamala Visweswaran. The remaining deficiencies of this installment are no fault of theirs.

1. Bronislaw Malinowski, *A Diary in the Strict Sense of the Term*, trans. Norbert Guterman (New York: Harcourt, Brace, and World, 1967); see also George W. Stocking, Jr., *The Ethnographer's Magic and Other Essays in the History of Anthropology* (Madison: University of Wisconsin Press, 1992).

2. For the outlines of some of this literature, see James Clifford and George E. Marcus, eds., *Writing Culture: The Poetics and Politics of Ethnography* (Berkeley: University of California Press, 1986); as well as Ruth Behar and Deborah A. Gordon, eds., *Women Writing Culture* (Berkeley: University of California Press, 1995); James Clifford, *The Predicament of Culture: Twentieth Century Ethnography, Literature, and Art* (Cambridge, Mass.: Harvard University Press, 1988) and *Routes: Travel and Translation in the Late Twentieth Century* (Cambridge, Mass: Harvard University Press, 1997); Richard

Fardon, ed., *Localizing Strategies: Regional Traditions of Ethnographic Writings* (Washington, D.C.: Smithsonian Institution Press, 1990); Richard G. Fox, ed., *Recapturing Anthropology: Working in the Present* (Santa Fe, N.M.: School of American Research Press, 1991); Clifford Geertz, *Works and Lives: The Anthropologist as Author* (Stanford, Calif.: Stanford University Press, 1988); Akhil Gupta and James Ferguson, *Anthropological Locations: Boundaries and Grounds of a Field Science* (Berkeley: University of California Press, 1997); Dorinne Kondo, "Dissolution and Reconstitution of Self: Implications for Anthropological Epistemology," *Cultural Anthropology* 1 (1986): 74-96; George E. Marcus and Michael Fischer, *Anthropology as Cultural Critique* (Chicago: University of Chicago Press, 1986); George Marcus, ed., *Critical Anthropology Now: Unexpected Contexts, Shifting Constituencies, Changing Agendas* (Santa Fe, N.M.: School of American Research Press, 1999); Kirin Narayan, "How Native is a 'Native' Anthropologist?" *American Anthropologist* 95 (1993): 671-686; Sherry Ortner, *The Fate of "Culture": Geertz and Beyond* (Berkeley: University of California Press, 1999); Paul Rabinow, *Reflections on Fieldwork in Morocco* (Berkeley: University of California Press, 1977); George W. Stocking, Jr., ed., *Observers Observed: Essays on Ethnographic Fieldwork*, (Madison: University of Wisconsin Press, 1983); and Kamala Visweswaran, *Fictions of Feminist Ethnography* (Minneapolis: University of Minnesota Press, 1994). While the hysteria over "postmodernism" in the discipline partly emanated from the methodological concerns raised in reflexive questions by a small (if professionally well-situated) group of practitioners (and partly from a series of political assaults on neutral authority, led perhaps most successfully by feminism), anthropologists of varying persuasions tend to unite in finding other cultural studies insufficiently engaged with the details of everyday practice beyond formal representations. Here we should also note that when we write "anthropology" we generally mean the North American configuration of the discipline, which, in the international relations of the contemporary academy, represents an imperial center of power and influence. Like our illustration of "exile" with the Eastern European case, not every general remark made would apply to every particular case worldwide and through time; our purpose is not to make universal claims but rather to expose connections between very visible sites of representation (ones, furthermore, whose gender is neutralized in masculine norms). To that end, wherever possible we have used sources available in English, the metropolitan language of this essay. Rather than deploying frequent translations as an authoritative device, we will admit jointly implicated identity as a sometimes displaced Anglophone anthropologist and a Czech-Slovak émigré Canadian archaeologist resident in the United States.

3. Yossi Shain, *The Frontier of Loyalty: Political Exiles in the Age of the Nation State* (Middletown, Conn.: Wesleyan University Press, 1989), 1-2.

4. Ewa Thompson, "The Writer in Exile: The Good Years," *Slavic and East European Journal* 33, no. 4 (Winter 1989): 499.

5. Joseph Brodsky, "The Condition We Call Exile," in *Altogether Elsewhere: Writers on Exile*, ed. Marc Robinson (Boston: Faber and Faber, 1994), 3. For distinctions between categories of displacement see Liisa Malkki, "Refugees and Exile: From 'Refugee Studies' to the National Order of Things," *Annual Review of Anthropology* 24 (1995): 512-515; Mary McCarthy, "A Guide to Exiles, Expatriates and Inner Émigrés" and Edward Said, "Reflections on Exile," in *Altogether Elsewhere*, 49-54, 143-4. Also see the critical discussion of the term in Caren Kaplan's *Questions of Travel: Postmodern Discourses of Displacement* (Durham, N.C.: Duke University Press), especially 101-142.

6. Liisa Malkki's *Purity and Exile: Violence, Memory, and National Cosmology among Hutu Refugees in Tanzania* (Chicago: University of Chicago Press, 1995), a study

of Hutu refugees in Tanzania, provides a vivid reminder that displacement plays an active cultural role for masses represented as a distant object of suffering. Also see Michael Fischer, "Starting Over: How, What, and for Whom Does One Write about Refugees? The Poetics and Politics of Refugee Film as Ethnographic Access in a Media-saturated World," in *Mistrusting Refugees*, ed. E. Valentine Daniel and John C. Knudsen (Berkeley: University of California Press, 1995), 126-150; and Luc Boltanski, *Distant Suffering: Morality, Media, and Politics* (Cambridge: Cambridge University Press, 1999).

7. Randolph Starn, *Contrary Commonwealth: The Theme of Exile in Medieval and Renaissance Italy* (Berkeley: University of California Press, 1982), 1.

8. Michael Seidel, *Exile and the Narrative Imagination* (New Haven, Conn: Yale University Press, 1986), 1.

9. Starn, *Contrary Commonwealth*, 1-2.

10. Starn, *Contrary Commonwealth*, xv.

11. By "Eastern Europe" we mean the political empire and satellite states of the former Soviet Union, as experienced by intelligentsia living in Central European and Russian urban centers, revolving linguistically around a core of Slavic languages. Our focus rests on the post-Stalinist period when, especially after the events in Hungary in 1956 and those in Czechoslovakia in 1968, the ideological bankruptcy of state socialism became more apparent to erstwhile sympathizers in the West. Eastern European émigrés came to occupy a morally privileged position, representing the virtue of idealism to many would-be radicals as well as would-be conservatives, uniting the disparate inheritors of the Enlightenment. Moreover, for intellectuals they held out the appeal of political relevance in writing. In the context of an authoritarian regime, literature cannot help but be political; the term *samizdat* ("self-published") could never be translated literally from a system where the act signified a crime against the state to one where it signified an inability to find a commercial publisher. This fact cloaked otherwise sardonic works in a mantle of virtue, e.g., Josef Škvorecky's *The Engineer of Human Souls* (New York: Alfred A. Knopf, 1984). In contrast, the redemptive tone that pervades current discussions of identity in anthropology—in which metaphors of "exile" are often invoked (see, e.g., Behar and Gordon's *Women Writing Culture*)—depends on earnest liberatory politics and more diffuse formulations of oppressive censorship. For a comparative, ethnographic study of East and West in this context, see John Borneman, *Belonging in the Two Berlins: Kin, State, Nation* (Cambridge: Cambridge University Press, 1992).

12. Thompson, "The Writer in Exile," 513.

13. The responsibility of testimony for a would-be writer would apply, regardless of the extent to which exile is a result of state oppression, although its political inflection (and reception) might vary accordingly. On the limits of Aijaz Ahmad's criticism of the postcolonial expatriate, see Kaplan, *Questions of Travel*, 105-110.

14. See Geertz, *Works and Lives*, as well as Gupta and Ferguson, *Anthropological Locations*, on the significance of this expression and its implication of presence within the ethnographic project. For further background on the legacy of natural history, see Henrika Kuklick and Robert E. Kohler, eds. *Science in the Field* (Chicago: University of Chicago Press, 1996).

15. See Stocking, *Ethnographer's Magic*, for a more careful account of the rise of fieldwork in anthropology. Here we are privileging the received folklore, on the simple grounds that the selective, progressive narratives of "Whig" history are crucial to the construction of disciplinary boundaries and identity.

16. Bronislaw Malinowski, *Argonauts of the Western Pacific* (New York: E. P. Dutton, 1961), 21.

17. Talal Asad, ed., *Anthropology and the Colonial Encounter* (New York: Humanities Press, 1973) and Edward Said's *Orientalism* (New York: Vintage, 1979) represent two sources of criticism. George Stocking's *Ethnographer's Magic* provides a more detailed and historically nuanced account. Arjun Appadurai's *Modernity at Large: Cultural Dimensions of Globalization*, (Minneapolis: University of Minnesota Press, 1997) and Akhil Gupta and James Ferguson, eds., *Culture, Power, Place: Explorations in Critical Anthropology* (Durham, N.C.: Duke University Press, 1997) render the spatial logic transparent, while Fardon's *Localizing Strategies* sketches a number of different area genealogies. See also Edwin Ardener, "'Remote Areas': Some Theoretical Considerations," in *Anthropology at Home*, ed. Anthony Jackson (London: Tavistock, 1987), 38-54; Melville Herskovits, *Franz Boas: The Science of Man in the Making* (New York: Charles Scribner's Sons, 1953); Carl Pletsch, "The Three Worlds, or the Division of Social Scientific Labor, circa 1950-1975," *Comparative Studies in Society and History* 23, no. 4 (October 1981): 565-590; Han Vermeulen and Arturo Alvarez Roldán, *Fieldwork and Footnotes: Studies in the History of European Anthropology* (London: Routledge, 1995); and Noam Chomsky, Laura Nader, Immanuel Wallerstein, R. C. Lewontin, Ira Katznelson, and Howard Zinn, *The Cold War, the University: Toward an Intellectual History of the Postwar Years* (New York: New Press, 1997).

18. See Robinson, *Altogether Elsewhere*, and Clifford and Marcus, *Writing Culture*, for testimony.

19. Behind its originality, the name "Tamina" contains linguistic resonance lost in translation, since in Czech *tam* means "there" and *jiná* is the feminine form of "different."

20. Milan Kundera, *The Book of Laughter and Forgetting* (New York: Alfred A. Knopf, 1981), 79.

21. Vladimir Nabokov, *Speak, Memory* (New York: Mentor, 1966), 203-204.

22. Stanislaw Baranczak, "Tongue-tied Eloquence: Notes on Language, Exile, and Writing," in *Altogether Elsewhere*, 242, 251. Jan Novak's "The Typewriter Made Me Do It" provides an amusing and insightful account of the pressures contributing to the preservation and gradual loss of language in emigration, culminating in the crucial lack of a typewriter equipped to make diacritical marks. Novak, "The Typewriter Made Me Do It," in *Altogether Elsewhere*, 261-266. For amplification, see Eva Hoffman, "Obsessed with Words," in *Altogether Elsewhere*, 229-233.

23. Ivan Diviš (selection in K. Hvížd'ala, *České rozhovory ve světe*. Index: Köln. BRD, 1981), 228, our translation.

24. Ludvík Vaculík (selection in K. Hvížd'ala, *České rozhovory ve světe*), 7, our translation.

25. Michel-Rolph Trouillot, "Anthropology and the Savage Slot: The Poetics and Politics of Otherness," in *Recapturing Anthropology*, 17-44.

26. Susan Sontag, "The Anthropologist as Hero," in *Claude Lévi-Strauss: The Anthropologist as Hero*, ed. E. Nelson Hayes and Tanya Hayes (Cambridge, Mass.: The MIT Press, 1970): 185, 196.

27. Claude Lévi-Strauss and Didier Eribon, *Conversations with Claude Lévi-Strauss*, trans. Paula Wissing (Chicago: University of Chicago Press, 1991), 67.

28. Claude Lévi-Strauss, *The View from Afar*, trans. Joachim Neugroschel and Phoebe Hoss (New York: Basic Books, 1985).

29. Sherry Ortner, "Reading America: Preliminary Notes on Class and Culture," in *Recapturing Anthropology*, 163-189; Laura Nader, "Up the Anthropologist: Perspectives Gained from Studying Up," in *Reinventing Anthropology*, ed. Dell Hymes (New York:

Pantheon, 1972), 284-311. The estrangement of anthropology from its immediate surroundings has perhaps been more distinct in the British variant; in the early American context, the "field" was never as conveniently separated from home by oceans (see Fox, *Recapturing Anthropology*, and Fardon, *Localizing Srategies*). Ruth Benedict and Margaret Mead—publicly central and yet relatively marginal in institutional terms—would demand attention in writing a more complicated history of foreignness in anthropology, as would the variegated identity of early practitioners beyond Boas and Malinowski (e.g., Lloyd Warner, Hortense Powdermaker, or the ever difficult to locate Zora Neale Hurston). Here we simplify to highlight a suggestive pattern, one that would translate into received wisdom for an expanding postwar generation of anthropologists who, with the assistance of greatly increased funding for social science, institutionalized disciplinary norms. See George W. Stocking, Jr., *Anthropology at Chicago: Tradition, Discipline, Department*, an exhibition marking the fiftieth anniversary of the Department of Anthropology, October 1979-February 1980, the Joseph Regenstein Library, the University of Chicago (Chicago: The University of Chicago Library, 1979).

30. Witness the recent admission of one established practitioner: "After I finished the project on middle-class London magic, it was quite plain to me that to sustain an identity and a salary as an anthropologist I would have to do some fieldwork in the exotic third world." T. M. Luhrmann, *The Good Parsi: The Fate of a Colonial Elite in a Postcolonial Society* (Cambridge, Mass.: Harvard University Press, 1996), ix. We should also not forget that disciplines are externally as well as internally defined; the expectation of practitioners of other academic disciplines (not to mention the reading public) is often even more rigid on this point, and the romanticization of exotic experience more extreme.

31. Claude Lévi-Strauss, *Tristes Tropiques*, trans. John and Doreen Weightman (New York: Penguin, 1973), 85.

32. Raymond Firth, "Bronislaw Malinowski," in *Totems and Teachers: Perspectives on the History of Anthropology*, ed. Sydel Silverman (New York: Columbia University Press, 1981), 110.

33. See Stocking, *Ethnographer's Magic*, 40-51; and Lévi-Strauss and Eribon, *Conversations*, 87-88. At the end of the century it is precisely such imperfections of historical position that preoccupy Malinowski's intellectual descendents.

34. Letter quoted in Grazyna Kubica, "Malinowski's years in Poland," in *Malinowski between Two Worlds: The Polish Roots of an Anthropological Tradition*, ed. Roy Ellen, Ernest Gellner, Grazyna Kubica, and Janusz Mucha (Cambridge: Cambridge University Press, 1988), 96.

35. Stocking, *The Ethnographer's Magic*, 44.

36. Stocking, *The Ethnographer's Magic*, 51. For background on earlier social history of scientific witnessing, and who could and who could not fill the testimonial role, see Steven Shapin, *A Social History of Truth: Civility and Science in Seventeenth-Century England* (Chicago: University of Chicago Press, 1994). While Malinowski was indeed a member of the cosmopolitan European intellectual elite of his day, he was born to a subordinate branch, and had to master a dominant language to achieve authority and recognition.

37. In *Argonauts*, Malinowski writes, "It is very nice to have a base in a white man's compound for the stores, and to know there is a refuge there in times of sickness and surfeit of native. But it must be far enough away not to become a permanent milieu in which you live and from which you emerge at fixed hours only to 'do the village'" (6-7). The *Diary* makes explicit the frustration and sometimes revulsion behind the phrase.

38. Joan Vincent, "Engaging Historicism," in *Recapturing Anthropology*, 57.

39. In addition to the plates published in *Argonauts*, see Michael W. Young, *Malinowski's Kiriwina: Fieldwork Photography 1915-1918* (Chicago: University of Chicago Press, 1998) for images of the ethnographer in the field.

40. Sylvie Richterová, "Nezávislá literatura a závislá kritika," in *Česká nezávislá literatura po pěti letech v referátech* (conference proceedings), ed. František Kautman (Prague: Primus, 1995), 38, our translation.

41. Malinowski, introduction to *Facing Mount Kenya: The Tribal Life of the Gikuyu*, by Jomo Kenyatta (London: Secker and Warburg 1956), vii-viii. Recent literature on "native" anthropology—variations on the theme of studying one's "own"—helps return ethnography to the complicated moment of Malinowski's definition of method. See Narayan's "How Native is a 'Native' Anthropologist?"; Visweswaran's *Fictions of Feminist Ethnography*; and Lila Abu-Lughod's "Writing Against Culture," in *Recapturing Anthropology*, 137-162.

42. See Appadurai, *Modernity at Large*, for a sketch of emerging global topography and George Marcus, "Ethnography in/of the World System: The Emergence of Multi-Sited Ethnography," *Annual Review of Anthropology* 24 (1995): 95-117, for some of the methodological issues involved. Richard Price and Sally Price's *Equatoria* (New York: Routledge, 1992) blurs diary and ethnographic insight in describing contemporary variations on the nineteenth-century tradition of museum collecting.

43. Cited in Leopold Damrosch, Jr., "Myth and Fiction in Robinson Crusoe," in *Daniel Defoe's Robinson Crusoe*, ed. Harold Bloom (New York: Chelsea House Publishers, 1988), 109.

44. Appadurai, *Modernity at Large*, and Homi Bhabha, *The Location of Culture* (London: Routledge, 1994).

45. Donna Haraway, "Situated Knowledges: The Science Question in Feminism and the Privilege of Partial Perspective" *Feminist Studies* 14, no. 3 (Fall 1988): 575-600. For further confusion with the categories of situation, see Judith Butler's *Gender Trouble: Feminism and the Subversion of Identity* (New York: Routledge, 1990). For a rendition of hybridity different from Bhabha's, see Bruno Latour's *We Have Never Been Modern* (Cambridge, Mass.: Harvard University Press, 1993).

46. Said, "Reflections on Exile," 147.

Chapter Six

Foreign Bodies: Engendering Them and Us

Margot Badran

How is the foreign created? How is it gendered? How is it experienced? I shall consider these questions in the context of the Arab world and especially of Egypt and Islam. It is important to foreground that we always experience the foreign through gender. Thus we cannot fully chart and analyze the foreign without attending to its gendered manifestations. National and cultural contexts influence the articulations of gender. Thus to live as a foreigner in (other) national and cultural contexts is to live one's gender differently. The foreign is difficult to define, to pin down; it is slippery and elusive. Yet, it is insistently present. The foreign is like a shadow; it moves with one, is outlined by one, it only has its existence in relationship to the thing it silhouettes.

One way to begin to chart the foreign is to describe how it is experienced. Such a description assists us in seeing the uses to which it is put and the ends it is made to serve. Also, attending to names for the foreign—how they are constructed, when and by whom, how they are deployed—offers insights into the life of the foreign and the lives of foreigners. In this paper, I thus draw upon my own experience of the foreign, of living in Egypt as a foreigner, as well as upon my academic study within the disciplines of women's studies and history, to explicate and theorize the constitution and deployments of the foreign. This is in part, then, an autobiographical project, but one that my research suggests extends beyond a single experiencing self, having multiple echoes in the lives of others.[1] Unpacking my story will, I hope, contribute to the project of clarifying how the foreign is constructed and how foreign selves are en/gendered. It will reveal an intricate and intimate choreography between those who construct the foreign, and the self that is made foreign, and unmask its political workings.

Excavating the self to uncover the workings of the foreign is a form of exposure not fully comfortable to the narrating self. Exposure fractures the protective borders the self erects in negotiating the foreign, the borders through which one attempts to retain a prior, ostensibly non-foreign, self. Exposure can also be threatening to those whose "othering" practices and agendas may be laid bare. Autobiographic exposure propels the subject to name small acts, for it is in the telling detail, as much as in the grand theory, that we see the workings of the "foreignization" of others. In living our daily lives, we may be quite aware of the invisible electric fences that constructions and impositions of the foreign erect, but we often choose not to draw attention to them because it is easier to pretend they are benign, or that they, and the politics they entail, simply do not exist. Exposure rips through this invisibility.

In order to explicate how the foreign is en/gendered and experienced, I draw on a theoretical framework based on a set of intersecting arguments. My first two arguments concern patriarchy and feminism. First, constructions and experiences of gender and foreignness are directly related to specific patriarchal systems, which are rooted in time and place, and refracted through constructions of class, race, ethnicity, and religion, and to deliberate efforts to maintain these systems. Second, there also exist feminist resistances to patriarchal practices of gendering the foreign and of making gender foreign, resistances primarily staged by women, who are both insiders and outsiders. These resistances (like collusions) are always part of complicated agendas. Issues of classification, control, and power—both imposed and resisted—are thus central to projects of en/gendering the foreign, as they are to en/gendering its other.

My third argument concerns constructions both of the indigenous woman and of the foreign woman who, through marriage-in, is conceived as an "outsider within," and which will be explored in the specific context of Egypt, though it is an example that may resonate in other Arab and Muslim societies. The indigenous woman herself, at one level, is conceived as "the foreign" or the (alien) disturber of natural and social order. She is *fitna* or chaos, the disruptive foreign element, the *unnatural*; yet at the same time, paradoxically, she is *nature* itself, as Fatima Mernissi has deftly elucidated.[2] The woman is perceived as a sexual being, or as Mernissi puts it, "an omnisexual being," unlike the man whose sexuality only partly defines him. The woman is sexually voracious and therefore threatening both to herself and to the entire social order. This disruptive alien element must be tamed and controlled—*domesticated*—by the patriarchal family. Through this taming, the (unruly, frightening) foreign becomes naturalized. However, the indigenous woman also symbolizes the authentic— "the purest of the pure," "the most indigenous of the indigenous," "the most inside of the inside." As symbols of the authentic, women are often hyper-mobilized in times of national peril, as in the cases of colonial invasion in Algeria and India, as Marnia Lazreg and Partha Chatterjee have elaborated respectively.[3] As symbol of the indigenous, of the nation itself, the woman becomes both house and flag—the abode and the sign—of national identity and authenticity. The foreign woman is thus doubly foreign: by being woman, she is cast (by popular ideology) as inherently a foreign element, a condition she shares with indigenous women; and by originating from another country and culture, she is rendered foreign again. The foreign woman who becomes an insider through marriage-in, what I have called the "outsider within," is both *domesticated* and *estranged*: the indigenous patriarchal family and the patriarchal state set out to absorb and control her. Yet because of her origins (conceived both in terms of place and ethnicity), she, unlike the indigenous woman, cannot symbolize the authentic.

Becoming Foreign

In my twenties, when I went to live in Egypt, I suddenly became a foreigner. Foreigners were persons who found themselves in countries other than their own, other than the country of their birth or citizenship, and so this status was laid upon me. But to myself I was never a foreigner. The me is not foreign, so I thought. Of course, I was well aware that when outside one's own country one is foreign and that, while not foreign to myself, I *was* foreign to others. And so, I wore foreignness like a new coat—one that did not quite fit and was often eyed oddly. As foreignness was bestowed upon me, so was this foreignness gendered. My status as a female foreigner was thickened and further mediated by my marriage to an Egyptian and by my intent to settle in Egypt. I became the "foreigner within." I was not a traveler, a visiting short-term resident, nor a long-term expatriate: all quite different ways of being a foreigner. A woman as a foreign traveler typically is viewed as an "honorary male"; as a short-term resident she is simply a transient; and as a long-term expatriate she may claim a zone of immunity or live in a cocoon of eccentricity.[4] The female foreigner within, whose marriage-in narrows the gap between the outside and inside, is subjected to pressures to conform and observe local rules of propriety, fine-tuned by family and class. Ways I was foreign and ways I was re-gendered locally were constructed through both the nation (Egypt) and religion (Islam). In looking at how nation, religion, and culture (as well as family, class, etc.) structure foreignness, it is necessary also to consider the historical moment. Any set of configurations constructing the foreign are dynamic and in a continual process of change and permutation. And persons who are "foreignized" are also themselves always changing.

Thus, in scrutinizing the foreign through the window of experience, it is germane to speak of the times and of the person I was at the moment of my initial experience as a foreigner. I was an American graduate student in the Center for Middle Eastern Studies at Harvard when I came to Egypt in 1966 just weeks after my marriage. The civil rights, anti-war, and feminist movements were sweeping through the United States and many of us, as students, both defined our lives in terms of these liberation movements at home and identified with the national liberation movements of Africa and Asia. It was a moment of exhilaration, promise, and hope, of breaking old rules and making new ones. It was a moment of reaching out, of reaching beyond borders and boundaries, of brotherhood and sisterhood. Ideas of the foreign were *foreign* to us and quite irrelevant. It thus came as a shock to discover that I, suddenly, had become foreign.

The first year of my new foreignness was the first year of my marriage. How the two were linked and the ways they were to saturate each other I could never have known when I set out on my multiple journeys. In 1966, Egypt—the foreign country where I sought to make my home (and to resolve the apparent contradiction between *foreign* and *home*)—celebrated the tenth anniversary of President Nasser's nationalization of the Suez Canal and the final expulsion of the military remnants of British occupation. Arab socialism and pan-Arabism were active projects of hope for better lives, as were the many African liberation movements headquartered in Cairo. The 1960s were also the time of the Cold War world with its rigid and bitter polarities, a world in which Egypt and America stood on opposite sides. Nine months after I arrived in Egypt, the Arab-Israeli war of 1967 broke out. Suddenly I was not simply the "foreigner within" but, by virtue of my nationality, I was the "enemy within."

Meanwhile, I came face to face with another kind of "foreignizing," this at the hands of fellow Americans, with whom I shared birthplace, upbringing, education, and citizenship, and to whom, presumably, I should not be a foreigner. These were American residents and expatriates, more specifically white Americans, who manifested an anxiety to guard clear-cut borders and the privileges secured by maintaining a distinct foreign status. They displayed condescension toward their co-nationals, especially female co-nationals who blurred the boundaries by marrying-in, and undertook to distance these "transgressors."[5] Perhaps the French term *déraciné* best describes this sense of being uprooted—in this case, by others and without choice. Thus to such compatriots *cum* expatriates, I had, through marriage, crossed a forbidden line; in part it was seen as a "racial" line (though it tangled together "race," ethnicity, and culture); in part, as a line between the West and the so-called, and implicitly lesser, "rest." What seemed to be like a treacherous hijacking, or at least manipulation, of my national identity and legal status, could not only be used to assuage these individuals' anxieties about their own status, but to shore up a wall behind which they could secure their privileges and take advantage of "the other." When I felt the sting of this behavior, it led me to think about, and learn from, the experience of black Americans—both in the United States and in Egypt.

White Americans were not the only Americans in Egypt. In the 1960s, during the time of anti-racist struggles in the United States and anti-colonial struggles in Africa, many black Americans, mainly men, gravitated to Egypt. They had little desire to mix with white Americans. Even though, like myself, many of the Muslim African Americans were studying at Al-Azhar University, we had no interaction because there, they as men and I as a woman were kept carefully segregated by gender. It would not be an exaggeration to say that black and white Americans in those days were foreigners to each other.

The experience of African Americans in Egypt adds other layers to an understanding of how the foreign is constituted and operationalized. David Du Bois, in his memoiristic novel of the period . . . *And Bid Him Sing*, captures the experience of male black Americans in Egypt in the 1960s. The author, a black liberation militant, journalist, recent editor of the Black Panthers' journal, and the adoptive son of W. E. B. Du Bois, came to Egypt at the beginning of the 1960s. Du Bois draws out the layers of identity construction of a brutally uprooted people, foreign in their own country, who, in going to Egypt, perceived themselves to be "coming home." Du Bois's chief protagonist, the poet Sulaiman, upon descending the airplane in Cairo, "knelt down and kissed the earth of Mother Africa."[6] However well Egyptians received the black Americans as friends, they did not see them as African brothers but as *Americans*; nor, in fact, did the Egyptians see *themselves* as Africans. Sulaiman complained that an Egyptian friend "called me *khawaga*" (a term used in addressing a Western man); "I had to tell him we had the same ancestors."[7] Even Sulaiman's marriage to an Egyptian woman did not confer insider status, as it would for a foreign woman marrying an Egyptian man. As Du Bois's novel depicts, the acid test of who was an insider and who was an outsider came with the War of 1967, when all Americans, like other foreign nationals, were ordered to leave, *except* wives of Egyptians. Du Bois's Sulaiman, who had illusions about belonging, and was married to an Egyptian, was expelled. I, who had no illusions about *not* being a foreigner, was allowed to remain because of my status as the wife of an Egyptian.

In Egypt, I attempted to transcend my new foreignness, to become something new while retaining something old. I could see how the foreign was constructed through patriarchy and perhaps see it all the more vividly because *I was foreign* and *I was female*. It is not infrequent that women outsiders see and experience more acutely the manifestations of other patriarchies, against which they have neither inherited nor honed coping mechanisms.

History, the shadows of colonialism and its bitter postcolonial traces, Egyptians' identities and agendas, Western residents' identities and agendas, my own origins, my gender, and my new positioning all swirled into the shifting configurations of my experience of becoming foreign. The foreign, I realized, was an imposed category thrust upon one, rather than being willfully chosen; it happened in spite of one's wishes. And it was saturated with cultural constructions and power politics, which bore gender markings.

One way I have sorted through these intersecting layers is to examine the ways the foreign is named, to learn its terms and meanings, which also involves knowing what the foreign is *not*. Hence, I wish to detour momentarily from my narrative to explore Arabic terminology: words for the foreign and its others that have circulated in Egypt. In this lexical mapping, I look for practices of naming that provide clues to how the foreign, and its necessary foil, the indigenous, have been conceptualized.

Naming the Foreign/er: Terminology and Its Determinants

Names for the foreign/er and its others are historical fabrications. They are concocted at particular moments and places to set borders, to define the self, as much as, and maybe more than, to delineate the (alien) other. Arabic, as a Semitic language, builds words from a set of root consonants through which radiate related as well as opposing meanings. When words are coined they display this "magnetic field" of meanings, although these meanings often shift over time so that original inflections are obscured. When people choose words, they are often unaware of their original meanings and are not necessarily signaling the nuances words may originally have carried. I am more interested here, however, in how certain conceptualizations of foreignness and foreigners were formulated and the ideas embedded in these words. For in their shifting significations, words leave traces of their previous meanings. They leave sediments that linguists, in an archaeology of terminology, might excavate. Thus, despite the volatility of words and their meanings, roots offer telling clues in my search for constructions of the foreign and its others.

Writing this paper in English about Arabic terms for the *foreign* and *indigenous* involves shuttling between two languages without fully parallel words. In English there appear to be fewer words for *foreign* than in Arabic and even the most generic inflection of *foreign* is different in the two languages.[8] The English word *foreign* derives from the Latin *foras*, or outside, while probably the most generic, and certainly the most commonly used, word in Arabic for foreign is *ajnabi/yya,* which comes from a root that means to run alongside or parallel to (Wehr, 139). Conveying less distant othering, this etymology does not suggest an inside/outside binary and ostensibly connotes a less hierarchical version of coexistence.

Various Arabic words for *foreigner* appear in different registers of the language—classical Arabic, modern standard Arabic (the written language), and spoken Egyptian—and signal specific spacio-cultural mappings. For example, the word *gharbi/yya,* derived from *gharb* [West], is used to designate a foreigner, and specifically connotes a Westerner or European (Wehr, 668). Other words for Western foreigners are *franji/yya* (Franks or Europeans) and *rumi/yya* (Byzantine, Roman), though both are now archaic as applied to people (Wehr, 710, 369). Another word that connotes place is *'ajami/yya* referring to those coming from Persia (Wehr, 593). This term is common in the Arab countries of the Gulf, signaling Arabs of Persian origin who constitute a significant part of the local populations. Wehr contends that the adjectival form *'ajami/yya* denotes "speaking incorrect Arabic and even speechlessness" (593). Explaining that *'ajami* refers to foreignness, Mernissi remarks that the term, "literally [refers to] those who cannot speak Arabic correctly, who either speak it badly or have not mastered its subtleties."[9]

Gharbi/yya (Westerner) is a heavily loaded term for *foreigner*. The term carries associations with colonialism and thus is freighted with overtones of the culturally imperialistic. It is often used to express, and certainly evokes, a polarity between an "inauthentic" Westerner and the "authentic" native. It can also be used to express an exaggerated approval or disapproval. Thus, unlike the more generic and neutral term *ajnabi/yya*, the term *gharbi/yya* sets up a distinct distancing that implies cultural and political difference. *Gharbi*, when gendered female (*gharbiyya*), often carries additional connotations of sexual promiscuity in a way that *ajnabiyya* does not.

Terms of address serve as markers and maintainers of the indigenous and the foreign. They are potent classificatory devices constantly repeated at the point of individual social interaction. Egypt has historically welcomed and accommodated diverse communities of Westerners. During the nineteenth century, Europeans began arriving in increasing numbers due to state-sponsored modernizing programs, expanding trading opportunities and, later, the swelling British colonial apparatus. The term *khawaja/khwajayya*, of Persian origin (from the word *huja* or teacher), is a form of address applied to Western foreigners (Wehr, 264), as are the borrowings *monsieur* and *madame* for Francophone, or mister and misses for Anglophone, foreigners.[10] *Effendi, bek,* and *basha,* loan words absorbed into Arabic from Turkish, and bearing the traces of Ottoman suzerainty, were forms of address that designated rank and were used in addressing Eastern men: Egyptians, Arabs, and Turks. *Basha* and *bek* were officially bestowed titles; *effendi* was used to address men from the professional classes. These titles were proscribed after the revolution of 1952 with its egalitarian socialist ideology. Similarly, *hanim,* or Lady, another loan word from Turkish absorbed into Arabic, was a form of address used for upper class Egyptian and other Eastern women that faded after 1952 (although it was never officially outlawed) in favor of *Madame,* which had meanwhile become increasingly common with the spread of French as the everyday language of the Egyptian elites.[11]

Idiosyncratic deployments of terms of address can also confuse boundaries and cunningly appear to dilute the notion of the foreign. During British occupation and partial independence (1882-1952) colonial officials appropriated Egyptian titles; for example, Thomas Russell, Commandant of the Police, was called Russell Pasha. By contrast, *hanim* was never appended to the names of Western women in colonial service (who were mainly engaged in education and health), which might lead us to ponder the gendered logic of "cross-titles." Male British colonial officials' use of "native titles" that symbolically blurred the distinctions of foreign and indigenous—and their relations of unequal power—contrasted with insistence on women's strict adherence to boundary maintenance by all means, including terms of address.

Naming the Indigenous: Terminology and Its Determinants

The foreign can only be understood in relation to the "non-foreign" through which it is formulated.[12] It is thus instructive to look at formulations for the indigenous. In Arabic, there are more words for indigenous than for foreigner. Words for the non-foreigner cluster around three organizing principles: one, place—including, but not limited to, the territorial modern nation state; two, lineage—conceived of as a people, a social, cultural, or religious community, or an individual or family genealogy; and three, the concept of "the natural."

The modern nation state has created its own categories for indigenous and foreign: they are typically *muwatin/a* (citizen), derived from *watan* (the territorial nation state), and *ghair muwatin/a* (noncitizen).[13] These are legal constructions by which the state defines and controls categories of people within its geographical borders (Wehr, 1080). Female citizen and male citizen are not, however, parallel categories in law but, rather, express two ways of being citizens, challenging the tenet of equality implied in the notion of (democratic) citizenship. An adjective for the indigenous that is connected with place is *baladi*; used in reference to a native, fellow citizen, or countryman/woman, the word derives from *balad*, which signifies country, especially a particular part of the country such as a town or village (Wehr, 72). During the colonial period, the British and other Westerners used the word *baladi* pejoratively to indicate something inferior or "tacky"; Egyptian elites also used the term disparagingly to refer to people of the popular classes. Another way the indigenous is connected with place is seen in the adjective *mahalli/yya*, which means local, native, or indigenous and comes from the root *mahal*: a stopping place, encampment, way station (Wehr, 200). In United Nations parlance, *mahalli/yya* (as well as *asli/yya*) is used to designate *indigenous*.

In addition to being grounded in place, Arabic words for the indigenous are also connected with lineages or constructions of a people or human community. *Qawm* designates a tribe, race, or people. *Qawmiyya* can also be used to signify nationalism (Wehr, 800). From *asl,* connoting origin, source, descent, or lineage, comes the word *asli*, which, as we have noted, functions in United Nations vocabulary to designate *indigenous*. The word connotes the original, genuine, authentic, or pure; it stresses the significance of roots and is still often heard in the more highly tribal cultures of the Arabian Peninsula.[14]

A term similarly implying lineage, but focused more upon the idea of kin, relatives, family, and the domestic, is *ahl*, which likewise denotes *native* or *indigenous* (Wehr, 33). In Egypt, from the late nineteenth century to the 1952 revolution (that is, during the colonial period), the National Courts were called the *ahli* courts and were distinguished from the Mixed Courts where cases involving foreigners were held (in accordance with the privileges and protections bestowed upon them by the Capitulations).[15] Finally, the word *sha'b* constitutes the indigenous as the populace or folk, as well as nation or tribe, and became important in the Marxist lexicon of postrevolution socialist Egypt because it connoted an egalitarian construction of nationality (Wehr, 472).

Two words that signify *indigenous* are specifically connected with "nature" or "the natural." The more common of these, *tabi'i/yya*, the primary meaning of which is *natural*, is also used to connote the native, inborn, ordinary, usual, or regular (Wehr, 552). A less common word, *fitri/yya*, could be translated as native, natural, inborn, or instinctive—and implicitly conflates these meanings (Wehr, 720).

The most complex term conveying a sense of the indigenous in Arabic is *jins*, which refers to race and nation, as well as sex, and, more abstractly, to genus, class, or species; it is also the name for gender as a grammatical category (Wehr, 141). *Jins* in contemporary everyday parlance is used for sex. *Al-jins* is a loanword that linguists tell us came into Arabic from Syriac *genso* and Greek *genos*, which denote genus, kind, ethnicity, nation (of believers), race, and sex, and also function as grammatical terms. Most scholars claim that *al-jins* as a designation for sex only came into circulation within the past two or three hundred years. The first Arabic term for gender to circulate in Egypt was *nau 'al-jins*—a kind or species of sex.[16] In any case, *al-jins* and related words in Arabic today carry multiple connotations.[17] *Jinsiyya* is the standard word for nationality or citizenship. *Tajannus* is the acquisition of citizenship or naturalization and *mutajannis/a* is a naturalized citizen.[18] On an immigration card, one is asked to mark one's *jins* (male or female) as well as one's *jinsiyya* (nationality).

Concepts of the foreign and the indigenous are also constructed within the context of religion, specifically Islam. The word for the community or nation of believers coined at the beginning of Islam is *umma* (the related Arabic word *umm* is mother), which retains its original meaning. The person who belongs to the nation of believers is called *mu'min/a*, a believer, one bound by *iman*, faith or belief (Wehr, 29). In contemporary Arabic parlance, *umma* can also connote the Arab nation and the term used for the United Nations is *Ummum al-Muttahida*, a community of nations united (*al-muttahida*) by adherence to, or belief in, a covenant.

The foreigner to Islam can simply be called a non-Muslim, *ghair muslim/a*. She or he can also be called, pejoratively, a *kafir/a*: unbeliever, infidel, or atheist. Completely anathematizing is the term *murtadd/a*—the apostate—one who has defected, or is accused of straying from the faith through words or deeds, and is subject to punishment by death according to Egyptian law, which is derived from (a reading of) the *Shari'a* (Islamic religious law). In Islam, there is also a construct for those in the middle space between foreign and indigenous, outsider and insider, which is *ahl al-kitab* or "people of the book," referring to Jews and Christians, who as *dhimmis*, according to Islam, are free non-Muslim subjects, entitled to protection. However, protective status whether for individuals, women, peoples, or countries (such as Egypt's under the British Protectorate from 1914 to 1922) can be problematic and function euphemistically for various forms of subjection.

While the Muslims in the Ottoman Empire constituted the *ra'iyya* or subjects, the Empire organized its non-Muslims into *millets:* communities or "nations," based on combinations of religion and ethnicity—Armenian Orthodox, Armenian Catholic, Syrian Orthodox, etc.—internally governed by the community's own laws (Wehr, 312). Under the Capitulations system, these "foreign minorities" enjoyed extraterritorial legal rights and special privileges—a system of protection which they, not surprisingly, welcomed. In Egypt, the Capitulations which extended special legal and economic privileges to the foreigners in Egypt ended only in 1937, fifteen years after the (quasi-independent) secular nation state was established. Long-term foreigners, known as "indigenous foreign minorities," many of whom had been in Egypt for several generations, enjoyed this privileged foreigner status and, even after the Capitulations ended, chose to remain legal foreigners. After the 1952 revolution, however, persons of the formerly protected Eastern foreign minorities—Armenians, Greeks, and others— were forced to choose between assuming Egyptian citizenship or emigrating.

The foregoing lexical excursion reveals the wide range of constructions of the foreign and the indigenous with their permuting inflections. It transmits hints, signals, and warnings.

Mechanisms for "De-foreignizing"

The Egyptian state and the Islamic religion both have distinct, gender-specific mechanisms for "de-foreignizing" or including the other: the state, through naturalization, a legalizing-domesticating operation; and religion, through conversion, a legalizing-ideological operation.

For the Egyptian state, which divides individuals into the categories of citizen and noncitizen, being a "foreign citizen" is a contradiction in terms, though people born into their citizenship often, in practice, "foreignize" new citizens. States can confer citizenship on individuals, but the naturalization laws of virtually all Arab states, Egypt included, are restricted to offering citizenship to wives of male citizens. By contrast, male spouses of female Egyptian citizens are not eligible for Egyptian nationality. Such a policy effectively genders as female the pool of new or naturalized citizens. The children of a (non-Egyptian) woman married to an Egyptian man may, and if in Egypt *must*, assume Egyptian nationality, while the children of an Egyptian woman married to a non-Egyptian citizen cannot inherit Egyptian citizenship through their mothers. Feminists and human rights activists are fighting this form of gendered "foreignizing" that does not give male spouses of Egyptians the option to become citizens and that casts Egyptian mothers' children by a noncitizen father as aliens.[19] The patriarchal backbone of these policies is not difficult to detect. Through such policies, the state attempts to control its women citizens, to pressure them to "marry in," that is, to effect endogamous marriages and to punish them, short of stripping them of their citizenship, if they do not. This is also a way of regulating the construction of male citizenship and fusing a necessary link between birth, background, and citizenship for men only.

In contrast, the vehicle for becoming an insider to Islam, that is, conversion to the faith, is open equally to women and men. The only requirement is attesting to belief; when a non-Muslim converts to Islam, that person becomes a full member of the *umma*, "nation" or community of believers. Both male and female Muslims must pass their religion to their offspring. When non-Muslim men wish to marry a Muslim woman, according to Islam, they can only do so after becoming Muslim, hence marriage and conversion for men are often linked. We see a salient difference between Islam and the state: a non-Muslim man *must* become Muslim to marry a Muslim woman, but a non-Egyptian man who marries an Egyptian woman *cannot* become an Egyptian citizen.

Experiencing the Foreign as an Outsider Within

In this and the following section, I return to my experience in Egypt in the late 1960s and 1970s. I shall look at state structures of classification and control that affected me as a foreign woman married to an Egyptian citizen, at religious structures of classification and control (as expressed in Egypt) that affected me as a non-Muslim woman married to a Muslim, and at those less distinct, but very tangible, cultural controls that take the form of pressure to conform (though such conformity does not ultimately confer full acceptance, the status of "one of us"). I shall then analyze how and why certain other Americans resident in Egypt positioned me as an outsider because of my status as the wife of an Egyptian citizen and note consequences of this positioning. These concrete examples will help unpack the layers through which foreignness is constructed.

The state enables the foreign spouse of an Egyptian citizen to obtain an official long-term residence permit.[20] As already mentioned, the state also allows a foreign wife access to citizenship, unlike the foreign husband. Such privileges accorded the foreign wife protect the Egyptian man's right to marry a woman of his choice, including a foreign woman, without penalty and at the same time protect the patriarchal structures of the family (headed by an Egyptian-born husband) and state. While Egyptian women have the right to marry a foreigner, they are made to pay a price for exercising that right for, as we have seen, neither their husbands nor their children may become citizens. The foreigner and her or his Egyptian spouse are always located in this grid of Egyptian patriarchal culture. While I gained residency privileges as a foreign wife, I also was controlled by the state because of this status. If I wanted to leave the country, for example, I, like other Egyptian wives, could not do so without obtaining the signed permission of my husband—an official requirement for the issuance of my exit visa—despite the fact that I was not an Egyptian citizen. A husband could control his wife's movements, not only in and out of the country, but in and out of the house as well, by a provision in the *Ahwal Shakhsiyya* (Personal Status Code) known as *bait al-ta'a*, enabling a husband to forcibly return, with police help if necessary, a wife who left the conjugal residence without his permission.[21] The state would thus perform virtually the same function for the husband regarding his wife's ability to move beyond national borders. This caused many women, both foreign and Egyptian, many difficulties, complicating their movements or curtailing their ability to move abroad. In this instance, we can see how the patriarchal state erased the distinction between foreign and Egyptian women, regulating alike the movements of both. While feminists and human rights activists have assiduously fought against the restrictions on Egyptian women's rights to move freely within and outside the country, it was only in 2001 that it became legally possible for an Egyptian woman to obtain a passport and to travel abroad alone without the permission of her husband.[22]

There was, however, one instance in which the state treated me strictly as a foreigner; this was related to a question of national security. During the years between the 1967 war and the first stage of signing the rules of disengagement in the late 1970s, I, like all foreign nationals, was prohibited from moving outside the major cities in the Nile valley as most of the country was considered a "military zone." In this case, my foreign status was absolute and clear-cut; my marital status as the wife of an Egyptian had no effect.

Meanwhile, I discovered that Islam also controls the non-Muslim through her status as the wife of a Muslim. According to Islam as commonly interpreted, a Muslim man is able to marry a woman belonging to *ahl al-kitab* (a "people of the book"), but a Muslim woman, as noted, is not able to marry a non-Muslim man. Such a reading of religious prescriptions likewise upholds a patriarchal family order: the man as head of the family controls, and is responsible for, his wife and children; a Muslim woman must not fall under the control and responsibility of a non-Muslim husband. While the non-Muslim woman has the right to marry a Muslim man, in so doing she becomes subject to Muslim laws regarding marriage, divorce, child custody, and inheritance. She has no rights at all regarding child custody and inheritance and, in divorce, her rights, like those of Muslim women, are heavily restricted. The state and religion interact in Egypt in legally regulating family matters through the *Ahwal Shakhsiyya*, which is statutory (state) law built upon interpretations of the *Shari'a*. Thus, interpretations of Islam as expressed in Egyptian state law shore up the patriarchal structure of the Muslim family by assuring that wealth and offspring are not siphoned off by a foreign, non-Muslim wife. Reform of the Egyptian Personal Status Law has been a perennial women's demand since the first wave of Egyptian feminism.[23]

Consequently, as a non-Muslim married to a Muslim, I fall under the jurisdiction of the Egyptian Muslim Personal Status Law with its various forms of gender inequalities. While there are separate Personal Status Codes for Muslims and Christians, a single Islamically based law of inheritance (a matter of personal status) applies to all Egyptians regardless of religion. Non-Muslim foreign wives, as well as Muslim and Christian women without sons, are subject to inequities under inheritance laws; the former inherit nothing and the latter inherit less than do mothers of sons.[24] Governed by Muslim personal status legislation myself, I obviously have a direct stake in how the law is formulated. Thus, in 1987, I joined the newly-formed Network of Women Living under Muslim Law (WLML), an international activist and research organization which works to eliminate gender injustices in the construction and application of Islamic laws, often by exposing their contradictory formulations.[25] I also began to conduct activism, as well, through research and writing about new forms of Islamic feminism, promoting more gender-egalitarian readings of the *Qur'an*.[26]

Turning attention to culture, we see that it operates in divergent ways and can be deployed both as an inclusionary or exclusionary device. It is often expressed in binary oppositions between the indigenous and the foreign, "ours and theirs," "us and them," and is articulated through notions of the authentic, the moral, and the pure. Culture can be deployed to construct and regulate the foreigner, to give the foreigner space, or to retract that space; indeed it often does both at the same time in ways that can be disconcerting. In Egypt, as in many other cultures, there is more potential for, and actual manipulation of, the foreign woman than the foreign man, a price she pays for greater inside status. While the state and Islam control the female foreigner within from above and implement their various forms of legal regulation at particular moments in people's lives, culture seeks to control her through impositions in the routines of everyday life. Cultural discourses (discourses of do's and don'ts) can be highly manipulative of the foreigner; in a sense, discourse is to culture what law is to the state. It was in the arena of "culture" that my experience of being an inside foreigner in Egypt was most unnerving. The laws of the state and religion may be understood and, as such, more directly confronted or circumvented, whereas the discourses of culture are more elusive, certainly to the uninitiated, and decidedly more volatile.[27]

In my earlier years as a foreign woman living my everyday life in Egypt, I felt that the disadvantages connected with my "foreigner within" position in the culture outweighed whatever benefits the state accorded me. I experienced what I felt to be undue and unfair attention paid by family, friends, and acquaintances to the smallest details of everyday life, to my dress and movements. (This was before the appearance of the new "Islamic dress" in the 1970s.) While I found the microscopic monitoring of my everyday behaviors and the delivery of admonishments irritating, I was most offended by the *idea* that people accorded themselves such authority over me. I also found attention to the myriad details about my deportment absurd because they did not fit into any logical framework of my own. It became clear that the attention to my dress and behavior revolved around me as a *young* woman. I became more conscious of myself as a sexual being. Later, when I encountered Fatima Mernissi's elaboration of the woman in Islamic Arab culture as an "omnisexual being," it crystallized for me theoretically what I had sensed through my own experience in Egypt.[28] What all the surveillance was telling me was that it was not I who could command respect by my own modes of behavior, which I felt to be decent even if different—and which I modified out of consideration for different sensibilities—but that respect would come from my conformity to what I often thought of as trivial conventions imposed by others.[29] Dress or simple modes of public deportment, for example, became important; what I thought was appropriate, decent, and acceptable by my own upbringing and standards was suddenly open to discussion and sometimes censured. What was happening was that I was losing *authority* over myself, over the smallest details of my everyday life. I could also see that there were variations on the advice given me depending upon who was dispensing it (variations relating to class background and personal proclivities) and that "culture" was often used as a legitimizing device for behaviors particular individuals wished to impose upon me. Things were not made easier when advice was dispensed from my elders, mainly women, as failing to heed this counsel would be taken as impolite or lacking in respect. As I was the "foreigner within," I had greater access to the interior spaces of the culture, but once in this inside space my own (too foreign) cultural habits had to be either restyled or jettisoned. I became aware of a certain irony: the less foreign I became to Egyptians through this redesign, the more foreign I became to myself. Yet I was determined not to lose myself and cede authority over my life to others. Thus, very early on I staged everyday acts of resistance, mainly in the form of refusals to comply. It was a way of demanding the freedom to be different and the right to be myself. In the following section I shall speak of how I found allies in this resistance in pioneering Egyptian feminists.

Another way in which I experienced a new foreign status was, as I have mentioned, in relation to other Americans in Egypt for whom, because of my marriage-in, I had stepped over a boundary. Motored by their own interests, they reconstructed my identity as the "other." I offer two examples from the late 1960s to illustrate. In a discussion about the possibility of my teaching at the American University in Cairo, I was informed that I would not be paid as an American but be given the lower salary offered to Egyptians (an injustice to Egyptians which I protested as well). The head of the department's condescending explanation was: "You married one [an Egyptian] so we are going to treat you like one." With that, he accorded himself, as did the university policy he was willing to represent, the right to decide my nationality and to discriminate against me.[30] The other example involved my enrollment at the American University in Cairo. Immediately upon my arrival in Cairo I enrolled in an Arabic class; apart from simply wanting to continue my Arabic for everyday purposes, I needed to sit for a qualifying Arabic examination in order to get my M. A. at Harvard, which the university agreed to have administered in absentia. But after one semester, I was informed that Arabic as a foreign language was for foreigners who were temporarily in Egypt (students from abroad and temporary residents), but not those, like me, who had come to settle. Fortunately, this dismissal led to my application to Al-Azhar University, the venerable Islamic university, where I was accepted as a foreign student and granted a stipend. Not only did this move protect my education, but it opened up to me new avenues into the culture.

In sum, I felt the worst thing about being "foreignized" was the denial of a basic right to a self—a "non-foreign" self—and one's right to authority over one's own life. As a new "foreigner within" I was determined to claim more space, and the right, to be myself.

Experiencing Feminism as "De-foreignizing"

While I was chaffing at ways people were trying to reshape me, I met some first-wave Egyptian feminists. I discovered that many things that I had been told were part of Egyptian culture—things that I, the female foreigner, must accept—*they* called injustices perpetrated against women and they encouraged my resistance. Patriarchal controls imposed on women were not part of a sacrosanct culture, they insisted, and must not be given the gloss of indigenous culture or religious prescription to be preserved. Saiza Nabarawi, whom I met in 1967, and who became a mentor and elder friend, had, along with *her* mentor and elder, Huda Sha'rawi, removed the veil from her face thirty-four years earlier in an act that signaled their refusal to conform to patriarchal control cunningly imposed in the name of Islam and "indigenous culture."[31]

The unveiling was enacted on the eve of the feminist movement they would help lead for a quarter of a century. In telling me the story of her unveiling, Nabarawi was urging me to investigate and question restrictions and injustices imposed in the name of culture; she was teaching me that there was also a local tradition of dissent and resistance against injustices to women and that this was as much a part of the culture as the restrictions it opposed. She told me about the feminist movement of which she had been a part from the 1920s until the mid-1950s and how, after the dissolution of an independent feminist movement in 1956 by the state under President Nasser, she had kept a low profile at home and had become more visibly active in the international arena.[32] Had I not met Saiza Nabarawi, Hawa Idris (the niece of Huda Sha'rawi), Inji Aflatun (a communist and feminist writer, activist and artist), Duriyya Shafiq (leader of the *Bint al-Nil* feminist movement), and others in whose homes I visited, I would not have been aware of the continuation of a behind-the-scenes feminist discourse. I could point to them and their activism as examples of a tradition of *insider resistance*: I could make their arguments mine—arguments framed in the discourses of culture, nation, and religion. I did not have to be the dutiful pupil forced into remedial learning.

Early this century, when Egyptian feminists exposed and confronted patriarchal oppression, *they* were branded foreign. They and their feminism were discredited as Western despite the fact that these disturbing "aliens" were Egyptian women with impeccable nationalist credentials, who had been active in the nationalist movement against British colonial rule, and whose nationalist activism—inseparable from their feminism—was enthusiastically accepted. Thus, it was with Egyptian activist women castigated as foreigners that I began my journey through the minefields of the gendered "us-es" and "thems." From these women, I learned about ways of thinking and behaving that were alternative to the conventions that had been presented to me as obligatory in the discourses of nation, culture, and Islam. I learned from them how they had fought to construct a new identity for Egyptian women, initially simply as persons with the right to move in public space, to alter their dress and habits, and to be respected while exhibiting new forms of decent behavior; and I learned how they later demanded their rights to be fully participating citizens of a modern, independent state. These women, who had bridged colonial and postcolonial society, found that their own subject positions had changed from fully accepted participants in the militant nationalist struggle to second-class citizens in the new quasi-independent state in 1923.

From them, I learned how *they* experienced being foreign. This was first, by not being accorded in practice the full and equal rights of citizenship that the Egyptian constitution granted them and, second, by being labeled as "Western" and thereby delegitimized because they dared to object. I was reinforced in my own will not to succumb to the attempts of others to define and control me, not to bow indiscriminately to inherited modes of behavior. I saw firsthand that it was not simply one set of Egyptians—or only conservative Egyptians—who could admit one into society, nor one set of conventions, to which one must adhere to become "properly" Egyptian. I learned that the epithet "Western" used in a pejorative sense could be applied to anyone in an attempt to place her outside the borders of acceptability, to "foreignize." The last of the "first-wavers" accepted me as "one of them," in Saiza Nabarawi's words. She, Hawa Idris, Amina al-Sa'id, Inji Aflatun, and others understood that I had not come to Egypt to perch on the fringes, enjoying the easy social and economic benefits that accrued to expatriates, but to settle, to live the hard times with them, to become one of them. Intentions and actions mattered as they dissolved the borders between themselves and me. These feminists, who well understood the manipulative, delegitimizing, and stigmatizing uses of the foreign, gave me the chance to become an insider and to choose what to accept and reject, and the chance to shape my own identity.

My interactions with these Egyptian feminists drew together two projects: the personal project of becoming an insider in Egypt and a professional project of academic research on the history of the rise of feminism in Egypt. The two projects worked to reinforce and enhance each other. I felt that my research was a path to a deeper understanding of Egypt and a grasp of its culture—of both its plural realities and its possibilities for change. My relationships with my elder mentors, meanwhile, helped me *live* Egypt differently.

Second-Wave Feminism: Feminist Activism, Identity Politics, and the Foreign

By the mid-1980s, Egypt had been my home for twenty years, although during these years I came and went frequently. Several years earlier I had finished my thesis on the first wave of Egyptian feminism for my doctorate at Oxford University. Throughout the process I had continued to mesh personal and professional projects.[33] Twenty years was a long time and my sense of being foreign in Egypt had become muted. I had staged resistances and had made accommodations. If I felt that people had given me more space to be myself, I also was a different person than I had been before. And it would not be long before I would lose my early feminist mentors and guides: Saiza Nabarawi, Hawa Idris, Inji Aflatun, and Amina al-Sa'id, all of whom died in the late 1980s and early 1990s.

Egypt was a different place from the country I had first entered. In the aftermath of Nasser's death in 1970 and with the coming to power of Anwar Sadat, Arab socialism was dismantled, "open door" capitalism was introduced, a multiparty system was permitted to surface, and formerly silenced voices and ideologies were once again allowed in public space. This period saw the rise of Islamism, or political Islam, and with it the dissemination of a reactionary discourse on women and gender. But feminism, too, found expression once again in this new, more open public space. If first-wavers I met in Egypt lent me a hand in pulling me in and mentoring me, I participated alongside second-wavers in enacting our feminism. We came together as women and formed our own feminism from the base of shared experience and common problems we faced in living in Egypt.

Second-wave feminism inside Egypt was constructed around our shared experience and positionings as women. A major concern of the new second-wave feminism was the rise of a reactionary discourse about women articulated by political Islam. As participants in the construction of second-wave feminism, we articulated what we *lived* in Egypt, or witnessed at close hand in a place where we spent our daily lives; we were conceiving a new wave of feminism from within (although the perennial and ignorant allegations that feminism was Western could be heard in certain quarters). Ethnicity, race, and origins were not constitutive of the "us." The "us" of Egyptian feminism accommodated difference; it was pluralistic; it included foreigners; it included men. My participation in this second-wave feminism, which continued the fight against patriarchal, social, and economic injustices women faced, brought me further inside.

In the 1980s, Nawal al-Saadawi, who combined socialism and feminism, encouraged me to join the Arab Women's Solidarity Association (AWSA) in Cairo, which she had recently founded. I attended the monthly *nadwas* (public seminars) held at the AWSA headquarters where women and men debated gender issues affecting our lives in Egypt. As a historian, I gave papers at AWSA analyzing aspects of women's nationalist and feminist past in Egypt.[34] I published both scholarly papers and articles in the local Arabic and English press. In 1990, Sana' al-Bissi invited me to write an essay on the meaning of feminism for the mass circulation magazine she had founded called *Nisf al-Dunya* [*Half the World*].[35] Through such projects, I participated in Egyptian intellectual and activist life, exploring and experiencing Egyptian feminism as pluralist rather than particularist.

In the 1980s and early 1990s, identity politics was rampant both in Egypt and in the West, though its reverberations and concepts of foreignness were markedly different in these two settings. In Egypt and other parts of the Middle East, identity politics pivoted around secular and religious poles. Second-wave feminists were concerned with what we saw as the dangers of a spreading, gender-conservative Islamism. Feminists wanted to hold the ground and Islamist women activists wanted to change the ground as part of a larger movement intent upon establishing an Islamic state. In 1990, Valentine Moghadam organized a conference on Women and Identity Politics in which I participated along with many other scholars from the Middle East.[36] At this conference, we discussed the dissatisfaction we detected on gender issues from women associated with Islamist movements, specifically the older Islamist movements in Egypt and Iran. We were seeing the seeds of what was later to be called Islamic feminism.

Meanwhile in the West, identity politics and feminism took a different shape. By the early 1970s, second-wave feminism in the United States had given birth to the new academic field of women's studies, which our generation had participated in creating.[37] African American studies had grown out of the civil rights movement and, in the wake of national liberation movements, postcolonial studies was on the rise. In 1978, Edward Said published *Orientalism*, elaborating how the West had packaged the Eastern "other" and demonstrating the operations of power behind this orientalism. I remember attending a conference in 1978 dedicated to the creation of the upstate New York branch of the new National Women's Studies Association and feeling distinctly uncomfortable that middle class white American's experience was generalized to all women. The kinds of women's experience I had both lived and observed in Egypt did not fit the narrow paradigm being articulated. By the 1980s, however, women's studies in the United States had understood—had been made to understand—that it had focused too exclusively on white women and theorized solely from their experience. African Americans, Chicanas, and women from Asia and Africa took women's studies in America into a new realm, introducing the terms "women of color" and "third world women" as categories of both identity and analysis. Increasingly in the 1980s, identity politics in the United States and other parts of the West pivoted around national origin, ethnicity, and race.

Accordingly, the legitimate voices were perceived to be the voices from within various groups: third world women, women of color, Arab women, Egyptian women, and others speaking about themselves. After all, women had, as feminists, demanded to represent themselves, rather than be represented solely by men. People who had not represented themselves must assume this task, must acquire authority to speak on their own behalf. Both as a feminist and as someone who had earlier felt her own authority to represent herself threatened, this position had strong resonance for me. But I realized that the problem arises of how to honor the rights of people and groups to speak for themselves without delegitimizing the rights of others to speak, without denying our ability to speak about each other as well as ourselves.[38]

In the Western academy in the 1980s, identity was configured around ethnic, racial, and national affiliation; it was a moment of focusing on the constitution of selves and others. And in constituting and claiming selves, the "foreign" or the "other" was a residual category. The foreign—here, the inauthentic or distorting—appeared in opposition to the selves constructed around ethnicity and race. Within this discursive project being articulated by feminists in the academies of the West, there was little room for an "us" constituted around shared gender experience, nor for the articulation of a past or future in a shared space undefined by ethnicity, "roots," and race. If the pluralist space that second-wave feminism occupied in Egypt was "de-foreignizing," identity politics in the United States served a "foreignizing" or "othering" function. These two paradigms offered different definitions of insiderness: the performative and experiential on the one hand, and the ascriptive and essentialist on the other. The former opened up possibilities, transgressed borders, and dismantled the foreign; the latter legitimated and maintained borders sustaining the foreign.

Globalization and Dis/solving the Foreign

Recent questioning of the nation, nationalism, and national identity implicitly interrogates the concept of the foreign. The spread or revival of religion throughout the globe possesses its own ways of dismantling borders set up by nations, race, and ethnicity, while, at the same time, making clear its own lines of demarcation. With an intensifying focus on globalization and elaborations of globalist discourses, the idea of the foreign is being implicitly reconfigured as the local becomes part of the global and the global part of the local.

Yet, the foreign still retains currency in (local) cultures as an opposition to the indigenous. Even among citizens of the same nation, a naturalized citizen may be seen as foreign if s/he does not share common racial and ethnic marks. Thus one can decide to become a citizen but cannot decide not to be foreign. Foreignness would appear to be a status conferred upon one by others and not a result of personal choice. Categorizing and treating one as foreign is an othering process that preempts individual agency and dismantles the notion of equality.

In trying to explicate the foreign, and particularly the female foreigner, through drawing upon my experience in Egypt, I have used the term "foreigner within" to name the way my marriage-in defined me, thrusting me into a middle space between the outside and the inside. I gained a form of entry through this patriarchal door—a form of entry that placed me under the control and protection of the patriarchal state and religion. In exchange for obeying the rules I would be protected. But conformity and protection were not acceptable prices to be paid for passage in. I found another door—the door of feminism. This was the one that led me by way of contestation and struggle to a space where I could assume some control over my own life. I am now a naturalized Egyptian but I am still considered foreign. Citizenship alone does not dissolve the foreign nor constitute the indigenous. Since naturalized or new Egyptians are virtually all women (because, as noted, only spouses of male Egyptians are eligible for citizenship), this ambiguous middle space is a female space. Refiguring this space and its inhabitants poses a feminist challenge yet to be taken up.

Notes

1. This paper is part of a larger autobiographical project recalling and reflecting upon more than three decades of life lived in, and in relation to, Egypt. It draws upon journal entries, letters, and memory.

2. See Fatima Mernissi, *Beyond the Veil: Male-Female Dynamics in a Modern Muslim Society*, rev. ed. (Bloomington: University of Indiana Press, 1987).

3. Marnia Lazreg, *The Eloquence of Silence: Algerian Women in Question* (New York: Routledge, 1994); Partha Chatterjee, *The Nation and Its Fragments: Colonial and Postcolonial Histories* (Princeton, N. J.: Princeton University Press, 1993).

4. There is an extensive literature by and on foreign women as travelers in Arab and other Middle Eastern countries. On Western women re-gendered as travelers, see, for example, Dea Birkett, *Spinsters Abroad: Victorian Lady Explorers* (New York: Blackwell, 1989); on Western women travelers and residents, see Billie Melman, *Women's Orients, English Women, and the Middle East 1718-1918: Sexuality, Religion, and Work* (Ann Arbor: University of Michigan Press, 1992). On long-term residents in the nineteenth century, see, for example, Lucy Duff Gordon, *Letters from Egypt*, centenary ed. (London: Routledge, 1969) and Katherine Frank's biography of Gordon, *A Passage to Egypt: The Life of Lucie Duff Gordon* (Boston: Houghton Mifflin, 1994). For an example of female expatriate literature in the late twentieth century, see Elizabeth Fernea, *A View on the Nile* (Garden City, N.Y.: Doubleday, 1970). There is also a significant literature touching on "gender role flexibility" and immunities accorded foreigners (especially Western women) in Asia and Africa. See, for example, Hannah Papanek, "The Woman Fieldworker in Purdah Society," *Human Organization* 12, no. 2 (Summer 1953): 160-63; Carol McC. Pastner, "Rethinking the Role of the Woman Fieldworker in Purdah Societies," *Human Organization* 41, no. 3 (Fall 1982): 262-64; Carolyn Fleuhr-Lobban and Richard A. Lobban, "Families, Gender, and Methodology in the Sudan," in *Self, Sex, and Gender in Cross-Cultural Fieldwork*, ed. T. L. Whitehead and M. E. Connoway (Chicago: University of Illinois Press, 1986), 182-195; and Laura Nader, "From Anguish to Exultation," in *Women in the Field*, ed. P. Golde (Chicago: Aldine Publishing Company, 1970), 97-116.

5. When American and other Western men married Egyptian women, a reverse process was set in motion, which is not to suggest that this was not problematic for the Egyptian wives.

6. David Du Bois, . . . *And Bid Him Sing* (Palo Alto, Calif.: Ramparts Press, 1975), 187.

7. Du Bois, . . . *And Bid Him Sing*, 122.

8. For translations and definitions I use *The Hans Wehr Dictionary of Written Modern Arabic*, ed. J. M. Cowan (Ithaca, N.Y.: Spoken Languages Services, 1976), hereafter referred to as "Wehr." The original Hans Wehr dictionary was published in German in 1952 and was translated, edited, and enlarged by Cowan in 1960. Most of the words were collected between 1940 and 1944 through searching books, newspapers, periodical literature, letters, and radio.

9. Fatima Mernissi, *The Forgotten Queens of Islam*, trans. Mary Jo Lakeland (Minneapolis: University of Minnesota Press, 1993).

10. In the seventeenth century, the term *khawaja* signified a merchant (who might or might not be of foreign origin) coming from the region rather than from the West. See also Nelly Hanna, *Making Big Money in 1600* (Syracuse: Syracuse University Press, 1998), 18.

11. It appears that the Turkish mode of address disappeared faster among women whose social language was French than among men whose titles signaled their rank in society. The titles *Basha* and *Bey*, moreover, were bestowed by the ruler, whereas *hanim* was simply an upper class convention.

12. Geographer Klaus-John Dodds, in speaking of the construction of foreign policy, stresses how identity requires differentiation and that the foreign is a loaded and interested project. See "Geopolitics and Foreign Policy: Recent Developments in Anglo-American Political Geography and International Relations," *Progress in Human Geography* 18, no. 2 (1994): 186-208. See also M. Shapiro (cited by Dodds), who argues that "The making of the other as something foreign is thus not an innocent exercise in differentiation. It is clearly linked to how the self is understood." *The Politics of Representation* (Madison: University of Wisconsin Press, 1998), 1.

13. I say typically because there are variants such as Kuwait, where there are three categories of inhabitants: full or first-class citizens, second-class citizens or *mutajannisin* (who have been naturalized), and *bidun* or stateless but settled in the country (primarily Bedouin who did not register to become citizens by a state mandated deadline).

14. The notion of roots as defining the indigenous or insider was mobilized by the six women authors of *Arab Women in the Field: Studying Your Own Society*, ed. Soraya Altorki and Camillia Fawzi El-Solh (Syracuse, N. Y.: Syracuse University Press, 1988). Three grew up in the Arab world and two were raised in the West; two had foreign mothers (one raised inside and the other outside the Arab world). All had had higher education in the West and all but one was then living and working outside the Arab world. While the contributors defined *indigenous* as denoting "the researchers' membership in a cultural area or in a specific community," ethnic roots or ancestry more specifically united them as Arab women than did the vaguer notion of membership in a cultural area or community which could well include ethnically non-Arab women. *Arab Women in the Field*, 7.

15. The first Capitulations were a system of agreements between the Ottoman Empire and foreign nations under which foreign citizens and subjects were allowed to live in the Empire, enjoy special rights, and remain exempt from both taxes and the Turkish legal system. In modern Egypt, Capitulation treaties made directly with foreign countries were modified at various times and remained in effect until 1937.

16. For further discussion of the term *al-jins* and its origins, see my paper "Gender Journeys in/to Arabic," *Languages and Linguistics*, special issue on Languages and Gen-

der in the Arab World (forthcoming). Rendering the term *gender* into Arabic is highly fraught and the subject of intense debate. *Nau'* *al-jins* became problematic because of widespread objection to the use of *jins* [sex] in public discourse; now a more common term for gender in Egypt is simply *nau'*. There is considerable objection by Arabic speakers, in Egypt and elsewhere, to using the foreign word *gender*, to appropriating it as a loanword. However, *gender* has been appropriated into Arabic as the loanword *al-jandar* in Yemen; this happened via the Empirical Research and Women's Studies Center at San'a' University where the term passed into the academic vocabulary. But after virulent criticisms of the Center by conservative forces in the Fall of 1999, the Center was reorganized and the term *gender* was removed from all curricular materials; currently, it is not allowed in academic discourse at the Center.

17. *Jins* has also been deployed for *race* and the term *racist* has been used for sexist. For example, Egyptian feminist Saiza Nabarawi applied the term *racist* to gender in her writing. As I noted in *Feminists, Islam, and Nation: Gender and the Making of Modern Egypt*, Nabarawi's "use of 'racist' in French [the language in which she wrote], clearly signifies 'sexism'" (Princeton, N.J.: Princeton University Press, 1995), 161. I was referring to her article "A la dérive," *l'Egyptienne* (Sept. 1931), 9. *Feminists, Islam, and Nation* was among those texts the Supreme Council of Culture in Egypt selected for translation into Arabic in commemoration of the centenary of Qasim Amin's book *Tahrir al-mar'a*; it appears in Arabic under the title *Ra'idat al-haraka al-niswiyya al-misriyya wa al-islam wa al-watan.*

18. As noted above, *mutajannis/a* in Kuwaiti Arabic is the term applied to a "second-class citizen" or a person who arrived from nearby in the region (typically, Saudi Arabia or Iraq) in the middle decades of the twentieth century.

19. Among the activists I have interviewed on this subject are Sumaiyya Ibrahim, a development practitioner and herself married to a foreigner and Fu'ad Riyad, former professor of law at Cairo University. The issue is also currently high on feminist agendas in other countries in the region.

20. It might be noted that during the June War of 1967 the only category of foreigners not expelled from the country were female spouses of Egyptian men.

21. Although *bait al-ta'a* was abolished in 1967, the notion that a husband might control his wife's movements lingers.

22. See Badran, *Feminists, Islam, and Nation*, 126-35.

23. See Badran, *Feminists, Islam, and Nation.*

24. The standard argument in defense of gender inequalities in inheritance is that they are counterbalanced by the legal requirement of a Muslim husband to financially provide for his wife and children.

25. On WLML, see Seema Kazi, "Muslim Law and Women Living under Muslim Laws," in *Muslim Women and the Politics of Participation*, ed. Mahnaz Afkhami and Erika Friedl (Syracuse, N.Y.: Syracuse University Press, 1997) 141-46; Farida Shaheed, "Linking Dreams: Network of Women Living under Muslim Laws," in *From Basic Needs to Basic Rights*, ed. Margaret A. Schuler (Washington, D.C.: Law and Development International, 1995), 305-26; and Shaheed, "Controlled or Autonomous: Identity and Experience of the Network Women Living under Muslim Laws," *Signs* 19, no. 4 (1994): 997-1019.

26. Recently, in a debate among (mainly) Muslim intellectuals in which I took part on the notion of equality in Islam, I responded to Rached al-Ghannouchi's suggestion that there were some exceptions regarding equality that had to be accepted concerning women and non-Muslims by asking for clarification because, theoretically, *mu'mina* is not a par-

allel construction to the *mu'min*. On the proceedings of these debates see *Islam and Equality: Debating the Future of Women's and Minority Rights in the Middle East and North Africa* (New York: Lawyers Committee for Human Rights, 1999).

27. One way I confronted the state requirement for the signed permission of my Egyptian husband was to enter the country on a tourist visa (this was especially important if my husband were out of the country himself at a time I might need his signed permission).

28. See Mernissi, *Beyond the Veil*.

29. In the context of a temporary fieldwork experience, Lila Abu-Lughod writes concerning the expectations placed upon her to behave in a way signifying moral conformity: "They included me in their moral community, a position that imposed a set of imperatives and constraints on me. I wanted to be accepted, and I also felt that I *was* a moral person—it was just that I did not define morality by some of the terms they used, particularly for women." "Fieldwork of a Dutiful Daughter," in *Arab Women in the Field*, 149. This description captures how I felt, but in a context not of a temporary fieldwork situation, but of everyday living as a new insider.

30. Some of the more egregious inequalities in pay and benefits among staff of different nationalities at the American University in Cairo have been ameliorated in recent years.

31. Saiza Nabarawi herself had had insider-outsider problems when, after having been raised ostensibly as a "French girl" in her early teens, she returned to live in Egypt in her country of birth. Her periodic recounting of this story told me that she never quite got over a sense of displacement, even though she felt intensely Egyptian and was a fervent nationalist. See my article "Alternative Visions of Gender," *Al Ahram Weekly* (Feb. 13-19, 1997), 11.

32. My book, *Feminists, Islam, and Nation* tells the story of the first-wave feminist movement.

33. My doctoral thesis is entitled, "Huda Sha'rawi and the Liberation of the Egyptian Woman," presented to Oxford University in 1977. The thesis, which is available at the Bodleian and certain other university libraries, contains materials not published in my book.

34. One of the papers I presented is "Al-Nisa'iyya ka quwwa fi al-'alam al-'arabi" ["Feminism as a Force in the Arab World"] which was published in *Al-Fikra al-mu'asira al-'arabiyya wa al mar'a [Contemporary Arab Thought and the Woman]* (Cairo: Arab Women's Solidarity Association, 1989).

35. The article is called "Ma hiyya al-nisa'iyya?" ["What is Feminism?"] *Nisf al-Dunya* 34, no. 7 (Sept. 21, 1990): 85.

36. The conference was held in Helsinki in the fall of 1990; many of the papers were published in a volume edited by Valentine Moghadam called *Identity Politics and Women: Cultural Reassertions and Feminisms in International Perspective* (Denver: Westview Press, 1993). My chapter in this book is titled: "Gender Activism: Feminists and Islamists in Egypt," 202-27.

37. Berkshire Women's History and Women's Studies Conferences were important sites in the process of creating women's studies. I have written on the rise of the study of women in the Middle East and Muslim societies within the contexts both of the new women's studies and Middle Eastern Studies in the United States. "The Institutionalization of Middle East Women's Studies in the United States," *Middle East Studies Bulletin* 22, no. 1 (July 1988): 9-18.

38. Thus, in women's studies, history, literature, and anthropology, for example, we

can benefit both from studying ourselves and from what others see in studying us. A distinction can be made, moreover, between speaking about, and speaking for, others.

Chapter Seven

Expedition into the Zone of Error: Of Literal and Literary Foreignness and J. M. Coetzee's *Waiting for the Barbarians*

Rebecca Saunders

I know of no direct route to this obscure territory, so I shall ask you to follow me through the series of detours by which I happened to arrive there. It will require several stops: at the intersection of literature and foreignness; at J. M. Coetzee's novel *Waiting for the Barbarians*; at the language of South African apartheid.

Literature has long been conceived as a site of foreignness. Not only has it often been valued for its ability to transport a reader to faraway places, but it functions, in its institutionalized form, as a primary purveyor of foreign culture: "Language and Literature" departments, segregated by national, ethnic, or regional distinctions, are where students go to learn a foreign language or study a foreign culture. This cohabitation of the concept of the foreign with the study of literature is the institutional index of the primary relation that the concept of the foreign bears to language. Indeed, the paradigmatic foreigner in the Western tradition—the barbarian—is precisely one who speaks a different language, and among the most identifiable marks of everyday foreignness are an accent, a mismanaged idiom, an alterity in expression.[1]

Literature, moreover, speaks a language that is foreign to everyday language. Its nature is to be "foreign" within its own culture.[2] In the 1920s, the Russian formalists, attempting to designate the distinguishing feature of literariness, defined literature as *ostranenie* [defamiliarization], as a process of estrangement and alienation. If perception is automatic and habitual, they argued, literature functions to eradicate the automatism of perception; it makes the familiar foreign. "The purpose of art," wrote Viktor Shklovsky, "is to impart the sensation of things as they are perceived and not as they are known. The technique of art is to make objects 'unfamiliar.'"[3] Literature, in other words, makes our own world seem foreign in an effort to dissolve the ideologies that separate us from "genuine existential contact with things and the world."[4] If Shklovksy's early manifestoes attempted to isolate literature from history, politics, psychology, and ethics, to forge "an absolute separation of poetic language from the language of everyday communication,"[5] they nonetheless did so by invoking a concept with decidedly social connotations (*ostranenie*) and by a theoretical endeavor that, in its very resistance to the dictates of Marxist-Leninist aesthetics, was inescapably political. But it was Berthold Brecht who, after his 1935 trip to Moscow, translated the aesthetic effect of *ostranenie* into the explicitly social *Verfremdungseffekt* [alienation effect].[6] Drama, Brecht argued, should strive for an effect of alienation—a foreignness—in which "the audience [will be] hindered from simply identifying itself with the characters in the play."[7] This technique, aimed at disrupting what the formalists called "automatism of perception" and Brecht called "the bourgeois narcotics business,"[8] was even more specifically aimed at subverting the audience's assumption that the present is "natural" and eternal, to encourage it to see its own time as impermanent, as foreign to past and future generations:

> [W]e must drop our habit of taking the different social structures of past periods, then stripping them of everything that makes them different; so that they all look more or less like our own, which then acquires from this process a certain air of having been there all along, in other words of permanence pure and simple. Instead we must leave them their distinguishing marks and keep their impermanence always before our eyes, so that our own period can be seen to be impermanent too.[9]

What both Shklovksy and Brecht perform, I would argue, is a revaluation of the rhetoric of foreignness that permeates the hermeneutic tradition. For hermeneutics—which Schleiermacher, for example, defines as "understanding all foreign or strange speech"[10]—consistently depicts error, uncertainty, or absence of understanding *as* foreignness and treats that foreignness as a problem to be solved, a deviation to be disciplined. Shklovksy and Brecht, however, rather than resolve the crisis that foreignness produces in understanding, cultivate the transformative effect of the crisis itself; they valorize as epistemologically and socially significant the moment prior to interpretative determination. If hermeneutics prescribes what we should do with the foreign, Shklovsky and Brecht examine what the foreign does to us.

Yet if literature is a process of making foreign, such a "making" is less a hostile incursion into everyday language than the cultivation of a foreignness that inheres in the structure of language itself, in what Saussure calls the arbitrary and differential nature of the linguistic sign and in what Derrida describes as "the spacing which constitutes the written sign: the spacing which separates it from other elements of the internal contextual chain . . . but also from all the forms of a present referent."[11] If ordinary speech sublimates this foreignness—through what Paul de Man calls "the myth of semantic correspondence between sign and referent"[12]—literature cultivates it. It bears witness to the uncanniness of a world living in the diaspora of language.

But isn't this merely to spin metaphors? Does this figural, literary foreignness have anything at all to do with literal foreignness, with the demarcations that designate who belongs in a place and who doesn't, with the segregation of ethnicities or "races," or with the material reality of armed borders or access to education and medical care? For reasons I shall spell out over the course of this chapter, my contention is that, yes, the regulation and suppression of what we have called "linguistic" or "literary foreignness" is a primary technique for producing and disciplining "literal" foreigners. The grounds for this wager lie coiled within words themselves for the English word *foreign*, like French *étranger*, Spanish *extranjero*, and Greek ξένος, all carry the telling connotation of "improper" and can be used as a synonym for inappropriate.[13] Indeed, both the prefix and the root of *improper* mark significant attributes of foreignness. On the one hand, the privative constructs an entity that is comparative and dependent; it signals the fact that foreignness is conceived negatively. On the other hand, the root *proper* designates what the foreigner by definition lacks: identity (what identity he possesses is fundamentally derivative, a repository for what the domestic conceives itself not to be); propriety (she misreads signs, responds inappropriately, makes errors); purity (he is imbedded in stereotypes of both physical uncleanliness and metaphysical confusion); literality (her words fall outside of proper meaning); property (he is, by quite logical extension, prohibited from owning property).[14]

Synonymous with the *improper*, the foreign is extraneous to proper meaning; and indeed the concept of the foreign itself is characterized by an errant figurality. For the originary denotation of words such as the French *étranger*, Spanish *extranjero*, German *fremd*, and Greek ξένος is merely strange or odd, and thus what we currently take to be the "literal" or "proper" meaning of the foreign—one who is from another country, one who is not a native or a citizen—is already a figurative meaning. Yet rather than elucidate an abstract concept by reference to a concrete object, this figure articulates the materiality of foreignness through the abstract notion of strangeness; rather than represent "an idea under the sign of another idea that is more striking or better known,"[15] this metaphor operates under the sign of the unknown itself. It is not only difficult, on this view, to determine at what point foreignness becomes figural, but impossible to speak of "literal foreignness" at all: for to be foreign is to become a figure, to be dematerialized, to fall outside of proper meaning.[16]

To say that the foreign falls outside of proper meaning is also to say that (produced by an unsound opposition, recalcitrantly non-literal, and persistently destabilized by the migrations and transformations of peoples, boundaries, and customs) the foreign is a "concept" perilous to the standards of respectable metaphysicians. It is, in short, a *zone of error*. To name the foreign a zone of error as I do in this essay is, first, to describe its impure metaphysical status, for the term simultaneously is characterized by, and refers to, the irrational, the ambiguous, the confused, the anomalous, the uncertain, the imaginative: what cleanly thought sweeps hurriedly under the rug of untruth. Second, it is to recognize the foreign as a site of trial and error, of non-mastery and risk, crucial to contesting the logic of the proper and akin to the "strategic and adventurous" journey that Derrida associates with (the delineation of) *différance*:

> Strategic because no transcendent truth present outside the field of writing can govern theologically the totality of the field. Adventurous because this strategy is not a simple strategy in the sense that strategy orients tactics according to a final goal, a *telos*, or theme of domination, a mastery and ultimate reappropriation of the development of the field.[17]

Third, to name the foreign a zone of error is to evoke the everyday experience of foreignness, the error that results from the inability to read culturally inflected signs with precision: the fumble for protocol, the inadvertent offense, the unintended meaning.[18]

The tension between the conceptual instability of foreignness and its regulation by law—the apparent contradiction between what we have called a "zone of error" and the unambiguousness of a passport or a passbook—might also be articulated as a varying relation to, or possession of, *context*. Context is, before the department of justice or the bureau of immigration, the court that governs the zone of error; in linguistic terms, it is the series of syntagmatic relations that regulate the semantic relation between signifier and signified. It is, further, the law to which hermeneutics turns to regulate epistemological foreignness: hermeneutics draws a clear equivalence between being foreign, in error, and out of context. Schleiermacher, for example, warns of the "completely mistaken ideas" that result from extracting sentences from their context.[19] And St. Augustine insists on context as the criterion through which the ambiguous (the unstable, moving in two directions) is stabilized into hermeneutic determination (bound, limited, fixed): "In the event that there are several [meanings that] remain *ambiguous* . . . then it is necessary to examine the *context* of the preceding and following parts surrounding the *ambiguous* place, so that we may *determine* which of the meanings [is] consistent."[20] While for hermeneutics (which insists on a master context that corrects error) context functions to regulate foreignness, for the Russian formalists (who prompt us to shift through multiple contexts) it is central to producing foreignness: "The various devices of defamiliarization," writes Jameson, "resembled the relationship of words to expected or unexpected contexts."[21] And Shklovksy notes that a writer like Tolstoy tends to describe things out of their normal context, to depict the domestic as a foreigner might see it. This is why, according to Shklovsky, poetic language often appropriates foreign languages.[22]

This contextual regulation of literary foreignness is not only analogous to, but often coincident with, the regulation of "literal" foreignness: it is a lack or an overabundance of context that conditions the foreigner's social impropriety, her error. An insufficient grasp of those unspoken background assumptions that comprise cultural context—what Bultmann calls "pre-understanding" or "the context of life"[23]—lead the foreigner to misinterpret, to be improper, to err. Similarly, a *surplus* of context—the availability of differing and competing cultural contexts—condition the foreigner's uncertainty, ambiguity, errancy. If context (from Latin *contexere*) is the fabric woven by a culture, foreigners make the errant stitches that turn the pattern into something else.

The literary theorist who doubtless has paid the most attention to context is Stanley Fish. His argument runs something like this: we are never not in a context and, though it may be so widely shared that it seems to disappear, this context—or "interpretive community"—produces understanding, certainty, "the ordinary, the normal, the usual, the everyday, the straightforward, the literal."[24] Texts are thus always stable—they always only mean one thing—because contexts make them so and because we are never not in a context. It is highly significant, however, that Fish's theory of context disregards the existence of foreigners. When he contends, for example, that "all utterances are understood by way of relying on 'shared background information,'" he tacitly excepts and logically excludes the foreigner who does not possess that background information.[25] For while Fish may well be right that we are always in a context, he assumes that that context is singular and homogenous, that it is evenly distributed, and indeed that it is synonymous with "situation." For example, in the essay "Is there a Text in This Class?" he poses the question: "How does communication ever occur if not by reference to a public and stable norm? The answer," he contends:

> is that communication occurs within situations and that to be in a situation is already to be in possession of (or to be possessed by) a structure of assumptions, of practices understood to be relevant in relation to purposes and goals that are already in place; and it is within the assumption of these purposes and goals that any utterance is immediately heard.[26]

Yet it is precisely that "structure of assumptions" that the foreigner (to a greater or lesser degree) lacks and that simultaneously produces and adjudicates her "error." Not everyone in a "situation," in other words, possesses the same (degree of) context: indeed to be a foreigner is to be in a situation where one is out of context. Fish's invocation of "a public and stable norm," moreover, relies on the assumption that the "public" is homogenous (that it has been purified of foreign elements) and that context is singular (that the multiplicity of contexts characteristic of foreignness has been eradicated). This passage is also telling in the implicit synonymy it establishes between possessing context and apprehending literal meaning: to be at home in a context is to have access to (ostensibly) immediate meaning; to be foreign to a context is, by contrast, to be encumbered by an awareness of mediation, to be detained by language itself, to make a detour through its forgotten figurality.[27]

From this stop at the intersection between literal and literary foreignness, I take three souvenirs: first, the figural—and in a larger sense—*improper* nature of foreignness; second, the conception of foreignness as a zone of error, in a sense both epistemological and quotidian; and third, the recognition that this error is regulated not only by legislation, but, above all, by the law of context.

My next stop is at South African author J. M. Coetzee's novel, *Waiting for the Barbarians*, an allegorical text that is, I would argue, both thematically and structurally about foreignness and, hence, an exploration into the relationships between "literal" and literary foreignness. Thematically, it is a tale of "barbarians" on whom foreignness has been brutally imposed and of "a country magistrate, a responsible official in the service of [a generic] Empire" who places himself in foreign territory—both in the land of the dark "barbarians" and in a zone of error—a subjective dislocation that allows him to conceive of himself as other and to become foreign to the identity mapped out for him by historical circumstances.[28] The novel narrates, that is, not only his journey(s) into barbarian territory, but his willingness to concern himself with uncertain signs, his insistence on error in the language through which the empire signifies *barbarian*, and his attempt to recuperate the foreignness in signification that the certainties of empire have sought to eradicate.[29]

The novel, further, is structured as an allegory; and allegory is a kind of language in which a text's literal meaning is foreign to its proper meaning.[30] It is the "extreme case," writes Jon Whitman, of a fundamental "dislocation of words from their objects," a "language at one remove from what it claims to present."[31] From Greek ἄλλος (*allos*: other) and αγορεύιν (*agorein*: to speak), allegory means literally to speak other than one seems to speak; and the root *allos* imbricates allegory in a series of associations conspicuously related to foreignness, to words, for example, like ἄλλου (*allou*: elsewhere, in another place); αλλοτριάζειν (*allotriazein*: to be estranged, alienated); αλλότριος (*allotrios*: belonging to another); αλλοφύλος (*allofilos*: of another people, strange, foreign).[32] Allegory is, we might say, an exiled language: it does not belong to the meaning closest to it, does not speak the local tongue, does not have the same customs as everyday language.

And if allegory is structured by a fundamental foreignness between its literal and proper meanings, it is also characterized by that zone of error through which we have described foreignness. For the dislocation of meaning from sign characteristic of allegory structurally inscribes a space in which hermeneutic error is inevitable. Indeed, the first known use of the word allegory was as a replacement for the archaic term ὑπόνοια (*uponoia*: suspicion, surmise, literally "beneath sense"); and Heraclitus and Philo both use the terms interchangeably. *Allegory* was employed, that is, to designate thought tinctured by uncertainty. Both Aquinas's anagogical level of allegory, which points toward "future glory," and the sixteenth-century identification of *enigma* with allegory, mark that aspect of its structure that resists containment within the known, the unlatched window of signification that perpetually precludes closure of the hermeneutic act. This zone of hermeneutic error that inheres in allegory has historically, however, been governed by a code that disciplines its wanderings and regulates its error. The allegorical sign refers not only to a proper meaning, but to a code that stabilizes that foreignness, interprets the sign, and domesticates meaning within a coherent ideology.[33] Indeed, the allegorical sign is disciplined, above all, by *context*. Being at home in a particular context, understanding its conventions and customary meanings, both guarantees one's ability to read the allegorical sign and demonstrates one's inclusion in the code-knowing culture. The word allegory itself bears this nuance of exclusivity: allo-agorein is to speak in secret, outside the public *agora*, to be included in the group that understands, that has access to proper meaning.

Not only does Coetzee's text dramatize the zone of error that characterizes both "literal" and literary foreignness, but it insists that a consequential relationship exists between them. For the novel demonstrates, I would argue, that a primary technique for disciplining "literal" foreignness is the suppression of linguistic foreignness. Fearing a barbarian uprising, the "emergency powers" have stationed a certain Colonel Joll at the frontier; he has embarked on a program of capturing, imprisoning, and torturing the native peoples. The following report, informing the magistrate of the death of a barbarian prisoner, illustrates the language of empire:

> During the course of the interrogation contradictions became apparent in the prisoner's testimony. Confronted with these contradictions the prisoner became enraged and attacked the investigating officer. A scuffle ensued during which the prisoner fell heavily against the wall. Efforts to revive him were unsuccessful. (2)

This reportorial language, in which words do not signify something other than what they literally say, is devoid both of the hermeneutic foreignness that calls for interpretation and of the defamiliarization that disrupts perception. It is a language in which every trace of foreignness has been deported: direct, literal, certain. And that certainty is fortified by a careful management of context. The report tacitly disavows any significant relation to a larger text—its literality renders it discrete, autonomous. Through the passive voice, moreover, it transports events from the untidy context of active, responsible agents to the far more stable context of objective description and inevitability in which, for example, "contradictions becom[ing] apparent" is stabilized as (universally true) fact, rather than, say, an interpretation of one of the investigators. In other words, the empire controls both (literary) foreignness and ("literal") foreigners by regulating context, in this case by virtually erasing it, by making *étranger au sujet* who witnesses this contradiction, what circumstances led to it, what criteria determined it a contradiction, how a scuffle ensued, what constitutes a scuffle, what caused the prisoner to fall, what efforts were used to revive him.

The magistrate, by contrast, departing from the tranquil familiarity of his interpretive community, insists on the uncertainty of such signs and on error in the empire's language. Thus, rather than "skimming over [the report] with an incurious eye," he questions "what the word *investigations* meant, what lay beneath it like a banshee beneath a stone" (9).[34] Disclosing the multiple significations that the word conceals—intimidation, mutilation, torture, murder—necessitates recontextualizing language in diverse discursive and material conditions, looking for meaning in foreign places, reading allegorically. Hence, before going to bed, the magistrate crosses the square, wakes the sleeping guard and slits open the shroud where the prisoner's body is sewn. The dead man's beard is caked with blood, his lips crushed, teeth broken. Turning to the guard, the magistrate says, "They say that he hit his head on the wall. What do you think?" (7) Rendering the event a product of interpretive activity, the magistrate's interrogative language recuperates the foreignness in signification that the empire has attempted to banish, introduces uncertainty into the knowledge it produces about itself, and simultaneously renders interpretation possible and determination impossible.[35]

The magistrate's reluctant venture into the zone of error becomes an apparently permanent exile, a migration from the reassuring certainties of empire to the shaky ground of uncertain signs. That exile is characterized by the labor of a close reading that grants asylum both to allegorical meanings and to the contexts (linguistic, social, political, and material) disfigured or banished by the empire. The magistrate, for example, rereads the language of uniforms, converting the empire's system of signs—its ostensibly unambiguous signifiers of rank—into a contextualized and uncertain allegory: "His insignia say that he is a warrant officer. Warrant Officer in the Third Bureau: what does that mean? At a guess, five years of kicking and beating people; contempt for the regular police and for due process of law; a detestation of smooth patrician talk like mine" (77). In similar fashion, the magistrate reads the marked body of the barbarian girl to whom he has given shelter and the suspiciously unmarked walls of the room where Joll's "investigations" have been carried out. He labors over deciphering the cryptic script of a lost civilization and habitually peruses the uncertain signs of landscape: the migrating waterfowl, "the ghost of a new warmth on the wind, the glassy translucence of the lake-ice" (57). And with equal attentiveness, he reads

himself, his works and words, the obscure signs of his desire: "I search for se-
crets and answers, no matter how bizarre, like an old woman reading tea-leaves"
(44).[36]

This close reading is characterized both by error—"the snow was not a good
sign after all!" (66-67)—and by erring: in his effort to record his "readings," for
example, the magistrate roams through the regions of testament, memoir, confes-
sion, history. Indeed the uncertainty of textual and contextual signs and the inac-
cessibility of the past whose traces they bear move the magistrate to *imagine*; to
adopt a practice, that is, ostensibly even more uncertain than reading and as contrary to truth as error itself. The magistrate struggles, for example, to formulate
an image of the barbarian girl before she was disfigured and, examining the
blanched site where she and others were tortured, "close[s his] eyes and make[s]
an effort to imagine the room as it must have been two months ago during the
colonel's visit" (35). Likewise, he shapes an imaginative, metonymic past out of
the ruins unearthed on his avocational digs:

> Perhaps in bygone days criminals, slaves, soldiers trekked the twelve miles to the
> river, and cut down poplar trees . . . and transported the timbers back to this
> barren place in carts . . . Perhaps ten feet below the floor lie the ruins of another
> fort . . . Perhaps when I stand on the floor of the courthouse, if that is what it is, I
> stand over the head of a magistrate like myself. (15)

The magistrate's errant reading practices are, moreover, contrasted with "wisdom,"
which is not only to say that they are personally disadvantageous, but that they
recuperate what the empire has relegated to meaninglessness; they defamiliarize
and contest the discursive "wisdom" through which the empire maintains power: "if
without reading it, or after skimming over it with an incurious eye, [I had] put my
seal on his report, with no question about what the word *investigations* meant, what
lay beneath it like a banshee beneath a stone—if I had done the wise thing. . . ."
(9).[37]

In no doubt the most patently allegorical moment of the novel, the empire
and the magistrate face off over a box of signs. Demanding that the magistrate
decipher a series of wooden slips that he has uncovered in his archeological digs,
the officers of empire attempt to banish the threatening foreignness from those
signs by simultaneously staging an inquiry and strictly delimiting the possibilities
of response: "A reasonable inference is that the wooden slips contain messages
passed between yourself and other parties, we do not know when. It remains for
you to explain what the messages say and who the other parties were" (110). The
empire thus regulates meaning by demarcating the context in which it can take
place, rendering the magistrate's interpretation a mere remainder of an already
established context. Further, it guarantees its contextual knowledge ("the slips
contain messages passed between you and other parties") by contrasting it with
uncertainty ("we do not know when"), surreptitiously solidifying an inference
into fact. The magistrate, nonetheless, formulates an interpretation of the wooden

slips that injects uncertainty into that "structure of assumptions," to return to Fish's terms;[38] though the magistrate does not know what the signs stand for, he "translates" them—erratically, erroneously, imaginatively—into signifiers of linguistic foreignness.

> "Now let us see what the next one says. See, there is only a single character. It is the barbarian character *war*, but it has other senses too. It can stand for *vengeance*, and, if you turn it upside down like this, it can be made to read *justice*. There is no knowing which sense is intended. That is part of barbarian cunning.
> "It is the same with the rest of these slips." I plunge my good hand into the chest and stir. "They form an allegory. They can be read in many orders. Further, each single slip can be read in many ways. Together they can be read as a domestic journal or they can be read as a plan of war, or they can be turned on their sides and read as a history of the last years of the Empire—the old Empire, I mean." (112)

In this response, the magistrate repatriates the foreignness in signification that the empire has attempted to eradicate and indeed insists that meaning cannot be confined to a proper location; he makes mordant parody of the empire's association of barbarians with linguistic foreignness; he demonstrates the perspicacity of epistemological barbarism and its capacities for destabilizing imperial knowledge; and he employs a trope—a literal turn of the sign and a figural invocation of what de Man calls "the rhetorical basis of language"[39]—to recontextualize: to expose the meaning of the empire's practices and language in alternative contexts and thereby indict its fixed reading of the barbarian presence as unprovoked aggression.

But if the magistrate persistently props open a door in signification through which foreignness may enter, the sun never sets on the empire's efforts to keep it shut. In a phrase emblematic of the empire's drive to stabilize meaning, Colonel Joll entirely collapses signifier and signified: "Prisoners are prisoners," he declares, in a hermetic tautology that is simultaneously apotropaic and powerfully performative. For Joll's word produces the identity it names: when he calls you a prisoner, you are a prisoner. And the performative power of the empire's language is fortified through a reiteration that passes for a stable context, naturalizes and literalizes the meanings read within that context, and—with formidable social effects—secures the "one meaning" of which Fish speaks that "will seem so obvious that one cannot see how it could be otherwise."[40] The empire's context—its hermeneutic law—is secured by just such reiteration: "I interview those men who were on duty while the prisoners were being questioned," records the magistrate. "From each I get the same account" (35). Similarly, on his arrest, he notes the citational nature of the empire's accusation: "'Treasonously consorting:' a phrase out of a book" (77). That reiteration is also effected by passive consent: by the doctor who, avoiding impropriety, "does not ask how the [prisoner] sustained his injuries" (11), by the young *lieutenant*—the "place-holder"—who, unwilling to be caught out of context, decides "it was not [his] place to argue with [Joll]" (22), by the uninterfering guard who, refusing to enter the zone of error, declares, "I did not want to become involved in a matter I did not understand!" (37).

It is just such performative reiteration—the word barbarian running like fire from neighbor to neighbor—that frames and conditions Joll's public display of his prisoners, a grotesque spectacle of imperial power that, transforming the barbarian body into a sign, sets up a telling homology between eradicating enemies and stabilizing signs:

> The colonel steps forward. Stooping over each prisoner in turn he rubs a handful of dust into his naked back and writes a word with a stick of charcoal. I read the words upside down: ENEMY . . . ENEMY . . . ENEMY . . . ENEMY. He steps back and folds his hands.
> Then the beating begins. The soldiers use the stout green cane staves. . . . The black charcoal and ochre dust begin to run with sweat and blood. The game, I see, is to beat them till their backs are washed clean. (105)

Thus does the empire attempt to eradicate foreignness through a radical coincidence of sign and referent and perform precisely that dematerialization that characterizes foreignness—that transformation of a literal body into a figurative enemy.

If the empire's simultaneous chastening of linguistic foreignness and "literal" foreigners is significant, so too is the magistrate's terse response. When in this scene Colonel Joll proceeds to exhibiting his subsequent instrument of torture—a hammer—the magistrate responds with a single word: "No!" The word of the magistrate does not, strictly speaking, refer to the world, but, like the language of allegory as de Man describes it, back to language. Yet far from recoiling into linguistic hermeticism, that negation performs multiple and significant tasks within the world; and it does so by making language foreign to itself, by legitimizing and employing the foreignness laying low in language. Most significantly, the magistrate's word creates a hiatus, a disruptive and defamiliarizing lacuna, in the empire's performative reiteration. It transforms the empire's statement about itself into an uncertainty, into a question that can be answered affirmatively or negatively, into a proposition inhabited by truth or by error. The magistrate's "No!" is, moreover, a rejection with indefinite boundaries—does it negate the hammer? Joll? inhumanity? empire?—and not without its affinities to nihilism. For this "No!" marks an unstable and transitional moment characterized by an incipient denaturalization of the highest values, by a radical reassessment of such metaphysical categories as knowledge, goodness, and humanity, and by an indictment of that "infinitely superior whole" that works through subjects, imbeds them in a meaningful context and guarantees their value.[41]

The magistrate's "No!" is, in short, a distilled version of the zone of error: of its negativity, its conceptual instability, its disruption of context and threat to hermeneutic law, its socially ostracizing effects. And we might add: its risk. For not only does the zone of error bear personal consequences for the magistrate—he is imprisoned, beaten, tortured, treated like a foreigner—but it bears epistemological consequences for his "interpretive community." Once foreignness has settled down in signification and uncertainty set up camp in knowledge, once "figures . . . [have] infiltrat[ed] the defenses of rightful meaning," as Thomas McLaughlin puts it, the literal, proper, determined, and natural meanings of that community are put at risk; they are defamiliarized; they bear within them their own *verfremdungseffekt*.[42] And if this defamiliarization jeopardizes the divine right of meanings by demanding that they negotiate with other meanings, it also puts at risk the invisible law—the context—that legitimates their status. To inhabit the zone of error is to act in contempt of, and indeed to dismantle, the court that governs proper meaning, to insist on the legitimacy of a context that, however inevitably juridical, is heterogeneous, multiple and mutable. If the zone of error risks instances of lawlessness, instability, indeterminacy, and meaninglessness, it also invalidates those guarantees of meaning that, like other forms of "risk management," have been obtainable solely by those with the requisite cultural capital; it resists the reiterative practices that produce contextual hegemony; and it renders interpretation, in a more meaningful sense, possible. Indeed it is with this sense of risk that Coetzee's novel closes. Watching a group of children create a snowman, the magistrate muses: "Like much else nowadays I leave it feeling stupid, like a man who lost his way long ago but presses on along a road that may lead nowhere" (156). Though this line has been marshaled as incriminating evidence that the novel offers no hope of transcendence but merely a reprehensible and "suffocating despair,"[43] I would argue that it describes the zone of error: wandering in territory labeled "stupid" by a dominant morality, wagering the possibility of nothingness rather than reiterating the same, embarking on the kind of "strategic and adventurous" journey that, as we have noted, Derrida associates with *différance*. For if entry into the zone of error comes with no more guarantee than a border crossing at midnight, it also comes with its abundant possibility.[44]

From this stop at Coetzee's novel, I take a veritable trunk of souvenirs: first, the perception that "literal" foreignness may be disciplined through the suppression of linguistic foreignness; second, the recognition that that suppression of linguistic foreignness is effected by a regulation, and reiterative production, of context; third, the conviction that recuperating the foreignness in signification may not be contrary, but indeed imperative, to contesting the construction and treatment of "literal" foreignness; fourth, the hunch that such recuperation may well entail close reading, allegorical work, and contextual excavation; and finally, the premonition that such labor will be fraught with uncertainty and risk, will be, in short, an expedition into the zone of error.

When we arrive in apartheid South Africa, though we have apparently traveled from the literary to the literal, it is clear that we have seen this ground before. The novel's portrayal of "literal" foreigners regulated through the suppression of linguistic foreignness, of natives rendered foreign to their own land, of "civilization's" paranoid repression of dark "barbarians," of "emergency powers," detention, and torture: all unmistakably allegorize events in apartheid South Africa. And if the novel thematically allegorizes apartheid, the allegorical structure itself, I would argue, parodies the *language* of apartheid.[45] For the language of apartheid is characterized precisely by that "fundamental dislocation of words from their objects" that identifies allegory; or, as the *Commonwealth Report* puts it, the South African government, "has perfected a specialized political vocabulary which, while saying one thing means quite another."[46] But this is only half the picture. For while apartheid deploys a language that is highly allegorical, it also, like Coetzee's empire, disciplines and suppresses linguistic foreignness. Indeed it is this apparent contradiction—between the deployment of highly allegorical language and the suppression of linguistic foreignness—that is the hidden mechanism of the language of apartheid and, I would argue, key to the functioning of the entire regime. In short, apartheid both exploits and represses linguistic foreignness; it constructs and relies on highly allegorical texts but insists—and, through careful context management, ensures—that they be read literally. Just as statutory foreigners—black Africans—perform South Africa's labor while remaining statistically and physically hidden, so too does the foreignness in language perform the discursive work of apartheid beneath a veneer of highly polished literality.[47]

The term *homeland* might well illustrate this phenomenon. If in customary usage, *homeland* signifies the land of one's birth, a familial hub, the locus of either familiar belonging or nostalgic longing, the word in South Africa (transported from the controlled context of apartheid discourse to the material context of the homelands themselves) names barren and essentially uninhabitable wastelands set out as "reserves" for Africans, often far distant from the literal homelands of, and entirely unknown to, the people "repatriated" there. Read in this context, a homeland is a place conceived of, delineated, and imposed by apartheid policy, a place that physically separates people by "race" and black peoples by ethnicity, a justificatory ploy for rendering Africans statutory foreigners in their native land, stripping them of political rights, prohibiting them from owning land, and maintaining them in the role of "migrant workers" in urban areas. It is a dumping ground for the 3.5 million Africans forcibly removed from their homes to purify "white areas"; it is a contrived geography that radically disrupts family life by separating working men from their wives and children; a remote land that forces thousands to travel as far as two hundred miles a day to and from work and to expend a quarter of their earnings on bus fares; a fragmented territory comprised of multiple small pieces of land (often separated by white farms); an inhospitable space of poverty, disease, starvation, and among the highest infant mortality rates in the world.[48] The fact that apartheid succeeds in naming such a space a homeland evinces the degree to which it relies on the allegorical capacities of language, on the ability of allegory to become "purely figural," as de Man puts it, to "submit the outside world entirely to its own purposes."[49] Yet to call this denomination allegorical is also to recognize that homeland does not *literally* mean a foreign and uninhabitable place. On the contrary, for the word homeland to signify such a place one must engage in perversely figural, distorted, allegorical reading; one must wander perilously far from the borders of proper meaning. The foreignness between what *homeland* "says" and what it "means," however, is less an estrangement between signifier and signified than between signified and referent, between the semantic and mimetic functions of language.[50] Indeed the relationship between signifier and signified in this instance remains insistently literal: the government counts on the word *homeland* to generate so literal a signified in the minds of white South Africans (and of the rest of the world) that the referent is simply rendered irrelevant. The domestic and ostensibly natural relationship between signifier and signified simultaneously secures the appearance of literality, transforms allegorical reading into superfluous virtuosity, and legitimates the expulsion of the referent as a threatening foreign presence: improper, irrelevant, erroneous. Thus capable of determining perception itself, this referent-obliterating literality banishes the defamiliarization that disrupts perception and that warrants interpretation. The language of apartheid, like that of Coetzee's empire, ostensibly signifies nothing other than what it literally says: homelands are homelands.

But how guarantee that that language be read literally? How ward off the return of repressed referents? How prevent irksomely allegorical readers from letting loose the foreignness in signs? Apartheid's response to those questions is: through context. Indeed, within the context constructed and regulated by the South African government, signifiers coincide quite literally with their customary signifieds. *Homeland* does signify one's native land, for example, if, as a Standard-7 history book teaches, "the Bantu reserves [homelands] correspond roughly to the areas occupied by the Bantu when the Whites and Blacks first encountered each other in Southern Africa";[51] it does signify a place of familiarity and belonging if, as the *1978 South African Yearbook* states, "The Group Areas Act of 1949 gave legal status to the traditional residential segregation [of South Africa]";[52] if "History has over more than three centuries delineated South Africa into distinct ethnic territories"; and if this history determines "the physical basis for the present-day geopolitical relations between the territory of the White nation (the RSA [Republic of South Africa]) and those of the nine principal Black peoples within the boundaries of South Africa."[53] Homeland does signify a locus of nostalgic longing if removals to it, as the government has consistently maintained, are "voluntary." It does signify a nurturing familial environment if, as the *Yearbook* suggests, "Many [black] workers prefer a migrant type of job because they want to retain close links with their own territories [and because] they wish to shelter their families from some of the less desirable aspects of urban-industrial life."[54]

The self-reinforcing efficiency of this literality should not be under-estimated: context both determines and is determined by the word *homeland*. On the one hand, the context of apartheid—the interpretive community, in Fish's terms—ensures that the benign, positive meaning of the word will be taken as "the ordinary, the normal, the usual, the everyday, the straightforward, the literal."[55] On the other hand, the very denotation of the word homeland contributes to the performative construction of that context. Lest one have any doubts what the word means, one can consult a dictionary which will, with formidable authority, determine the meaning of the word and thereby validate and reinforce the context consistent with (and productive of) it.

Entrusted with the discursive transformation of wastelands into homelands, the allegorical language of apartheid is also charged with rounding up threateningly heterogeneous phenomena and detaining them within the confines of a stabilized name. As the *Commonwealth Report* notes, words such as *terrorism*, *treason*, and *communism* are "in the South African lexicon" not only "so far removed from [their] ordinary meaning as to be unrecognizable," but deployed to cover an "extraordinarily wide" field of meaning.[56] Under the Terrorism Act of 1967, for example, terrorism encompasses any activity which might "endanger the maintenance of law and order," create "hostility between the white and other inhabitants of the Republic," further or encourage "the achievement of any political aim, including the bringing about of any social or economic change," cause "prejudice" to "any industry or undertaking," or result in "embarrassment" to the "administration of the affairs of the State."[57] The term *communism* seems likewise to stick to all unfamiliar surfaces. For example, the section of the 1978 *Yearbook* entitled, significantly, "Communism, Subversion, and Terrorism," includes discussions of the African National Congress (ANC) and Pan-African Congress (PAC), the Rivonia trial (*the State v. Mandela and others*), the concept of "Black Power," the South African Students' Organization (SASO), and the "new radical movement" associated with Black Consciousness which, it avers, "culminated in the 'Soweto rebellion' of 16 June 1976."[58] Indeed the Suppression of Communism Act, as John Laurence observes, "made 'furthering an aim of communism' a criminal offense—then classed multi-racialism and even spontaneous public protests against apartheid as 'aims of communism.'"[59] Accordingly, in 1953, ANC leaders were convicted of furthering the aims of communism on the grounds that the defiance campaign "had advocated a scheme aimed at bringing about political, industrial, social, or economic change—by 'the abolition of laws differentiating between Europeans and Non-Europeans.'"[60]

It should not be overlooked, however, that the functional differences between our two examples—homelands and terrorism—signal two opposing trajectories inherent to the structure of allegory. On the one hand, allegory insists on the *divergence* between apparent and actual meanings and thereby conditions apartheid's most outrageous obfuscations (e.g., "homelands"). It is this trajectory of divergence present in Coetzee's novel that, interpreted as distance from historical and material circumstances, has been the largest source of critical reproach. On the other hand, allegory can obscure difference by insisting on *correspondence*, by containing heterogenous elements within a single, essentializing name. This is the role that personified virtues—Love, Honor, Courage—have often played in the allegorical tradition, the role that *communism* and *terrorism* play in apartheid discourse, and indeed the role that "the empire" and the "barbarians" play in Coetzee's novel. But this is still not the whole picture, for it is equally crucial to recognize the distinguishable traditions of allegorical *composition* (the practices that we have primarily been attending to in apartheid discourse) and allegorical *interpretation* (the practices that characterize Coetzee's magistrate). As we have witnessed in South Africa, even the most allegorical language can be read literally, and, as we have learned from the magistrate, even the most literal language can be read allegorically. Moreover, if reading practices negotiate the boundaries of proper and figural meaning, the two trajectories we have identified within allegory condition significantly dissimilar reading practices. The trajectory of correspondence allows for a reading practice that submits compositional details to a code, that offers stability, truth, a tidy idealism, in short, all the hermeneutic comforts of the literal.[61] This is the trajectory I see endorsed by both the hermeneutic tradition and apartheid. The trajectory of divergence, by contrast, leads to a reading practice that is less a matter of reading an allegory than of attending to the divergence in all language, a practice that discloses the uncertainty of signs, exposes the profligacy of their meaning, risks crossing contextual borders, and follows meandering and unmarked trails through the semantic. This is the trajectory I see pursued by Shklovsky, Brecht, and Coetzee's magistrate.

If, skulking down the path of allegorical divergence, apartheid exploits linguistic foreignness by constructing a text that "say[s] one thing [and] means quite another," it also suppresses that foreignness through a referent-obliterating literality and essentializing names. But however craftily constructed, the meaning of apartheid's language will ultimately be determined by readers, and it is therefore crucial for apartheid to maintain a context in which its language will be read literally, in which the instability and error in language will be disciplined, and in which allegorical readings (and readers) appear (only as the) improper. This context production is a veritable South African industry, a web of performative reiteration spun, for example, by a government-controlled television and radio system (the South African Broadcasting Corporation [SABC]); by newspapers and other information sources clandestinely funded by the National Party; by ostensibly impartial political analysts (such as the Foreign Affairs Association of South Africa) funded by, and a vehicle for, governmental interests; by inculcation of military doctrine and enforced military service; and by school textbooks that portray white supremacy as inevitable and natural.[62] The work of weaving this context is, moreover, carried out by numerous individuals, for example, by the security police who extract testimony by torture,[63] by the judges who have, as Amnesty International puts it, "taken the position that the laws, good or bad, are determined by government, and that the judiciary exists merely to see that they are upheld"[64] and not least by voting citizens who have, in overwhelming numbers, kept the National Party in power.[65]

I have a sense of *déjà-vu*. And on closer inspection this context not only recalls the performative reiteration that characterizes Coetzee's empire, but uncannily echoes both the relative nature of foreignness and its conceptual negativity. The former is evinced in the customary opposition Prime Minster D. F. Malan, for example, invokes "between two irreconcilable ways of life, between barbarism and civilization, between heathenism and Christianity,"[66] the latter, for example, in terms like "non-white" and "non-homeland Blacks." Indeed, when I look back at my souvenirs, I am startled by the resemblance that this context bears to the nuances of the *improper* we encountered at the concept of the foreign: in South Africa those nuances seem to materialize before my eyes, the word becomes flesh. Like the privative (*im-*) which nullifies the root (*proper*), apartheid renders the native foreign to his own land and incarnates the foreigner's lack of *identity* by expurgating black history and culture from official memory, by banning black leaders and political organizations and by literally destroying black people; it regulates *propriety* by criminalizing black's political activities, indicting their presence in urban areas, teaching them, through the Bantu Education System, that their aspirations are improper. The conceptual lack of *purity* that characterizes the foreigner is, further, enacted in South Africa in stereotypes of physical and metaphysical defilement according to which the white "race" is threatened with defilement as long as ideological, economic, social, or sexual contact with "non-whites" is possible. Blacks' words and actions lack *literality*; they fall outside of proper meaning. Their access to *property* is severely obstructed and the property they do possess is routinely—as in Sophiatown, Magopa, Crossroads, or District Six—destroyed by bulldozers.

Tirelessly separating the proper from the zone of error, this context determines the "apparently uninterpreted meaning" of words, acts, and persons. In so doing, it camouflages its highly allegorical language with a mundane literality that facilitates, rather than disrupts, what Shklovksy called "the automatism of perception"; it renders allegorical reading impertinent and referents beside the point. And it makes those who produce meaning alien to it into barbarians babbling an incomprehensible language.

Before we leave South Africa, I wish to make one more stop: at an old synagogue in the center of Pretoria that has been transformed into a courtroom, where a magistrate and two assessors sit in the erstwhile holy place and where a stained-glass window in the ceiling drops shards of colored light onto the faces of an audience in pews. I am led here, however errantly, by Coetzee's novel, where an inquest is taking place into the death of Stephen Biko.[67] Written the year following the Biko inquest, *Waiting for the Barbarians* is studded with details that evoke both testimony at, and information revealed by, the inquest.[68] For example, the empire's report that "the prisoner became enraged and attacked the investigating officer" and that "a scuffle ensued during which the prisoner fell heavily against the wall" (6) clearly recalls Major Snyman's testimony that Biko "went berserk" and hit his head against a wall during a scuffle with security interrogators (Woods, 243). Detainees in the novel are, like Biko, held incommunicado, naked and bound, their hands swollen from being shackled. Like Biko, whose injuries caused him to hyperventilate, to be unable to eat or move to the toilet, prisoners in the novel "breathe strangely, very deep and fast" (36), do not eat anything, and smell of old urine. Just as officers of Coetzee's "Third Bureau" neither keep records nor operate under statute, so too at the inquest security police admit to the absence of records and Colonel Goosen flatly declares, "we [the security police] don't work under statutory authority" (Woods, 259). Like the doctor in the novel who "does not ask how the boy sustained his injuries" (11), doctors at the inquest reveal that they did not investigate the causes of Biko's symptoms. Like the novel's guards who are instructed by officers what to tell the magistrate about tortured prisoners, security police admit to reiterating phrases fed to them by investigating officers. But even more significant than these thematic allusions, I would argue, is the novel's dramatization and indictment of the *language* of the inquest. For the inquest clearly evinces the way in which the foreigner is banished from proper meaning, encountered as a figure that must be stabilized by a hermeneutic code; the way in which reiteration, both active and passive, produces context; the way in which that context polices the borders of the proper and determines meaning; and the way in which apartheid regulates "literal" foreigners by disciplining linguistic foreignness—by at once exploiting and repressing the zone of error.

Colonel Goosen's testimony that "The security police . . . regarded Biko as nothing else than a terrorist leader in South Africa" (Woods, 256) was inadvertent witness to the fact that Biko's words and actions were consistently interpreted through the detour of figurality; they were not taken at face value, but assumed to be allegorical, to say something other than what they seemed to say.[69] Indeed, in response to questions about why the family had not been notified of Biko's condition, Goosen stated: "The circumstances were special. We were trying to prove that Biko was somebody quite different from what he had seemed to be" (Woods, 267). And just as security police read Biko's identity figurally, so too they heard his responses to interrogation not as direct, literal answers, but as figural errata that called for corrective interpretation: "he evaded questions concerning his visit to Cape Town," testified Major Snyman. "He would not answer questions directly" (Woods, 238). Consigned to the zone of error, Biko and his words were thus stabilized by an allegorical code, by the context of apartheid in which black activists are improper and their activities signify *terrorism*: "Biko was a violent revolutionary," stated witness Snyman; "his plans included the formation of a united revolutionary front with the ANC and the PAC which are terrorist organizations" (Woods, 246). Colonel Goosen concurred, testifying that the BPC had been concerned with training terrorists and that Biko had been creating "a climate for bloodbath and revolution in South Africa" (Woods, 284).

Biko's lack of literality in the context of apartheid conspicuously coincided with a lack of propriety, purity, and identity.[70] Lieutenant Oosthuizen stated that, when arrested, Biko was "cheeky" (Woods, 234) and Officer Hansen testified that when detained in 1976, Biko had "adopt[ed] a cheeky attitude and refused to provide the information required" (Woods, 255). In a December 5, 1977 broadcast, the SABC depicted Biko's death as an inevitable result of ideological impropriety and, further, portrayed that impropriety as a threateningly contagious social defilement that warranted banishing Biko from the pure and proper:

> To say that Biko's death resulted from a system which permits gross mistreatment and violation of the most basic human rights is absurd. . . . It would be nearer the truth (to say that he) was a victim of a confrontation in South Africa which has been recklessly supported from abroad, the victim, more particularly, of instilling among black activists the notion that it is their right to rule all of South Africa—and to hell with the established order. (Bernstein, 116)

In this broadcast, the apartheid spin doctors not only set up a tacit and telling homology between supporting Biko, moral impurity ("recklessness"), and being foreign ("from abroad"), but also contribute to the ongoing apartheid project of effacing black identity: assuming both that political ideas cannot be proper to blacks themselves (they are unwitting "victims" of others' thought) and that black rule would be tantamount to no rule—to chaos, anarchy, barbarism.

Indeed this conceptual lack of identity facilitates apartheid's simultaneous exploitation and repression of linguistic foreignness and, thereby, its regulation of foreigners; in other words, it allows the most exotically allegorical language to appear literal and guarantees that referents disruptive to that literality will be dismissed as intrusive and irrelevant. Accordingly, the SABC radio broadcast that announced Biko's death deployed a language ostensibly purged of foreignness, in which signifier and signified coincide in a literality that is comfortably secluded from both material referents and impudent feats like allegorical reading:

> Biko, who can be regarded as a leader among certain radical black elements in the country, was arrested in mid-August. . . . From 5 September he refused meals and threatened a hunger strike. . . . Should Biko's death be the result of suicide it would fit into a pattern which has become common among detainees in South Africa. . . . [N]umerous detainees, who have been detained following

communist training and indoctrination have testified that they receive specific instructions to commit suicide rather than divulge information to the police. (Bernstein, 22-23)

Such an explanation is rendered plausible by a context that simultaneously drains the statutory foreigner of identity, obliterates improper referents from signification and, like the famed defensive laager of the Trekboers, wards off black Africans from territory claimed by whites.

Indeed, long before his detention, Biko was banned; it was illegal for him to publish anything, to speak publicly, or to be quoted in any form, and thus whites knew little or nothing about him or his views. As Pollak puts it, he was "consigned to the legal status of isolation from the community, and indeed of virtual non-identity."[71] And once he was detained, he disappeared not only from public but from private view. He was, like other Section 6 detainees, held indefinitely without trial, incommunicado, with no access to lawyers, family, or acquaintances; he was guarded only by white members of the police force; he was transferred only after dark; he was not allowed any exercise lest it afford him the opportunity for communication; no one other than state officials could have access to him.[72] His identity was even concealed from Dr. Keely, the consulting neurosurgeon on his case, and from lab personnel who tested Biko's spinal fluid for signs of brain damage (the fluid was labeled with the name "Stephen Njelo").[73]

If the inquest laid bare the manner in which Biko was simultaneously read as a figure and obliterated as material referent, it also revealed the microphysics of context control through which apartheid was reiterated in the space of the prison. The reading of Biko as allegorical sign extended, for example, to his physical symptoms, which were not read as literal signs of injury resulting from torture, but as allegorical signs of "shamming." Goosen's description of Biko's slurred speech and lack of appetite (both of which ostensibly resulted from head injuries inflicted during interrogation) evinces the way uncertain signs were stabilized by a context in which political detainees' behavior inexorably signifies deviousness, sabotage, recalcitrance:

> I spoke to Biko as before and he mumbled incoherently. At this stage I was honestly of the opinion that Biko was playing the fool with us as neither the district surgeon nor I could detect any scars or signs of illness. While I was in the office, I again asked whether Biko had partaken of any food or drink. It was reported to me that he flatly refused to eat or drink. (Woods, 257)

Indeed every one of Biko's alarming physical symptoms were ultimately interpreted by a hermeneutic code in which they signified either malingering or lack of cooperation: his paresis as "pretend[ing] that one arm was slightly weak" ([Goosen] Woods, 268); his inability to speak as a "stubborn refusal to answer" ([Snyman] Woods, 243); his hyperventilation as "deliberately breathing in an unnatural way" ([Goosen], Woods, 257); his unconsciousness as "a technique of putting up a veil between himself and interrogators" (Goosen).[74] This context determined how even Biko's doctors read his symptoms. Dr. Tucker, for example, testified that Biko "was unwilling to walk" (*Record*, 786) and that "the reflexes of his lower limbs could not be elicited properly owing to a lack of cooperation" (*Record*, 850). And Dr. Lang explicitly affirmed that physical signs mean something different in the context of "prison medicine":

> I would like to point out to the Court that I find prison medicine a little different from general medicine, that there are . . . cardinal things that one has to keep at the back of one's mind, and the one is the question of the shamming because this is the—it is not a natural thing to do, but it is a frequent thing that those prisoners do get up to, that is to sham something. (*Record*, 753-754)[75]

Cloaking this allegorical reading with the mantle of proper meaning was enabled by a double reiteration: not only was this reading—that Biko's symptoms signify shamming—incessantly repeated, but it was posited as a recurrence of Biko's (and other prisoners') previous behavior. Goosen, who asserted that he "had had experience before with this tendency" (Woods, 263), told Drs. Lang and Tucker that "Biko's behavior in previous detention had been similar to his present behavior" (Woods, 310) and that he had manifested similar symptoms. When Dr. Lang gave neurology specialist Dr. Hersch a verbal history of Biko's condition, he told him "that while in detention previously Biko had shown difficulty in talking and had dragged his left leg" (Woods, 322). And Dr. Hersch stated in his affidavit that "the circumstances of the onset of his slurred speech and paralysis seemed to point to a functional [non-organic] condition [shamming], and I believe when he was last detained he evidenced similar physical signs" (*Record*, 1003).

This context was fortified by a reiteration not only of speech, but of silence. While security police admitted at the inquest that Biko might have received an injury to the head during a "scuffle" with interrogators, at no point did any of them mention this possibility to the doctors caring for Biko. Van Zyl, the doctor who examined Biko in Pretoria on the day he died, testified that he had been informed by phone that Biko had refused to eat anything for a week and that he had been examined by a doctor who could find nothing wrong with him. Van Zyl received no medical record; he was not told about Biko's signs of neurological damage; no one told him the case was urgent. And if this context was woven through with significant silences, it was also considerably strengthened by a passive reiteration synonymous with refusing to enter the zone of error. When questioned as to why he did nothing to correct Minister Kruger's false statements on national television (implying that Biko had died of a hunger strike), Goosen replied that "it was certainly not his duty and lay outside his function to do so" (Woods, 281). When asked why Biko had been kept naked and in leg irons, Snyman responded that "he had acted on instructions" (Woods, 242). Though in his autopsy the state pathologist immediately noted an obvious wound on Biko's forehead, Lt. Kuhn, Sgt. Van Vuuren, Captain Siebert, and Major Snyman all stated that they had not noticed it. Although all three pathologists at the inquest testified that Biko's injury must have resulted in a period of unconsciousness of at least ten minutes and possibly up to an hour, none of the police officers, according to their testimony, had discerned that Biko was unconscious.[76] Similarly unwilling to risk impropriety or be caught out of context were Biko's doctors. Although by the morning of September 8, Biko exhibited recognizable signs of brain injury—including an extensor plantar reflex, echolalia, left-sided paresis, slurred speech, and an ataxic gait—neither of the doctors attending him asked whether he had been injured; neither insisted that he be hospitalized; neither challenged the police decision to send Biko seven hundred miles in the back of a Land Rover to a hospital in Pretoria; neither bothered to inspect the vehicle, arrange for medical personnel to accompany Biko, or send medical records with him. Indeed much of the doctors' testimony at the inquest was a model of passive reiteration:

> KENTRIDGE: Why did you not ask, as the obvious question, whether the man received a bump on the head?
> TUCKER: I did not ask it, and that is all I can say.
> KENTRIDGE: . . . You did not ask?
> TUCKER: No, I did not. Where persons are brought to me for examination, my report is completed on a special form. This is all I am required to do. (Woods, 314)

Asked why he had not questioned Biko about abrasions to his wrists and lip, Tucker responded that "Biko had not volunteered any information" (Woods, 312). Asked why he had not investigated why Biko wet his bed, he stated "it could have been that he was unwilling to inform anybody that he wished to pass urine" (*Record*, 861). Asked whether he had taken any steps to verify Goosen's "shamming" story, Dr. Hersch replied, "Not at all, no" (*Record*, 1030). Asked why they didn't insist that Biko be hospitalized at a local hospital, both Drs. Tucker and Lang responded that they "didn't know that in this particular situation one could override the decisions made by a responsible police officer" (Bernstein, 93-94).[77]

If the context which exiled Biko from proper meaning was both actively and passively constructed by security police, the police investigation into his death was clearly nothing more than a reiteration of that context. Investigator Kleinhaus "questioned" police by means of duplicated forms containing a series of questions with alternative answers. He did not search police offices, did not ask for documents, did not subject Goosen to inquiry, and only belatedly interviewed doctors whose responses he clearly prompted:

> KENTRIDGE: Aggressive. That is how General Kleinhaus put it to you.
> TUCKER: Yes.

KENTRIDGE: So General Kleinhaus put the words in your mouth.
TUCKER: I wouldn't say he put the words in my mouth, he asked the questions and I answered them. (*Record*, 853)[78]

This context was, finally, micromanaged both by the legal structure of the inquest and by Magistrate Prins who regulated the propriety and admissibility of evidence. Under the rules of the inquest, counsel for the Biko family had no right to subpoena witnesses, but could only probe evidence made available by the court. Magistrate Prins, for example, rejected Kentridge's petition to include a statement made by Brigadier Zietsman (which contradicted aspects of Colonel Goosen's testimony) and the September 16 telex message from Goosen to police headquarters that made direct reference to an injury "which was inflicted on Mr. Biko at 0700 hours on 7 September after which he refused to speak" and that described Biko as having been in a "semi-coma" at the time he was sent to Pretoria (Bernstein, 26). He also rejected as "hearsay" transcripts of Minister Kruger's public statements.

The weight of my baggage tugs loose a memory as I linger at this scene: of the antithesis dramatized in Coetzee's novel between the certainties of empire and the erring of the magistrate. For much like Coetzee's imperial "devotees of truth" (9), security police at the inquest explicitly allied themselves with the illustrious forces of certainty and dismissed uncertainty as foreign, error as irrelevant. Major Snyman, for example, insisted that the police's sole method of interrogation had been to confront the zone of error—in this case Biko—with certainties. "We had to confront the man with facts," he stated. "He had to know that his friends had spoken. I confronted him with these facts" (Woods, 248). And Colonel Goosen, asked why he never suggested in his affidavit that Biko might have bumped his head, dismissed such inexactness as improper:

GOOSEN: I thought of it as a possibility.
KENTRIDGE: The possibility was mentioned nowhere in the affidavit.
GOOSEN: It didn't allow for possibility. (Bernstein, 50)

Similarly, Van Rooyen, barrister for the security police, implicitly contrasted his own case with Kentridge's as an opposition between the factual and the errant: "It is our submission that cross-examination should not be inflammatory, it should be factual, it should not be emotional, it should be factual. It must not be based on mere supposition it must be factual" (*Record*, 889).[79]

An unwillingness to deal with the foreignness in signs likewise characterized Biko's doctors who invoked the uncertainty of symptoms as a defense for not having treated Biko. When questioned as to why they had not had Biko treated for head injury, doctors testified, for example, that "this was a person who showed certain vague signs" ([Tucker] *Record*, 956), that "he was very vague about [his head pains] and when I asked him where they were he couldn't give me a satisfactory reply" ([Lang] *Record*, 725), that "there was a query about [the plantar reflex], there was a doubt about whether or not the toe actually went up or whether the toe remained in the horizontal position" ([Lang] *Record,* 725).[80] As Barrister Van Rooyen summed up the doctor's position, "one cannot treat without a diagnosis being made. No treatment could be given because there was nothing to treat" (*Record,* 956).

Indeed because the zone of error was, to security police and their associates, a site of impropriety, irrelevance, and insignificance, a place of metaphysical impurity with which contact should be avoided, it also functioned as a space where thought could be sent for delegitimization, as a dustbin for untoward details. Thus the presence of error functioned not as an epistemologically significant *Verfremdungseffekt* calling for interpretation, nor even as a figure to be stabilized by a code, but rather as cause for swift expulsion from significance. For example, the very possibility of error in the results of the lumbar puncture performed on Biko functioned as an excuse for expelling them from the diagnostic process. In fact, the results indicated a significant number of red blood cells in the spinal fluid: a sign of brain injury. Dr. Lang, however, dismissed the results as erroneous, as resulting from a "bloody tap," that is, as containing blood drawn from a blood vessel rather than the spinal fluid. Although the ease with which the puncture was performed decreased the probability of it being a bloody tap and although there exists a simple method for distinguishing a bloody tap (by xanthochromia), Dr. Lang's bed letter of September 10 simply stated that Dr. Hersch (who performed the lumbar puncture) "could find no pathology on Biko and that the lumbar puncture test was normal" (Bernstein, 90).[81] Similarly, when confronted with the error in their own language, doctors and security police repeatedly resorted to a distinction between falsity and error—between, that is, significant and deliberately produced misinformation and a negligible *lapsus* foreign to both the essence of one's intention and the substance of significance:

> KENTRIDGE: You say you have informed [Biko] that both Dr. Hersch and myself can find no pathology. That was false.
> LANG: No, this was incorrect it should have . . .
> KENTRIDGE: Why should you give a false reason for returning him to the police cells?
> LANG: I did not give a false reason for returning him to the police cells.
> KENTRIDGE: It was false to say that no pathology could be found.
> LANG: I didn't give him a false reason.
> KENTRIDGE: You wrote down a false reason.
> LANG: I gave an incorrect statement on this bed letter. (*Record,* 1108)

Similarly, Dr. Tucker testified that the declaration in his affidavit that Biko exhibited no positive signs of organic disease was "an incorrect statement" (*Record,* 910) and that his failure to include in the medical record abrasions on Biko's ankles and wrists "was an error" (*Record,* 865). Lieutenant Kuhn told the court the statement made in his affidavit concerning the times he had visited

Biko was not false, "just faulty" (Woods, 235). If security police at the inquest demonstrated a singular unwillingness to deal with ambiguous signs, the task of the Biko family and their counsel, Mr. Kentridge, was, by and large, repatriating such ambiguity into significance, questioning incessantly what lay beneath the inquest's language "like a banshee beneath a stone."[82] They, like Coetzee's magistrate, concerned themselves with uncertain signs—with reading the signs on Biko's dead body, piecing together shards of circumstantial evidence—and positioned those signs in differing contexts: of other detainees' experiences with torture, for example; of Biko's prior words, comportment, and health; of medical knowledge about the effects of brain injury.

From this stop at the language of South African apartheid, I take dismal souvenirs: first, the conviction that the language of apartheid functions by both exploiting and repressing linguistic foreignness, that it counts on the domestic circle of signifier and signified to produce a referent-obliterating literality; second, the conviction that the meaning of language will be determined by context, that context is constructed by both active and passive reiteration and that the context of apartheid, bearing a striking resemblance to the nuances of *improper*, is subtended by an obliteration of black identity, propriety, purity, literality, and property; and third, the recognition that while allegorical reading may, by insisting on correspondence and conformity to a code, efface the foreignness in language, it may also, by wagering on divergence, repatriate foreignness into language, contest the production of proper meaning, and throw open the gates to the zone of error.

When, arriving home, I place my motley assemblage of souvenirs on the mantle, it becomes clear to me that the figural, literary foreignness from whence I departed has much to do with "literal" foreigners, that demarcating borders between the literal and the figural, the proper and the improper, the native and the foreign, are processes with formidable social consequences: patrolling and suppressing linguistic foreignness is a standard procedure for disciplining "literal" foreigners. And so, unpacked, on native soil, I ostensibly return to the familiar. But I sense an uncanny *Verfremdungseffekt* and I begin at once to realize that, with souvenirs like these, you can't go home again.

Notes

I am grateful to Laura Chrisman for her astute and detailed comments on this essay.

1. As Sander Gilman notes, "even more brutally simple categories underlie these [distinctions]. For language implies the correct and meaningful use of language. Any other use is 'crazy.' Thus one of the inherent definitions of any linguistic group is that it

is the norm of sanity." *Difference and Pathology: Stereotypes of Sexuality, Race, and Madness* (Ithaca, N.Y.: Cornell University Press, 1985), 129. Mary Louise Pratt formulates her notion of "contact zones" from the use of the term *contact* in linguistics, where "contact language refers to improvised languages that develop among speakers of different native languages who need to communicate with each other consistently, usually in the context of trade. Such languages begin as pidgins, and are called creoles when they come to have native speakers of their own. Like the societies of the contact zone, such languages are commonly regarded as chaotic, barbarous, lacking in structure." *Imperial Eyes: Travel Writing and Transculturation* (New York: Routledge, 1992), 6.

2. This idea has been hotly contested, primarily in the form of debates over figural language. I wish neither to maintain the "literary" as a value-laden term nor to make "everyday" and "literary" into essentialized categories that function as a mechanism of exclusion. I would, rather, describe literary and everyday language as differing in degree rather than in kind and read the figurality often associated with "literariness" as an intensified version of the foreignness in all language that tends to be sublimated in ordinary speech. On the argument for the distinctive nature of "literariness," see Victor Shklovsky, "Art as Technique," in *Russian Formalist Criticism: Four Essays*, trans. Lee T. Lemon and Marion J. Reis (Lincoln: University of Nebraska Press, 1965); Victor Erlich, *Russian Formalism: History, Doctrine*, 3rd ed. (New Haven, Conn.: Yale University Press, 1981); and Paul de Man, *Allegories of Reading: Figural Language in Rousseau, Nietzsche, Rilke, and Proust* (New Haven, Conn.: Yale University Press, 1979). For arguments that the everyday is (or can be read as the) literary, see George Lakoff and Mark Johnson, *Metaphors We Live By* (Chicago: University of Chicago Press, 1980); and Stanley Fish, *Is There a Text in This Class? The Authority of Interpretive Communities* (Cambridge, Mass.: Harvard University Press, 1980). On the literariness of philosophical language, see Jacques Derrida, "White Mythology: Metaphor in the Text of Philosophy," *Margins of Philosophy*, trans. Alan Bass (Chicago: University of Chicago Press, 1982).

3. Shklovsky, "Art as Technique," 12. On Russian formalism, see also Erlich, *Russian Formalism*; and Fredric Jameson, *The Prison-House of Language: A Critical Account of Structuralism and Russian Formalism* (Princeton, N.J.: Princeton University Press, 1972).

4. Shklovsky, "Art as Technique," 55.

5. Jameson, *The Prison-House of Language*, 4.

6. See Berthold Brecht, *Brecht on Theatre: The Development of an Aesthetic*, trans. John Willett (New York: Hill and Wang, 1964). The product of contact with foreigners—of a German viewing Chinese theater in Russia—*Verfremdungseffekt* first appears in Brecht's writings after his attendance at a 1935 performance by Mei Lan-fang's company in Moscow and is, ironically, deployed in the service of precisely the political theory (Marxism) that the formalists wished to oppose through *ostranenie*.

7. Brecht, *Brecht on Theatre*, 91.

8. Brecht, *Brecht on Theatre*, 179.

9. Brecht, *Brecht on Theatre*, 190.

10. Fredrich Schleiermacher, "The Academy Address of 1829: On the Concept of Hermeneutics, with Reference to F. A. Wolf's Instructions and Ast's Textbook," *Hermeneutics: The Handwritten Manuscripts*, ed. Heinz Kimmerle, trans. James Duke and Jack Forstman (Missoula, Mont.: Scholars Press for the American Academy of Religion,

1977), 175.

11. Jacques Derrida, "Signature Event Context," in *Margins of Philosophy*, 317.

12. De Man, *Allegories of Reading*, 6.

13. *Etranger* and *extranjero* both derive from a Latin root (*extraneus*) that simultaneously signifies externality, impropriety, and irrelevance.

14. This prohibition may take the form of law, economic exclusion, or milder forms of social disapprobation: disparagement for taking away what "rightly belongs" to natives or citizens, or for using property improperly (e.g., furnishing the home, business, or body in "poor taste"). On the semantic field of the proper, see chap. 1, note 1. This figure of the *improper*, it should be noted, corresponds to, and is a specific version of, the Manichean allegory identified by Frantz Fanon and elaborated by Abdul Jan Mohamed as "a field of diverse yet interchangeable oppositions between white and black, good and evil, superiority and inferiority, civilization and savagery, intelligence and emotion, rationality and sensuality, self and Other, subject and object." Abdul Jan Mohamed, "The Economy of Manichean Allegory: The Function of Racial Difference in Colonialist Literature," in *"Race," Writing, and Difference*, ed. Henry Louis Gates Jr. (Chicago: University of Chicago Press, 1986), 82.

15. Du Marsais, cited in Derrida, "White Mythology," 235.

16. Significantly, Aristotle's terms for what we call the literal and the figural are, respectively, the κύριος (*kurios*: authoritative [or, substantively, an owner, possessor, familiar]) and the ξένος (*xenos*: foreign). See the *Rhetoric* Book 2. Moreover, if metaphor is, as Du Marsais would have it, a concept "in a borrowed dwelling" (cited in Derrida, "White Mythology," 253), then the foreigner is a literalized incarnation of metaphor: of the movement, the transport of baggage from one realm to another, and the "highly suspect exchange of properties" that characterizes metaphor. Derrida also notes the potential classification of metaphors which "supposes an indigenous population and a migration" and which classifies metaphors "according to their native regions." "White Mythology," 220. On the indeterminable border between figural and proper meaning, and the "explo[sion of] the reassuring opposition of the metaphoric and the proper," see "White Mythology," 270.

17. Derrida, "Différance," in *Margins of Philosophy*, 7. My attempt to recuperate foreignness and error from the epistemological dustbin and the asylum of pathology coincides with the critical practice deployed by Gayatri Spivak, in which, for example, the "bungling" dismissed from significance by Kant becomes "a synonym for intervention" and the "mistaken reading" is given its say. See Gayatri Spivak, *A Critique of Postcolonial Reason: Toward a History of the Vanishing Present* (Durham, N.C.: Duke University Press, 1999), 10, 49.

18. The *zone of error* thus names a range of positions: the everyday experience of being a foreigner; an image projected onto one as a result of being *named* foreign; or an epistemological position one may assume which entails risking identity, becoming improper and impure.

19. Schleiermacher, "The Academy Address," 197.

20. St. Augustine, *On Christian Doctrine*, trans. D.W. Robertson, Jr. (New York: Macmillan, 1986), 79, my emphasis. See also Rudolf Bultmann: "[E]very interpretation incorporates a particular prior understanding—namely that which arises out of the context of living experience to which the subject belongs." "The Problem of Hermeneutics," in *The*

Hermeneutic Tradition: From Ast to Ricoeur, ed. Gayle L. Ormiston and Alan D. Schrift (Albany, N.Y.: SUNY Press, 1990), 73.

21. Jameson, *The Prison-House of Language*, 63.

22. "According to Aristotle, poetic language must appear strange and wonderful; and, in fact, it is often actually foreign: the Sumerian used by the Assyrians, the Latin of Europe during the Middle Ages, the Arabisms of the Persians, the old Bulgarian of Russian litera-ture, or the elevated, almost literary language of folk songs." Shklovksy, "Art as Technique," 22.

23. Bultmann, "The Problem of Hermeneutics," 75.

24. Fish, *Is there a Text in this Class?*, 318.

25. Fish, *Is there a Text in this Class?*, 285.

26. Fish, *Is there a Text in this Class?*, 318.

27. Fish's theory not only conceptually obliterates "literal" foreigners, but explicitly reassures those critics fearful of the threat of literary foreignness; for polysemy, uncertainty, error, and such threats are, he argues, always already disciplined by context. Rather than in-vestigate the implications of this fear itself, he aims to demonstrate "how baseless the fear of these dangers finally is." Yet the "level of observation or discourse at which meanings are obvious and indisputable" by which Fish claims texts are stabilized is also, I would argue, the mechanism through which ideology functions; it is the invisible law that regulates pro-priety and disciplines foreignness. Indeed there are moments when Fish's interpretive com-munities bear a conspicuous resemblance to ideological hegemony: they render texts "al-ways stable," repress the processes through which that stability is constructed, and make meanings appear "natural." "[I]n every situation," he writes, "some or other meaning will appear to us to be uninterpreted because it is isomorphic with the interpretive structure the situation (and therefore our perception) already has." Fish, *Is There a Text in this Class?*, 305, 270, 277. That "apparently uninterpreted meaning," I would add, renders foreignness irrelevant and reinstates the "automatism of perception" against which Shklovsky deployed defamiliarization. On the "structural nonsaturation" of context, see Jacques Derrida, "Signa-ture Event Context," 310.

28. J. M. Coetzee, *Waiting for the Barbarians*, (New York: Penguin, 1980), 8. Cita-tions hereafter in the text. I am indebted here to Susan Gallagher who has argued that the novel demonstrates that "a complete binary opposition of self and Other is both oppres-sive and false." Gallagher, *A Story of South Africa: J. M. Coetzee's Fiction in Context* (Cambridge, Mass.: Harvard University Press, 1991), 118; and to David Attwell who de-scribes the magistrate as "attempt[ing] to reject the subjective space that his circum-stances and history have prepared for him." Attwell, *South Africa and the Politics of Writing* (Berkeley: University of California Press, 1993), 82. It is perhaps worth noting that in South Africa, magistrates are appointed from the ranks of the civil service, per-form both judicial and administrative functions, and were responsible for trying most of-fenders under the laws of apartheid. On the role of magistrates in South Africa, see John Dugard, *Human Rights and the South African Legal Order* (Princeton, N.J.: Princeton University Press, 1978), 280-303.

29. There exist numerous insightful readings of *Waiting for the Barbarians*. On the novel's discursive relation to events in South Africa, see Gallagher, *A Story of South Africa*; on the novel's critical reception and constructions of apartheid, see Clive Barnett, "Con-structions of Apartheid in the International Reception of the Novels of J. M. Coetzee," *Jour-*

nal of South African Studies 25, no. 2 (1999): 287-301; on the novel as a deconstruction of liberal humanist novelistic discourse, see Teresa Dovey, *The Novels of J. M. Coetzee: Lacanian Allegories* (Johannesburg: A.D. Donker, 1988); on the position of the novel within Coetzee's literary development, see Attwell, *South Africa and the Politics of Writing*. On the novel's treatment of torture, see Gallagher, *A Story of South Africa*; Barbara Eckstein, "The Body, The Word, and the State: J. M. Coetzee's *Waiting for the Barbarians*," *Novel: A Forum on Fiction* 22, no. 2 (Winter 1989): 175-198; and Jennifer Wenzel, "Keys to the Labyrinth: Writing, Torture, and Coetzee's Barbarian Girl," *Tulsa Studies in Women's Literature* 17, no. 3 (Spring 1996): 61-71. On its imagery of sight, see Dick Penner, *Countries of the Mind: The Fiction of J. M. Coetzee* (New York: Greenwood Press, 1989); and Debra Castillo, "The Composition of the Self in Coetzee's *Waiting for the Barbarians*," *Critique: Studies in Modern Fiction* 27, no. 2 (Winter 1986): 78-90. On debates over the political efficacy of Coetzee's style, see Eckstein, "The Body, The Word, and the State"; Attwell, *South Africa and the Politics of Writing*; Rosemary Jane Jolly, *Colonization, Violence, and Narration in White South African Writing: André Brink, Breyten Breytenbach, and J. M. Coetzee* (Athens: Ohio University Press, 1996); Stephen Watson, "Colonialism and the Novels of J. M. Coetzee," *Research in African Literatures* 17, no. 3 (Fall 1986): 370-392; Richard Martin, "Narrative, History, Ideology: A Study of *Waiting for the Barbarians*," *Ariel* 17, no. 3 (July 1986): 3-21; and Kelly Hewson, "Making the 'Revolutionary Gesture': Nadine Gordimer, J. M. Coetzee, and Some Variations on the Writer's Responsibility," *Ariel* 19, no. 4 (October 1988): 55-72. On the novel's treatment of colonialism, see Watson, "Colonialism and the Novels of J. M. Coetzee"; Michael Valdez Moses, "The Mark of Empire: Writing, History, and Torture in Coetzee's *Waiting for the Barbarians*," *The Kenyon Review* 15, no.1 (Winter 1993): 115-127; and Paul Rich, "Apartheid and the Decline of the Civilization Idea: An Essay on Nadine Gordimer's *July's People* and J. M. Coetzee's *Waiting for the Barbarians*," *Ariel* 20, no. 2 (April 1989): 69-79. On the novel's use of the present tense, see Anne Waldron Neumann, "Escaping the 'Time of History'? Present Tense and the Occasion of Narration in J. M. Coetzee's *Waiting for the Barbarians*," *The Journal of Narrative Technique*, 20 (Winter 1990): 65-86; and James Phelan, "Present Tense Narration, Mimesis, the Narrative Norm, and the Positioning of the Reader in *Waiting for the Barbarians*," in *Understanding Narrative*, ed. James Phelan and Peter Rabinowitz (Columbus: Ohio State University Press, 1994). On its indeterminate setting, see Gallagher, Dovey, Penner, and Attwell. For a reading of the novel's intersections with deconstruction, see Lance Olsen, "The Presence of Absence: Coetzee's *Waiting for the Barbarians*," *Ariel* 16, no. 2 (April 1985): 47-56. On the significance of Constantinos Cavafy's poem from which Coetzee draws his title, see Moses, Attwell, Penner, and Gallagher.

    30. Many critics, including Neumann, Rich, Dovey, Moses, Gallagher, Penner, and Attwell, have described *Waiting for the Barbarians* as an allegory. Dovey elaborates allegory via Lacan as "a mode implying the recognition that to speak is to speak as Other." Dovey, *The Novels of J. M. Coetzee*, 43. Stephen Slemon contends that postcolonial allegorical writing constitutes a challenge to the traditional relation between allegory and history. His argument, which coincides on a number of points with my own, is that "Coetzee's tactic in this novel is to portray imperial allegorical thinking in the thematic level of his novel and to juxtapose it with the allegorical mode in which the novel itself is written. The juxtaposition foregrounds the discontinuity between the two kinds of allegorical discourse, one based on imperial codes of recognition and the other on resistance to totali-

tarian systems." Stephen Slemon, "Post-Colonial Allegory and the Transformation of History," *Journal of Commonwealth Literature* 23, no. 1 (1998): 163. Barnett assesses the work of various critics who read the novel as moral or political allegory; see Barnett, "Constructions of Apartheid." On allegory, see John Whitman, *Allegory: The Dynamics of an Ancient and Medieval Technique* (Cambridge, Mass.: Harvard University Press, 1987); Paul de Man "The Rhetoric of Temporality," *Blindness and Insight: Essays in the Rhetoric of Contemporary Criticism*, 2nd ed. (Minneapolis: University of Minnesota Press, 1983), 187-228; and de Man, *Allegories of Reading: Figural Language in Rousseau, Nietzsche, Rilke, and Proust* (New Haven, Conn.: Yale University Press, 1979); Angus Fletcher, *Allegory: The Theory of a Symbolic Mode* (Ithaca, N.Y.: Cornell University Press, 1964); Walter Benjamin, *The Origin of German Tragic Drama*, trans. John Osborne (London: NLB, 1977); Stephen Greenblatt, ed., *Allegory and Representation* (Baltimore, Md.: Johns Hopkins University Press, 1981); and Gordon Teskey, *Allegory and Violence* (Ithaca, N.Y.: Cornell University Press, 1996).

31. Whitman, *Allegory*, 2.

32. Similarly, Quintillian notes that *allegory* is translated by Latin *inversio*—a term that captures both the relative and negative nature of foreignness. Medieval grammarians described allegory as *alieniloquium*, "other speaking."

33. Augustine's law of Charity and the systematization of exegesis during the early Christian era are paradigmatic. See Whitman on ensuring "the coherence and integrity of Christian doctrine," *Allegory*, 78; and Teskey on "the ideological coherence of the medieval culture of the sign," *Allegory and Violence*, 148.

34. The image of the banshee—a kind of fairy or imp that wails under the windows of a house where someone is going to die—marks both the tricky instability beneath the word's apparent solidity and the sense of foreboding associated with uncovering it.

35. Of course this is not to say that one cannot wager on a more or less correct meaning; in fact, it is precisely the act of reading an event, object, or word in multiple contexts that enables such a decision. It *is* to say, however, that the magistrate's interpretative activity is not a matter of recovering an original or proper context.

36. On the novel's thematization of indeterminacy, see Dovey, who argues for the subversive effects of "avoid[ing] fixation in a particular meaning," *The Novels of J. M. Coetzee*, 52; and Attwell, *South Africa and the Politics of Writing*. Recognizing the significance of the magistrate's reading otherwise is not to be confused with a categorical endorsement of all of his activities or interpretations. Indeed, the magistrate's reading of the barbarian girl as sign arguably repeats the dehumanizing gestures of the empire, confirms Teskey's argument for the violence of allegory, and adumbrates apartheid's reading of Biko (see below). However, this position, I believe, needs further refinement: the magistrate does not read the girl according to a code (as apartheid does Biko); indeed it is precisely the absence of such a hermeneutic code that conditions the magistrate's obsessive exegesis. Further, I would argue that humans, their bodies, acts, and words *do* signify; it is neither possible nor "humanizing" to take them out of the realm of signification. What is most reprehensible about the magistrate's reading of the barbarian girl is, from my perspective, the fact that he reads only a fragment of her and does so within a singular, obsessive context (the empire's program of torture) and, further, that he largely disallows her from producing proper meaning.

37. Those injudicious reading practices are also a resistance to facile moral verdicts. When he attempts to elicit the sentiments of his torturer, for example, the magistrate explicitly distinguishes understanding from blame: "Do not misunderstand me, I am not blaming you or accusing you, I am long past that. . . . I am only trying to understand. I am trying to understand the zone in which you live. I am trying to imagine how you breathe and eat and live from day to day." *Waiting for the Barbarians*, 126.

38. Fish, *Is There a Text in this Class?*, 318.

39. De Man, *Allegories of Reading*, 8.

40. Fish, *Is There a Text in this Class?*, 277. I am extending J. L. Austin's linguistic concept of the "performative" much as Judith Butler has in describing the construction of gender; this performativity should be conceived "not as a singular or deliberate 'act,' but, rather, as the reiterative and citational practice by which discourse produces the effects that it names." Judith Butler, *Bodies that Matter: On the Discursive Limits of "Sex"* (New York: Routledge, 1993), 2. Dovey argues that Coetzee's "re-writings" resist precisely this kind of normative reiteration through a defamiliarizing dislocation, that they "involve a *displacement* of the ideological position available to the subject in language, rather than the passive *repetitions* involved in normative reading and writing." Dovey, *The Novels of J. M. Coetzee*, 59.

41. It should be evident from this elaboration that I use the term "nihilism" in the specific sense sketched by Nietzsche in *Will to Power*, Section 12, trans. Walter Kaufmann and R. J. Hollingdale (New York: Vintage, 1967), 12-14.

42. Thomas McLaughlin, "Figurative Language," in *Critical Terms for Literary Study*, ed. Frank Lentricchia and Thomas McLaughlin (Chicago: University of Chicago Press, 1990), 85.

43. Martin, "Narrative, History, Ideology," 20.

44. If we dwell a little longer in the culture of this text, it becomes disconcertingly evident that, although the novel itself indicts the suppression of linguistic foreignness as a primary technique for oppressing "literal" foreigners, it is precisely for housing linguistic foreignness that Coetzee has been most consistently criticized. Nadine Gordimer, for example, disparages Coetzee's use of allegory as "a kind of opposing desire to hold himself clear of events and their daily, grubby, tragic, consequences." "The Idea of Gardening," *New York Review of Books* 31, no.1 (February 1984), 3. Similarly, Martin objects that "[an] alienation from itself, from its linguistic and historical constitution, marks the text of *Waiting for the Barbarians* at every level and prevents it from transcending itself." "Narrative, History, Ideology," 20. Moses writes of the "troublesome political implications" that follow from Coetzee's "poststructural understanding of interpretation." "The Mark of Empire," 122. And Paul Rich contends that "Coetzee's novel . . . indicates that literary postmodernism in a postcolonial context such as South Africa . . . is a moral dead end." "Apartheid and the Decline of the Civilization Idea," 389. Identifying Coetzee's offense alternately as "allegory," "postmodernism," or "poststructuralism," this reprimand is also symptomatic of a much more diffuse suspicion of literary foreignness that is not uncommonly encountered in critical discourses committed to mediating cultural foreignness. This suspicion—which has put in conspicuous appearances in feminism, identity politics, cultural studies, and postcolonialism, for example—is evinced by a reliance on a strictly transparent and referential model of language that discreetly banishes the inconvenient impropriety that deconstructive reading practices let loose in language; the assumption that a necessarily antagonistic rela-

tion obtains between textual and "real" foreignness; and a marked absence of "close reading"—shunned as if it carried the defiling taint of a critical community with which one would not want to be caught associating. For a reading of the "feeling stupid" of the novel's final line as "neither despair nor humiliation," see Eckstein, "The Body, the Word, and the State," 198.

45. What or who constituted apartheid is by no means self-evident. I include in my use of the term not only the political program and system of laws imposed by the Afrikaner National Party (NP), but also the active and passive reiteration of practices, discourses, and attitudes that enabled and maintained its power. *Apartheid* is an Afrikaans word meaning "apartness." It was first used to designate political policy in the "Sauer report," a statement on the "racial problem" prepared for the Afrikaner National Party in 1946. Building on existing discriminatory laws, apartheid began to be implemented as state policy after the National Party came to power in 1948. It is Hendrik Verwoerd, prime minister from 1958-1966, who is largely responsible for transforming the concept of apartheid into a "drastic, systematic program of social engineering." Leonard Thompson, *A History of South Africa*, rev. ed. (New Haven, Conn.: Yale University Press, 1995), 198. "At the heart of the apartheid system were four ideas," writes Thompson: "First, the population of South Africa comprised four 'racial groups'—White, Coloured, Indian, and African—each with its own inherent culture. Second, Whites, as the civilized race, were entitled to have absolute control over the state. Third, white interests should prevail over black interests, the state was not obliged to provide equal facilities for the subordinate races. Fourth, the white racial group formed a single nation with Afrikaans- and English-speaking components, while Africans belonged to several (eventually ten) distinct nations or potential nations—a formula that made the white nation the largest in the country." Thompson, *A History of South Africa*, 190.

Although apartheid as a political program has been abolished and its legal structure, since 1994, largely dismantled, many of its economic and social effects remain. Hence I adopt an uneasy historical present tense in this essay that refers primarily to the period between 1948 and 1994, but that also shades into the literal present. On the history of the apartheid era, see Thompson, *A History of South Africa*; Allister Sparks, *The Mind of South Africa* (New York: Knopf, 1990); David Mermelstein, *The Anti-Apartheid Reader: The Struggle Against White Racist Rule in South Africa* (New York: Grove, 1987); and Hilda Bernstein, *No. 46-Steve Biko* (London: International Defense & Aid Fund, 1978). For a nuanced analysis of the material circumstances and discursive articulations that conditioned apartheid and its multiple transformations, see Aletta J. Norval, *Deconstructing Apartheid Discourse* (New York: Verso, 1996). For a summary of apartheid laws, see Roger Omond, *The Apartheid Handbook: A Guide to South Africa's Everyday Racial Policies*, 2nd ed. (New York: Penguin, 1985); Muriel Horrell, *Race Relations as Regulated by Law in South Africa 1948-1979* (Johannesburg: South African Institute of Race Relations, 1982); and Fiona McLachhlan, "The Apartheid Laws in Brief," *The Anti-Apartheid Reader*, 76-78. On apartheid policies, see "A Special Mayibuye Supplement," an insert published by the African National Congress for the Truth & Reconciliation Commission. August, 1996, http://www.anc.org.za/ancdocs/pubs/mayitruth9608.html Feb, 1998; and John Dugard, *Human Rights and the South African Legal Order* (Princeton, N.J.: Princeton University Press, 1978). For a glossary of key terms of apartheid, see Hilda Bernstein, *For Their Triumphs and For Their Tears: Women in Apartheid South Africa* (London: International Defense &

Aid Fund, 1985).

46. The Commonwealth Group of Eminent Persons, *Mission to South Africa: The Commonwealth Report* (New York: Penguin, 1986), 81. *The Commonwealth Report* is the result of an extended visit by seven senior Commonwealth politicians (the so-called "Eminent Persons Group") to South Africa in 1986, led by Malcolm Fraser of Australia and Olusegun Obasanjo of Nigeria. While the group succeeded in establishing a dialogue between the South African government and Nelson Mandela, it terminated its stay on May 19 when the South African Defense Force (SADF) attacked alleged ANC bases in Harare, Lusaka, and Gaborone.

47. If, as Allister Sparks has argued, "from the beginning [white South Africans] have regarded the people of Africa as 'aliens,' foreigners from beyond the hedge or beyond the frontier or beyond the city limits, people whose real home was somewhere else, in a 'homeland' far away, out of sight," this conception was, under apartheid, solidified into laws—the 1950 Group Areas Act and the 1958 Bantu Self Government Act—that rendered Black Africans statutory foreigners in South Africa. Sparks, *The Mind of South Africa*, xvii.

48. Successively created through the Native Land Acts of 1913 and 1936, the Group Areas Act of 1949, and the Black Homelands Citizenship Act of 1970, the homelands (formerly referred to as "native reserves" or "bantustans") facilitate the migrant labor system in which blacks, who do not hold political rights outside of these areas, work as "foreign labor" within white South Africa, where they are not entitled to reside, hold citizenship, possess civil rights or, as Member of Parliament G. F. L. Forneman put it, "be burdened with superfluous appendages such as wives, children, and dependents who could not provide service." Cited in Bernstein, *For Their Triumphs and For Their Tears*, 14. "The goal," declared Cabinet Minister Cornelius Mulder "is that eventually there will be no black South Africans." Cited in Sparks, *The Mind of South Africa*, 136-137. Removals to these areas were carried out forcibly with armed police, bulldozers (which demolished black's homes in "white areas"), arrests, and numerous forms of intimidation. In 1976, the government began declaring these areas "independent" and calling them "black states" (though they were unrecognized by any other nation): a process the South African government compared to decolonization and described as "creative withdrawal of the Whites from the Black territories." *South Africa 1978: Official Yearbook of the Republic of South Africa*, 5th ed. (Johannesburg: South African Department of Information, 1978), 201, hereafter abbreviated to *Yearbook*. For a political analysis of the conception of homelands, see Norval, *Deconstructing Apartheid Discourse*, 142-151. On removals to, and conditions in, the "homelands," see the Surplus People Project Report, *Forced Removals in South Africa*, Vol. 1-2 (Cape Town: Surplus People Project, 1983); Muriel Horrell, *The African Homelands of South Africa* (Johannesburg: South African Institute of Race Relations, 1973); and Hilda Bernstein, *For Their Triumphs and For Their Tears*. In recent Truth and Reconciliation Commission (TRC) hearings, the ANC has indicted forced removals as one of apartheid's crimes against humanity. See *Truth and Reconciliation Commission of South Africa Report*, Vol. 5 (New York: Grove, 1999).

49. De Man, "The Rhetoric of Temporality," 203.

50. This is to distinguish not only signifier (word) from signified (concept or mental image), but signified from referent (a phenomenal object). I do not, however, mean to suggest the availability of an unmediated referent exterior to, prior to, or distorted by discursive context. Nor are my distinctions between the figural and proper, the allegorical and the lit-

eral, meant to suggest a fixed or natural domain of the literal. Indeed this would be to erase precisely the genesis of literality that I am attempting to map and to subscribe to as normative that "proper meaning" I am attempting to critique. I am interested, rather in investigating how the literal is constituted, what it includes and excludes, in tracing proper meaning as an effect of context, and in examining how context regulates both the proper meaning of words and the perception of referents.

51. Cited in Marianne Cornevin, *Apartheid: Power and Historical Falsification* (Paris: Unesco, 1980), 121.

52. *Yearbook*, 54.

53. *Yearbook*, 203. A history textbook puts the matter this way: "The established nationhood of the Whites has to be protected and maintained in that part of the country that *has always been theirs*. At the same time, the policy provides for the development of each separate Black nation to full autonomy. The focal point of this development is the Black States. These states are those parts of the country that *originally belonged* to the Blacks and still belong to them." Cited in Elizabeth Dean, Paul Hartmann, and Mary Katzen, *History in Black and White: An Analysis of South African School History Textbooks* (Paris: Unesco, 1983), 77.

54. Dean, Hartmann, and Katzen, *History in Black and White*, 231. Indeed even the most recalcitrant material details can, with some creative context management, be reconciled with the literal meaning of homeland. For example, bits and pieces of unconnected land—Bophuthatswana contains nineteen fragments, some hundreds of miles apart; KwaZulu comprises 29 major and 41 minor fragments—can constitute a homeland if, as the *Yearbook* claims, "The fragmentary appearance of these areas is chiefly the result of tribal wars and succession disputes: [if] the Blacks settled in comparatively small areas because their migrations were tribal movements rather than major population shifts involving full-fledged nations" (*Yearbook*, 204). For a detailed refutation of this position, see Cornevin, *Apartheid: Power and Historical Falsification*, 121-126.

55. Fish, *Is There a Text in this Class?*, 270.

56. *Commonwealth Report*, 52, 53.

57. Amnesty International Report, *Political Imprisonment in South Africa* (New York: Amnesty International, 1978), 21. Section 6 of the Terrorism Act authorizes "any police officer of, or above the rank of lieutenant-colonel, to arrest, without warrant or charge, anyone suspected of being a 'terrorist' as defined, or of possessing information relating to terrorists or terrorist offenses." Conviction under the Terrorism Act carries a mandatory minimum sentence of five years imprisonment and a maximum sentence of death. The Internal Security Act of 1976, which empowered the Minister of Justice to detain any person without trial for an indefinite period, allowed its terms to be even more radically inclusive—neither "security of the State" nor "maintenance of public order" are defined in the Act—and the criterion of "reasonable belief" is suspended. See Dugard, *Human Rights and the South African Legal Order*, 122. In 1985, during the state of emergency, "power to make mass arrests and detention without trial was extended to every single member of the police force, the railways police, the prison service and the army. . . . [A]nd in advance all state officials were made immune from liability both civil and criminal for all unlawful acts." *Commonwealth Report*, 55.

58. *Yearbook*, 319-320.

59. John Laurence, *Race, Propaganda, and South Africa* (London: Victor Gollancz,

1979), 175.

60. Cited in Dugard, *Human Rights and the South African Legal Order*, 156. "[A] skillful attempt to divert attention from the domestic causes of black resistance in South Africa" (Thompson, *A History of South Africa*, 216), apartheid's rhetoric of communist threat was also insistently deployed by South African delegate to the United Nations, Eric Louw, who argued before the General Assembly, for example, that "It is common knowledge that for the past five or six years there has been an infiltration into some of the emergent States of Africa of Communist agents of various kinds—commercial, technical, and also political," that "a number of the leaders of the African National Congress, which is a subversive organization and which largely contributed to the Sharpeville riots earlier this year, are well-known Communists, some of them having been trained in Russia," and that "the aim of Communistic penetration on the continent of Africa appears to be to create conditions of unrest and later on chaos in the emergent African States and territories." Eric Louw, *The Case for South Africa* (New York: McFadden Books, 1963), 62-64.

61. It is this trajectory of correspondence that underlies what Fletcher calls the "dualism associated with allegory which implies the radical opposition of two independent, mutually irreducible, mutually antagonistic substances," as well as the personifying process that "treats real people in a formulaic way so that they become walking Ideas." Fletcher, *Allegory*, 28. It is also presupposed in Fletcher's contention that allegory "does not accept the world of experience and the senses; it thrives on their overthrow, replacing them with ideas." Fletcher, *Allegory*, 322. It is not without significance that these assertions both depict the power of allegorical codes to eradicate foreignness *and* describe material circumstances in South Africa. Along similar lines, Teskey argues that "allegory [must] somehow capture the substantiality of beings and raise it to the conceptual plane. But for this to occur any integrity those beings may have must be negated. The negation of the integrity of the other, of the living, is the first moment of allegory's exertion of its power to seize and to tear." Teskey, *Allegory and Violence*, 18.

62. The press scandal in April 1978 brought to light the extent to which national news and information sources were surreptitiously funded and controlled by the National Party, exposing that the party had financed nearly 150 front organizations for pro-apartheid propaganda. See Laurence, *Race, Propaganda, and South Africa*; and John Phelan, *Apartheid Media: Disinformation and Dissent in South Africa* (Westport, Conn.: Lawrence Hill, 1987). TRC hearings have confirmed the broad influence the National Party exercised over the tone and content of news, including its power to "plant" stories. See *Truth and Reconciliation Commission of South Africa Report*, Vol 4. Sparks notes that it is not only during the obligatory years of military service that white boys are infused with military doctrine, but that "the educational process itself has been militarized. Some 200,000 schoolboys are formed into school cadet detachments, where they are drilled and psychologically prepared for national service." Sparks, *The Mind of South Africa*, 309. On South African textbooks, see Dean, Hartman, and Katzen, *History in Black and White*.

63. See, for example, the statements of Patrick McGluwa, William Tshimong, and Ian Rwaxa to Amnesty International. *Political Imprisonment in South Africa*, 31-32.

64. *Political Imprisonment in South Africa*, 28.

65. Teskey argues for the role of allegory in maintaining such a context: "allegories do not just reflect ideological structures," he contends, "they engage us in the practice of ritual interpretation by which those structures are reproduced in bodies and expressed through the

voice. As a substitute for genuine political speaking, allegory elicits the ritual repetition of an ideologically significant world." Teskey, *Allegory and Violence*, 132.

66. D. F. Malan, "Apartheid: Divine Calling," *The Anti-Apartheid Reader*, 95.

67. On September 12, 1977, Black Consciousness leader Stephen Biko died while in detention under Section 6 of the Terrorism Act. Biko had been central in establishing the South African Student Organization (SASO), the Black People's Convention (BPC), and numerous local programs in black communities. On Biko's life, work, and writing, see Steve Biko, *I write what I like*, ed. Aelred Stubbs (San Francisco: Harper and Row, 1979); Hilda Bernstein, *No.46—Steve Biko*; Donald Woods, *Biko*, 3rd ed. (New York: Henry Holt, 1987); N. Barney Pityana, Mamphela Ramphele, Malusi Mpumlwana, and Lindy Wilson, eds. *Bounds of Possibility: The Legacy of Steve Biko and Black Consciousness* (London: Zed Books, 1991); and Tim Juckes, *Opposition in South Africa: The Leadership of Z. K. Matthews, Nelson Mandela, and Stephen Biko* (Westport, Conn.: Praeger, 1995). On September 13, Minister of Justice James T. Kruger issued a statement that read in part: "[Biko] was arrested in connection with activities related to the riots in Port Elizabeth, and *inter alia* for drafting and distributing pamphlets which incited arson and violence. He was detained at the Walmer Police Station in Port Elizabeth since September 5. Mr. Biko refused his meals and threatened a hunger strike. But he was, however, regularly supplied with meals and water which he refused to partake of. . . . After consultation with the District Surgeon it was decided to transfer Mr. Biko to Pretoria. He was taken to Pretoria the same night. On September 12, Mr. Biko was again examined and medically treated by a district surgeon in Pretoria. Mr. Biko died the same night." Cited in Dean Louis Pollak, *The Inquest into the Death of Stephen Bantu Biko: A Report to the Lawyers' Committee for Civil Rights under Law* (Washington, D.C.: The Southern Africa Project, 1978), 7-8. Activists and journalists pressed for an inquest which was ultimately held between November 14 and 29, 1977. The inquest (which has less formal procedures than a trial) was presided over by a magistrate—Marthinus Prins—assisted by two assessors (who played an advisory role); Sidney Kentridge functioned as lead barrister for the Biko family and Retief van Rooyen as lead barrister for the security police. For legal opinions of the inquest, see Pollak and Sir David Napley, "Stephen Biko Inquest" in Bernstein, *Steve Biko*, 137-147. At the inquest, State Pathologist J. Loubser testified that Biko had died of "extensive brain injury," that his injuries were "clearly indicative of severe traumatic brain contusions" originating from "a mechanical origin." Cited in Woods, 328. Professor of Anatomical Pathology N. Proctor concurred. Witnesses at the inquest included six security police officers, Colonel P. J. Goosen, the physicians who attended Biko in detention (Drs. Lang and Tucker), and consultant specialist Dr. Hersch. The magistrate's final ruling at the inquest was that "the deceased was Bantu Stephen Biko, a black man aged thirty, that he died on September 12 and that the cause of death was brain injury which led to renal failure and other complications"; that "the head injuries were probably sustained on September 7 in a scuffle in the Security Police offices in Port Elizabeth"; and that "on the available evidence the death cannot be attributed to any act or omission amounting to a criminal offense on the part of any person." Cited in Woods, *Biko*, 353-354. My analysis of the inquest is based on transcripts contained in the "Record of the Inquest into the Death of S. B. Biko, November 1977, 688-1119," *Biko Doctors Case Collection*, Microfiche, hereafter cited in text as *Record*; Bernstein, *Steve Biko*, hereafter cited in text as Bernstein; and Donald Woods, *Biko*, hereafter cited in text as Woods. The latter is a compilation of notes taken by Wendy Woods, Roger Omon of the *Daily Dispatch*,

and Helen Zille of the *Rand Daily Mail*.

68. Both Gallagher and Attwell have previously noted this connection.

69. It perhaps warrants more explicit statement that the difference, as I see it, between apartheid's allegorical reading and the magistrate's is the difference between, on the one hand, making another foreign in order to establish one's own meaning as proper and, on the other hand, recognizing the foreignness in oneself and others as a way of allowing for differing meanings; between stabilizing meaning by a code—that is eradicating the foreignness from language—and allowing the foreignness in language to speak; between concentrating solely on the trajectory of allegorical correspondence and insisting on the trajectory of divergence; and between the genesis amnesia characteristic of meaning commodities and a genealogical excavation that indicts those meanings.

70. It also entailed a confiscation of property: he "wanted to take his private possessions with him to the cell, but this was not permitted." Woods, 234.

71. Pollak, *The Inquest into the Death of Stephen Bantu Biko*, 1.

72. Under Section 6, "No person other than the Minister or an officer in the service of the state acting in the performance of his official duties, shall have access to any detainee, or shall be entitled to any official information relating to or obtained from any detainee." Cited in Pollak, *The Inquest into the Death of Stephen Bantu Biko*, 4.

73. If a material referent for the name Biko was systematically erased from both public and private view, nearly anyone capable of making reference to that referent was similarly disciplined: following Biko's death, the BPC, SASO, and Black Women's Federation were banned; BPC officials, including Malusi Mpumlawana, Tehnmiwe Mtintso, and Kenny Rachidi were detained; journalists and activists pressing for an inquest, including Donald Woods, Percy Qoboza, Beyers Naude, Theo Kotze, David Russell, Cedric Mayson, and Brian Brown were banned and their newspapers were summarily shut down.

74. "Summary of Evidence Given by Col. Goosen at the Inquest," *Biko Doctor's Case Collection*, 1.

75. Recontextualizing, Kentridge described Biko's symptoms appearing in a white schoolchild on holiday and asked Dr. Tucker whether he would have the child hospitalized. Tucker responded, "I think that there are a certain—there is a certain difference in shall I say circumstance. . . . I would insist that the child go into hospital, yes" (*Record*, 919).

76. However, a telex dated September 16 from Colonel Goosen to police headquarters makes it clear that he recognized that Mr. Biko was in a "semi-coma". Napley, "Stephen Biko Inquest," 143.

77. The doctors' treatment of Biko generated a long and widespread controversy in the medical community. The South African Medical and Dental Council established a committee to investigate the matter, which in April 1980 found "no *prima facie* evidence of improper or disgraceful conduct on the part of the practitioners." Mary Rayner and the Committee on Scientific Freedom and Responsibility, *Turning a Blind Eye: Medical Accountability and the Prevention of Torture in South Africa* (Washington, D.C.: American Association for the Advancement of Science, 1987), 36. The committee's resolution was adopted by the Council the following June. Outraged members of the medical faculties of the Universities of Cape Town and the Witwatersrand took the case to the Medical Association of South Africa, a voluntary professional organization, which at first expressed its solidarity with the SAMDC but, subsequent to further pressure from members and negative in-

ternational publicity, appointed an Ad Hoc Committee that reviewed the available evidence and found that "Dr. Lang and Dr. Tucker acted in an improper and disgraceful manner in that: (1) They did not take a proper history either from the police or Mr. Biko; (2) Their physical examination was inadequate; (3) They ignored and misrepresented the opinion and advice given to them by Dr. Hersch and Dr. Keely; (4) They did not tell the police that Biko had unequivocal evidence of brain damage; (5) They falsified certificates; (6) They did not insist on hospitalization; (7) They accepted that the interests of their patient were subordinated to those of the security police; (8) They exhibited callous disregard for Biko's comfort" *Record*, 8. No punitive action was, however, taken against the doctors and a group of physicians took the case to the Supreme Court which ultimately upheld the charges of the ad hoc committee, abrogated the resolutions adopted by the SAMDC, and ordered it to establish a disciplinary committee. This committee, meeting in 1985, issued a caution and reprimand to Dr. Lang and suspended Dr. Tucker's license for three months.

78. Dr. Lang admitted that the possibility of Biko having a head injury "was in the back of [his] mind," but as Kentridge pointed out, "It might have been at the back of your mind but it was not in the forefront of your affidavit." Bernstein, 77. This silence concerning Biko's injuries rested on a well-established foundation of resistance to legally acknowledging torture; as Bernstein notes, "It was generally agreed that to complain about torture in the setting of the terrorism trial would inflame the prosecution and the judge. It was not in the best interests of the defendants, who were on trial for their lives, to assume this risk." Bernstein, 133. While affidavits were ultimately necessitated by the imminence of an inquest, none of the 28 affidavits made in connection with Biko's death mentioned him falling with his head against a wall or described any other scene of injury.

79. This insistence on certainty arguably extended to the judgment itself which, as Pollak has noted, offers no rationale, but attempts to rest on its own self evidence: "As a matter of judicial craftsmanship, the verdict is defective not so much because it is not persuasive as because it does not undertake to persuade. It merely declares a result." Napley, "Stephen Biko Inquest," 26.

80. A method for detecting possible brain injury, testing the plantar reflex entails stroking the bottom of the foot which should make the toes curl down (and not upwards).

81. Dr. Gluckman, pathologist for the Biko family, stated of the results of the lumbar puncture: "This report has contradictions. The analysis reports show the spinal fluid to be colorless, and at the same time containing 1655 red cells. Spinal fluid containing this count could not possibly have been clear. Anything from two to three hundred red cells is slightly turbid, and this increases as the number of red cells increases. It is not possible to have fluid containing over 1600 red cells, and for that fluid to be clear. One or the other is incorrect." Bernstein, 73. Dr. Hersch testified that he had "made it clear [to Goosen] that there were positive findings" from the puncture. Bernstein, 89.

82. Coetzee, *Waiting for the Barbarians*, 9. I wish to stress that while my emphasis in this chapter has been on apartheid's manipulation and repression of linguistic foreignness, that this focus is in no way a dismissal of the multiple and highly successful forms of organized resistance and everyday opposition that have been crucial to ending apartheid and conceiving a new South Africa. Indeed it could be demonstrated that many of these forms of resistance, perhaps particularly those theorized and practiced by Biko, were synonymous with what I have been describing as venturing into the zone of error.

Chapter Eight

Encountering Alien Otherness

Michael E. Zimmerman

As if the old struggle to respect all people regardless of differences and the emerging endeavor to esteem all terrestrial life were not enough to occupy human attention, our species may have to cope with the discovery of radically different beings—possibly extraterrestrials (E.T.s) that seem mentally and technologically superior to humans. Ever since Galileo opened the closed medieval cosmos, people have been both fascinated and repelled by the possibility that we are not alone in the universe. Although scientists conclude that no reliable evidence has yet been found that E.T.s exist, many people believe that such evidence *does* exist, in the form of unidentified aircraft sighted by thousands of trustworthy observers since the 1940s.[1] More striking, however, is the astonishing claim made by thousands of contemporary people that they have been abducted by highly intelligent, non-human aliens. In this essay, I examine the extent to which such an encounter would undermine anthropocentric humanism. Moreover, I investigate whether human reactions to truly radical otherness—in the form of non-human alien intelligence—resembles human reactions to the terrestrially foreign, in the sense of people from other countries or lands.

Accounts of alien abductions differ from one another in some respects, but they also reveal important similarities.[2] In a typical abduction, a person is (or persons are) taken from a bedroom, car, boat, or footpath, "floated" into a strange room (sometimes on board a hovering craft that resembles a classic flying saucer), subjected to painful physical examinations, told momentous information (whose details are usually forgotten) or shown scenes of an ecologically devastated planet, informed that they will remember their abduction "when it is time," and, in most cases, returned to the point where the abduction occurred.[3] Though many abductees realize that a period of time is unaccountably missing from memory, they often cannot recall what has happened to them, though about one fourth of abductees claim to have conscious memories of their abductions. Other abductees recover memories through hypnotic regression, the trustworthiness of which is the subject of considerable debate. Abduction is usually not a one-time affair, but begins early in childhood and continues through the reproductive years. A number of abductees report that the aliens remove sperm and egg samples, which are allegedly used to generate "hybrid" babies, half-human, half-alien. Speculation abounds about the possible significance of this bizarre practice, but no one really knows what is taking place.

Sleep disorders, hallucinatory states, fantasy proneness, temporal lobe seizures, and other psychological and/or physiological disorders may shed light on certain aspects of the abduction experience, but no single explanation or group of explanations has yet been able to account for the full range of phenomena associated with it.[4] Abductees who have undergone psychologically evaluative testing usually score within the "normal" range.[5] My own discussions with more than two dozen abductees have revealed nothing unusual about their personalities, though tests indicate that some of them suffer both from posttraumatic stress disorder and from a measure of inexplicable fear—symptoms that might be expected from people who repeatedly experience being abducted by aliens. Having argued elsewhere that the abduction phenomenon does not seem to be explicable as psychopathology, I take seriously the possibility that the phenomenon is a new one, currently unknown to Western science.[6]

According to the exclusionary either/or that prevails in modern Western science, however, the abduction phenomenon must either be psychological in nature, and thus subjective, or physical in nature, and thus objective. Even though conceding that most abductees are sincere in claiming that they had an abduction "experience," skeptics insist that this experience must be intrapsychic, i.e., the alleged aliens have no more independent otherness than do the figures encountered in dreams and hallucinations. In contrast, literalists believe that abductions are the work of real, flesh-and-blood extraterrestrials, whose intentions are either sinister or beneficent, depending in part on the projections of the interpreters.

Still other researchers, however, caution that abductees may be encountering a strange otherness that resists being adequately explained in terms of these mutually exclusive conceptual categories—either mental or physical. Such speculation disturbs defenders of modern rationalism, who fear that both the phenomenon itself and widespread interest in it are signs of an outbreak of irrationalism that threatens the hard-won achievements of science and democratic politics. Some abduction researchers, however, suggest that the phenomenon does not involve irrationalism and psychological-social regression, but instead is a process of psychic integration necessary for the evolution of consciousness. Understanding this process, should it in fact be taking place, would obviously alter prevailing views about the nature and meaning of human existence. What may be needed to understand the abduction phenomenon, then, is an expansion and transformation of current views about rationality, reality, and consciousness.

Driven by complex motivations, including the desire to free inquiry from religious dogmatism and the urge to understand the world in terms of physical sciences that best promote prediction and control of nature, modern "man" has either denied altogether, or explained away as psychopathology, dimensions of consciousness, planes of reality, and spiritual (non-material and non-psychological) beings that have long been taken for granted by the great majority of human cultures.[7] For these reasons, even more disturbing to modern thinking than the two possibilities that the aliens are either flesh-and-blood E.T.s or merely psychological phenomena is the possibility that they come from a different dimension than the space-time realm of modern science.

Obviously, alien abduction is usually not taken seriously in "better" academic neighborhoods. This is so partly because researchers fear being ridiculed for openly investigating the seemingly preposterous allegations that people are being abducted by non-human aliens, and partly because verifiable discovery of highly intelligent non-human beings—whether flesh-and-blood E.T.s or beings from other dimensions—could have a devastating effect on many people, perhaps especially on academics adhering to the view that humankind alone is the source of all meaning, purpose, and value. Academics concerned with the plight of immigrants and the consequences of colonialism, however, have something to learn from examining the psychological consequences that occur when people experience abduction by apparently non-human others, whatever may be the nature or origin of these perceived others. In addition to helping to alleviate the suffering and isolation experienced by so many abductees, academic study of the abduction phenomenon would help to shed light on the universal human fear of, and attraction to, otherness. Finally, research needs to be done on the social, cultural, and political consequences of the widespread public belief that the government knows far more about Unidentified Flying Objects (U.F.O.s), E.T.s, and alien abduction than it is willing to admit. To what extent does official ignorance about the abduction phenomenon fuel the fires of right-wing paranoia about government support of, and intrigue with, "aliens" of all kinds?[8]

Recently, concern about foreign immigrants has grown in Western countries to which people from poorer countries (including former colonies) are flocking to escape political oppression and to find work. For many tourists, encountering otherness—distinctive clothing, different skin color, odd cultural practices, unusual cuisines—is the whole point of traveling. Having those exotic others immigrating to one's own country is another matter altogether, however. Politicians frequently try to unify their supporters by turning foreigners—and even citizens who can be portrayed as sufficiently other—into scapegoats for a country's woes. In the United States, for example, immigrant-bashers play on fears about losing jobs to immigrants, even though job loss is more often due to decisions taken by powerful transnational economic interests. Even people not immediately threatened by outsiders will often join in expelling them (or worse) because people believe that in this manner they will achieve internal social unity, while also vanquishing their own mortality and evil.[9] By dominating the death- and evil-bearing other, the domineering group feels as if it has conquered death and evil. Due to surging human populations, rapid shifts in capital investment, environmental degradation, and greater ease of travel, we can expect that mass migrations—and thus international social tensions—will increase. In view of the unparalleled capability of modern weaponry, humanity may either have to come to terms with otherness, or else risk self-destruction.

Just as people have used differences in skin color, religion, gender, cultural practices, language, ideology, and economics to justify violence against other humans, people have also used differences between humans and other life forms to justify needless violence against plants, animals, and entire ecosystems. The idea of Manifest Destiny proclaimed that a united American people (white, of European descent) was bound to "develop" the continent's natural resources from coast to coast. Worldwide adoption of anthropocentric humanism, according to which nature is merely raw material for value-creating humankind, generates ecological problems that may endanger human survival. In "othering" nature, people have claimed that one trait or another—from tool-using to linguistic ability—demonstrates human superiority over other life, even though a number of naturalists have tried to refute such claims. There are good reasons for arguing that the emergence of humankind constitutes a significant advance in evolutionary history. Unfortunately, efforts to elevate humankind to the top of the cosmic heap have generally come at the expense of other life forms, although dolphins, whales, and non-human primates have received some consideration because of their apparently high intelligence. Even if humans are more fully conscious or intelligent than (most) other animals, this fact does not justify insensitive treatment of so-called "lower" species. The capacity for greater awareness brings with it an obligation to exhibit care and respect for all sentient life. Many religious and democratic traditions have called for an end to dehumanizing attitudes found in racism, sexism, and xenophobic nationalism. Similarly, many environmentalists now urge humankind to acknowledge its kinship with, and dependence on, the rest of terrestrial life. Attempts to dominate both nature and other human beings remain attractive, however, partly because they alleviate anxiety about personal and social mortality and evil. Success in curbing the human urge to dominate hinges on increased psychological and social integration, which leads individuals and groups to face up to their own mortality and proclivity toward evil, instead of projecting them onto others.

The first part of this essay briefly studies how colonial Westerners reacted to their encounter with New World populations and, conversely, how those "non-

Europeans" reacted to their encounter with technologically superior Europeans. We know that non-Europeans often suffered from that encounter, but what is less well known is the extent to which European culture never quite recovered from the culturally decentering blow of contact with native peoples in the New World, even though those people were colonized and often enslaved. Descartes's search for an indubitable foundation for truth was motivated partly by the skepticism that arose after discovery of New World peoples. Arguably, the brutal cultural and ecological practices of Western colonialism reflect Western man's desperate effort to reassure himself about his own cultural centrality. Having treated allegedly inferior human others so ferociously a few centuries ago, how might Westerners expect to be treated if discovered and colonized by technologically superior others?

The second part of this essay investigates the extent to which the phenomenon of alien abduction can shed light on human experience of the foreign, the other, the "alien." Temporarily bracketing the question of the ontological status of these aliens, I focus on the *experience* reported by abductees. Even if such experience is ultimately explicable in terms of complex psychological processes, and thus even if the aliens turn out not to be "objectively" present, much can be learned by examining the experience involved in encountering what at least *seemed* to be radically other. Moreover, study of such experiences may suggest that mainstream views of "reality" need to be expanded. Because the abduction experience is too complex to be studied exhaustively in an essay of this length, I will focus on one particular aspect of it: the experience of being apprehended by the alien gaze.

Western Anthropocentrism and Radical Otherness

In using hyberbolic doubt methodologically to establish an indubitable foundation for certainty, Descartes maintained that the doctrine of solipsism is difficult to refute. For all I know, he argued in his Meditations, the "people" whom I encounter are really complex automata, lacking the self-consciousness that characterizes my own existence. Only the goodness of a non-deceiving and necessarily existing God justifies concluding that there are others who are endowed with rational intelligence similar to my own. Many of Descartes's contemporaries denied the validity of his proofs for the existence of God. Hence, they had to find different ways of overcoming skepticism in general and solipsism in particular, i.e., skepticism about the reality of minds other than one's own. Addressing the problems of skepticism and solipsism led many philosophers into an epistemological thicket, but others dealt with these problems either by arguing that the individual mind cannot be understood apart from the social interaction that gives rise to it, or by simply *assuming* that other people do have minds of one sort or another. Some of the latter doubted, however, whether commoners, women, and

New World natives possessed rational minds, that is to say, minds like those of modern, educated, male Europeans. Contemporary critics charge that those thinkers ratified an ethno-logo-theo-phallo-centrism that justified subordination of non-Western peoples, women, and lower class males, whose subjectivity allegedly lacked the rationality necessary for inclusion in the class of fully human beings.

Here it may be useful to remind ourselves that, in seeking an indubitable basis for certainty, Descartes sought to overcome the skepticism generated by the discovery of New World peoples whose dramatically different cosmological framework, customs, and religious beliefs made them seem other than human: either noble savages or brutal beasts. In affirming the universal rationality of humankind, and thus in putting a particular spin on the Christian doctrine that all people are children of God, Descartes was attempting to do something besides privileging a certain kind of subjectivity. He was trying to restore coherence to a world shattered by contact with the other, even though in so doing he provided Europeans with a category—rationality—that was misused to marginalize non-Europeans and other social groups who were allegedly less than rational and thus not fully human.

Extant firsthand accounts show a variety of native American responses to first encounters with those European others, mounted on horseback, arrayed in metal armor, equipped with advanced technology, and often driven by goals (e.g., lust for gold) that the natives either could not comprehend or regarded with contempt. Many Native Americans, exhibiting a nearly universal human response, regarded the powerful aliens with a mixture of "hope and fear."[10] According to James Axtell, "The Indians regarded the Europeans' ability to fashion incredible objects and make them work less as mechanical aptitude than as spiritual power."[11] Many natives interpreted mass deaths in villages (actually caused by diseases introduced by colonists) as a sign that Europeans had shamanic powers, capable of slaying from a distance without visible weapons. Though such apparently godlike powers led to worldview collapse for some native cultures, others remained convinced of their superiority in comparison with European greed and selfishness.[12]

Since the voyages of Columbus, Westerners have never encountered a technologically more advanced culture. In view of the deleterious consequences that colonization had on New World cultures, some people are concerned about the potential repercussions of human contact with technologically superior aliens. Aware of the frequently deleterious consequences of Western colonization, contemporary science fiction writers often describe the "prime directive" of future interstellar exploration as non-interference in the development of technologically less-developed cultures. Although encountering morally and technically superior aliens might be a boon for humankind, many people are understandably concerned about the religious and political repercussions of such an encounter. Hence, in 1961, federally-funded researchers concluded that NASA should consider concealing from the public any discovery of non-human intelligent life, whether existing or extinct.[13]

In fact, even though New World cultures were obviously profoundly influenced, and often destroyed, by colonial contact, Old World civilization was hardly left unscathed. The discovery of alien cultures on continents that were not even supposed to be there posed an enormous challenge to Occidental self-understanding. Though conquests brought wealth, discovery of native others also caused Western man a narcissistic trauma perhaps even more serious than that brought about by the Copernican revolution, and later by those of Darwin and Freud. Far from being at the center of the universe and thus the main preoccupation of divine providence, European civilization, after contact with New World societies, was confronted with being simply one civilization among many others. Cultural foundations tottered as the attention of Europeans was drawn to maps on which vast new lands were being inked in as fast as explorers could survey them. What critics of modernity describe as the West's hegemonic drive to transform the other into the same, to incorporate difference into self-identity, was a reaction formation and has complex roots. In part, however, it may involve an obsessive attempt to digest what ethnocentric and anthropocentric Westerners could not assimilate: the possibility that Occidental culture is not the culmination of human life, not the goal of Creation, and not the source of all truth, value, and meaning.[14]

Western man is hardly alone in thinking that he and his culture stand at the center of the cosmos. Claude Lévi-Strauss—who helped to fuel anti-colonialism in the postwar West by criticizing the pretension that only the European "mind" is rational—maintains that the vast majority of cultures regard themselves as standing at the center of the cosmos. Combating the skepticism generated by discovery of New World peoples, Descartes maintained that scientific method, exemplified by mathematical physics, was a reliable method for gaining universally valid truths. But the success of scientific method promoted mechanistic materialism, which further undermined the European cosmology already damaged by contact with New World cultures. If New World cosmologies collapsed soon after contact, European cosmology disintegrated in slow motion. The successes of modern science, the capital provided by precious metals stolen from colonized peoples, and the wealth generated by applying industrial manufacturing methods to raw materials extracted from New World colonies, helped to cushion the wounded pride of European man as he left behind the comfortable medieval world and entered a brave new world that was bereft of theological and metaphysical comforts, and that defined man as a clever animal bent on furthering his own power and security.

Many Enlightenment thinkers, showing the influence of the Biblical tradition, emphasized that man was special because he alone was endowed with reason and moral freedom, by virtue of which (so concluded a number of *lumières*) he has the right to dominate the planet to further human progress. Following

Nietzsche, however, who warned of the nihilism resulting from a scientific-utilitarian cosmology, Heidegger (and others) argued that technological man frames the world such that entities can reveal themselves only in terms amenable to his own categories and instrumental goals. Instead of being the object of the gaze of the classical gods or the Biblical creator, modern man elevated himself to the status of all-seeing subject, for whom the world is merely an object to be known and controlled for human ends. Eventually disclosing himself as a complex natural entity, technological man becomes the laborer who is disciplined for, and consumed in, the process of gaining control of the planet, and eventually of the universe.[15] The truculent character of this project suggests that technological man is "acting out" so as to conceal something from himself, namely, that the technological project will not succeed in achieving Western man's goal of immortality.[16]

In this discussion of Western anthropocentrism, I hasten to add that many educated moderns, including Enlightenment philosopher-scientists such as Kant, have been enthralled by the possibility of extraterrestrial intelligence. Progressive thinkers have often believed that discovery of E.T.s would show that the cosmos is, in fact, everywhere evolving toward greater complexity, differentiation, and freedom. Darwinists such as Jacques Monod and Stephen Jay Gould are far more skeptical about the existence of E.T.s, however, because evolutionary processes are allegedly so subject to random events that life would probably never again emerge even on Earth, should life be extinguished here, much less on other planets. By devising a cosmology in which human life is a weird accident, modern science has not only discouraged belief in God and cosmic purpose, but has also encouraged people to conceive of human life primarily in terms of survival, for which the acquisition of power over others is essential. Contrary to such Darwinism, however, postmodern cosmologists maintain that the basic structures of the universe tend to promote the progressive emergence of ever more complex systems, including intelligent life. Physicist Paul Davies opines that:

> The most important upshot of the discovery of extraterrestrial life would be to restore to human beings something of the dignity of which science has robbed them. Far from exposing homo sapiens as an inferior creature in the vast cosmos, the certain existence of alien beings would give us cause to believe that we, in our humble way, are part of a larger, majestic process of cosmic self-knowledge.[17]

Despite significant modern interest in E.T.s, and despite the fact that a progressive postmodern cosmology is beginning to come into its own, Western institutions, ideologies, and philosophies—including, despite its vaunted "anti-humanism," much of contemporary continental philosophy—remain anthropocentric. Elements of anthropocentrism (or at least terracentrism) are discernible not only in the work of outspoken humanists like Sartre, but also in the writings of Heidegger, Levinas, Derrida, and Foucault. Most continental philosophers have agreed (though often in highly qualified and indirect ways) that humans are the most intelligent (linguistically endowed, ontologically open, guilty, creative/productive, or self-conscious) of all beings.

Early Heidegger, for example, radically distinguished between human *Dasein* and other entities. Lacking human language, he maintained, animals cannot constitute a "world" in which entities can be encountered as entities. Describing solipsism as a psuedo-problem, he insisted that human *Dasein* is always already "with" others in a world of shared concern. Even in later years, as he sought to overcome a residual anthropocentrism, Heidegger insisted that an abyss lies between animals and humans, who alone are appropriately capable of "dwelling on the earth."[18] Hence, he ignored the possibility that other beings—including dolphins and whales, not to mention E.T.s—may be endowed with ontologically disclosive capacities analogous, and possibly even superior, to our own. Opposed to space exploration, he was horrified by photos taken of the hidden side of the moon by a space probe.[19]

Until recently, the status of non-human others was only infrequently addressed by continental philosophers, including those, such as Levinas and Derrida, who have explored in much greater depth than did Heidegger the moral claims that the other makes upon me, the sociolinguistic constitution of self and other, and how the binary of majority ("self") vs. minority ("other") is used to justify oppression. In his ethics of heteronomy, Levinas argues that the look of the other makes upon me a moral claim, obligating me to intervene on behalf of the weak and oppressed. Though such attempts to emphasize the other are laudable, they have assumed that *only human beings constitute the class of the "other."*[20]

This assumption has legitimated harsh and even contemptuous treatment of living nature. Recently, however, some continental philosophers have begun questioning the anthropocentric assumptions which deny that animals can be "other" to humankind and which thereby routinely exclude animals from the moral landscape. In *Daimon Life*, for example, David Krell challenges Heidegger's suggestive, but tendentious analysis of the being of animals.[21] Further, Derrida has begun speaking critically of the Jewish-Greek-Christian "carnophallogocentrism," a "sacrificial economy" that involves human-centered, meat-eating acts of slaughter.[22] Commenting on Derrida, John D. Caputo notes that Heidegger and Levinas, despite their great differences, share "a common devalorizing of the animal." Attempts sharply to discriminate between humans and animals ultimately fail, Caputo asserts: "Killing tends to generalize itself. Killing (other) animals bleeds into killing other people. The dominant scheme is a generalized anthropophagic, man-eating violence."[23]

Though challenging one assumption of anthropocentrism, namely, that humans are "above" animals, Caputo is not ready to challenge another assumption, namely, that there are no entities "above" humankind. Echoing the despair associated with Western nihilism, reinforced a century ago by the conclusion that our entropic universe will eventually suffer "heat death," Caputo maintains that Kant's "starry sky" fills him not with awe, but instead reminds him that the cosmos—"so much will to power . . . a veritable monster of energy, decreasing here, increasing there, blessing itself in its sheer innocence"—is indifferent to "our fragile mortal fates."[24] Caputo writes that "no one we know of knows we are here, on the little star. We are like orphans—and widows and strangers. The stars do not care, do not take care of us. We are disasters all."[25] Lost in a monstrous, dying universe from which the gods have fled, we frail humans feel ourselves to be suffering "others," but there is no one—no higher "self"—to affirm our humanity and to intercede on our behalf. Though emphasizing human weakness, Caputo seems to think that human intelligence—even if less grandiose than that customarily envisioned by anthropocentric humanists—still leaves us alone at the top of the dying, meaningless cosmic heap.

In echoing in certain (but by no means all) respects Nietzsche's fatalism and *fin-de-siècle* despondency, Caputo ignores the postmodern cosmology that, as we discussed earlier, maintains that the universe exhibits a nisus toward ever greater complexity, differentiation, and consciousness.[26] That the universe may be evolving so as to become self-conscious suggests that there is *meaning* in cosmic history.[27] Far from being a sheer accident, human life may be only one of many instances of self-conscious life that has evolved in the universe, the number of whose galaxies has been increased tenfold according to photos recently taken by the Hubble Telescope. Quite probably, then, we are *not* alone.[28] But would "they" be so dramatically different that communication would be virtually impossible?

If Heidegger was right that meaningful encounters, including those involving foreigners, can occur only because humans exist in "worlds" articulated by language and shared practices, the question becomes: will "being-in-the-world" be a feature of E.T.s? Since E.T.s might possess vastly superior technology, questions about their mode of being would have to be posed from a perspective different from that adopted by colonizers inquiring into the mental and moral capacities of New World others. Most people seem to presuppose that humans could understand alien intentions. Science fiction typically portrays those intentions in terms that are consistent with the projections governing initial human encounters with foreigners: the aliens are either threatening or helpful, evil or good. Some people are simply indifferent to the prospect of contact with nonhuman intelligence because they consider such contact so unlikely. Most people, however, are either horrified at, or excited by, that prospect.

On the one hand, fear of being colonized by (indisputably other) aliens leads some people to be anxious about running into someone "out there," or about letting them know that we are "here." On the other hand, hope that technologically superior aliens would also be morally advanced leads other people eagerly to anticipate contact. In the event of a verifiable manifestation of alien presence, such powerful projections (sinister invaders vs. benevolent space brothers) would prevent most people from being able to perceive the aliens competently, much less to discern their intentions (assuming that "intentions" could be ascribed to such non-human intelligence).

The binary projections of "evil alien" and "good alien" may influence the perception both of abductees and of researchers persuaded that the abduction phenomenon involves an encounter with alien otherness. Often emphasizing the remarkable power of the alien gaze, some abductees claim that it terrifies and depersonalizes them; others maintain, however, that by stripping them of egoic subjectivity, the alien gaze challenges abductees to achieve a higher level of consciousness. Based on typical responses to encounters with sufficiently different human others, it is not surprising that some people view the aliens as pernicious invaders, others view them as benign beings trying to assist humankind. If films like *Close Encounters*, *E.T.*, and *Star Man* portrayed aliens as beneficent superior beings, more recent films such as *The Arrival* and *Independence Day* depict aliens as intent upon destroying humankind. That so many accounts of the alien gaze fall into one or the other of these projective categories suggests that great caution must be exercised in evaluating the truth value of such interpretations.

Nevertheless, because the experiences reported by abductees are so robust, I believe that it is reasonable to maintain that abductees are encountering some kind of otherness, even if such encounters are at least partially shaped by projections. Regardless of the ontological status of alien otherness, abduction narratives reveal how contemporary people react to what they themselves experience as radical alterity. In future centuries, today's abduction narratives may be regarded as first-person accounts of humanity's initial reaction to contact with others whose appearance is stranger, whose technology is more advanced, and whose intentions may be more incomprehensible to contemporary humans than were the *conquistadores* to Native Americans five centuries ago.

In the next part of this essay, I examine the alien gaze, first in terms of Sartre's dismal view that the "look of the other" deprives a person of her subjectivity and freedom. Then, I explore the possibility that the alien gaze constitutes a challenge and opportunity to move beyond the limits of ordinary egoic consciousness. Finally, I examine the kinds of questions that the abduction experience raises with regard to the human encounter with the Other.

Encountering the Alien Gaze

The Objectifying Gaze

Abductees report encountering several different kinds of aliens, especially gray-colored ones, short and tall, who can evoke abject terror. So bizarre are the aliens and so advanced are their technological capacities that some abductees report experiencing an almost complete worldview collapse—whether that worldview be secular humanism or some traditional religion—as well as a crushing blow to the personal identity connected with, and dependent on, that worldview. Many abductees report that the aliens treat them indifferently and with cold efficiency, as if abductees were little more than laboratory animals. Apparently, being paralyzed, floated through walls into a non-human aircraft, and physically probed by strange life forms is frightening enough, but an extraordinary terror often arises when abductees are forced to look into the large, almond-shaped, intensely black, and seemingly impenetrable eyes of the aliens. The overpowering alien gaze often leaves one feeling drained of personhood and agency.

In *Being and Nothingness*, Sartre offered a devastating account of the dehumanizing, objectifying "look of the other" (*le regard de l'autrui*). Influenced at least as much by Cartesian solipsism as by Hegel's social ontology, Sartre wrote that human interaction involves a constant struggle for supremacy. This struggle culminates not in mutual self-recognition, as Hegel argued, but rather in a binary opposition: one of the contesting parties becomes a free subject, while the other is reduced to an object held captive in the gaze of the victorious other. As a subject, I experience freedom to initiate activity within the world. But as objectified and frozen in the gaze of the other, e.g., when I hear footsteps in the hallway as I am peering through a keyhole, I lose that freedom. If I am sitting in a park alone, Sartre added, I feel myself to be a free subject, the central figure in terms of which the whole world takes on significance. When someone else comes on the scene and sees me, however, his subjectivity becomes an abyss toward which my freedom and subjectivity begin to drain away. Hence, for Sartre, a reciprocating subjectivity would seem impossible.

Analogously, so it would seem, the alien gaze sometimes deprives people of their subjectivity, so that no reciprocal social recognition is possible between human and alien. Readers unwilling to accept the possibility that aliens involve genuine "otherness" of one kind or another may hypothesize that abductions are very intense nightmares that reflect a person's feeling of powerlessness in social relationships. Feminists, African Americans, and formerly colonized people, for example, have asserted that the arrogant gaze of the powerful other can objectify individuals, thus depriving them of personhood. By studying abduction "nightmares," then, we may learn something about human responses to particularly powerful experiences of the objectifying gaze. Of course, even if thousands of people were having nothing more than remarkably similar, vivid, life-changing, persistently occurring nightmares about being abducted by aliens, this fact alone merits serious investigation.

The "nightmares-reflecting-everyday-powerlessness" hypothesis, however, must take into account the fact that minority groups are not disproportionately represented in abductions, that about half of abductees are men, and that many abductees have relatively high social status. The reader might reply that virtually everyone in contemporary society feels powerless in the face of three threats: nuclear war, ecological devastation, and economic decline. For decades, the United States was threatened with nuclear annihilation by "the evil empire," the former U.S.S.R. Moreover, ever since the 1960s, many people have become increasingly concerned that industrialization and human population growth will irreparably damage the biosphere on which all life depends. Finally, foreign competition has diminished the United States's former economic superiority, thereby undermining the confidence of those postwar Americans who set out to recolonize the planet in terms of "American values." Could these factors explain why so many people are having "nightmares" in which they are being oppressed and colonized by technologically superior aliens? Are these "dreams" a "return of the repressed," in which Americans experience the powerlessness once felt by Native Americans at the hands of invading Europeans? Is it, further, a widespread sense of personal helplessness that leads many abductees to generate a compensatory fantasy, in which they are singled out to give birth to a new cosmic race? Or does this alleged fantasy play within the dream itself the compensatory role of ameliorating the horror involved in the abduction? Answers to these questions are worth pursuing, though doing so would require careful interviewing of abductees, rather than simply drawing conclusions based on a cursory examination of published narratives.

Another objection to the nightmare hypothesis is that the abduction experience is sometimes said to be more "real" than anything abductees have ever experienced, whether in dreams or in waking life. Further, the alien gaze is reported to be devastatingly powerful, apparently far more so than any imaginable human gaze. Hence, the alien gaze does not seem to be a nightmare appearance of the "big Other," representing what Lacan calls the "law of the father." After all, the big Other demands that an individual remain a subject, however unsatisfying and alienating such a condition may be, by conforming to the norms of the symbolic order. Abductees often report, however, that they are deprived of human subjectivity when looking into the huge, slanted, almond-shaped, and intensely black eyes of the "grays."

Interviewed by Temple University professor David Jacobs, abductee Lydia Goldman describes being spellbound by alien eyes:

GOLDMAN: I'm looking into those eyes. I can't believe that I'm looking into eyes that big. . . . Once you look into those eyes, you're gone. You're just gone. JACOBS: How do you mean that? GOLDMAN: I can't think of anything but those eyes. It's like the eyes overwhelm me. How do they do that? It goes inside you, their eyes go inside you. You just are held. You can't stop looking. If you wanted to, you couldn't look away. You are drawn into them, and they sort of come into you. JACOBS: Are your eyes open or closed? GOLDMAN: My eyes are open, but my mind is sort of gone. I have no will. I have no will. I am absorbed and I'm not fighting it.[29]

The fact that many abductees report being dehumanized by the alien gaze suggests some parallels with Sartre's account of the look of the human other. After all, the aliens usually exhibit a humanoid appearance, with heads, eyes, torsos, bodies, and legs.[30] But the benumbing alien gaze is often followed by an appalling procedure called "mindscanning" that has no analogue in Sartre's paranoid study of the human gaze. According to Jacobs,

> This "mindscan" procedure involves a taller [alien] being staring deeply and penetratingly into the abductee's eyes from a distance of roughly six inches to actually touching foreheads. During this agonizing procedure, the abductee cannot close his eyes, nor can he look away.[31]

While undergoing mindscanning, "abductees commonly feel that data of some sort is being extracted from their minds."[32] According to Jacobs,

> One person said that he had the feeling that his mind was being played back like a video tape recorder. Often abductees will say that specific emotions can be elicited during the Mindscan. The aliens can bring out profound feelings of fear, terror, anger, rage, shame, guilt, and the like.[33]

If the alien gaze can call forth profoundly disturbing negative emotions, it can also alleviate terror, assuage sharp physical pain, and even generate powerful feelings of love. Indeed, some abductees claim that they have never felt so completely loved and understood as they did when being gazed upon by the aliens. Does the experience of such deep love correspond to genuinely loving intentions on the part of the aliens? Or are abductees so depersonalized by the gaze that they regress to infantile status, in which they ultimately experience the gaze as the all-encompassing, loving look of their mothers? That abductees can quickly shift from fearing and hating their abductors to loving and feeling cared for by them suggests that abductees may project onto their captors the same ambivalent feelings that natives project onto unexpected and very strange foreigners—on the one hand, suspicion, fear, hostility; on the other hand, trust, curiosity, and love.

The situation is made more complex by the fact that "the aliens will also generate sexual feelings."[34] Before concluding that such feelings are consistent with an infant's erotic attraction to his or her mother, we should note that abductees often report that their "involuntarily increasing sexual feelings can be embarrassing, and when they lead to orgasm, they can be humiliating and enraging."[35] Replying to the claim that sexually-oriented abductions are nothing but apparitions generated by fantasy-prone masochists seeking to surrender their selfhood, clinical psychologist Caroline McLeod argues that the emotional intensity of abduction experiences far outstrips that involved in masochistic experiences; moreover, abductees rarely say that they obtain any of the sexual satisfaction that a masochist receives in the process of being humiliated or dominated in connection with masochist sexual activity.[36]

Although fear is a significant component in some abduction experiences, many abductees report a minimal amount of it, while still others say that by staying with, and passing through, the fear, they undergo a psychological expansion that makes possible a developing relationship with the aliens. As we shall see in the next section, such accounts lead some investigators to read the abduction phenomenon in positive terms, as an opportunity for humankind to move beyond the ancient fear of otherness that generates persecution, war, and genocide. Of course, researchers with a dark reading of alien intentions, such as Budd Hopkins, David Jacobs, Karla Turner, and others, regard such beneficial psychological developments as an unintended byproduct of interacting with beings who intend nothing good for humankind.[37] The disparity between these two views suggests that in dealing with the radically other, researchers may be casting projections (the "evil invaders" vs. "benevolent brothers" binary noted above) that are misleading enough when projected onto human others.

The Challenging Alien Gaze

So far we have examined three kinds of alien gazes: (1) the cold, efficient, but relatively indifferent gaze of a researcher studying a laboratory animal; (2) the malevolent gaze of an enormously powerful other seeking to dominate and enslave; (3) the loving gaze of a benevolent being. The first and second gazes have certain similarities with Sartre's account of the objectifying look of the other, though the alien gaze is reportedly far more powerful than any human gaze. The third kind of gaze, however, the loving gaze, has no Sartrian parallel. Among other things, this gaze may either be a projection by abductees who have regressed to an infantile state, or a ruse designed to mislead the abductee about the alien's dark intentions, or a manifestation of genuine benevolence by the alien other. According to researchers with a positive view of the abduction phenomenon, the loving gaze suggests that aliens are deeply concerned about the fate of humanity. Hence, even though human encounters with aliens often evoke terror, such terror might constitute a challenge which, if successfully met, may enable humankind to develop the higher form of awareness needed to alleviate social strife and ecological destruction.

Researchers such as John Mack, Kenneth Ring, and Whitley Strieber, who focus on the potentially positive aspects of the alien gaze, maintain that a skewed sample population leads Jacobs and Hopkins to overemphasize the unpleasant aspects of the abduction experience. In other words, Jacobs and Hopkins attract abductees who have been particularly terrified by their experience. Strieber, author of best-selling books about his own abduction experiences, reports receiving tens of thousands of letters from abductees, the great majority of whom report a positive account of, and attitude toward, their experience.[38] Of course, Jacobs and Hopkins retort that Strieber, Mack, and Ring not only attract abductees with a positive outlook, but also encourage them to interpret their experience in terms consistent with the idea that the aliens are a positive force encouraging human spiritual evolution.[39]

But Strieber, Mack, and Ring insist that their optimistic reading is more consistent with what abductees actually say. Although positive projections may influence that reading, it does have the advantage of exhibiting a nuanced stance toward the ontological status of the "aliens." Regarding them neither as flesh-and-blood E.T.s literally inventing a hybrid race, nor as complex mass hallucinations, Strieber, Mack, and Ring search for vocabulary adequate to describe not only the "high strangeness" of the encounter with alien otherness, but also the personal and spiritual growth that, at least sometimes, accompanies such encounters. For many abductees, as Mack has explained on several occasions, being apprehended in the gaze of apparent non-human otherness generates "ontological shock" on the part of abductees, who have a very difficult time integrating this finding into their conventional Western ideas about the limits of "reality." Mack maintains that, while it is appropriate to alleviate the trauma suffered by some abductees, researchers must also recognize that psychological and spiritual development often follows for abductees who can move beyond their original shock and terror. The abduction experience may be akin to a shamanistic initiation procedure that leads not only to a higher, more integrated, less ego-constricted mode of awareness, but also to a vastly expanded conception of reality. Such an initiation is particularly terrifying, insofar as it dismantles both the worldview and the ego-structure with which people identify so closely.[40]

The alien gaze, revealing the finitude of the ego-structure, may also trigger powerful emotions in which the ego has an investment (whether in clinging to, or fleeing from, those emotions). Spiritual traditions such as Buddhism encourage meditative practices in which one is forced to confront the insubstantiality of the ego-structure, while experiencing fully, but dis-identifying with, the ever-changing emotions associated with that structure. The spiritual aspirant must experience his or her darkest fear and deepest shame, as well as his or her most alluring fantasies and desires. By undergoing such disillusioning experiences, portrayed symbolically in spiritual traditions as the fierce "guardians" blocking the gateway to higher consciousness, the aspirant may be freed from the ignorance that leads to suffering.

Strieber has described his own changing attitudes toward abduction experiences. Originally, his fear during an abduction experience was so great that he considered calling his first abduction book *Body Terror*, but changed the title to *Communion* in order to emphasize the potentially transformative dimension of his encounters with non-human intelligence. In a more recent book, *The Secret School*, he emphasizes the inadequacy of viewing the alien others as either evil or benevolent:

> We tell ourselves that the visitors are evil and to be hated, that we are justified in not trying to understand. Conversely, we call them saviors, which is equally an illusion. In any event, we tell ourselves that we know what they are; we make them concrete as aliens and even give them names. About all we really know is that something very different from us—or that wishes to appear that way—is hiding in the shadows of the night and the depths of the mind.[41]

Strieber recognizes the moral issues involved in the fact that the "visitors" take him against his will. Once, he told his captors that they had no right to take him. Much to his astonishment, a low voice replied: "We do have a right."[42] Seeking to understand this reply a decade later, Strieber notes that even though compulsion is incompatible with the ideal of autonomy, people do use compulsion appropriately in some situations, e.g., in dealing with children, with people judged to be dangerous to themselves or society, and with patients who (perhaps because of impairment connected with their illness or injury) resist treatment necessary to save their lives.[43] Strieber speculates that rough treatment by the aliens is partly an effort to awaken people from "soul blindness," which "is a disease incalculably worse than cancer, and [of which] we are all, to some degree, victims."[44] He concludes:

> So maybe the violence and the coercion are really an attempt to get us to notice something that we want very badly not to see. If this is true, the ferocity may be a kind of demand for a response. They could be so far outside our expectations—so unreal, as it were—that only the most intense effort on their part will enable us even to become aware of their presence. They may be in the bizarre position of literally swarming through our world—and yet being unable to get us to notice them.[45]

Regarding Strieber's approach, two comments are in order. First, some people object strongly to his conclusion that abduction, rape, and humiliation constitute "tough love" aimed at provoking growth in transpersonal awareness, psychic ability, and a sense of "cosmic purpose" in hard-hearted, benighted humans. Psychological or spiritual developments may simply be unintended byproducts of practices, such as abduction and rape, that ought not to be portrayed as acceptable means, however good the alleged end might be.

Second, given the superior power of the aliens, we cannot interpret what Strieber calls their "demand for a response" as analogous to Hegel's famous account of the challenge involved in the life and death struggle for recognition. The preindividuated humans involved in that struggle were roughly equal in strength, but this is evidently not the case with aliens and humans. Indeed, in view of the sometimes cold, physically painful, or humiliating treatment that (some) abductees reportedly receive, the alien-human encounter may more readily call to mind Hegel's account of the master-slave relationship. In that relationship, however, the master demands work, not recognition, from the slave. Eventually, the slave displaces the master, who has become dependent on the slave's productive activity. In view of the remarkable powers exhibited by the alleged aliens, however, some researchers maintain that the outcome of the alien-human relationship would not be the same as the outcome of the master-slave relation. That is, humanity would not eventually displace the aliens, but would be permanently subjugated to them.

Although taking such considerations into account, researchers like Mack contend that the aliens seem to demand something besides compliance, namely, a psychological and spiritual awakening necessary for humankind to enter into a more equal relationship with the aliens.[46] Abductees report that the aliens themselves seem to need things that humans possess, namely, vitality, personality, and emotional range. Perhaps the "breeding" program is to be read not literally, but symbolically, as a process of mutual exchange, in the course of which humans will achieve higher consciousness, while aliens will receive greater emotional range and personality. It would seem, however, that the aliens are the agents of change in this relationship. Perhaps they are prodding humankind to grow psychologically and spiritually in ways needed for mutual and reciprocal exchange to take place, assuming of course that the aliens, however they are to be understood, have such exchange in mind.

Many of Mack's clients see a connection between their awakening concern about terrestrial environmental problems, on the one hand, and the personal and spiritual growth that the abduction experience seems to promote, on the other. Some abductees have developed a complex cosmology that portrays the universe as an interrelated whole with many different levels of "reality" in addition to the material and psychological planes, which are the only ones recognized by modernists and most postmodernists. The evolutionary interpretation of abduction would be met with suspicion not only by abduction researchers with a dimmer view of the abduction phenomenon, but also by postmodernists who deny that humankind has any *telos*. Convinced that one can do no more than tweak at the boundaries of the repressive regimes of modernity, many postmodernists lack both a cosmology and a conception of human potential capable of envisioning non-human others whose gaze might prompt a transformation of human self-understanding.

The human yearning for transcendence motivates the love for wandering mentioned at the start of this essay. Robert M. Torrance describes humankind as "the questing animal" striving to transcend its given circumstances. Behind the tribal "vision quest" lies the same creative impulse that leads the spiritual aspirant to meditate, the artist to explore new possibilities of expression, and the scientist to understand the workings of empirical phenomena. Commenting on William James's remark that all religions "suggest a possible salvation through 'making proper connection with the higher powers,'" Torrance asserts:

> The "objective" truth of religious experience thus lies not in a changeless entity outside or beyond the human but in the continuity or interrelation between the individual and a kindred other—call it futurity, potentiality, or spirit—through which the individual self is expanded; this very transcendence is the object of a spiritual quest continually engendered by uneasiness or dissatisfaction with the given.[47]

Genuine transcendence requires the death of one's current identity, personal and cultural. The abduction phenomenon occurs in connection with widespread dissatisfaction with anthropocentric modernity, which forces everything to show up in terms of human categories, i.e., as either material or psychological phenomena within an apparently meaningless universe.[48] Unwilling to live in this spiritual desert, countless people are reporting encounters with extraordinary realms and entities long regarded as the products of primitive imagination. Instead of concluding that near-death experiences, past-life regressions, encounters with angels, and alien abductions are instances of escapism, delusional thinking, irrationality, or psychosis, we might entertain the possibility—as did William James—that these phenomena reveal dimensions of reality that are hidden to ordinary consciousness and that invite spiritual and personal development on the part of those who encounter them.

According to unapologetic modernists like the late Carl Sagan, however, by suggesting that abduction reports reveal aspects of reality not acknowledged by natural science, researchers are contributing to a dangerous eruption of irrationalism that may seem relatively impotent if viewed merely as an aspect of New Age frivolity, but that takes on a far more ominous cast if regarded as a contemporary reprise of the irrationalism and cultism that, for example, helped to give rise to National Socialism in Germany. Of course, one should be concerned about the social and political consequences of a wholesale renunciation of rational inquiry in favor of rank superstition. Most abduction researchers, however, are not irrationalists; indeed, they call on scientists to expand their horizons in order to make room for studying anomalous phenomena being reported by reliable observers. For those whose very identity depends on the vision of man as conqueror of nature, however, paranormal phenomena are threatening because they suggest that there are realms not charted and controlled by discursive intelligence. A modernist may be willing to speculate about the possibility of intelligent extraterrestrial life somewhere in this enormous cosmos, but he or she may reject the possibility that non-human intelligence may be interacting with human beings. Hence, Sagan's *a priori* assumption that alien abductions are explicable in terms either of human imagination or of psychopathology, even though he did not undertake any empirical research into the phenomenon.[49]

Of course, cultural and psychological categories should be brought into play when analyzing the abduction phenomenon, for novel experiences are usually described in terms of categories available to the experiencer. Hence, Carl Jung attributed the Cold War flying saucer craze in part to the psychological need for humans to project into the heavens the healing mandala symbol—the saucer-shaped U.F.O.—that promised to integrate a fractured world. Jung wrote that flying saucers could not be adequately interpreted as a psychological projection, since such projections cannot be photographed and tracked on radar at 6,000 miles per hour. "Something is seen," Jung wrote, "but we know not what it is." Analogously, abductees seem to encounter something, though we don't know what it is.[50]

Jung's concept of "synchronicity" (an acausal process involving meaningful coincidence) enables us to acknowledge that the behavior of alien abductors is morally reprehensible, while also agreeing that abductions may contribute to psychological and spiritual advancement for humankind. Even if we suppose that the aliens have no regard for human advancement, there may be something more than accidental about their arrival at this particular moment, in which humanity is arguably in such dire need of transformation.[51] The alien-human encounter may have arisen through cosmic processes or patterns that are not discernible in terms of the history, causal trajectory, or self-understanding of either aliens or humanity. Nevertheless, through this unanticipated human encounter with a powerful and possibly evil alien adversary, humankind may rise to a new level of consciousness.

Hence, Michael Grosso argues that whatever the aliens may be, they are playing some role in the attempt by "mind at large" to correct today's dangerous cultural imbalance.[52] Terence McKenna maintains that the alien presence should be understood in terms of "the human oversoul," an enormously intelligent "organism" that regulates "human culture through the release of ideas out of eternity and into the continuum of history."[53] Finally, Carl Raschke asserts that aliens and U.F.O.s may be remolding "not just peripheral religious or metaphysical ideas, but entire constellations of culture and social knowledge. In this connection, U.F.O.s can be depicted as what I would call ultraterrestrial agents of cultural deconstruction."[54]

Conclusion

In concluding, it may be useful briefly to compare and to evaluate such speculation about the possibly positive effects of such cultural deconstruction with the historical effects of the deconstruction of Native American cultures by European *conquistadores*. There is no point in adopting a romantic view of pre-contact American cultures, including the Aztec and Inca empires, the cruelty of which was not necessarily bested by that of the European empire-builders.[55] Indeed, Cortéz was able to recruit many native Americans to help him overthrow the oppressive Aztecs. Another reason for Cortéz's astonishing victory over the Aztecs, however, was the fact that an ancient prophecy had predicted the return of a bearded, white-skinned man who would transform society. His men's horses and firearms confirmed his status as an extraordinary other to be greeted less with fear than with awe, and perhaps with hope for a brighter future. The experience of suspicion and wonder, fear and hope, were played out countless times throughout North and South America during the centuries of contact and conquest. Many hundreds of tribal cultures were destroyed in the process, partly as the result of the introduction of new diseases against which native populations had no immunity, partly as a the result of the imposition of new social and economic practices, and partly as the result of the "ontological shock" associated with having their own worldviews dramatically challenged by the arrival of others who possessed not only a new cosmology, but also the weapons to enforce acceptance of it.

In the best-case scenario, surviving members of native cultures adapted to their new circumstances and ultimately benefited—along with everyone else— from technological advances, economic development, and political democratization. In such circumstances, nostalgia for the "old ways" is tempered by recognition that the new ways have a lot going for them, including longer life spans and modes of self-consciousness that were probably not widely available in tribal situations. On the other hand, losing the languages, cultural practices, beliefs, and natural settings of so many hundreds of tribal cultures is something to be mourned, even if some "good" came out of such grievous losses. Moreover, for millions of Native Americans, the best-case scenario mentioned above has not come to pass. As second-class citizens in the countries established by European colonizers, their self-consciousness can scarcely be said to have been improved by the deconstruction of the cultures of their ancestors.

Assuming for a moment that contact is now occurring between aliens and some humans, we would do well to ask whether its consequences would parallel those that characterized contact between Europeans and Native Americans. Would some humans ultimately benefit from a kind of transformation or evolution of consciousness, and would others experience personal disorientation and cultural destruction? What can we learn from the experience of Native Americans who most successfully negotiated the terms of their new status in, and relationship to, the alien cultures imposed upon them? What can we learn from spiritual seekers who have undergone egoic-deconstruction when encountering non-human powers, but who reportedly gained a more encompassing mode of awareness in the process? In view of the stakes involved in the possibility of an alien-human encounter, such questions, and many others, need to be addressed by everyone concerned about the fate of humankind. Even if the present wave of "alien abductions" proves to be explicable in terms of previously unknown psychological mechanisms, alien-human encounter of some kind seems increasingly likely as more and more scientists conclude that the universe is hospitable to the evolution of life, including intelligent life. Even if the "aliens" ultimately arrive not from another dimension or the soul-plane, but from another planet, humankind must begin now to prepare itself for this encounter with a most extraordinary kind of otherness.

Notes

1. For an analysis of the postwar U.F.O. controversy by a well-known astronomer and historian, see Steven J. Dick, *The Biological Universe: The Twentieth-Century Extraterrestrial Debate and the Limits of Science* (New York: Cambridge University Press, 1996).

2. "Literalist" researchers, who minimize differences in abduction narratives, may conceal the extent to which psychological and cultural factors are not incidental, but central, aspects of abduction phenomena.

3. Sometimes abductees are returned to the wrong spot, however, or at least find themselves inexplicably far from their homes.

4. An excellent review of these accounts is to be found in David Jacobs, *Secret Life: Firsthand Accounts of UFO Abductions* (New York: Simon and Schuster, 1992). *Psychological Inquiry* 7, no. 2 (1996) devotes its entire issue to the abduction phenomenon.

5. Most recently, see the essay by research psychologist Caroline McLeod, "Anomalous Experience, Psychopathology of Socially Constructed Reality: The Example of Alien Abduction" (forthcoming). Based on a comparison of forty reported abduction experiences with a control group of forty individuals recruited from the general community, this study indicates that "more complex mechanisms" than psychopathology and fantasy proneness are needed to understand the alien abduction phenomenon.

6. See Michael E. Zimmerman, "Forbidden Knowledge of Hidden Events: The Strange Phenomenon of Alien Abduction," *Philosophy Today* 41, no. 2 (Summer 1997): 235-254. In *Abduction*, Harvard Psychiatrist John E. Mack argues that alien abduction cannot be diagnosed in terms of our current knowledge of psychopathology. John E. Mack, *Abduction*, rev. ed. (New York: Ballantine, 1995). See also Mack's latest book, *Passport to the Cosmos: Human Transformations and Alien Encounters* (New York: Crown Publishers, 1999). For other insightful approaches to this phenomenon, see Michael Craft, *Alien Impact: A Comprehensive Look at the Evidence of Human/Alien Con-*

tact (New York: St. Martin's Press, 1996) and Patrick Harpur, *Daimonic Reality: Understanding Otherworldly Encounters* (New York: Arkana, 1994).

7. Whenever I use the term "man," I do so advisedly, in order to stress patriarchal dimensions of Western culture.

8. See Jodi Dean, *Aliens in America: Conspiracy Cultures from Outerspace to Cyberspace* (Ithaca, N.Y.: Cornell University Press, 1998).

9. See Ken Wilber, *Up from Eden: A Transpersonal View of Human Evolution* (Boston: Shambhala, 1981), and René Girard, *Things Hidden since the Foundation of the World*, trans. Stephen Bann and Michael Metteer (Stanford, Calif.: Stanford University Press, 1978).

10. James Axtell, *After Columbus: Essays in the Ethnohistory of Colonial North America* (New York: Oxford University Press, 1988), 131. See especially chap. 8, "Through Another Glass Darkly: Early Indian Views of Europeans."

11. Axtell, *After Columbus*, 131.

12. Axtell, *After Columbus*, 135.

13. The relevant portions of this report, "Proposed Studies of the Implications of Peaceful Space Activities for Human Affairs," are cited in Stanley J. McDaniel, *The McDaniel Report* (Berkeley, Calif.: North Atlantic Books, 1993), 160.

14. On this topic, see Jean-François Lyotard, *Heidegger and the Jews*, trans. Andreas Michel and Mark S. Roberts (Minneapolis: University of Minnesota Press, 1990).

15. See Michael E. Zimmerman, *Heidegger's Confrontation with Modernity* (Bloomington: Indiana University Press, 1990).

16. See Michael E. Zimmerman, "Ontical Craving vs. Ontological Desire," *From Phenomenology to Thought, Errancy, and Desire*, ed. Babette Babich (Dordrecht: Klewer, 1995), 503-525.

17. Paul Davies, *Are We Alone?* (New York: Basic Books, 1995), 129.

18. Martin Heidegger, "Letter on Humanism," *Basic Writings*, ed. David Farrell Krell (New York: Harper & Row, 1978).

19. Martin Heidegger, "Only a God Can Save Us: *Der Spiegel*'s Interview with Martin Heidegger," trans. Maria P. Alter and John D. Caputo, *Philosophy Today* 20 (Winter 1976): 267-284.

20. Unfortunately, Levinas has said that only a member of one's own people can be considered an other who has a claim on me. In this way, he excluded Palestinians from inclusion in the class of morally significant beings. See *The Levinas Reader*, ed. Sean Hand (Cambridge, Mass.: Basil Blackwell, 1989), 294-295.

21. David Farrell Krell, *Daimon Life* (Bloomington: Indiana University Press, 1992).

22. Jacques Derrida, "'Eating Well,' Or the Calculation of the Subject: An Interview with Jacques Derrida," in *Who Comes after the Subject?*, ed. Eduardo Cadava, Peter Conner, and Jean-Luc Nancy (New York: Routledge, 1991).

23. John D. Caputo, *Against Ethics* (Bloomington: Indiana University Press, 1994), 198.

24. Caputo, *Against Ethics*, 17.

25. Caputo, *Against Ethics*, 225.

26. See David Ray Griffin, *The Reenchantment of Science* (Albany: SUNY Press, 1989).

27. See M. A. Corey, *God and the New Cosmology: The Anthropic Design Argument* (Lanham, Md.: Rowman & Littlefield, 1993).

28. For a dissenting view, see Robert Naeye, "OK, Where Are They?" *Astronomy* 24, no. 7 (July 1996): 36-43.

29. Jacobs, *Secret Life*, 98-99.

30. Some aliens, however, are said to resemble giant insects and reptiles.

31. David Jacobs, "Medical Examination and Subsequent Procedures," in *Alien Discussions*, ed. Andre Pritchard, David E. Pritchard, John E. Mack, Pam Kasey, and Claudia Yapp (Cambridge: North Cambridge Press, 1994), 54.

32. Jacobs, *Secret Life*, 97.

33. Jacobs, "Medical Examination and Subsequent Procedures," 54.

34. Jacobs, "Medical Examination and Subsequent Procedures," 54.

35. Jacobs, "Medical Examination and Subsequent Procedures," 54.

36. See Caroline C. McLeod, Barbara Corbisier, and John E. Mack, "A More Parsimonious Explanation for UFO Abductions," *Psychological Inquiry* 7, no. 2 (1996): 156-167.

37. Jacobs, *Secret Life*; Budd Hopkins, *Intruders: The Incredible Visitations at Copley Woods* (New York: Ballantine Books, 1987); Karla Turner, *Into the Fringe: A True Story of Alien Abduction* (New York: Berkley Books, 1991) and *Taken: Inside the Alien-Human Abduction Agenda* (Roland, Ark.: Kelt Works, 1994).

38. Whitley Strieber, *Breakthrough* (New York: Harper Collins, 1995). See also Richard J. Boylan and Lee K. Boylan, *Close Extraterrestrial Encounters* (Tigard, Ore.: Wild Flower Press, 1994); Raymond Fowler, *The Watchers* (New York: Bantam Books, 1991); Kenneth Ring, *The Omega Project* (New York: William Morrow, 1992); and Mack, *Abduction*.

39. See David Jacobs, "Are Abductions Positive?" *International UFO Reporter* 21, no. 2 (Summer, 1996): 21-25. See also Jacobs's book, *The Threat* (New York: Simon and Schuster, 1998), for a particularly dark assessment of the plans that the aliens allegedly have for humankind.

40. There are numerous Western counterparts to such a viewpoint. For example, early in this century Karl Jaspers argued that "limit situations" (e.g., close calls on the battlefield) provide the opportunity for transformation of a previously constricted and taken-for-granted personal existence. Jaspers's views, along with those of St. Paul, Kierkegaard, and Nietzsche, profoundly shaped Martin Heidegger's concept of authenticity. See Michael E. Zimmerman, *Eclipse of the Self: The Development of Heidegger's Concept of Authenticity* (Athens: Ohio University Press, 1986).

41. Whitley Strieber, *The Secret School: Preparing for Contact* (New York: Harper Collins, 1997), 82.

42. Strieber, *Communion* (New York: Beech Tree Books, 1987), 107.

43. Strieber, *Communion*, 116.

44. Strieber, *Communion*, 116-117.

45. Strieber, *Communion*, 117.

46. Mack, *Abduction*. Regarding such spiritual growth, Keith Thompson writes: "It's possible that UFOs, the near-death experience, apparitions of the Virgin Mary, and other shamanic visionary encounters are as much of a prod to our next level of consciousness as rapidly blooming sexual urges are a prod to a teenager's move from childhood to adolescence." Cited by Kenneth Ring in "Near-Death and UFO Encounters are Shamanic Initiations: Some Conceptual and Evolutionary Implications," *ReVision* 11, no. 3 (Winter 1989): 20. For further development of this theme, see Thompson's excellent book, *Angels and Aliens* (Reading, Mass.: Addison-Wesley, 1991).

47. Robert M. Torrance, *The Spiritual Quest: Transcendence in Myth, Religion, and Science* (Berkeley: University of California Press, 1994), 285.

48. See Harpur, *Daimonic Reality.*

49. Carl Sagan, *The Demon-Haunted World: Science as a Candle in the Dark* (New York: Random House, 1995).

50. Carl G. Jung, *Flying Saucers: A Modern Myth of Things Seen in the Sky*, trans. R. F. C. Hull (Princeton, N.J.: Princeton/Bollingen, 1959).

51. See Jung, *Flying Saucers*; and Gregory L. Little, *The Archetype Experience* (Moore Haven, Fla.: Rainbow Books, 1984).

52. Michael Grosso, *The Final Choice* (Walpole, N.H.: Stillpoint, 1985); and "UFOs and the Myth of the New Age," *ReVision* 11, no. 3 (Winter 1989): 5-13.

53. Terrence McKenna, cited in Ring, *The Omega Project*, 245.

54. Carl Raschke, "UFOs: Ultraterrestrial Agents of Cultural Deconstruction," *Cyberbiological Studies of the Imaginal Component in the UFO Contact Experience*, ed. Dennis Stillings (St. Paul, Minn.: Archaeus Project, 1989), 81-98.

55. On the problems that characterize many small-scale, tribal societies, see Robert B. Edgerton, *Sick Societies: Challenging the Myth of Primitive Harmony* (New York: Free Press, 1992).

Chapter Nine

Xenotropism: Expatriatism in Theories of Depth Psychology and Artistic Vocation

Coco Owen

Introduction

In the tradition of depth psychology—that psychology, including psycho-analysis and Jungian analytical psychology, which posits an unconscious—images of the foreign have universally been put to work in the manufacture of theory, just as they have, as fantasies and dreams, served the needs of personal psychology. One need, in particular, which these images have filled is to represent potent initiations and potential identities for artists in search of vocation.[1] Images of the foreign as used in psychology, and specifically as folk nosologies of the psychology of the artist, incarnate Otherness as pathology or as wildness, and present multiple readings of how we are simultaneously ourselves and not ourselves. Images of the foreign have been imported *Gastarbeiter* in the construction of theories of personality and pathology and have lived through the same vicissitudes as, in the larger sphere, have people and cultures classified as foreign by the existing order. As we will see in this essay, the image of the foreign has undergone analysis and a working-through since Freud, just as the figure of the artist, in depth psychology, no longer represents the exemplary neurotic but an exemplar of self-creation. We will see how the artist, as figure of the foreign, provides, in an expatriating turn to the foreign—what I am calling *xenotropism*—a script for psychology's account of otherness and of self-development.

Depth psychologists have invoked the foreign to explain everything from the otherness of unconsciousness to the genesis of pathology and of artists' rebel antics.[2] In the hands of these theorists—Europeans, émigrés, exiles, and Americans—evocations of the foreign served to define pathology as the not-us we say it is; as the documented, reified alien slippingly permitted to work against domesticity's absolutist aspirations to normalcy; and inevitably, against Western psychology's rationalist, objectivist fantasies of itself.

In psychologies of the unconscious (including later elaborations of the schools of object relations, self-psychology, and archetypal psychology), the foreign has represented the subversive in psychic and cultural life: the threat posed by both the unconscious and its symptoms is the incursion of the psychotic in the guise of the foreign. In the work of uncovering the unconscious, depth psychology has made art and artists, along with the symptom, a significant *topos* of the foreign. The image of the crazy artist has been fruitful for analysis: rather than being utterly other, like a "barbaric" symptom, Western artists have, since Plato, been labeled foreigners among us, and art the destabilizing force in the *polis*. As the "familiar" foreign, art and artists are intoxicating, disruptive, and deranging; then ultimately critiqued, interpreted, diagnosed, naturalized.

In the first part of this essay, I will consider how Freud and several later theorists—Heinz Kohut, D. W. Winnicott, and James Hillman—used the image of the foreign. All of these theorists used images, whether as the outer barbaric or inner creative, to delineate their theoretical territory. I will also show how each of them, figuratively and often literally, expatriated from his theoretical place of origin in order to attain the perspective necessary for his particular vision of psyche. Each theorist envied, resisted, or covetously lusted to incorporate artists' innovations and methods of work into their theories and did so either by approximating or pathologizing the unfamiliar and radical (that is, foreign-to-psychology) elements of those innovations. Because of psychology's manifest wish to establish itself as an empirical science, however phenomenological its early emphasis, most analytical theorists, whether of the Freudian or Jungian schools, have felt that rationality rather than imagination was their genre. As a consequence, artists undertook what became vicarious emigrations into modernism and postmodernism for the psychologists who stayed closer to philosophical home, schematizing their own intellectual emigrations from their predecessors: Freud's from Breuer; Winnicott's from Freud and Klein; Kohut's from Freud (and Germany); and Hillman's from Jung.

In the second half of the essay, I will examine artists' impulse to expatriate in light of the psychology of the foreign, and the status of art as the foreign, described in the first half of the essay. Artists—and in this essay I will limit my focus to writers—have long been seen as double agents frightening the collective with their *unimaginables*, as individuals often marked not just by the supposed foreignness of art but by a "deviant" sexuality or untoward passions.[3] I will discuss the figure of the American writer seen as estranged from her milieu because of her dissatisfaction with conventional satisfactions: someone who experiences a cultural melancholy and longs for a more *simpático* elsewhere, a foreign which would feel like family. I will also analyze the *topos* of expatriatism (which, for British and American writers, has so often meant Paris, "the city of writing"),[4] in the establishment and consolidation of the artist's self and vocation and offer a thumbnail typology of expatriate artists. We will see how expatriating, especially early in one's career, can be read as a sign of vocation and may provide the portfolio supporting a claim to be the "real thing." I hope to show that expatriation is undertaken, most often intentionally, to bracket out what is—paradoxically—foreign, or alien, about the familiar. In expatriation the writer can claim and consolidate the foreign within the self—that which is actually one's own. To do this, I have taken accounts of writers' expatriation principally from the *Paris Review* "Writers at Work" interviews, and will conclude the essay by focusing on Henry Miller, an avidly self-explicating expatriate.

We shall see how the difficulty of sloughing off one's homegrown self for an artistic one often inspires writers, in reaction, to self-medicate with an experience of cultural displacement. This displacement itself may then merely repeat and reinscribe artists' experience of estrangement within their family and immediate culture; it may also effect a transformation. Although leaving home entails a risk that writers might lose connections and traditions, they may succeed in remaking themselves into the image of the foreign they often felt they were at home—and may in fact have been. In expatriating there is an attempt to (re)create an identity congruent with the artists' own sense of self, and artists may be able to reimagine their return, *with a difference*, to their own tradition when their identities as the writers they felt they should become are secured and feel less vulnerable.

By reading expatriatism psychologically, with the interpretive strategies of our expatiating (wandering, digressing) theorists, I will venture not just to narrate, but to imagine, the workings and resolution of the play of selves behind artists' recourse to the foreign as a means of self-creation and affirmation of vocation. Here we will see xenotropism as these writers' gesture toward the reinvention and reanimation of self-exiled selves; as an attempt to repatriate their otherness—and ours—into a more cosmopolitan, more at-home-in-our-skin *us*.

Coco Owen

Psychological Geographies

Theories are plots.

—James Hillman, *Healing Fiction*

Each theorist I will consider had a particular relationship to the foreign as rhetorical device and as literal place, whether through exile, expatriatism, or (as in the case of Freud and Jung) through a touch of neurosis.[5] Each also had a personal sense of the arts and preferred artists in whom he tended to see his own shadow. Each used the artist as a prototype for the highest level of development his theory identified (i.e., as someone who had learned to coexist with the unconscious) and as an inspiration—however tinged the admiration was with what I think of as genre envy. Thus art has served as the shadow of depth psychology by working outside of psychology's self-policed borders of genre and its privileging of "normalcy."

In this half of the essay, I will consider how four theorists—Freud, Winnicott, Kohut, and Hillman—employed the figure of the foreign in their schemata of psyche and moved into foreign territory, imagining their way into new psychological topoi, psychic topography, and cultural geography. The fruit of these intellectual and personal sojourns in areas of investigation foreign to their predecessors was, in each case, a new story about the psyche.[6] Each thinker I will consider (except Hillman, it seems) looks at the artist ambivalently—queerly, we might say—and always as an instance of the foreign. This opinion held particularly true for those artists contemporary with Freud, from Picasso onward, whose work either engendered or echoed the cultural displacements of religion and rationalism—an effect replicated by the psychoanalytic revolution's "discovery of the unconscious," which Shoshana Felman refers to quite simply as "a cultural trauma."[7]

For the three theorists whom I would call modernists, Freud, Winnicott, and Kohut, inquiry into the foreign functioned as an imaginal site for self-definition through theory-making. For Freud and Jung, as pioneers of the modern unconscious, the turn to the foreign was clearly a turn inward to the strangeness of the images, instincts, and impulses frowned on at home. Just as writers (and I will speak mainly of British and American writers here) have long used expatriation as an initiation and a confirmation of their calling, these theorists confirmed their sense of self and their analytic vocation through xenotropism, a turn to the foreign.

Freud's Foreign Body

Before I consider how Freud used images of the foreign to portray his discoveries about the psyche, I want to situate Freud's intellectual endeavor in terms of its own trajectory of expatriatism. The word *expatriatism* comes from the medieval Latin *expatriatus* and the verb *expatriare*, which means to leave one's own country and, specifically, one's father. It is, according to Webster's, "to withdraw (oneself) from residence in or allegiance to one's native country." In the case of Freud's intellectual innovations, to call them the result of intellectual expatriation is to read a very old word through oedipal lenses which Freud himself ground. With Freud, the related word *expatiation* is also to the point: from the Latin verb *exspatiare* (to wander, digress), to expatiate is "to move about freely or at will."

Freud's intellectual expatriatism and wandering, his errancy, began with his first psychological work on the "talking cure" with Breuer and "Anna O," and with his experiments in hypnosis. It continued in his self-analysis and culminated in the publication of *The Interpretation of Dreams*.[8] Freud's expatriation as a thinker began in his dissatisfaction with his ability to treat hysterical patients and in his own distress. He invoked images of the foreign numerous times, particularly when discussing the "topography" of the psyche and the mechanism of the symptom—a formulation now classic in psychoanalysis: the unconscious as trope of instability.[9] In elaborating the concept of the unconscious inductively, from its manifestations in the supposed irrationalities of dreams and parapraxes, Freud, like so many artists and innovators, worked by xenotropism, claiming the unconscious as his territory and irrationality as its foreignness. *Xenotropism*, technically, is used in microbiology to refer to a class of viruses, inactive in a host, which require the exogamy of yet another species in order to replicate. So here I invoke a foreign discipline—that of physiology, which Freud used as a frame of reference for legitimizing his psychoanalytic theories—to describe expatriation's role in creativity.

As we will see, Freud employed the image of the foreign to describe his concepts of the unconscious, the structural model of psyche, the symptom, empathy, and treatment. The word *foreign* itself comes from the late Latin *foranus*, "on the outside." It is related to the Latin *foris*, from which "forum" derives, and also includes the phenomenon of something "occurring in an abnormal situation in the living body and often introduced from outside," i.e., the foreign body, a usage of Freud's which passed into psychoanalytic discourse. Both of these notions—of the foreign as the outside and as assembly for adjudication—adhere in Freud's Adamic naming of the psyche's regions and in his explanations of their interrelations: the superego judges the id's difference and deviance in the presence of Citizen Ego. However, for a psychology originally situated in homely German notions of the *Ich*, the *Uberich*, and the *Es*, the translation of Freud into English actually doubled rather than merely translated its foreignness. Use of the Latin terms id, ego, and superego, an attempt to make Freud's system appear more taxonomical and scientific, rendered Freud more foreign, expatriated both through translation and level of diction.[10]

Freud's background in neurology continued to form the discourse of his developing psychological system. In an extended meditation on the organization of pathogenic material, Freud stated that it "behaves like a foreign body, and that the treatment, too, works like the removal of a foreign body from the living tissues."[11] He goes on to say that the "foreign body" does not enter into any relationship with the ego, but its presence increases its distinction from the ego. Then he shifts and says that the psychic pathogen is not like a foreign body, but like an "infiltrate";[12] this is an attempt to represent the effect of the foreign's presence on the ego: it becomes, through its defense against the foreign body, the very image of its resistance. Freud does not give a simplistic model of psychological treatment of the pathogenic: "Nor does the treatment consist in extirpating something," he says.[13] Rather than focus on the removal of the foreign body, he focuses on the ego's resistance, the reification of which becomes a defense mechanism. The foreign body, then, falls back into the unconscious—or perhaps it never in fact lifts from the unconscious; its existence and incursions must be inferred through the existence of resistance.

Freud also used the foreign to explain symptom formation, likening the symptom to a foreigner whose presence signals the failure of repression, of borders. Thus the symptom, like a dream, also derives from secondary revision and is a dream of the original foreign disturbance which could have manifested, but did not. Symptoms, Freud noted in "The Dissection of the Psychical Personality," are "of all the contents of the mind, most foreign to the ego."[14] He goes on to say that symptoms are "foreign territory to the ego—internal foreign territory—just as reality (if you will forgive the unusual expression) is external foreign territory."[15] For Freud, the unconscious becomes conscious through the foreignness of its parapraxes, symptoms, and dreams through which, in another *dédoublement*, images of foreigners often import the pathology, the "alien" symptom telling out the neurosis and telling on it.[16] And for Freud, resistance to the foreign's incursive courtship of the ego—that is, xenophobia—constitutes yet another pathology, the ego's failure to reconcile with "primitive" impulses and infantile wishes.[17]

Images of the foreign reenter Freud's tableau later in the "Dissection of the Psychical Personality" essay. He imagined the structural dimensions of the psyche (superego, ego, and id) as "provinces, realms, landscapes" and as a "mixed population (Germans, Magyars, Slovaks)." But, as he continued, "you will find less orderliness and more mixing, if you travel through the region."[18] Here we have some imaginative, and loaded, nationalistic material which may help explicate Freud's (and Jung's) xeno-neurosis: if one enters the foreign, rather than awaiting its incursion, the ego's primacy, and all identity politics dependent on it, lose their alleged, essentialist objectivity. Here Freud is describing a way in which his own nascent theory, carefully imagined as a science, could itself be altered by a foreign exchange: the inside for the outside, the foreign for the ego. (Hillman, as we will see, devotes himself to an archetypal analysis of precisely such perspectives.)

Always, the archetypal Western fear of the barbarian hordes, of losing ground, of being overrun. And a travel interdiction: don't go there.

Freud, famously, received the Goethe Prize for literature instead of equivalent scientific recognition. This was a prophecy: that psychoanalysis would spread to the humanities and find its way into literature as a tool, and sometimes as a thorn, of its self-analysis. Freud said that art represented an uneasy feat—that of sublimation, the transmutation of instinct and infantile wish into a palette more palatable to the ego. Freud, unlike Jung, was not tempted to be an artist, his *Weltanschauung* being so staunchly that of a medical scientist believing in determinism. He admired Goethe, Shakespeare, Leonardo da Vinci, and others, but within reason.[19] And yet: Freud opened up regions of the interior for exploration and provided tools—free association; the diagnosis of symptoms, pathology, and neurosis; and the interpretation of dreams, parapraxes, and myth—by which the strange within, that which is foreign to us, enters and schools us in the illusions of civilization while seeing in the dark, speaking in tongues.

Winnicott's Country of Infancy

D. W. Winnicott is known as a founder, not so much of his own school as of an ingenious analytical style. His work focused on the mother-child dyad, advocacy of the "true self," and the role of "transitional objects" in the development of a capacity to play and use symbols. His own development as a psychoanalytic theorist took him into the previously underexamined region of infancy, and of intimacy between caregiver and child. In this work, he followed two émigré analysts, Anna Freud, who did the first systematic child analysis, and Melanie Klein, who looked at the preverbal development of object relations. For Winnicott, what better way to proceed from the father of psychoanalysis than to precede him, to go "prior to the Oedipus complex," to "the self of the infant" as it emerges from its merger with the mother?[20] Winnicott himself was never an expatriate, though he did come from a small town to a big hospital in London, from a tradesman's family to the world of medicine and psychoanalysis. Poetry was a temptation, written but concealed. Another divagation of Winnicott's was his taste for educating lay audiences about psychoanalysis by communicating, in the simplest terms, the fruits of his clinical observations and theoretical errancies.

Perhaps because of his respect for the material arising from the transitional realm between infancy and autonomy, Winnicott respected artistic work. He classified it as adult play distinguished by a "ruthlessness" in service of the true self's demands and as an admirable kind of health, that of having the "courage to be in touch with primitive processes." With this observation, I would say Winnicott makes a subtle indictment of the socializing, moralizing trends in society which seem to demand complete capitulation of one's authenticity in what he called "pathological accommodation" to conventional social requirements.[21]

In addition to the inspired creativity he showed in making his own journey away from Freud and Klein to the country of infancy, Winnicott spoke for the revelatory and quasi-literary status of psychoanalytic inquiry:

> The psycho-analyst, as I have already said, can be looked upon as a specialist in history-taking. . . . A psycho-analytic case description is a series of case histories, a presentation of different versions of the same case, the versions being arranged in layers each of which represents a stage of revelation.[22]

Here we hear echoes of the archeological fantasy companioning psychoanalysis since Freud's (and Jung's) image of the psyche as a house of many strata, a claim of expertise in "history-taking," and a view of the patient's story as not only polysemous but as *gospel*.[23] With Winnicott, the move is from a drive-based, egocentric psychology, in which the unconscious is the foreign and pathology is a foreign body, to psychologies of the self and internalized object relations. Now, with the foreign within—however ill-assimilated—the companion pathologies also evolve. Rather than Viennese hysteria and pathologies of repression, for Winnicott and the object-relations school, the new pathologies are distresses of the self-in-relation.[24]

In two major papers, "Mind and Its Relation to Psyche-Soma" and "The Capacity to Be Alone," Winnicott sketches a trajectory of individual development applicable to the expatriation experiences of the writers I will discuss later.[25] In the first paper, Winnicott describes optimal development as proceeding from a seamless psychosomatic experience arising out of the "holding environment" which the mother creates. This environment allows only age-appropriate frustrations, which the infant can tolerate if they occur in a climate of empathy. If, however, the maternal matrix does not adequately hold with "good enough" mothering, Winnicott says "the thinking of the individual begins to take over and organize the caring for the psyche-soma" with *"mental functioning becoming a thing in itself."*[26]

This premature method of self-maintenance is what Winnicott calls "mind:" a portion of self experienced as autonomous and fictitiously located in the head and fantasized to be disconnected from the somatic fabric of self. In its inappropriately precocious self-caretaking, this "mind" becomes the nucleus of what Winnicott calls the "false self" and mind nothing other than a pet fiction.[27] The characteristic, self-protective symptomography of mind is a (compulsive) cataloguing—mind as librarian, archivist. And it is precisely here that the familiar trope of the foreign body appears: "But this cataloguing type of mental functioning acts like a foreign body if it is associated with environmental adaptive failure that is beyond understanding or prediction."[28] Winnicott identifies construction of a "false self" (the self which is often the pleasing and well-adjusted one parents like) as essentially the result of a successful colonization by the ruling order.[29]

In the second essay, "The Capacity to Be Alone," Winnicott locates integrity and health in the ability to tolerate solitude. He traces this capacity to the reliable, empathic presence of the caregiver who sustains the child's ability to immerse him- or herself in play. Though he identifies the skin as the border between self and other, Winnicott does not call the other foreign; nor does he believe pathology arises from an infectious-diseases model of intrusion by "foreign bodies" or "primitive mental mechanisms." Rather, pathology arises from the immature psyche's attempt to adapt to, and survive deficits in, the "facilitating environment."[30] In Winnicott's thinking, it is the domestic and familiar, not the foreign or other, which disrupts creative adaptation.

With this significant shift in stories about pathology's etiology, cure comes from reparative work in a state of regression, from something which a good-enough environment recreates in the transitional zone of the symbolic. With this shift, we have a basis for a new psychology of expatriatism, which the earlier Freudian model, built on a classical fantasy of the ego as the city-state in conflict with "barbaric" drives and of art as a sublimation of drives, does not adequately address. Freud's model explains how to pacify and colonize the id ("where id was, there shall ego be," as the famous analytic adage has it) or how to understand the mourning and melancholy of exile, but not how to redress pathologies of anomie or self-loss which are, shall we say, the modern or post-Nietzschean pathologies.[31] The new psychology of expatriatism situates expatriation as a move into, as a search for, a more congruent holding environment mirroring the "foreign" true self.

Winnicott's dual notion of self—"false" and "true"—is a heuristic with which some tendencies of normalcy and ego adaptation can now be explicated as inauthentic gestures of accommodation doing harm to self-integrity. He thereby identifies external demands requiring a false adaptation as a most common pathogen, and privileges the needs of the individual above that of family or society. The foreign is no longer the enemy; it is now the familiar which is pathogenic. Henry Miller, whose story of expatriation we will look at in detail later, gives a terse and searing depiction of a life lived according to the dictates of a false self:

> My liberation seemed to involve pain and suffering to those near and dear to me. Every move I made for my own private good brought about reproach and condemnation. I was a traitor a thousand times over. I had lost even the right to become ill—because "they" needed me. . . . Had I died I think they would have galvanized my corpse into a semblance of life.[32]

Winnicott's vision of the child's developmental journey from dependence to independence provides a schema for looking at artists' expatriatism, when it is in the service of vocation: there must be a preservation of the capacity for authentic play and a refusal to be denatured by "pathological accommodation."[33] Ruthlessness in sacrificing the false self and its obscuring of the qualities of play, authenticity, and vulnerability is required for creative work. There is a search for the reparative, mirroring environment—not only for its "holding" capacity, but as an instance of the ego-ideal: a vision of what one longs to become. Winnicott's own innovative imagination (as well as his *agon* with both Sigmund and Anna Freud) linked development in general with artistic development, yet contrasted the two:

> A mother and father do not produce a baby as an artist produces a picture or a potter a pot. They have started up a developmental process which results in there being a lodger in the mother's body and then in her arms and then in the home provided by the parents, and what this lodger will turn out to be like is outside anyone's control.[34]

Generally, Winnicott holds parents quite accountable, but here I think he is talking not about general well-being and the need for good-enough parenting, but about the individual destiny which falls into the Fates'—or art's—realm. The "lodger," Winnicott is telling parents, is a foreigner, and that is a sign of the child's mysterious, individual integrity and creativity; the sign that the child does not "belong" to them, but to his or her own soul. Winnicott does not grant parents creative control nor encourage them to confuse childrearing with art; he is too attuned to the autonomy needs and individuality of the child to grant parents that power. At best, an individual gets enough environmental support for development of the "true self" and can then make use of innate gifts to lead a creative, authentically adaptive life. This would be, as Winnicott envisions it, a creative life drawing on the ability to play and ride the liminal state between the id's wishes and society's requirements—a life, in effect, of openness to the foreign.[35] As we shall see, Winnicott's emphasis on the infant-mother dyad and on preoedipal issues of self-formation are in many ways consonant with the self-psychology of Heinz Kohut, who developed a particular vocabulary for identifying the effects of impaired early caretaking on the healthy and necessary narcissism of the child's self-in-creation.

Kohut's Empathy with the Foreign

Another third-generation psychoanalyst, Heinz Kohut, developed his theories in the course of what he styled empirical, scientific, psychoanalytic observations emphasizing the use of empathy as a tool for making theoretical inferences about the psyche.[36] He was raised in Vienna, went to medical school at the University of Vienna, and emigrated to the United States as a consequence of World War II. For Kohut, the crucial issues of development are narcissistic ones: does the developing child have the occasion to experience two new transferences he identifies, the mirroring and idealizing transferences? These transferences, the first not to be considered drive derivatives, invoke what Kohut calls the child's grandiose selfobject and the idealized selfobject.[37]

Kohut observes that the literal "uplift" the baby experiences when handled by a reliable mother is the source of the same uplifting feeling "of looking at a great man or woman . . . or a wonderful piece of music, etc."[38] Here is the link between the healthy (and necessary) narcissism of childhood and what Kohut calls, as we will soon see, the world of cultural selfobject relations. Kohut characterizes development as a story of object relations rather than of oedipal struggles, making a place for himself by specializing, as did Winnicott, in phenomena of the psyche anterior to those which most concerned Freud. Kohut's narrative of development, re-envisioning the Freudian conflict of instinct and "civilization," focuses on the emergent self as a microcosm of relationships and places infant narcissism at the crux of psychological development.

An émigré himself, Kohut was concerned with history and interested in the application of self-psychology to groups and nations. He read history as analogous to, and in a sense as derived from, individual development. He felt that the national self replicates the emergence of the "nuclear self"—or is it vice versa?—and explicitly conflated the artist's fate with the fate of rejected aspects of the national self. Art and the artist's vocation must then also be attempts to heal not only the "nuclear self," but the national cultural self as well. This focus on the collective function of art characterizes much of Kohut's thinking and is recorded in the collected essays and interviews of *Self Psychology and the Humanities*, the primary Kohutian text that I will use here.[39]

Kohut's images of the foreign occur principally in reference to the collective. For example, he notes that "so long as another culture is totally foreign to us, it is like psychosis."[40] But he goes on to undercut this seemingly easy (and typically Freudian) distinction between the known and the foreign by noting that, by the use of an "empathic bridge," what might look foreign is not, and what classical analysis used to call psychosis often is not.[41] He makes this case explicitly, essentially by recasting the classical psychoses as self disorders which signal a history of disturbed internal object relations rather than an invasion or infection by foreign pathogens.

However, he does acknowledge that there is an *archai* of foreignness in which something he considers beyond empathy—the past—still inheres. Kohut says that "everything from yesterday backwards" is effectively "a foreign culture."[42] Here we have the same association we saw in the previous mention of the "foreign culture," but now Kohut unhooks foreignness from nationalistic images used to describe psychosis and situates psychosis in the fantasy of (literal) history. The Freudian psychosis is cured by a shift in definition of the self's boundaries, by empathy for what was pathologized as the foreign deviance threatening to undermine the privileged domestic norm. Then, after saying the past is a foreign culture, Kohut adds that "it is very difficult to *think* oneself into another person."[43] This highlights the paradox that, despite his emphasis on empathy, Kohut relies on the image of the foreign to depict that which is beyond (his) empathy: not psychosis—an us versus them version of it—but the *past*. All of our histories.

Kohut also used the type of physiological analogy for the foreign we saw earlier with Freud's descriptions of pathogenic "foreign bodies," but uses it affirmatively. In the essay "On the Continuity of the Self," Kohut describes our absolute dependence on others as a xenotropic need for the "foreign protein" which the body requires to break down and reconstitute experience into usable form: for we cannot mirror ourselves or, to use Winnicott's image, provide our own good-enough environment.[44] What we need is someone and something in correspondence to us, a foreign correlative. I will argue that the artist, for whom existing familiar and cultural self-objects may of necessity be inadequate, a xenotropism, a mirroring exogamy, is imperative—if not prescribed—in this view of artistic development.

Kohut also swerves from Freud in his reading of culture. He does not believe its "discontents" are the inevitable residue of instinctual repressions and sublimation. He distinguishes between "civilization," which he equates with the socializing and moralizing aims of society, and "culture," the material production of the highest work humans are capable of: "You think of culture only as supportive or as nonsupportive of the maintenance of the self. . . . The *Unbehagen* [discontents] can only be when support is not provided."[45] Kohut identified a specifically *cultural* conception of the "object," that imaginary internal representation of significant others, which he called the "cultural selfobject." It can be a cultural figure or work of art which a person can cathect in the service of idealization needs. With this move, Kohut, as in his observation that the past is a "foreign culture," again links the microcosm of individual subjectivity to the collective by describing cultural selfobjects as "a replica of the culture" which the "group self" uses for mirroring and idealizing object transferences.[46] This is analogous to the way the self uses the parental *imagoes* and may be the site where a disjunction between the self and the home culture arises, and one or the other, the individual or the culture, is experienced as foreign: a cultural transference.

Kohut follows an Aristotelian view of great drama as representing a "cosmic self" which has therapeutic effect inasmuch as it permits a vicarious experience, not of catharsis, but of a fully realized nuclear self: "The broken self is mended via the creation of the cohesive artistic product."[47] It is emphatically not mended through a mindless mimicry of the culture's (and, indeed, the family's) image of normalcy, which results in a self relying on "borrowed cohesion."[48] Here Kohut is distinguishing, I believe, between true creative work on the self and what is essentially a self-pathology simply imitating cohesion in the absence of thorough-going creative work. For Kohut, the resulting "well-adjusted" individual has in fact been overtaken by a foreign self (i.e., a perfectly-at-home false self) and is crazy.

Since creativity demands, as Kohut observed in the essay "Creativeness, Charisma, Group Psychology," that one go "into lonely areas that had not been previously explored by others," he sees artistic work as analogous to, and perhaps in fact literalized by, a move abroad.[49] The figurative expression "new territory" which Kohut employs here to describe creative work is accompanied by a recurrent image of outer space or moonscape and becomes what, along with the "past," is still foreign for him, still beyond empathy. The foreign is no longer simply represented by people who speak a different language or observe different customs, but by the apparently non-human, that which is beyond earth's—and empathy's?—gravitational pull. This, for Kohut, is the border of foreignness, the otherness once again being used to represent that which exceeds our current capacity for empathy.

Hillman: Going South

The archetypal psychology of James Hillman begins in the wake of C. G. Jung's analytical psychology. Though Jung's swerve from Freud constituted the most significant *agon* in the early history of psychoanalysis, I will not consider that break here, but, following one of Jung's most prominent (and heretical) heirs, will shift to work within the Jungian constellation where archetypes, rather than drives, constitute the primary material.[50] Hillman's own move away from Jung is explicitly to run the boundaries between therapeutic psychology and culture, or the realm of the "Western cultural imagination."[51] Hillman explicitly leaves behind the world of "medical and empirical psychologies" with which Freud and Jung could never break because of their identification with scientific empiricism and their desire to establish depth psychology in that tradition.[52]

Hillman's own expatriations have been multiple: from America to Europe to India and to Zurich by 1953, and back to the United States more than twenty years later; from intellectual North to South; from the empirical, materialist tradition to the scene of the "Western cultural imagination"; from a "monotheism" to "polytheism" of ego psychology.[53] Hillman works less in behavior and treatment than he does in imaginal geography and cultural *topoi*. In *Inter Views*, source of the only autobiographical information in his works, Hillman locates his work in the metaphorical Mediterranean South, in Renaissance Italy and classical Greece, in contradistinction to the "Northern" psychology of Freud and Jung, which Hillman characterizes as in fact belonging to the tradition begun with the Reformation.[54] Hillman instead identifies his archetypal psychology with the Renaissance and enters a play of polarities contrasting the literal with the imaginal and the dayworld of ego consciousness with the underworld of dream and fantasy.[55] Hillman has sought to locate psychology in a third position, that of "soul," a perspective of fantasy and fantasies of seeing, and seeing-through, by means of myths, *archai*, and "values" which seeks to evade, destabilize, and illuminate the binary, metaphysical concepts Jung emphasized—and often reified—in his theories. Hillman has extended Jung's hermetic model of working with the unconscious. No longer does a stable ego observe the unconscious; it is decentered through the use of an archetypal perspective:

> Hermes inhabits the borderlines; his herms are erected there, and he makes possible an easy commerce between the familiar and the alien. . . . For Hercules [i.e., the heroic ego], however, it is a wrestle and a sweat to move in and out, to entertain differing alternatives, languages, customs—psychic realities and physical realities—at the same time. His world is oppositional.[56]

Here we see Hillman juxtaposing his own approach with that of Jung, and, as he would have it, all of nineteenth-century Western psychology. Having adopted a polytheistic, decentered view of the image as primary material, Hillman no longer takes any stance which opposes the foreign to something; the foreign is seen in its absolute relativity as a perspective—that is, the foreign was always an artifact created by over-identification with the ego. There is no absolute other, either sociopolitically or in the unconscious; there is only what the ego construed as other when its own biases and perspective were unexamined. Hillman offers depth psychology access to borderline realms rather than Iron Curtains, liminality rather than the Jungian problem of the opposites. He proposes both pathology and subjectivity as gods' play, as their stories and reflections, rather than as reified entities existing because they have been named or corralled into categories:

> Yet these symptoms and quirks are both me and not me . . . they are visitations, alienations, bringing home the personal/impersonal paradox of the soul: what is "me" is also not "mine"—"I" and "soul" are alien to each other because of soul's domination by powers, daimons, and Gods.[57]

What Hillman does is to tell us not (to quote Gertrude Stein) that "there's no there there," as people have feared about social constructionism's critiques of the self, but that our *axis mundi* is fluid and should not be reified into any literalistic fantasy of stability—into any theology, materialism, or positivism. For archetypal psychology, "The artificial tension between soul and world, private and public, interior and exterior thus disappears when the soul as *anima mundi*, and its making, is located in the world."[58] And, I would add, following Kristeva, that old reified fictions dividing the domestic and the foreign disappear too.[59]

Hillman also leaves behind the Kantian idealism in Jung's view of archetypes and limits archetypes to the phenomenal world, their aspects to imagination's metaphors. He tracks the *archai* in everything, as everything is a production of the imagination. He will not translate images into concepts, and this rage against nominalism and metaphysical reification is the polemical premise of his seminal work, *Re-visioning Psychology* (1975). He rejects, as we have seen, many philosophical genres (empiricism, scientism, materialism, rationalism, idealism), preferring less monolithic, hegemonic genres to the heroic: the picaresque to the epic; imagism to narrative; a "poetic basis of mind" to either physiological, structural, or developmental data. There is, Hillman insists (following Wallace Stevens), "always 'a poem at the heart of things.'"[60]

Therefore, Hillman takes rhetoric rather than observation as his method, and the image, symptom, or dream rather than the case history or adaptation as his subject. He aims to see through rather than explain, and to see through with the perspective of myth, of fantasy, of the gods. The aim is also to "save" soul by honoring the pathologized and demonized, a function which Hillman claims for both archetypal psychology and art: "It is this pathologized eye which, like that of the artist and the psychoanalyst, prevents the phenomena of the soul from being naively understood as merely natural."[61]

Clinically, working in the tradition of Jung, Hillman's approach to the foreign in analysis would be to make the patient's viewpoint conscious rather than to uncritically interpret the patient's clinical material. For example, any images of foreigners or dream visits to foreign countries which a patient presented might be dissected, amplified, and honored—but not explained away. He would not translate these images into conceptual allegories of the psyche. He hails images as real, as complementary, Dionysian rites through which Eros (the unconscious) gestures at Logos (the ego), seducing its attention and attempting its correction. To use this approach therapeutically, the archetypal analyst would be "giving support to the counter-ego forces, the personified figures who are ego-alien" and encouraging a patient to consider experience as broad as the imagination.[62]

With Hillman, we are no longer situated in the domestic and foreign commonplace, we are seeing all of culture and human activity as psychological and, consequently, as material for psychologizing, or seeing-through. Hillman has ambitions of putting psychology on "a poetic basis of consciousness."[63] Cure, then, does not come by any quasi-medical, martial, or diplomatic operations of cleansing the self of foreign bodies and managing the Foreign Office; cure is only the recognition that one is multiply foreign, always both stranger and insider, depressed and manic.[64] This move brings "provincial" strategies of seeing into a cosmopolitan awareness.

"The Great American Ache"

"Foreign": the music in me from elsewhere.

—Hélène Cixous, *Coming to Writing*

One's destination is never a place
but rather a new way of looking at things.

—Henry Miller, *Sexus*

While, as Hillman says, American writers go to Europe, psychologists leave Europe—often as refugees or exiles—for the United States. He observes elsewhere that many of those important figures in European psychology who emigrated used to be Freudians, "each of whom identifies Freud with pathology, pessimism, and thanatos, and then leaves him for greener fields. These fields were literalized by the American continent; leaving Freud, thanatos, and pessimism meant finding America, love, and optimism."[65] Hillman himself took the writers' trajectory, eventually finding in Europe precisely that darker "fantasy of antiquity" which is closer to thanatos.[66] Clearly, something of the same philosophical and psychological impulses underlie the draw continental Europe has for Anglophone artists.

Here I want to consider the experience—and to make a composite *case*, in effect—of the aspiring writer seeking cultural initiation and vocation, or the established writer seeking refuge or renewal, in a turn to the foreign: a sojourn abroad, expatriation. Edna O'Brien wrote her first novel, *Country*

Girls, in the few weeks after her arrival in London, saying that she felt "*alien*," so "lost—an outsider," that the book wrote itself, encompassing her "experience of Ireland and my farewell to it."[67] Why did this rupture birth the book? Why did Gertrude Stein, in a piece called "Why I Do Not Live in America," say that "your parent's home is never a place to work it is a nice place to be brought up in . . . she [America] is a rich and well nourished home but not a place to work"?[68] Stein invokes an image of parents, of home, of place, and of work—ingenuously? What doesn't she say? She does not say what the work is and what it required that was beyond the purview of home and family. Being "nice" and "rich and well nourished" was not so much not "good-enough" as it was immaterial to work. Lawrence Durrell seconded this sentiment in a complaint about the impossibility of working at home as a British writer. In a perfect technical description of xenotropism, he says that:

> One goes to Europe because, like a damn cuckoo, one has to lay these eggs in someone else's nest. Here in France, in Italy, and Greece, you have the most hospitable nests, you see, where there's very little chi-chi about writing or artists as such, but which provide the most extraordinarily congenial frames in which a job of work can be done.[69]

I want to examine what these writers found lacking in the commonplace plenty of the New World or home, what the work was that it could not be done at home. Right away the "case" of the emigrating writer asks these questions: What did the family scene lack—privacy, support, reception, recognition, objectivity, a home, nourishment for the vocation? What was the culture unable to offer—a living connection to history, a regard for the arts, an elegiac consciousness, a paradoxical affirmation of one's cultural identity? Thus Durrell's observation: "It's the culture that separates, you see, and turns the artist into a sort of refugee. It's not a question of residence."[70]

Expatriatism encompasses both proximal psychological causes and distal archetypal influences, so I will read writers' own explanations for their expatriatism in light of the analytic reflections on the foreign explored in the previous section. We will hear motives for expatriatism ranging from Gertrude Stein's seemingly matter-of-fact search for a place to work to Henry Miller's sense that America rejects its artists and only a "rebirth" will help. As for the archetypal pull toward expatriatism, xenotropism is a type of turn to the Keatsian *via negativa*—a counterintuitive instinct to leave rather than go home—which both confers and confirms artistic vocation and illuminates vocation's odyssey. Writer and critic Hélène Cixous makes this point succinctly: "Yet this is the way we must go, leaving home behind. Go toward foreign lands, toward the foreigner in ourselves. Traveling in the un-

conscious, that inner foreign country, foreign home, country of lost countries."[71]

Therefore, we start with a sense that to yearn toward art marks one with
an otherness which one already was, making the foreign feel familiar, with a
sense that art is another country and that the tradition and the work itself are
the true family. Cixous, a writer marked as multiply foreign (Franco-
Spanish-German-Jewish in colonial Algeria, *pied noir* in France, woman in
letters) often presents the writer's experience as a constant dialogue with internal and external foreignness. For Cixous, not only does the writer become
strange to herself and others, but worse—everyone from writer to family to
nation experiences the writer's attraction to things beyond home's provi-
sions as a crime:

> The writer is a secret criminal. How? First because writing tries to under-
> take that journey toward strange sources of art that are foreign to us. . . .
> The writer has a foreign origin; we do not know about the particular na-
> ture of these foreigners, but we feel they feel there is an appeal, that some-
> one is calling them back. The author writes as if he or she were in a for-
> eign country, as if he or she were a foreigner in his or her own family. . . .
> The foreign origin of the book makes the scene of writing a scene of im-
> measurable separation. . . . We write, we paint, throughout our entire lives
> as if we were going to a foreign country, as if we were foreigners inside
> our own families.[72]

Here we have the layers of foreignness in a writer's experience—within the
self, within writing itself, and within one's culture—named and all presented
as disturbing, disruptive, or threatening.[73]

So how important are failures in the "facilitating environment" (Winnicott) or the "empathic responsive matrix" (Kohut) in engendering a sense of
alienation in the artist whose creative response is then experienced as criminal? In discussing the development of sociopathy, often attributed to artists,
Winnicott believes that privation precedes any consciousness of deprivation.
Many children drawn to art—indeed many children—are inadequately mirrored, getting little "holding" from their caregivers. Any resulting disruptions of self-cohesion reflect their caregivers' impoverished comprehension
and perception. And yet, writers must have enough ego-mastery or intellectual endowment to use their drives constructively, as Freud would maintain;
or at least to bring their creative powers to fruition without diminishing them
to fit the dimensions of a false self which would suit their family or their
culture, but be unable to bear any radical invention. There are, also, creative
people who lack enough sense of security and self for sustained, inventive
solitude or geographical mobility, yet still have the imaginative and ego resources to engage in creative work; not resources enough, however, to expatriate in pursuit of vocation, as we shall see in the case of Anne Sexton.

Artists have their own folk psychology of the motivations for expatriation. Artist Beauford Delaney's bittersweet explanation for his expatriatism, reported in John Ashbery's collected writing on art, serves as an example: "Life in Paris offers me the anonymity and objectivity to release long-stored memories of sorrow. . . . One never leaves home if one was never there."[74] Here expatriation merely affirms an internal condition of alienation which is true in current *and* remembered experience. Both Kohut and Winnicott would say that distresses of preverbal self-development underlie the sense of unreality, lack of vitality, and self-disconnection which both analysts see as *the* modern pathology. Delaney, notably, does not say he was looking for home, or a place which he imagined would feel like home, but that he was looking for a neutrality in which the truth of his earlier experience could represent itself to him; in doing so, he also very succinctly (and unconsciously?) describes the ideal scene of a classical analysis and the transference. It is that expatriation, motivated by a search for anonymity, memory's memorialization, and objectivity, could be described as an intuitive search for a better-than-analytic cure because expatriation is a total-immersion experience of objectivity; it is a forum for self-observation and divestment of foreign (i.e., imposed) aspects of selfhood. It may also be an alchemical vessel which, unlike analysis, is not intermittent, but constant.

The fantasy of cure by total immersion may be the perfect fit for the writer who needs to escape "impingement" from others and the environment in order to repossess her own intentions and achieve an experience in which the "*continuity of being is not disturbed.*"[75] The experience of relief ensues, as in analysis, from losing one's past; and, upon finding it, reframing it. In this mode of expatriation, which I will discuss in more detail later, I see what might be called a creative emptying (an artistic *kenosis*) by which expatriation mimics or enacts the proverbial "flight into health" which often happens to people entering psychological treatment. The emotional experience may be akin to weightlessness, and why shouldn't an invitation to buoyant mania or derealization's anonymity accompany an *invitation au voyage*, accepted?[76]

Are there any artists who can stay at home and realize their vocation? What would a good-enough home life have offered a creative child? Let us say: this child's play would have been permitted, her innovation and dreaming in solitude supported by, and contained within, the parents' overarching circle of care, in which the child's "capacity to be alone" engendered the capacity to create. I submit that this artist would not *need* to expatriate for most of the reasons I will discuss in this essay; this artist would be free to travel or sojourn for the pleasure of it, free to be compelled by illusions or desire rather than by the distress of developmental deficits demanding redress. These are the artists capable of creative self-enhancement and self-enlargement, rather than only self-reparative work, through xenotropism. I would propose that xenotropism is a homeopathic rather than prophylactic or allopathic curative gesture: if alienation is symptomatic of what is wrong in one's experience, in the strategy of "self-medication," the reflex is to go toward congruity with the ailment, seeking and intensifying it, literalizing the fantasy of its pathology. One then gives one's inner experience of being different a chemical bath in something really foreign—the midnight sun, the taste of durian, french fries with mayonnaise—to assuage and ground one's biographically-informed estrangement fantasies that the foreign is one's native state. Turning to the foreign permits (re)construction of the mirroring and internal dynamism necessary to persist and create—given a workable foundation and enough resilience to endure changes in the complexion of one's object relations—as one turns to the symbolic, to fantasy, image, memory. Eventually, the artist may recognize that one belongs to the tradition of one's art.

As we look at numerous writers who expatriated, we will find those who made therapeutic use of their expatriation, for whom leaving home functioned as Winnicott and Kohut predict such self-help might. There are also those, as we will see, for whom xenotropism was no help, who may not have had the inner resources to benefit from a *dépaysement* in the service of the self (to paraphrase Karl Abraham). They are those who were unable to locate either their "true self" or "personal way of being" because of too much early wounding, or who, lacking an adequate experience of mirroring and idealizing, were unable to reorient themselves through their art.[77]

The Genre of the Interview

My material on writers' experiences abroad comes mainly from the well-known *Writers at Work* series of collected interviews from the *Paris Review*. I have chosen to work with this material since the *Paris Review* interview has long been an imprimatur of artistic status, and because the conventions of the *Paris Review* interview include questions about how the writer became a writer, about where, when, and how she writes. Another question never missing asks about the significance and influence of any sojourn abroad. As a result, the interviews are miniatures conventionally framing expatriatism in the service of artistic vocation. Having an expatriation story is nearly *de rigueur* proof of artistic vocation in the same way that a "creative illness" became the sign of a calling to depth psychology.

The genre of the *Paris Review* interview itself, in appearance a souvenir of a dialogue, becomes a quasi-textual invention, what Genette called an *épitexte*.[78] The interview form is cast as a story of a meeting—*"toutes les interviews sont narrativisées* [all interviews are narrativized]"—telling the archetypal story of the writers' calling to art.[79] The writers interviewed in the journal have always had the opportunity to write their answers rather than to talk—talk, in its "naked orality," as Frank Kermode said, being a foreign medium for discussing one's writing.[80] The interview, Kermode continues, is "an unnatural medium" for the writers because of its pretense at spontaneity: the writers may review, touch-up, revise, or entirely hijack their interview; they may erase traces of the interviewer and turn the "interview" into personal essay. Though most of the writers do speak with the interviewer and revise later, Cynthia Ozick, for example, protesting that "conversation is air," asked if she could type her responses to the interviewer's questions rather than speak.[81]

It is the hybridity of the genre, its fictive immediacy and naughty, "naked orality," which entices both the writer and the reader into the interview, however numerous the loopholes in its verisimilitude. The fiction that we are getting a treasure map—however finessed or ideal—to the secret of the writers' vocation and art likewise entices and incites. For all its mix of pretended immediacy with revision-polish, the genre of the writer interview, like that of the clinical interview, promises a tightly framed character exposé. But perhaps most importantly, with respect to what Kohut said about the true salutary effect of great art, the interview awakens hope for a healing exposure to a fully realized self: a work of living art.

Another fiction inherent to the interview is, as Wilfrid Sheed said in introducing the fourth series, that the interview is democratic and that an interview with an interlocutor is "better for us than their [the writers'] own mysterious wanderings would have been."[82] At the same time, readers may or may not know that the writer had control over the final form of the interview. Even though the interviews are presented as a means of rendering "wandering" writers more accessible to us, the writers are expected to expatiate and expatriate from the conventions of that form. In the *Paris Review* interviews, expatriating defines form as well as content. Writers with enough cachet for an interview must, like divas, have both a democratic temper (they will appear before the public) and a temperament (they will let us know they are special). This display of the writers' wit and any excessive, transgressive (*c'est-à-dire*, foreign) gestures, which those who are stay-at-home non-*enfants terribles* can only admire, provides yet another proof of vocation and mastery. Readers cotton to the promise that the interview will be at once revelatory and demystifying, providing an intimacy with a personality judged worthy of scrutiny and admiration.[83]

Frank Kermode notes that it is the American writers in particular who have the most investment in the story of their vocation and take it the most seriously.[84] I would explain this by saying that North American writers have a socially constructed burden to manifest a respectably serious destiny. This reflects not only the historical cultural dilemma of America as Europe's stepchild but that of writers who grew up fearing that espousing art was unlikely to earn them parental approval, given art's unlikelihood to lead one to conventional definitions of professional success. American artists have had to fear that others, and family to be sure, will think little of their work unless they have proved themselves exceptionally worthy through acclaim and financial success. This interpretation is furthered by the perception that the United States is also a country where, as Nadine Gordimer pointed out, "'nobody's' at risk' except from their own demons."[85] How often, in America, such demons may be construed as familial.

The Expatriation Cure

For some writers, expatriating was their first self-defining embodiment of an artistic vocation, what Cynthia Ozick called "the delectable excitement, *the waiting-to-be-born* excitement, of longing to write."[86] Expatriating was a consciously curative response to pressures at home; whereas, for others it was due to political turmoil, war, genocide, economic depression, or blacklisting. However, with the American or British *Paris Review* interviewees, we are usually in the company of the voluntary expatriate, the Grand Tourist, a different being than the involuntary exile.[87] Many of these voluntary expatriates left for the reasons I have discussed and many went to Paris, a city which has served this century as true north for those wanting to recreate themselves as artists. As a city of pilgrimage and an *imago* for Western artists, Paris is what Thebes is to the mythology of the Oedipus complex: it has its place in the pantheon as one of art's *genius loci.*

John Ashbery, in his art criticism, describes an encounter of the American daimon with the Parisian as "American restlessness, energy, and visual know-how being released in a non-American space of great physical charm, of subtly different human relationships, whose real nature is elegiac and conservative rather than forward-looking and constructive."[88] With this description of the city, we recall Hillman's advocacy of the retro-move from America to Europe and from North to South rather than from Old to New. Hillman proposes that going back to the Old World is going forward to reclaim the world within, deepening rather than expanding it, burnishing rather than inventing.

J. E. Gedo, a psychoanalyst who writes about artists, explicates creative work in a way which dovetails into my analysis of the psychological efficacies of expatriation and the fateful function of an *imago* such as Paris. In reviewing the work of another analyst, Adrian Stokes, Gedo observes that:

> The aesthetic object is an ideal object that is seen as lively, complete, and stable. Whatever its subject matter, the aesthetic object is capable of giving pleasure through the poignancy of its facture; in this way, archaic as-

pects of the inner world that are ordinarily unacceptable to many persons may be made public through externalization into a realm of illusion without conflict.[89]

In this view, artistic vocation depends partly on an idealization of the created work as a good-enough mother, or a good God: a compass grounding the self. Vocation, then, fulfills Kohut's description of an idealized self-object as a stable, self-congruent figure which can absorb and survive the self's "catch and release" of attachment. This inner work of the vocation and its emblems—such as Paris—may arise to serve not only, but especially, when the environment fails to aid the growing child's evolving need for an idealized mirror of her innocent, fecund grandiosity.

Since expatriation is a literal move into a symbolic realm in which internalized object relations play out as a literal, libidinized relationship to art, we are clearly in Winnicott's realm of transitional space. Here, *in this place*, for the child, objects conventionally thought to be material may be animate; thought has the power to kill and create. Here, creation of the self is still occurring—the way volcanism creates islands—and is a process susceptible to intervention, whether through an analysis allowing for play and regression, through the self-reparative work of creation, or through expatriation. Here, the function of *elsewhere* is to receive the projection of a need to be received and facilitated, unimpinged upon, and subtly aided in, exploiting creative solitude.

Kohut described "a transference of creativity" he thought occurred for the artist in the creative phase of working: he believed that artists needed a cathected relationship to someone to sustain their work because their reserves were "enfeebled" as they "engaged in the daring exploration of the moon landscapes of the unknown."[90] I would extend this transference to include a transference onto geographical place. There is certainly as much of a "transference of creativity" to sites of high art as there is to companions, and artists are the disciples of those places, submitting themselves to their exigencies in return for their *darshan* and dispensation. As Dennis Porter observes in *Haunted Journeys*, "The burden of a subjective as well as of a collective, culturally transmitted past determines in complex and unpredictable ways our relation to foreign places and people."[91] Paris, London, and New York are such places; Florence and Rome. Kohut might describe an expatriation within the transference as a search for "a matrix of security" to support the creative process.[92] I believe a cathected site of expatriation enlivens a promise of being just such a good-enough matrix, of being a better matrix for nurturing the artist's work than the family or home culture, precisely because the family is too familiar (no matter how benign) to catalyze one's necessary move into the foreign which one's art is.

Those for whom expatriation did not alleviate the lacks of earlier development and facilitate a move into authentic autonomy are those who remain unable to form what I might call a xenotropic transference to any
place; these might be artists who, as Ashbery says, never shake "the feeling
of being a stranger even in moments of greatest rapport with one's adopted
home."[93] There is also the syndrome Ashbery felt he detected among some
of the expatriate American painters in Paris: a lack of "protest" in their
work.[94] He blamed this lack on expatriation itself, feeling that these artists
may have "already sufficiently expressed whatever protest they feel by expatriating themselves"; that, while expatriation may enrich the work or make it
possible, it may also consume creative energy and assuage the need to
make.[95] Leaving one's country may certainly encapsulate a protest in the
case of political exile and refugee artists, but this is not usually true for
those who expatriate voluntarily, as an assertion (to the family) of differentiation and authenticity. While an artist's decision to expatriate can always
be read as a message to one's family of origin, it is never only that. It is also
something strictly in the service of embodying one's vocation, or the part of
the self which is conceived of as an artist.

There is in going abroad, as artist Eric Wolf commented in *Art News*,
"an emptying of oneself, during which all local thoughts go away."[96] I propose that this self-emptying is both personally and archetypally necessary
for someone exploring a call to the vocation of artist: Empty? The better to
be filled with one's destiny. Vocation manifests when one becomes more attached to the possibilities of one's art than to making oneself in the image of
family. In many milieux and cultures, this move is experienced as a particularly European American style of betrayal, as an abandonment of the family
and its "face," of sacred local turf wars, or the race war, or the struggles of
identity politics. An artist pursuing vocation has either given up, or voluntarily turns away from, old alliances and seeks a new center of gravity around
which to realign work and fantasy. Vocation will be the new axis around
which the artist's, rather than the personality's, concerns revolve.

If the artist pursues expatriation in the service of vocation, there are
several possible modes of response to the new place: assimilation, integration, separation, or marginalization.[97] A neophyte artist can "go native" like
Gauguin, or create a hermetic retreat conducive to an increased focus on the
self—a retreat for sharper devotion to the work. Some crave the sensation of
anonymity and "neutrality" of being a stranger in a foreign city. Gertrude
Stein claimed that she maintained this kind of relationship to Paris and
France, that she purposely stayed outside of the French language in order to
render English more vivid to her. John Ashbery, writing about Stein, comments that "the foreign language that surrounded her was probably also a
necessary insulation for the immense effort of concentration this book [*The
Making of Americans*] required."[98] And later he says of her that Paris pro-

vided "a comfortable, *neutral*, cosmopolitan working space to a writer who did not wish to be disturbed."[99] I would propose that an artist chooses a city not only for its buzz as a "cultural selfobject" but for the accuracy of the mirroring and adequacy of support the artist fantasizes the place—as if a mother—will proffer. In any immigration or expatriation there are two mothers, as Salman Akhtar notes, the "mother of symbiosis" and the "mother of separation."[100]

Mary McCarthy is a writer who found a sympathetic place capable of fostering what Kohut would call a mirroring selfobject transference:

> Also, I felt a great, great congeniality . . . with the history of Florence, the Florentine temperament. I felt that through the medium of writing about this city I could set forth what I believed in, what I was for; that through this city, its history, its architects and painters . . . it was possible for me to say what I believed in.[101]

Here the sense of place matches the writer's image of the ideally congruent setting, the place seeming to promise that one's subjectivity will be perfectly realized and reflected back in a way which is experienced as permission and invitation to reveal one's vision of the "true self." Some artists, however, may carry guilt about abandoning their family and native country which prevents them from integrating or merging too completely into the new culture. They may have to participate in the new place only vicariously or at a remove, in a way which is not felt as transgressive to old loyalties. But to the degree an expatriating artist has the inner capacity to engage the foreign locale, and to the degree there is a "goodness of fit," I hold that the sojourn works reparatively on the self-as-medium: as the artist works on the medium, the medium works on the artist.

A Typology of Expatriatism

I propose there are, broadly, three different kinds of expatriate artists, reflecting three different psychological situations behind artists' expatriation. I will call these types "escape artists," "hunger artists," and "home artists." First, the escape artists are those pushed out by a sense of oppression, impingement, and intrusion, who need to leave overpowering relationships. Then there are the hunger artists, whose experience of neglect and compromised attachment at home sends them abroad because they need better mirroring and better nurturing. Home artists, the third type of expatriate, leave home because they crave a tonic experience of displacement which will either jump-start or renew their ability to create within their familiar parameters of identity.

Escape artists, the first type of expatriate, crave an experience of anonymity and neutrality in moving away from impingement. They desire solitude and may remain observers, outside of the world they've entered. At
home, the second type, the hunger artists, experience sensations of emptiness; they may never have felt at home anywhere. They desire affirmation of
their ability to work. The place of sojourn takes on the archaic maternal
function of "holding," but it can occur in many forms—aesthetic, sensuous,
or architectural, even culinary! The third type, the home artists, often simply
reaffirm their core cultural sense of identity through the welcome shifts in
the salience of identity's markers—when skin color, accent, religion, or par-
entage are unfamiliarly crucial. This experience of decentering the familiar
teaches the artist all she needs to know about the real ground of the self in
order to discover the compass point and the ground of the work.

In her *Paris Review* interview, Elizabeth Spencer vividly expresses the
experience of an escape artist who went abroad in response to a sense of impingement. While discussing her sojourn abroad and its necessity, the interviewer reminded Spencer of what she had said in her book, *The Voice at the
Back Door*: "In the South, it's nothing but family, family. We couldn't
breathe, even, until we left."[102] But Spencer also expressed the revival of
early separation/individuation trauma which separation through expatriation
can bring:[103] "I can never 'adjust' to losing anything I really love. . . . I don't
think I've ever really cut the root; I never wanted to."[104] One might say this
passage reflects the sentiments of someone whose roots held, someone who
indeed had both sufficient emotional attachment to family and home and
sufficient encouragement to be her own person. However, in the phrase, "I
can never 'adjust,'" I sense anxiety's intrusive twinge; a moralizing, self-
punishing thought that she "should" have been able to let go in a way she
could not, that her love was too needy, unfree, or fraught. Maintaining a
connection to one's origins may mean that indeed there was attachment, and
it need not be inimical to the development of an artistic identity. But, if one
is bound to home by anxiety, the attachment to home was an insecure attachment and may despoil any moves toward a creative autonomy.

Ted Hughes, in his *Paris Review* interview, sounds like an escape artist.
He describes not just expatriation but "exile" as a remedy for early impingement or intrusion, and pictures that impingement in the strongest
terms: "We're at the mercy of the groups that shaped our early days. We're
so helplessly social—like cells in an organ. Maybe that's why madness
sometimes works—it knocks out the oversensitive connection. And maybe
that's why exile is good."[105] What's interesting here is first, his acknowledgment of our dependence on our origins and our true interdependence
and, second, his characterization of us as being "at the mercy of" those connections. He portrays this helplessness as an inevitable accompaniment of
dependence and a hindrance to individuation. Hughes then says that mad-

ness seems like an almost unavoidable defense against the intensity of our interconnectedness, and that madness and exile (and, interestingly, he doesn't distinguish between exile and expatriation: getting away is all) are both life-preservers.

Edna O'Brien conveys the same sense of external oppression in her interview when she reflects on her childhood in Ireland: "My relationship with Ireland is very complex. I could not live there for a variety of reasons. I felt oppressed and strangulated from an early age."[106] O'Brien makes no explicit link between her experience of the nation's *imago*, its cultural self, and of her Irish family, but reactivity to the family haunts and infuses her reactivity to the country which "oppressed" and "strangulated": the violence toward the self she experienced is given an impersonal complexity in which the two transferences, to family and country, have become fused into one archobject. What the artist fleeing impingement seeks abroad, elsewhere, is the state of "fertile neglect" where the overweening impress of the family-country complex is lessened enough to allow the core self's desires to manifest.[107]

Artists who go abroad out of a sense of dearth, void, or neglect—the hunger artists—have a different experience. Here is Susan Sontag: "How many trips we have to undertake so as not to be empty and invisible."[108] Expatriation or repeated sojourns propelled by this lack do not have a good prognosis for creative remediation, unless the dearth is experienced chiefly as an apathy or as a result of truly lackluster surroundings. If one has tried foreign sojourns without being revivified and jump-started, expatriation will not cure. But if expatriation has been sought as a means of enlivening the self and it has, then the artist has enough inner resources and the necessary work of self-transformation can unfold. Stephen Spender's comment in his interview, "I always felt twice as much alive the moment I left England" is an example of a simple lack of vitality which leaving can redress.[109]

Unfortunately, sometimes warming oneself by a strange, welcoming fire cannot satisfy, and an unassuaged ache and disappointment follow the attempt. When this is the case, xenotropism cannot effectuate the desired "turn," and make it right. There may be no capacity for the purely artistic work when the sense of inner emptiness is too great, and Winnicott's zone of transitional space, of symbolic play, cannot be accessed.[110] In positing this, I follow Gedo's observation that there may be identifiable "developmental lines for aesthetic capabilities" and that creativity may involve "autonomous functions" which require "*unusual* growth in order to become available volitionally."[111] This observation supports my contention that an artist's development is dual: to be capable of creativity requires first, having enough resources within the self to support creative work and its duresses, and then second, the capacity to dream wildly within the discipline of one's craft.

Writers who are unable, because of their fragility, to expatriate—or even successfully sojourn abroad—certainly exist. Anne Sexton, so seriously disturbed and eventually a suicide, tells the story of a failed sojourn in her *Paris Review* interview. She recounts how she once got a grant to go abroad and hoped to recreate the trip a great-aunt, who was her best childhood friend, had taken years earlier and during which she had mailed letters to Anne. She had the idea of writing back letters to her great-aunt and making poems of them. But the great-aunt's original letters were stolen in Brussels and that was the end of the poems Anne intended to write. Instead of staying the year which her grant allowed, she was obliged to come home after only two and a half months because, she said, "I lost my sense of self. I had, as my psychiatrist said, 'a leaky ego' and I had to come home. . . . I need my husband and my therapist and my children to tell me who I am."[112]

Gedo believes that "the artistic product is an idealized object, tenuously distinguished from the self and therefore akin to an infantile fetish."[113] I would amend this to say that it is not the product alone which is idealized, but its making: the process becomes pleasurable in its resolution of tension or invention of a novel solution to an aesthetic or emotional problem. The realm of making then mediates between internal and external object relations—what Hillman calls the imaginal realm or world of images and Winnicott calls transitional space—where direct work on the soul, that oxygen which makes humans into *homo faber*, is possible. Cynthia Ozick calls this work, in a phrase Hillman could echo, "a parallel Eros."[114]

The artist's relationship to the process of imaginative work and to the place of expatriation may parallel or recapitulate one another just as the relationship to the work recapitulates primary object relations with one's parents. The place of expatriation then becomes the alchemical vessel of the adult's experiment with his or her capacity to re-parent the self. If this process works, and there are art objects as its documents, the resulting (psychological) work may look like this: the art object, depending on whether we are talking about an escape or hunger artist, is formed out of a void or chaos; it first becomes an object which soothes, then eventually is granted more autonomy if the artist is sure of her creation and her continued ability to create; finally, one might relate to the creative product with *jouissance*, appreciating it for its own mysterious being.[115]

The actual reparative and constructive function of making, as opposed to the repetitive, compulsive nature of the fetish and fetishization, is also neglected in Gedo's analogy between the art object and the fetish. A fetish's cathexis, by definition, remains unconscious and resistant to evolution or working-through. Rather than being a "fetish," the art object may be, as Edna O'Brien said, a "fetus."[116] She pinpoints the reparative and curative ability of the creative process to bridge old rifts between the false and true selves in this discussion of the narrative technique in one of her novels: "As a child you are both your secret self and the 'you' that your parents think you are. So the use of the second person [in *A Pagan Place*] was a way of combining the two identities."[117] Here we see the classic conflation of creative work with work on the self. This explanation of her first novel's etiology highlights what midwifes the writing process itself: "It was the separation from Ireland which brought me to the point where I *had* to write."[118] In O'Brien's view, writing is separation's segue into individual work; it is the self's expatriation in order to be. But it is not an emptying; it is self-transformation.

The third type of expatriate I've identified, the home artists, are writers who went abroad and discovered they belonged at home. Their artistic development follows a different trajectory than the first two types of expatriate artists because the gift and the work are able to unfold on home ground.[119] The separation which the two other types of expatriate artists feel is necessary to foster the self-as-artist and the work is of little importance. A salutary jolt of decentering suffices. Nadine Gordimer, as mentioned previously, is such a writer. She discovered her sense of identity as a South African as soon as she went to England. What she found was a sudden clarity about her true self and the acquired fantasies about identity which had obscured it. The simultaneous confirmation and disconfirmation of these rival versions of self only happened with the displacement of traveling abroad. For Gordimer, disconfirmation of the fantasy—the familial and cultural myth that England was really "home"—freed her to begin her work on what, for her, was an authentic and very viable basis.

Isak Dinesen is another writer who describes her arrival abroad without linking it to either a sense of neglect needing redress or a need to escape external impingement. She was, by her own account, more pushed by economic and political factors than driven by a need for psychological survival or rejuvenation. The joy she felt on arriving in Africa—but not just the continent itself, rather the farm which became her new home—is uncolored either by unresolved separation or a need to forget where she had come from: "The first day I arrived there, I loved the country and felt at home, even among unfamiliar flowers, trees, and animals, and changing clouds over the Ngong Hills, unlike any clouds I had ever known."[120]

Her recognition of an unexpected sense of "home" seems centered in her response to the landscape's lushness, which appeals because it is completely unprecedented. Her response is not linked to any vague longing for the exotic, nor was her intent in going there to make herself a writer. She went there to live and make her way. In this way too, she is different from so many who expatriated in order to facilitate their work. Her experience of a sense of home appears grounded in the place's particularity, more as if it were a lover she'd found than an antidote for earlier developmental injuries. The writing came retrospectively, when she found out she had to leave Africa: "Later, when I knew in my heart I should have to sell the farm and go back to Denmark, I did begin to write."[121]

By contrast, Dinesen's earlier experience in Paris, when she went there as a painter, was completely different; Paris overwhelmed her and took her away from painting. All she said in her *Paris Review* interview was that "the impact of Paris was too great," that there was too much Paris to see.[122] She was probably not meant to be a painter, or this expatriation might have launched her in that vocation, but it did not. Beyond this, she may not have been ready, as she was not yet ready then to be a writer, though she had already been published by the age of twenty. She explained this by saying, "I think I had an intuitive fear of being trapped."[123]

Dinesen does not really fit in any one of the three types of expatriates we have seen. I think that is because the motive of her expatriatism was not to become an artist, but was pragmatic, a way to make her life rather than her art. That the art followed was perhaps a compensation and a way of mourning the home the foreign had become when she repatriated to Denmark. This is somebody, then, who became a refugee and began writing out of loss; somebody who did not become an artist through expatriation but through repatriation. The writer she then became had roots in a need to preserve the person she had become in Africa, a way of preserving the important selfobject, the image of that lost home.

Having considered these three different psychological scenarios for expatriation and their theoretical underpinnings in depth psychology, I would now like to look more closely at one writer's story, that of Henry Miller. His story will help illustrate the reparative and constructive functions of xenotropism—of a turn to the foreign—which I am arguing for here. I will examine Miller's experience as an expatriate in light of the thumbnail sketch he gives in his *Paris Review* interview, then amplify that account from his other writings. His story exemplifies both the stages, and therapeutic potency of, an expatriation thoroughly and consciously in the service of artistic development. Though many might argue that his liveliest work was done in his Parisian years, his own view was that these years were years of apprenticeship not only as a writer, but as a person of vision.

Henry Miller: Expatriatism as Second Birth

Living in another language means growing another self.

—Alastair Reid, *The New Yorker*, June 24, 1996

Henry Miller's writing career, and the role his years in France played in it, provides a template of xenotropism's psychological function for a writer who expatriates, whether briefly or for decades, to serve the work. In Miller's case, we can test the foregoing observations and analysis about the function of the foreign in light of depth-psychological theory and see how they illuminate Miller's development as a writer in Paris. I am proposing that development of the vocation is inseparable from the child's history and its sequelae: this is the "eternal child" who tinctures the adult's experience, the child moving and suspended, as Hillman would say, in the *metaxy*—or middle realm—between the artist's past and the world of the present. The deep story of artistic vocation is inescapably a story of "bearing the child," of "carrying his incurable weakness" consciously into the work.[124]

I have advocated recognition that an artist's work is pivotal as an object in the artist's personal development, and I also want to enlarge the notion of expatriation beyond its stereotypical associations of escapism and dilettantism: expatriatism is coextensive with any artistic work which it engenders or informs. In Paris, Miller cast the realization of personal vocation into heroic terms and imagined his development as a "bloody struggle to liberate himself, to emerge clean of the past, a bright, gory sun god cast up on an alien shore."[125] In Gerald Kennedy's excellent analysis of expatriation, he writes that "the life of writing requires 'pilgrimage' and 'flight,' a deliberate forsaking of the known and familiar."[126] But what can appear to be a prerequisite for the artistic vocation, as we have seen, is as much a convention about artists as it is necessarily accurate about the psychological exigencies in any individual writer's experience: some writers, as we have seen, need to stay home.

In speaking of Miller, Kennedy comments that writing was transformative, gestational, and involved a second birth—the birth of the artist-self. Miller himself described Paris as "the cradle of artificial births"[127] and depicted the historical and contemporary power of Paris to draw what Kohut, as we have seen, called the cultural selfobject transference. What Paris provided for his writing, Miller continued, was a context which made it possible for him to be delivered "back into his soil."[128] This is analogous to the reparative work of "holding" on which Winnicott focused in such depth, except that Miller takes it further, beyond just reparation into the mythic realm of rebirth and resurrection.[129]

Miller's succinct description of the death and rebirth experience in expatriation is not just schematic, but archetypal:

> I had two beginnings really, one here in America, which was abortive,
> and the other in Europe. How was I able to begin again, one may well ask?
> I should answer truthfully—by dying. In that first year or so in Paris I lit-
> erally died, was literally annihilated—and resurrected as a new man . . .
> the transition, if I may say so, from the conscious artist to the budding
> spiritual being.[130]

Here is a writer not working from ego, but starting from a new center of
gravity in the self, from what Kohut might call his "cosmic self"—the apo-
theosis of the true self, with art as its representation. Thus, the mythic script
of the pursuit of vocation through expatriation: estrangement from the familiar, often actually felt to be foreign to the true self, drives or inspires one to
concretize and ground one's sense of otherness through expatriation. *Ostranenie*, the swerve from the familiar, yields a symbolic death of the old self
and makes way for a reframed emergence of the true self as artist. The psychological distance between the biographical self and the artistic self, literalized in the geographical move abroad, can function as a measure of two
things: first, the self-estrangement experienced by the child in the family,
and second, the qualitative difference between the biographical self and the
imaginal soul, or what Hillman—as a neo-Neoplatonist—calls the *daimon*.

Kennedy tells us that "the engendering of an expatriate self through 'artificial birth' produces a myth of personal origins which sublimates the
trauma of natural birth and maternal rejection."[131] While I understand the
evocative power of calling the transformation a rebirth (that potent
mytheme), Kennedy portrays it through the agency of sublimation, loosely
used, and consequently misapplies the notion of sublimation: he uses it both
as evidence of the wounded narcissism resulting from "maternal rejection"
and as a prescription for its cure. By definition, the defense mechanism cannot also be the cure; it is a stopgap, a repetitive, non-transformative strategy.
While some art may be a personal psychological strategy practiced defen-
sively and repetitiously to survive what ails, much art is self-transforming or
self-transcending, practiced with the hope that the work will make the artist,
just as much as the artist makes the work.

Both Winnicott and Kohut offer subtler analyses of the sequelae to maternal rejection and of the reparative efforts people make. What is notable is
that Kennedy's phrase, "natural birth," echoes Pauline use of the category
"natural man." The classic philosophy invoked implies that the artist needs
to be born again "artificially" in order to bring forth mature products of personal vision. I would reframe Kennedy's attempt to universalize this phenomenon by saying that not all artists seek a second birth, nor do all of those

who enact this rebirth do it in the same way. Rather, expatriation is a specific choice some artists make, and not always in service of recovering the true self in the vocation. Nor is it necessarily a search to undo the childhood trauma of maternal *rejection*—the grit for the pearl may as easily be maternal impingement, or impersonal neglect, or *paternal* rejection. But in all instances, we could say that expatriation for the sake of the work is a gesture toward the integrity of the vocation, toward the emergence of the "true self" or an authentic "personal way of life."

From Miller's experience comes this description of the conditions necessary to become an artist: "Personality is engendered at the point where the inner and outer landscapes are contiguous."[132] And from this personality comes the work. To propose a corollary: the successful expatriation should work to render an artist's inner and outer life compatible. Miller expatriated for reasons fitting both the hunger artist and the escape artist. In the United States, he experienced a sense of dearth as well as a strong sense of cultural impingement. He had the sense that "America is essentially against the artists, that the enemy of America is the artist, because he stands for individuality and creativeness, and that's un-American somehow."[133] He experienced the lacks in the home culture as edifying: "I am grateful to America for having made me realize my needs."[134]

At first Miller felt he was the kind of person who would have gone anywhere and tried anything to feel better, but it turned out that Paris worked for him: "I am a man of the old world, a seed that was transplanted by the wind, a seed which failed to blossom in the mushroom oasis of America. I belong on the heavy tree of the past."[135] For this type of expatriate writer, it is precisely one's outsider status and the felt rightness of the receiving foreign environment which combine to create the therapeutic equivalent of rapport in psychotherapy or the appearance of the transference in analysis—both instances considered a sign that the therapeutic process has in fact been joined, that it has "taken"—whatever the actual length of time in the professional relationship.

And what factors ensure that a place, a city, or an analyst is contiguous enough with inner experience to permit the self, the work, to unfold? This is a mystery of personal preference, cultural history, examples, myth, predisposition, archetypes. For a place to fulfill the needs of xenotropism, I suspect degree of foreignness from the home culture, which cross-cultural psychology operationalizes as "cultural distance," has to be significant, but not great. I believe the choice of place will also be affected by the artist's subjective degree of alienation, the intensity of need for a mirroring selfobject, the ego strength and inner resources of the artist (i.e., how much symbolic distance from home she can tolerate), and the presence of an idealizing transference to the place. Each art, like each school of psychotherapy, has its shrines.

For Miller, the move to Paris signaled the end of one life and the beginning of another one, as a writer, for which he could take responsibility. He describes a moment of understanding when he realized what had happened to him: while in the metro, the phrase, *"l'homme que j'etais, je ne le suis plus* [the man I was, I am no longer]" came to him.[136] Elsewhere he wrote about his death/rebirth as a writer in Paris—"Like it or not, I was obliged to create a new life for myself. And this new life I feel is mine, absolutely mine"—and with that the freedom, coeval with God's, to create his fate.[137]

Miller describes his "detachment" from America as a separation from the sun, like a satellite planet of matter splitting away, for which the sun no longer existed and "I had myself become a blazing sun. And like all the other suns of the universe I had to nourish myself *from within.*"[138] He says, again in mythic terms, that one would either become "more and more alive, or more and more dead" from having made this move to establish one's true, artistic self at the center of one's psychic universe.[139] He tells us, in essence, that the shift in center of gravity from the familial, but alienated, biographical self to an authentic self as an artist is a gamble, that it can go badly or not at all, and that it requires both a Promethean effort of ego and the support of a sympathetic person/place matrix.

No wonder the story of writers' vocation are as fascinating to us as the tragedies Kohut thought afford us vicarious, necessary, and satisfying glimpses of a realized self: these stories of expatriations undertaken to re-establish the self creatively and authentically are pure psychodrama. When renowned writers are telling us their stories, as in the *Paris Review* interviews we have examined, we are assured of a successful ending; we know they achieved, if not their own self-transformation, at least the work. For other artists who are works-in-progress—perhaps ourselves—the narrative line is not yet revealed and the fate is undetermined.

Ezra Pound, an unlikely informant on individuation perhaps, as an unreconstructed exile and "traitor," said this about the function of the foreign in his *Paris Review* interview, done toward the end of his life:

> Exotics were necessary as an attempt at a foundation. One is transplanted and grows, and one is pulled up and taken back to what one has been transplanted from and it is no longer there. The contacts aren't there and I suppose one reverts to one's organic nature and finds it merciful.[140]

The larger pattern of a life which Pound describes here points toward how the work of self-making through xenotropism prepares one for what Jung called individuation—the art of becoming who one really is—and, above all, for mortality. As Joyce Carol Oates observed in her interview, "the mere passage of time makes us all exiles."[141]

Xenotropism, as we have seen, can work as a strong, self-preserving instinct in the trajectory and narrative of self-realization. We have traced how depth psychology, with its narrative about people's fates, first feared the foreign, using it as an image of infection, psychosis, and threat, and now has extended it empathy. Depth psychology has, along with other postmodernist movements in the humanities, gone as far as decentering notions of self and other, of ego and alien.[142] Now the foreign is no longer an essential Other, it is a floating definition which may take a perspective or have its errancy across borders. But, most importantly, it no longer wears the face of pathology.[143] The understanding of self and artistic vocation, acquired chiefly from Winnicott's and Kohut's work, provides perspective for interpreting any expatriation undertaken expressly to allow development of the self-as-artist, or to find a containing milieu where one would have a chance to realign and nurture the authentic self according to what Hillman might term the soul's *axis mundi*. However far that world is from the coordinates an artist was originally given, the trajectory between these two worlds limns the development of the vocation, a true piece of work.

Notes

1. Archetypal psychology's apologist, James Hillman, succinctly defines depth psychology as "the modern field whose interest is in the unconscious levels of the psyche—that is, the deeper meanings of the soul." In a typical move, he links this modern definition back to Greek thought by citing Heraclitus's statement: "You could not discover the limits of the soul (*psyche*), even if you traveled every road to do so; such is the depth (*bathun*) of its meaning (*logos*)." Hillman, *Re-Visioning Psychology* (New York: Harper & Row, 1975), xi. As for the term *artistic vocation* that I have chosen here and will use throughout the essay, I intend to invoke both the primary meaning of vocation as a "call" or "summons" (from the Latin *vocatus* and *vocatio*) and its religious connotation to describe an artist's development. Especially here, connecting as I am the development of the artist's work with the development of the self-as-artist, the word *vocation* carries what feels like the necessary specific gravity honoring both the work and the calling.

2. As examples: Sigmund Freud, convinced art was at best the sublimation of primitive instincts; C. G. Jung, convinced Picasso was Western art's greatest schizophrenic; D. W. Winnicott, perhaps enviously and wistfully, describing artists' "ruthlessness."

3. There is no end to examples of artists' infamous eccentricities (tolerable deviance) and perversities (intolerable deviance). A short list: George Sand with her cigars and trousers; Oscar Wilde's passion for fine china; Proust's cork-lined room; Truman Capote's collection of French paperweights, some of which he always had to have with him when he traveled. A telling and simple definition of eccentricity from Patience Gray, an expatriate chef and artist, reveals one source of artists' perceived foreignness: "Eccentricity: living according to priorities established by one's own experience." Gray, *Honey from a Weed: Fasting and Feasting in Tuscany, Catalonia, the Cyclades, and Apulia*

(San Francisco: North Point Press, 1990), 111. Later in the paper I will discuss artists' alleged foreignness and subjective sense of alienation as a consequence of their insistence on what Winnicott calls the "personal way of life." Winnicott, "Morals and Education" in *The Maturational Processes and the Facilitating Environment* (New York: International Universities Press, Inc., 1965), 102.

4. This phrase comes from Gerald J. Kennedy's fine book on exiled and expatriate artists in Paris and, in context, reflects his consideration of "the predicament of the exiled, ungrounded writer searching for the city of writing." Kennedy, *Imagining Paris: Exile, Writing, and American Identity* (New Haven, Conn.: Yale University Press, 1993), 184. Kennedy explains how expatriate and exiled artists "underwent dislocation to achieve a new relation to their work" (192).

5. Hillman, a bit gleefully perhaps, recounts his precursors' geographical distresses: Freud was constitutionally unable to go to Rome until 1901 and had a "disturbance" on the Acropolis during his visit there. See Henri Ellenberger's classic work, *The Discovery of the Unconscious* (New York: Basic Books, 1970), 447, for more details, as well as for a thorough analysis of the biographical context of Freud's and Jung's ideas. Hillman also calls our attention to several articles on "Freud's Disturbance on the Acropolis" that appeared in *American Imago* 26, no 4 (1969). As for Jung, he fainted when he went to Rome and was deeply ambivalent about the disorienting pull of the foreign on his trips to Africa, the United States, and India. In India, he spent the last part of his trip on board his ship, fearing the power of the country and deciding he must concentrate on his work back home in Zurich. See C. G. Jung, *Memories, Dreams, Reflections*, trans. R. Winston (New York: Vintage, 1963), 269. Hillman reads these geographical neuroses as instinctive responses of a mind out of its element, as he contends that Freud and Jung's psychologies are fruits of a Northern, monotheistic mentality, and that therefore the move South (into the Italy of the Renaissance, and the polytheism of classical Greece) was constitutionally impossible for them. See Ellenberger, *Discovery of the Unconscious*, 447.

6. As critic Edward Said has said, "Exile, immigration, and the crossing of boundaries are experiences that can provide us with new narrative forms or, in John Berger's phrase, *other* ways of telling." Cited in Dennis Porter, *Haunted Journeys* (Princeton, N.J.: Princeton University Press, 1991), 5. Each theorist expatriated from received knowledge about psychology into a new "way of telling" the story of the psyche. As Jacqueline Chénieux-Gendron comments in an essay on the surrealists abroad, "self-analysis is built on the foundation of a lucid exile." Chénieux-Gendron, "Surrealists in Exile," in *Exile and Creativity*, ed. Susan R. Suleiman (Durham, N.C.: Duke University Press, 1998), 175.

7. Shoshana Felman, *Jacques Lacan and the Adventure of Insight: Psychoanalysis in Contemporary Culture* (Cambridge, Mass.: Harvard University Press, 1987), 63.

8. Sigmund Freud, *The Interpretation of Dreams* in *Standard Edition of the Complete Psychological Works of Sigmund Freud* 6 (London: Hogarth Press, 1960).

9. For example, in a work that might be categorized as applied psychoanalysis, Julia Kristeva follows Freud's commonplace in her analysis of the foreign and the foreigner when she remarks, "The foreigner is a 'symptom.'" Kristeva, *Strangers to Ourselves*, trans. Leon S. Roudiez (New York: Columbia University Press, 1991), 103.

10. See Bruno Bettelheim's popular work, *Freud and Man's Soul* (New York: A.A. Knopf, 1983) for an account of the translation of Freud into English and his view of the terminology's effect on the American perception of psychoanalysis.

11. Freud, *The Psychotherapy of Hysteria* in *Standard Edition* 2, 290-291.

12. Freud, *The Psychotherapy of Hysteria*, 291.

13. Freud, *The Psychotherapy of Hysteria*, 291.

14. Freud, "Dissection of the Psychological Personality," *Standard Edition* 22, 22.

15. Freud, "Dissection of the Psychological Personality," 57.

16. Homi Bhabha, who describes the result of this internal xenophobia both for the individual and for the group, speaks of "the Stranger, whose languageless presence evokes an archaic anxiety and aggressivity by impeding the search for narcissistic love-objects in which the subject can rediscover himself, and upon which the group's *amour propre* is based." Bhabha, "DissemiNation: Time, Narrative, and the Margins of the Modern Nation" in *Nation and Narration*, ed. Homi K. Bhabha (New York: Routledge, 1990), 316.

17. In a counterpoint to Freud's fantasy of the pathogenic foreign object, Dennis Porter quotes Abdelkebir Khatibi writing of his delectation and consumption of the foreign through eating and the resulting curative self-displacement: "Every foreign dish that defies our customs liberates our body from its earliest habits." Cited in Porter, *Haunted Journeys*, 298. Here is delectation of the foreign as hedonism made strange.

18. Freud, "Dissection of the Psychological Personality," 72.

19. Hillman notes that "Freud's associations are with literature, for which he uses—always a sign of affective importance—a foreign term, *roman à clef*, meaning 'a work which presents real persons and events, but disguised by the author.'" Hillman, *Healing Fiction* (Barrytown, N.Y.: Station Hill Press, 1983), 5.

20. Winnicott, "Analysis in Latency," in *The Maturational Processes and the Facilitating Environment*, 9th ed. (New York: International Universities Press, Inc., 1986), 116, 117.

21. Winnicott, "Classification: Is there a Psycho-Analytic Contribution to Psychiatric Classification? (1959-64)" in *The Maturational Processes*, 132.

22. Winnicott, "Classification," 132.

23. See James Hillman, *A Blue Fire*, ed. Thomas Moore (New York: Harper Perennial, 1991), 8.

24. Other well-known theorists of the British object-relations school are Ronald Fairbairn, Michael Balint, and Wilfrid Bion.

25. Winnicott, "The Mind and Its Relation to the Psyche-Soma" in *Through Paediatrics to Psychoanalysis* (London: Hogarth Press, 1975); Winnicott, "The Capacity to be Alone" in *The Maturational Processes and the Facilitating Environment*, 29-36.

26. Winnicott, "The Mind and Its Relation to Psyche-Soma," 246.

27. "A special case of the false self is that in which the intellectual process becomes the seat of the false self. A dissociation between mind and psyche-soma develops, which produces a well-recognized clinical picture. In many of these cases there is probably an especially high intellectual endowment, and this may contribute to the building up of the syndrome." Winnicott, "Classification," 134.

28. Winnicott, "Mind and Its Relation to Psyche-Soma," 248.

29. Unfortunately, the "false self" can become a sorcerer's apprentice, sure of how to begin, but unable to stop. Health, for Winnicott, is finding an appropriate balance between the demands of social identity and of the individual good, or "the personal way of life." Winnicott, "Morals and Education" in *The Maturational Processes and the Facilitating Environment*, 102. Winnicott also saw the "false self" as one of the introjects taken

in from the infant's environment. These introjects "are not exports reimported, they are also truly foreign goods." Winnicott, "Morals and Education," 99.

30. Winnicott, "The Capacity to Be Alone," 135.

31. See Homi Bhabha on "how easily that boundary that secures the cohesive limits of the Western nation [self] may imperceptibly turn into a contentious *internal* liminality that provides a place from which to speak both of, and as, the minority, the exilic, the marginal and the emergent. . . . So long as a firm boundary is maintained between the territories, and the narcissistic wounded is contained, the aggressivity will be projected onto the Other or the Outside." Bhabha, "DissemiNation," 300. And note Kristeva's terse comment: "There is nothing more dismal than a dead God." Kristeva, *Black Sun: Depression and Melancholia*, trans. Leon S. Roudiez (New York: Columbia University Press, 1989), 8.

32. Cited from *Sexus* in *Henry Miller on Writing* (New York: New Directions, 1964), 17.

33. Winnicott, "Dependence towards Independence," in *The Maturational Processes and the Facilitating Environment.*

34. Winnicott, "Dependence toward Independence," 85.

35. Winnicott makes explicit his sense of how creative capacity and creative work initially come into being:

    [T]he integrating tendencies of the infant bring about a state in which the infant is a unit, a whole person, with an inside and an outside, and a person living in the body, and more or less bounded by the skin. . . . [T]here is now a place in which to store things . . . the child is now not only a potential creator of the world, but also the child becomes able to populate the world with samples of his or her own inner life." Winnicott, "Dependence towards Independence," 91.

36. Kohut is certainly not original in recognizing the role of empathy, though he did much to defend it as a tool both for analytic cure and for analytic investigation. Freud had said much earlier about the role of empathy in bridging difference that it "plays the largest part in our understanding of what is inherently foreign to our ego in other people." Sigmund Freud, "Group Psychology," in *The Standard Edition* 22, 108.

37. Writing of these new transferences, Kohut observes: "Both are reactivations of frustrated developmental needs. They are not drive transferences. . . . One needs to be accepted and mirrored." Kohut, "Idealization and Cultural Selfobjects" in *Self Psychology and the Humanities: Reflections on a New Psychoanalytic Approach*, ed. Charles B. Strozier (New York: W. W. Norton, 1985), 226.

38. Kohut, "Idealization and Cultural Selfobjects," 227.

39. See, for example, Kohut's statement that "the artist prepares the way for the culturally supported solution to the conflict or for healing of the defect." Kohut, "Self Psychology and the Sciences of Man," in *Self Psychology and the Humanities*, 89.

40. Kohut, "One Needs a Twinkle of Humor," in *Self Psychology and the Humanities*, 251.

41. Kohut, "One Needs a Twinkle of Humor," 251.

42. Kohut, "Stranger, Take Word to Sparta," in *Self Psychology and the Humanities*, 267.

43. Kohut, "Stranger, Take Word to Sparta," 267, emphasis mine.

44. Kohut, "Stranger, Take Word to Sparta," 238.

45. Kohut, "Religion, Ethics, Values," in *Self Psychology and the Humanities*, 262.

46. Kohut, "Idealization and Cultural Selfobjects," 227.

47. Kohut, "The Self in History," in *Self Psychology and the Humanities*, 169.

48. A. Goldberg, ed., *How Does Analysis Cure?* (Chicago: University of Chicago Press, 1984), 167.

49. Kohut, "Creativeness, Charisma, Group Psychology," in *Self Psychology and the Humanities*, 192, 222.

50. For an even-handed treatment of the Freud-Jung schism from a psychoanalytic viewpoint, see the last section of J. E. Gedo's book on creativity, *Portraits of the Artist: Psychoanalysis of Creativity and Its Vicissitudes* (New York: Guilford Press, 1983).

51. James Hillman, *Archetypal Psychology: A Brief Account* (Dallas, Tex.: Spring Publications, 1983), 2.

52. Hillman, *Archetypal Psychology*, 1.

53. Hillman, *Archetypal Psychology*, 2.

54. James Hillman with Laura Pozzo, *Inter Views* (New York: Harper & Row, 1983).

55. Here is Hillman's elaboration on this point:

We seek in the fantasy of the Renaissance an Archimedean point by means of which we could gain enough purchase upon psychology so as to lift this great encumbered field . . . off and away from its old Reformational foundations to be set down again upon the back of the Mediterranean bull—Ortega's dangerous two-horned bull—its style of madness and its style of fertility. Hillman, *Re-Visioning Psychology*, 218.

56. James Hillman, *The Dream and the Underworld* (New York: Harper & Row, 1979), 180-181.

57. Hillman, *Re-Visioning Psychology*, 105.

58. Hillman, *Archetypal Psychology*, 26.

59. Kristeva explores how lost the post-Enlightenment mind would be without the familiar coordinates of rational thought: "If he were to wander to the end of his passion for altering, dividing, knowing, modern man would be a foreigner to himself—a strange being whose polyphony would from that moment on be 'beyond good and evil.'" Kristeva, *Strangers to Ourselves*, 134. Later, in what I might call an expatriation into fantasy, she says that this "strange[ness] occurs when the boundaries between *imagination* and *reality* are erased." Kristeva, *Strangers to Ourselves*, 188. In short, the perspective of archetypal psychology.

60. Hillman, *Archetypal Psychology*, 23.

61. Hillman, *Archetypal Psychology*, 40.

62. Hillman, *Archetypal Psychology*, 51.

63. Hillman, *The Dream and the Underworld*, 137.

64. Hillman's support for his view of the "poetic basis of consciousness" is this assertion: "*Every reality of whatever* sort is first of all a fantasy image of the psyche." Hillman, *The Dream and the Underworld*, 137. Hillman considers errancy in an extended aside on the Knight Errant, a hermetic, nomadic, anheroic figure, in the chapter "Psychologizing or Seeing Through" in *Re-Visioning Psychology*, 159-164. The Knight Errant is a psychopomp bringing "mordant insight" (162) to his episodic, not epic, narration of a journey which has no goal other than the gifts of its errancy.

65. Hillman, *Re-Visioning Psychology*, 241.

66. Hillman, *Re-Visioning Psychology*, 218.

67. *Women Writers at Work: The Paris Review Interviews* (New York: Penguin Books, 1989), 340.

68. Gertrude Stein, *How Writing is Written*, ed. Robert Bartlett Haas. Previously Uncollected Writings of Gertrude Stein Series, Vol I (Los Angeles: Black Sparrow Press, 1974).

69. *Writers at Work: The Paris Review Interviews*, 2nd Series (New York: Viking Press, 1963), 264.

70. *Writers at Work*, 2nd Series, 264.

71. Hélène Cixous, *Three Steps on the Ladder of Writing*, trans. Sarah Cornell and Susan Sellers (New York: Columbia University Press), 69-70. See also Hillman, who says, "integration of the shadow is an emigration. Not him [i.e., our shadow] to us; we to him. His incursion is barbarism, our descent is culture." Hillman, *Re-Visioning Psychology*, 225. From this it would follow that emigration is an integration of the shadow, and that the shadow of America is, according to Hillman, an awareness of death, and devotion to artisanal or art work which is unmarketable and unprofitable.

72. Cixous, *Three Steps on the Ladder*, 20-21.

73. Elsewhere Cixous remarks that "when somebody writes, somebody dies." Cited in Verena Conley, *Writing the Feminine: Hélène Cixous* (Lincoln: University of Nebraska Press, 1993), 140.

74. John Ashbery, *Reported Sightings: Art Chronicles, 1957-1987*, ed. David Bergman (Cambridge, Mass.: Harvard University Press, 1991), 93.

75. Winnicott, "Mind and Its Relation to the Psyche-Soma" in *Through Paediatrics to Psychoanalysis*, 245.

76. The poet James Merrill, in his memoir *A Different Person*, described the Kohutian sense of "uplift" he and his partner experienced as foreigners in Greece: "Thus labeled, we felt a great burden of personality—individual history—lifted from our shoulders, and set about playing our parts in the ancient Athenian comedy." Merrill, *A Different Person* (New York: Knopf, 1993), 190.

77. Salman Akhtar, writing on changes in identity through immigration, identifies "the extent to which an individual has achieved the intrapsychic capacity for separateness prior to immigration" as crucial in an immigrant's or, I would say, an expatriate's ability to tolerate the separations involved. Akhtar, "A Third Individuation: Immigration, Identity, and the Psychoanalytic Process," *Journal of the American Psychoanalytic Association* 4, no. 3 (Winter 1995), 1055.

78. See Dorothy E. Speirs, "Un Genre Absolument Moderne: l'interview," *Romance Quarterly* 37, no. 3 (August 1993), 303.

79. Speirs, "Un Genre Absolument Moderne," 303.

80. Frank Kermode, introduction to *Writers at Work*, 6th Series (New York: Viking Press, 1984), ix. Francine du Plexis-Gray, who introduced the 5th Series, calls the genre the "rewritten interview." *Writers at Work*, 5th Series (New York: Viking Press, 1981), xiii.

81. Cynthia Ozick, *Women Writers at Work*, 293.

82. Wilfred Sheed, introduction to *Writers at Work*, 4th Series (New York: Viking Press, 1976), xiv.

83. As Dorothy E. Speirs writes of the interview:

> A l'encontre du rapportage à la troisième personne, ces entretiens à la première personne rendent sympathique pour la plupart l'individu inter-

rogé en faisant pénétrer le lecteur dans l'intimité de l'homme ou de la femme célèbre. De là, l'illusion créée par le journalist d'un contact direct entre l'interlocuteur et le public, de la demystification du personnage interviewé. Speirs, "Un Genre Absolument Moderne," 303
[Contrary to third-person reportage, these first person interviews for the most part render the interrogated individual sympathetic by making the reader penetrate the intimacy of the famous man or woman. From this, the illusion created by the journalist of direct contact between the interlocutor and the public, the demystification of the person interviewed.]

84. "And it may be in the seriousness with which they are willing to speak of their vocation as a fate and a burden and also a privilege, that the Americans distinguish themselves from their British contemporaries." Frank Kermode, introduction, xv.

85. Cited in Frank Kermode, introduction, xvii. And apropos, in Katherine Anne Porter's *Paris Review* interview, the interviewer, Barbara Thompson, reminds Miss Porter of something she herself had said of family, that it is the "absolute point of all departure and return." *Women Writers at Work*, 51.

86. Ozick, *Women Writers at Work*, 297.

87. In the field of cross-cultural psychology, J. W. Berry is one of the most prolific theorists on the nature of cultural change and cultural transition. A recent comprehensive presentation of the work in this area to date is his article with D. L. Sam, "Acculturation and Adaptation," in *Social Behavior and Applications*, Handbook of Cross-cultural Psychology Vol. 3, ed. J. W. Berry, M. H. Segall, and C. Kiagitcibasi (Boston: Allyn & Bacon, 1997), 291-326.

88. Ashbery, *Reported Sightings*, 88.

89. J. E. Gedo, *Portraits of the Artist*, 29.

90. Kohut, "Creativeness, Charisma, Group Psychology," 195.

91. Porter, *Haunted Journeys*, 188. He also describes the "complex transferential network" we make of countries we visit even just once. Porter, *Haunted Journeys*, 170.

92. Kohut, "The Psychoanalyst and the Historian" in *Self Psychology and the Humanities*, 219.

93. Ashbery, *Reported Sightings*, 90.

94. Ashbery, *Reported Sightings*, 91.

95. Ashbery, *Reported Sightings*, 91.

96. Eric Wolf, *Art News* 94, no. 6 (June 1995), 87.

97. This is J. W. Berry's categorization of the acculturative strategies which immigrants and sojourners can take toward the new or host culture. The characteristics of both the acculturating immigrants and the receiving culture influence their choice of acculturation strategy. See Berry, "Immigration, Acculturation, and Adaptation," *Applied Psychology: An International Review* 46 (1997): 5-34.

98. Ashbery, *Reported Sightings*, 109.

99. Ashbery, *Reported Sightings*, 110.

100. Akhtar, "A Third Individuation," 1062.

101. McCarthy, *Women Writers at Work*, 198.

102. Spencer, "The Art of Fiction CX," *Paris Review* 31, no. 111 (Summer 1989), 189.

103. Separation/individuation is the name Margaret Mahler used to describe the developmental phase between birth and three years. She derived her widely accepted theory

of development from much close observation of American mothers and children after she emigrated from Europe. See M. Mahler, F. Pine, and A. Bergman, *The Psychological Birth of the Human Infant* (New York: Basic Books, 1975).

104. Spencer, "The Art of Fiction CX," 200.

105. Hughes, "The Art of Poetry LXXI," *Paris Review* 37, no. 134 (Spring 1995), 134.

106. O'Brien, *Women Writers at Work*, 351.

107. Ashbery, *Reported Sightings*, 94. Also, in an exposition of the relationship between alienation in the Russian formalist sense of *ostranenie* and exile in the lives of Victor Shklovsky and Joseph Brodsky, Svetlana Boym writes that many modernist artists' life stories "use alienation itself as a personal antibiotic against the ancestral disease of home." Boym, "Estrangement as a Lifestyle," in *Exile and Creativity*, 242.

108. In this essay, "Project for a Trip to China," Sontag explores the origin of her yearning and fascination for China. *Susan Sontag Reader* (New York: Vintage Books, 1983), 280. In another piece, "Unguided Tour," she examines the nostalgia of travel, its connection to loss, and what she feels is its hopelessness: "How far from the beginning are we? When did we first start to feel the wound? This staunchless wound, the great longing for another place. To make this place another." Sontag, *Susan Sontag Reader*, 380.

109. Spender, *Writers at Work*, 6th Series, 64.

110. This from a draft manuscript of Elizabeth Hardwick's which served as the frontispiece to her *Paris Review* interview: "When you travel your first discovery is that you do not exist." This version is actually a revision under which the original is still legible: "When you travel your first discovery is somehow that you no longer exist" (202). It is this "somehow" which, while a weaker word in a more indirect sentence, invokes the bewilderment and disorientation which the loss of the old and the shock of the new can engender. The "no longer" in the original reflects a dynamic in which leaving caused nonexistence rather than revealed it as an apriority.

111. Gedo, *Portraits of the Artist*, 29, 38.

112. Sexton, *Women Writers at Work*, 278.

113. Gedo, *Portraits of the Artist*, 29.

114. Ozick, *Women Writers at Work*, 297.

115. Kafka's famous comment on the function of writing strikes many writers, as it did Nadine Gordimer (who quoted it in her *Paris Review* interview), because it says writing and reading are ways out of the void: "A book ought to be an ax to break up the frozen sea within us." Cited in Gordimer, *Women Writers at Work*, 261. On the work affording pleasure, *jouissance*, see Roland Barthes's celebrated works, *The Pleasure of the Text*, trans. Richard Miller (New York: Hill and Wang 1975); and Barthes, *A Lover's Discourse: Fragments*, trans. Richard Howard (New York: Hill and Wang, 1978). Joyce Carol Oates also makes functional claims for the act of writing beyond even the attainment of pleasure, saying that creation is "a genuinely transcendental function—a means by which we rise out of limited parochial states of mind." Oates, *Women Writers at Work*, 366. Hillman imputes ontological status to the work: "We build body in writing . . . you actually create a *corpus*, a body, which becomes a person of its own." Hillman, *Inter Views*, 160. Annie Dillard also knows this "person" created out of writing—"It is a golem," she says ruefully in *The Writing Life* (New York: Harper & Row, 1989), 58.

116. O'Brien, *Women Writers at Work*, 356.

117. O'Brien, *Women Writers at Work*, 349.

118. O'Brien, *Women Writers at Work*, 340.

119. In a piece on Jane Freilicher, Ashbery writes of the kind of artists who find they are most themselves at home:

> The excitement of their craft comes not from the exotic costumes that reality wears in different parts of the world, but in the slight disparities in the sibylline replies uttered by a fixed set of referents: the cat, the blue pitcher, the zinnias, the jumble of rooftops or stretch of grass beyond the window. Ashbery, *Reported Sightings*, 244.

120. Dinesen, *Women Writers at Work*, 10.

121. Dinesen, *Women Writers at Work*, 10.

122. Dinesen, *Women Writers at Work*, 10. Like Dinesen, Katherine Anne Porter was a writer who picked the place of her sojourns carefully. For her first sojourn, she felt a need to avoid going anywhere too frequented or too overwhelming, so she went to Mexico "when everybody else was going to Europe." Porter, *Women Writers at Work*, 57. Porter felt it was important for an artist to follow his or her own path, to avoid groups and artistic movements.

123. Dinesen, *Women Writers at Work*, 10.

124. James Hillman, *Loose Ends: Primary Papers in Archetypal Psychology* (Dallas, Tex.: Spring Publications, 1975), 46.

125. Cited in Kennedy, *Imagining Paris*, 168.

126. Kennedy, *Imagining Paris*, 168.

127. Cited in Kennedy, *Imagining Paris*, 164.

128. Cited in Kennedy, *Imagining Paris*, 169.

129. See D. W. Winnicott, *Holding and Interpretation* (New York: Grove Press, 1987) for a case study of an analysis revolving around the importance of the analytic space and the regression which its "holding" function permitted.

130. Miller, *The World of Sex*, cited in *Henry Miller on Writing*, 119.

131. Kennedy, *Imagining Paris*, 170.

132. Cited in Kennedy, *Imagining Paris*, 183.

133. Miller, *Writers at Work*, 2nd Series, 178.

134. Miller, *Black Spring* in *Henry Miller on Writing*, 87.

135. Miller, *Henry Miller on Writing*, 91.

136. Miller, *Henry Miller on Writing*, 93.

137. Miller, *Henry Miller on Writing*, 96.

138. Miller, *Henry Miller on Writing*, 96.

139. Miller, *Henry Miller on Writing*, 96.

140. Pound, *Writers at Work*, 2nd Series, 56.

141. Oates, *Women Writers at Work*, 369.

142. In a succinct observation in the *American Psychologist*, Daniel White and Alan Wang write, "For postmodernists, the self is not obliterated, but situated." White and Wang, "Universalism, Humanism, and Postmodernism," *American Psychologist* 50, no. 5 (May 1995), 392.

143. Examples of this trend in academic psychology can be seen in the work of Kenneth Gergen and Edward Sampson. On the nature of the self, see especially Edward Sampson, "The Decentralization of Identity," *American Psychologist* 40, no. 11 (November 1985): 1203-1211. R. A. Shweder and Anthony Marsella have done important

work on the cultural relativity and origins of allegedly "universal" psychological concepts. In the clinical practice of depth psychology, Jacques Lacan, James Hillman, and Christopher Bollas (in very different ways) have redefined the self in analysis.

Chapter Ten

War to the Death: Nativism and Independence in Latin America

John Charles Chasteen

Whether in their ubiquitous role as chroniclers of war and empire or, Herodotus-like, as tellers of tall tales about the startling otherness of distant lands, historians have always been interpreters of foreign places and their inhabitants. The past, after all, is itself a foreign country, inhabited by people whose values and attitudes often differ substantially from those of today. Drawing back the veil of otherness, making the foreign familiar, is a valuable conceptual service, especially when the perception of difference is not the inevitable result of distance, but rather a matter of politics as, I will argue, it most often is.[1]

As a world phenomenon, production of the foreign (in its salient modern sense, referring to state citizenship) has been a function of the spread of nationalism. The spread of nationalism altered existing perceptions of social difference, intensifying some lines of cleavage, diminishing others, and making global patterns more uniform overall. Benedict Anderson has highlighted the repeatable, "modular" qualities of republican nationalism and its stunningly universal diffusion as a template of political organization during the nineteenth and twentieth centuries. The creation of a score of Latin American republics in the first half of the nineteenth century marks one of the most important moments in the establishment of that template, the first occasion on which nation states were, so to speak, mass produced, each with its own heroes of independence, republican constitution, uniformed army, flag, and other more-or-less standard paraphernalia of nationhood.[2] Almost invariably, the birth of Latin American nations was accompanied by an important redefinition of what was foreign, and by a strong nativist reaction against foreigners.

Indeed, popular nativism (the celebration of native birth coupled with vituperation of the foreign) must be reckoned one of the most potent political forces in the independence period. Something radical was afoot in 1813 when the liberator Simón Bolívar proclaimed a "War to the Death" in which all Venezuelans (*"Americanos"*) would be spared, irrespective of their crimes, while Spaniards and Canary Islanders would receive no clemency.[3] Bolívar's proclamation attempted to redefine his political enemies—formerly the personification of authority and political authenticity—as irreconcilably alienated and foreign. The attempt worked. Throughout Spanish America, wherever independence was conflictive, the nativist spirit blossomed during the fighting and continued to spread afterward.

Since the revolutionary 1960s and 1970s, Latin Americanists have stopped referring to the independence struggles of the 1810s and 1820s as revolutions,[4] but a revolutionary change certainly did occur in political culture and in definitions of what—or, more pointedly, *who*—was foreign.

Before independence, the Spaniards and Portuguese held virtually all the political power and much of the wealth in their American colonies, and they were clearly identified as European outsiders—but *not* as foreigners. In Spanish America they were called *Peninsulares* in reference to their birthplace in the Iberian peninsula, and in Brazil, *Renóis*, people "of the kingdom," meaning Portugal. Spaniards and Portuguese were most decidedly not *Americanos*, nor were they *extranjeros* or *estrangeiros*—these being the best (Spanish and Portuguese) translations for *foreigners*. Foreigners were English or French, for example, and they were most often Protestant. Etymologically, the words *extranjero* and *estrangeiro* came from French, which suggests the importance of Frenchmen as foreigners *par excellence* in Iberia. Related terms in Spanish and Portuguese add further specificity to the concept, suggesting an Iberian experience in which things foreign have excited both ridicule and imitation. The *Pequeño Larousse*, for example, defines Spanish *extranjerismo* ("foreignism") as "some people's ridiculous affectation of foreign customs." The *Dicionário prático ilustrado* includes an exact Portuguese equivalent, *estrangeirismo*, as well as *etrangeirice* (another, slightly more deprecatory, way of saying "foreignism"), *estrangeirar* (to "foreignize"), and *estrangeirado* (one who has undergone "foreignization"— become Frenchified, so to speak). Portuguese speakers can also avail themselves, if need be, of the word *estrangeirada*, defined as "a mob of foreigners," or *estrangeirinha*, a term offered in the spirit of "Dutch treat."[5]

These Spanish and Portuguese terms, it would appear, were coined by societies in which foreigners—particularly the French—have long been important, so what is the nature of the paradigm shift that occurred with the independence struggles of the early nineteenth century? To form an answer, we must examine the constructions of foreignness that came to Latin America as part of its colonial legacy. We must take a look at the colonizer's origins in the Iberian Peninsula before going on to explore the colonial evolution of collective identities and the rupture marked by independence-era nativism.

Iberia, poised between Africa and Europe and between the Atlantic and the Mediterranean, has historically been a meeting place of peoples, after all: Christians and Muslims interacted on Iberian soil—periodically at each others' throats—during the entire medieval period. In the 1400s, both Portugal and Spain became leaders in the European exploration of the rest of the world. Spain's rise to power in Europe under Habsburg rulers, beginning in 1517 with Charles V (known in Spain as Carlos I), brought Spaniards into contact with people from all over the Austrian dynasty's far flung domains. In 1700, a Bourbon prince (Felipe V) occupied the Spanish throne and for the rest of the century his descendants retained strong French connections not to the taste of many of their Spanish subjects.[6] Foreigners were, if anything, even more influential in tiny Portugal, whose population numbered only about one million inhabitants when it embarked on a course of world empire in the sixteenth century. *Renóis*, Portuguese "of the kingdom," were scarcely sufficient to staff key administrative posts, not enough really to populate the territories they claimed around the globe (between 1500-1800), not enough even to crew the sailing vessels that held their seaborne empire together. Of necessity, foreigners were ubiquitous in Portuguese Asia.[7] Add to this the overwhelming economic power wielded by northern European merchants in both Spain and Portugal, the indubitable prestige of French cultural models in both Iberian kingdoms, and the relentless entanglement of both countries in international rivalries and alliances, and one can easily understand why Iberians had developed so many words with which to talk about foreigners.

Extranjero or *estrangeiro* had a political, more than a cultural, definition during the Iberian colonization of Latin America. Language, ever a touchstone of social identities, illustrates the point. Left to their own devices, widely spoken languages tend to incorporate foreign borrowings willy-nilly. Linguistic purity, on the other hand, is a phenomenon of physical isolation or political will. Linguistic purity was a special preoccupation of Spanish royal policy, which sought to impose the Castilian variety of speech over all its competing Iberian cousins and then to standardize its written form as a proper instrument of imperial administration.[8] Portuguese, too, might have been subsumed by Spanish as part of this process, were not Portuguese, already in the thirteenth century, the language of an independent monarchy whose eventual alliance with England enabled it to resist Castilian domination. Thus, for political reasons alone, Portuguese is today a national language while Galician and Aragonese, for example, are reduced to the status of regional dialects. Spanish national consolidation and incipient imperial expansion resulted in the first written grammar of a modern European language, presented to the Spanish queen precisely in 1492.[9] In 1714, Felipe V established a Royal Academy to protect the Spanish language against insidious foreignism. Never mind that the academy was founded on a Parisian model or that Felipe himself spoke Spanish with a French accent. The Spanish and Portuguese empires might aspire to linguistic purity, but they were very far from achieving it, so foreigners were defined less by culture than by political allegiance. Foreigners were those politically outside the empire, especially its enemies, and this hardly applied to the king, whatever his accent.[10]

In 1800, on the eve of the wars of independence, Spanish and Portuguese territories in America were brimming with an ethnic complexity destined to complicate future attempts to create cohesive national communities. The Iberians themselves were a diverse lot. Symptomatically, the Spanish colonizers of Latin America often referred to their homeland in the plural, speaking of "the Spains."[11] The northern half of the Iberian Peninsula, with its regional languages or dialects, and the southern half, with its strong Moorish influence, presented a veritable mosaic of cultures. Immeasurably augmenting this diversity in America was the confluence of Iberian with African and indigenous American populations. Indigenous people and enslaved African people comprised a majority in the region as a whole in 1800, and these non-European groups were even more ethnically complex than the Iberians.

The slaves—particularly important in Brazil and the Caribbean—were from several widely separated parts of Africa and represented countless ethnic affiliations, loosely grouped by the slave trade into a much smaller number of categories: Congos, Benguelas, Mozambiques, Angolas, Lucumíes, to name a few.[12] These groups, each of which subsumed a variety of African ethnicities, were called nations. Completely uprooted from their native villages, kin groups, and tribes, enslaved Africans were forming new "national" identities as they gathered to dance and socialize as Congos or Mozambiques on Sundays and church holidays. In the festival of Corpus Christi, when official symbolism called for a parade representing the constituent elements of the imperial body politic, the African nations of colonial Latin America were expected to display their national dances in the streets. Overall, African slaves and their descendants in Latin America preserved more Old World antecedents in their New World identities than was the case in the United States—perhaps because the Iberians allowed them greater freedom, as has often been claimed, but surely, too, because of a greater intensity and duration of the slave trade.[13]

Indigenous people formed the demographic core of the Spanish American population before independence, and they too represented many different nations. In the sixteenth century, indigenous people had been segregated by the Spanish crown into a "Republic of Indians"—not a separate territory, but a parallel society organized in administratively designated "Indian towns" where Iberian colonizers were not to intrude. The Republic of Indians and the Republic of Spaniards were both theoretically loyal to the Spanish king, and the word *extranjero* referred to neither. Despite the colonizers constant habit of lumping indigenous people together as "Indians," those peoples themselves were slow to assign much importance to the category, which assumed a common identity among indigenous groups who felt as remote from each other as might Scots from Slovaks or Sicilians. For the most part, indigenous people presented themselves as "Indians" only when that brought them a specific advantage in interactions with the colonizers. For the most part, they were Nahuas or Aymaras, Quiché Mayas, or Tupinambás, according to their own sense of ethnic identity.[14]

Not only did the colonization of Latin America bring together three racial groups each of which was riven internally by ethnic diversity, but additional ethnic differences emerged as a result of the process of colonization. For example, the process of colonization displaced many indigenous people and separated them from their tribal origins. Indigenous migrants in the Andes, called *forasteros*, created significant population shifts as old communities withered in the face of colonial exploitation and new ones sprang up elsewhere.[15] Centuries of Portuguese slaving and proselytizing in the Amazon region created a floating population (literally and figuratively) of de-tribalized indigenous people called *tapuios*, who lived independently along the banks of the fluvial maze, moved about in canoes, and often spoke only Nheengatu, a kind of Amazonian Esperanto, a composite of indigenous languages cobbled together by Jesuit missionaries and spoken, at one time, throughout Brazil.[16]

Racial mixing was a second source of new distinctions born of colonization. The Spanish and Portuguese invaders were overwhelmingly male, and large numbers of biracial children resulted from their sexual encounters with African and indigenous women. The rapine of conquest played its ugly part, but the historian also encounters frequent tales of helpless Iberian castaways who were adopted by indigenous people and fathered literally scores of children among them. The Iberian crowns generally tried to discourage this racial mixing, even prohibiting it legally in some cases, but they never succeeded in stopping it.[17] People of mixed race occupied, at first, an uncomfortably marginal position— not European, not indigenous, not African—but, by 1800, they constituted perhaps a quarter of the population. Gradually, mixed-race (Spanish *mestizo* or Portuguese *mestiço*) became not a category but a congeries of categories corresponding to each individual's particular combination of racial ancestry, e.g., the person whose grandparents were a Portuguese, a Benguela, a Tupi, and a mulatto. Progressive intermarriage multiplied the possibilities in each generation.[18]

Race mixing thus inexorably undermined the caste system through which the colonizing powers tried to govern—a system in which the right to wear certain clothes or occupy certain offices, for example, was reserved for whites, indigenous people had to pay a special head tax, and so on. Children born to parents of different castes fell between categories and confounded the system, so more categories were created to accommodate them. The strains were most obvious in Spanish America, where official racial categories multiplied alarmingly in the late colonial period, reaching a dozen in common use and several dozen in theory. While some have viewed this as the zenith of the caste system, it was more like a desperate last hurrah.

In addition, over the course of three centuries of colonization had arisen a substantial class of native-born Brazilian and Spanish American whites, perhaps a fifth to a quarter of the population. In the eighteenth century, reinvigorated Iberian monarchies tried to tighten their imperial control over their American colonies, and men born in Spain or Portugal—detached from local roots and presumably more loyal to imperial purposes—seemed better agents for this purpose. An administrative policy of systematic preferment for European-born whites raised bitter resentment among the American-born whites, and Spanish *Peninsulares* and Portuguese *Renóis* reciprocated with animosity toward the American born. The general ideology of European colonization in America included ideas about the biological superiority of European organisms—crops and animals, as well as people—along with the notion that transplantation of European organisms to tropical America brought inevitable degeneration.[19] Spanish *Peninsulares* and Portuguese *Renóis* did not tire of citing the profligacy and indolence of American-born ne'er-do-wells as a case in point, and they often added innuendoes of racial impurity to their imputations of environmental determinism.

Finally, a profusion of Latin American provincial identities grew in importance during the colonial period. To begin with, the Spanish had gravitated toward large indigenous populations, and their most successful colonization tactic involved, in essence, taking over preexisting indigenous tribute systems. Therefore, the indigenous "provinces" that organized those tribute systems carried over to the colonizer's administrative map. This gave some provincial identities in Spanish America pre-Columbian roots that existed nowhere in Brazil, where forest or plains dwelling tribal people had no such large tribute systems to be coopted. The Brazilian provincial map was initiated purely by a different process of colonization, parceling out neat parallel strips of fertile coastal plain for sugar plantations to be worked by slaves uprooted from their former patterns of habitation. With or without an indigenous substratum, Spanish American and Brazilian provinces had been given more or less permanent shape by 1800.[20] On the eve of independence, feelings of territorial belonging among Spanish Americans and Brazilians were more focused on provinces than on larger administrative structures. Significantly, common names designating people's place of origin referred to provinces rather than viceroyalties. Inhabitants of the Viceroyalty of New Spain (today Mexico and Central America) would identify as *Poblanos* or *Yucatecos*, for example, according to their province of birth, avoiding the forced, erudite-sounding name *Novohispano*, that corresponded to New Spain as a whole. On the eve of independence, most people in Spanish or Portuguese America used the term *patria* (literally, *fatherland*, a word conveying warm feelings of belonging) for the province where they were born.[21]

Here, then, were differences aplenty—but very few "foreigners," almost none—because people who received that name had been rigorously kept out. The Spanish and Portuguese did not admit other European visitors to their American empires, unless they were in the service of an Iberian crown or the Catholic Church.[22] Yet, between 1810 and 1850, the political order of the continent was transformed partly by angry crowds denouncing the foreigners in their midst, and these foreigners were not newcomers. One might say that the political conflicts surrounding independence brought a sweeping *production of the foreign* by making birthplace the crucial determinant of political identity.

The carving up of Spanish America into more than a dozen aspiring nation states set a precedent in the spread of nationalism because these nations were not defined by linguistic community. All shared the same national language and a common history of colonization. What, then, differentiated them? Anderson himself has offered two pieces of the puzzle, suggesting that bureaucratic careers and patterns of newspaper readership had begun to delineate regions within which the elite class would imagine the nation.[23] But native-born bureaucrats were few before 1810, and newspapers fewer. Indeed, the puzzle of Spanish America's political fragmentation—clarified by the counter example of a unified Brazil—still has missing pieces. One obvious place to look is the tumultuous political process of independence which created the new nations: both the first wave of 1810-1825, in which the continent broke away from Spain and Portugal, and the further fragmentation of 1825-1850, which added a half dozen more sovereignties to the map of the hemisphere.[24]

Violent conflict swept the continent during these years, and nativist politics were at the center of that conflict in almost every case. Bolívar drew the nativist line with paradigmatic clarity in his War to the Death, but this is only one of countless examples. Nativist rebellions undermined Bolívar's aspiration to create a united republic embracing Colombia, Ecuador, and Venezuela. Mexico's wars of independence began with a massive insurrection of peasant armies that marched under the banner of Mexico's native Virgin of Guadalupe and shouted "Death to the Spaniards!" as their principle battle cry, and nativist agitation remained the most volatile aspect of Mexican politics long thereafter. Likewise in Argentina, a nativist identification with the independence movement carried over strongly into the politics of the 1830s and 1840s.[25]

Peruvian elites were the slowest on the continent to embrace independence precisely because indigenous rebels had already used nativist themes to convulse much of the Andean highlands during the 1780s (in the famous revolts led by Tupac Amaru, who claimed descent from the Inca emperor and rhetorically aligned all *Americanos* against Spaniards), but once patriot armies from other parts of the continent finished off the Spanish, the Peruvian elite called on the logic of nativism to free themselves from the patriots. Independence came peacefully to the United Republic of Central America, but nativist logic contributed to the break up of its five constituent provinces in the 1840s. In Brazil, nativism provided the central logic for separation from Portugal in 1822, then, nine years later, brought the downfall of Brazil's first emperor, Pedro I, accused of surrounding himself with ministers born in Portugal. During the years 1835 to 1845, a string of nativist uprisings in the provinces offered the greatest threats ever to the territorial unity of Brazil.[26]

The preceding enumeration serves to indicate the political salience of Spanish American and Brazilian nativism following independence. That salience is often overlooked today, perhaps because it seems unpleasantly commonplace.[27] But this nativist outbreak takes on more significance when viewed as part of a large-scale modeling of world nationalism. Nativist political emphasis on birthplace found an influential precedent in the independence of the United States of America. Indeed, the spread of nativism reflects, above all, its tactical utility for leaders of independence movements in situations of decolonization.

With a few notable exceptions, Latin American patriot leaders were members of the native-born white minority who sought not to remake colonial society but to assume control of it themselves. Independence promised them, above all, the opportunity to wrest political and economic privileges away from those born in Spain or Portugal. Their main problem was the other three-quarters or four-fifths of the population—the slaves, mixed-race, and indigenous people whose continued subjection defined those privileges and who had scant incentive to endorse the narrow interests of the native-born whites. Powerful bonds of group affinity would not easily be created here. The nativist formula—America for the Americans—finessed this thorny difficulty by rhetorically asserting affinities among the vast native-born majority in contradistinction to a vulnerable, neatly defined, "foreign" enemy. Focus on a common enemy had tremendous political utility in the creation of broad political alliances because, unlike problematical aspirations of national solidarity, anti-Spanish and anti-Portuguese sentiments were something Americans of all social classes did indeed share. Thus, the nativism of the military struggles against Spain and Portugal was largely *Americanism*, differentiating little among American nations.[28]

The political map drawn between 1810 and 1825 proved unstable, at least in part, because of a second stage of nativism. After independence, nativism became a force in internal politics, arguably the issue that most engaged the political energies of the common people in the hemisphere as a whole. In independent Mexico, liberal nativists directed their wrath at the Spanish-born who remained, many of them wealthy and well-connected, and expelled them. Even more violent agitation was directed at the Portuguese-born who remained in Brazil. In addition, distinguishing among Americans was now part of the nativist agenda. Conservative Argentine nativists baited cosmopolitan elites (Francophiles or Anglophiles) despite their native birth.[29] At issue now, in addition to birth, was culture. Without exception, the aspiring new nation states had been founded on a premise—usually a fiction, an aspiration full of ulterior motives, but still a premise—of profound cultural affinity, of nationhood. Now feelings of affinity had to be nurtured if the new nations were to survive for long. The years between 1825 and 1850 were dominated by an identity politics that has always been hard to explain in terms of economic interest. The wars of independence and their heroes became important reference points in the imaginative construction of new nationhood.[30] Patriot leaders ruled everywhere for a generation after independence. In addition, clothes, accent, music, dance, and food gained salience as markers of native identity. Nativists directed suspicion against those heedless of national customs. Such heedlessness betokened lack of patriotism or even suspicious foreign influence.[31]

Of course, traditional folkways varied considerably from province to province, and virtually all the new states contained more than one province. If folkways defined a nation, then many provinces could claim nationhood for themselves, and more than one nativist movement attempted to create a breakaway republic. Several such breakaway attempts failed in Brazil, though one, the Republic of Piratini lasted almost a decade. In Spanish America, many secondstage breakaways became permanent: Uruguay, Venezuela, Ecuador, Honduras, El Salvador, Nicaragua, and Costa Rica. Colombia's particularly intense preoccupation with regional folkways and its weak central state corresponds to the quasi-national status of its federated provinces in the mid-nineteenth century. Even leaders without a regionalist agenda (much less secessionist ambitions) often gained political legitimacy by demonstrating a personal affinity for the folkways of their province of origin.[32]

Spanish American and Brazilian nationalists have continued, ever after, to elaborate nativist themes in everything from history, poetry, and fiction, to music and folk dance movements. The systematic designation of Latin America's regional dishes and peasant costumes, the energy invested in them, and the pride with which they are displayed to foreigners, exceed in intensity analogous activities elsewhere. The ethnic and geographic diversity of the continent's rural life have provided the raw materials, but nativist ideology has given them prominence.[33] Clearly, these cultural elaborations of native identity have responded to the continuing need for evocations of nationhood. The construction of really inclusive national communities has, in fact, been arduous and halting. The phenomenon is not unique, however. A strong sense of inclusive national community remains conspicuous by its absence today in many countries around the world.

Nationalism is an ideology of ultimate commitment, an ideology that claims a loyalty beyond friendship, even beyond family, and links it to an imagined group of unseen millions who live within particular borders, marking all other people as foreign. This commonplace of the last two centuries is a remarkable historical development, a paradigm shift in the architecture of human communities. The rise of Spanish American and Brazilian nativism—driven by the political expediency of cross-class, multiracial alliances against the colonizers—played a significant role in that development by making the nation state into something like a standard model for decolonization. Nations were posited routinely where they did not yet exist. Gradually, steadily, they consolidated themselves. The recent weakening of the nation state, discussed in the 1990s, has had only trivial effects compared with the universal triumph of the nation state model since 1790.[34] Nationalism, it seems entirely fair to assert, is by far the most widely compelling political ideology in the world. Why? Where does it get its powerful affective charge? The preceding discussion illustrates a possible explanation. The explanation hinges on a sudden and enormous change in the scale of the social groups to which people have directed their primary loyalty.

People have many identities and potentially conflicting loyalties. Colonial Spanish America and Brazil were only a bit unusual in the multiplicity of their overlapping, interacting identities. Such multiplicity must be reckoned quite a normal state of affairs in the long term of human experience. For many thousands of years, human society has been composed of tribes, villages, provinces, clans, and so on—definitions of group identity that intersected in the lives of individual people. Moments of historical conflict are typically marked by tension and jostling, as changing situations oblige people to accept the new practical importance of one identity and subordinate others. The universal imposition of the nation state has precipitated the process, forcing even the most reluctant people to choose sides in countless "wars to the death."

The process has been uneven and is surely far from finished. Probably, it makes little sense to think that it will ever be finished, since collective identities have been reshuffling kaleidoscopically throughout recorded history. It will not be finished when every potential ethnic or national group has achieved self-determination—should that unlikely situation come to pass—because ethnicities and nations will themselves continue to take root in new places and wither away elsewhere. Viewing the ethnic strife that seems to characterize the post-Cold War international scene, recent commentators have made frequent use of the word "tribalism," but most of the groups in conflict today are ethnic or national groups whose social organization is decidedly not tribal.

Those who evoke the idea of tribalism while describing Bosnia or Sri Lanka in the 1990s refer to the tendency of groups in conflict to see each other as utterly and unalterably foreign, undeserving of the same consideration extended to one's own. Here is something that tribes of hunter-gatherers do indeed share with ethnic groups in conflict, and also with clans engrossed in blood feuds and with modern nation states embarked on total war. When groups come into sharp conflict, they very frequently construct an idea of their enemies as corresponding to a fundamentally different category of human—even infra-human—existence, oriented to an utterly different social world, bound by contrasting moral principles or lacking them altogether. Thus, the construction of what is foreign or what is irremediably other has a political utility well exemplified in the history of nativism, which is often characterized by mob violence toward those perceived as foreign.[35]

During the last two hundred years, nations have claimed group loyalties of an intensity formerly characteristic of clans and tribes. The change in scale has been enormous. Clans and tribes are human communities normally numbering no more than a few hundred individuals. These must have been the largest groups of primary loyalty in the lives of human beings throughout the thirty or forty thousand years of the paleolithic period. They must have continued to be the main groups of primary loyalty through the ten or so thousand years since the advent of agriculture. Until about 1800, the great majority of human beings from China and India to France and England lived in agricultural villages of about two thousand people, normally quite fragmented by cleavages of kin. Although bending a knee to a common king or emperor, members of different tribes or clans were not loyal politically to each other. Kingdoms could be large, and empires larger, but the political architecture of monarchy was not erected on the idea of loyalty to a group. Hence, the idea of the foreign often had relatively little significance even in sprawling political entities. The human group of primary loyalty was still defined, in most of the world, by blood kinship.[36]

Nationalism has worked a startlingly rapid massing of primary group loyalties. A human group numbering many millions, spread over a vast territory, cannot be experienced directly by its members. To call the group into being in people's minds, nationalist leaders and ideologues had to create ways to imagine the nation.[37] Partly, imagining the nation consisted simply in being able to define and understand it, to differentiate the national from the foreign. But in order to take on the affective power associated with primary group loyalties, the nation also had to be felt—the greatest challenge. Feeling unity with an absent group of many millions must necessarily be a mystical experience. Nativism gains its political potency from the clarity that it gives to people's experience of nationhood. Like membership in a family, nation becomes a birthright. The native-born basks in unconditional, irrevocable belonging, unachieved excellence. The nativist emphasis on customs, clothing, and music offers an easy way to affirm and enjoy national identity, as does nativist vituperation of the foreign. Nativist discourse excoriates foreignness in order to purge it—literally to cast certain people out of society—but also because the fire of exorcism serves temporarily to efface differences among those of native birth. Wars to the death take their desperate violence less from a human impulse to reject the other than from a political tactic to build group solidarity for a particular purpose.

Imagine the difficulties involved in the attempt to transfer people's primary commitment away from kin and personal alliances and toward large, diverse, conflictive, and sometimes ill-defined national groups. It is no wonder that such attempts often fail, no surprise when soldiers decline to die gloriously for anonymous strangers or when family priorities lead to misappropriation of official funds. Despite their historical contribution to the development of world nationalism, Latin American societies have continued to exhibit a powerful orientation toward family, as well as toward networks of person-to-person alliance that cross-cut and undermine the affective hold of the nation state. Then too, on a personal level, Latin Americans are generally welcoming to foreigners and attracted to things foreign. Nationalist politics aside, they often revel in the foreign. Otherwise, Simón Bolívar would never have needed to declare "War to the Death" in the first place.

Notes

1. I refer here to politics of the kind explored in Gilbert M. Joseph and Daniel Nugent, eds., *Everyday Forms of State Formation: Revolution and the Negotiation of Rule in Modern Mexico* (Durham, N.C.: Duke University Press, 1994). But I also intend politics in the very broadest sense to include gender politics, racial politics, identity politics, and all other processes of social domination and contestation. Such politics occur in the everyday practice of social honor and patronage described by Pierre Bourdieu, *Outline of a Theory of Practice*, trans. Richard Nice (Cambridge: Cambridge University Press, 1977). It inheres in the conceptual architecture of all language; see Richard Harland, *Superstructuralism: The Philosophy of Structuralism and Post-Structuralism* (London: Methuen, 1987).

2. Benedict Anderson, *Imagined Communities: Reflections on the Origins and Spread of Nationalism* (London: Verso, 1996).

3. On Bolívar, the standard source in English is still Gerhard Masur, *Simón Bolívar* (Albuquerque: University of New Mexico Press, 1969).

4. In accordance with the sociological emphasis of Latin American historiography in the 1960s, 1970s, and 1980s, "revolution" was thought to require *a reshuffling of the social deck*, which rarely occurred at independence. See, for example, Leslie Bethell, ed., *The Cambridge History of Latin America*, 8 vols. (Cambridge: Cambridge University Press, 1984-91).

5. Ramón García-Pelayo y Gross, *Pequeño Larousse ilustrado* (Paris: Ediciones Larousse, 1964); and Jaime de Séguier, *Dicionário prático ilustrado* (Porto, Portugal: Lello & Irmão, 1974).

6. See John Lynch, *Bourbon Spain, 1700-1808* (London: Basil Blackwell, 1989).

7. See C. R. Boxer, *The Portuguese Seaborne Empire, 1415-1825* (New York: A. A. Knopf, 1969).

8. See Angel Rama, *The Lettered City* (Durham, N.C.: Duke University Press, 1996).

9. Rama, *The Lettered City*, 35.

10. Anderson explores the contrast between national and dynastic patterns of political legitimation in *Imagined Communities*.

11. See François-Xavier Guerra, "Identidad y soberanía: una relacion compleja," in *Las revoluciones hispanicas: independencias americanas y liberalismo español*, ed. François-Xavier Guerra (Madrid: Editorial Complutense, 1995).

12. Meanwhile, the slave trade itself was creating a detribalized "African creole" culture surrounding ports of embarkation along the West African coast. This important phenomenon is only now coming to light.

13. Good looks at the phenomenon in widely separated parts of Latin America are George Reid Andrews, *The Afro-Argentines of Buenos Aires, 1800-1900* (Madison: University of Wisconsin Press, 1984); and Fernando Ortiz, *Los cabildos y la fiesta afrocubanos del Día de Reyes* (Havana: Editorial de Ciencias Sociales, 1992).

14. It is interesting to note, however, that their words for *outsider*—like *misti* in the Andes—tended to crowd most non-indigenous people into the same category.

15. See Karen Vieira Powers, *Andean Journeys: Migration, Ethnogenesis, and the State in Colonial Quito* (Albuquerque: University of New Mexico Press, 1995).

16. The *tapuios* are much less known than the Andean *forasteros*. See Carlos de Araujo Moreira Neto, *Indios da Amazônia, de maioria a minoria (1750-1850)* (Petrópo-

lis, Brazil: Editôra Vozes, 1988).

17. There were some rare occasions in which race mixing was administratively encouraged, e.g., in Amazonia by the eighteenth-century Portuguese reformist minister Pombal.

18. Magnus Morner, *Race Mixture in the History of Latin America* (Boston: Little, Brown, 1964) has long been the standard account. Claudio Esteva Fabregat's *Mestizaje in Ibero-America* (Tucson, Ariz.: University of Arizona Press, 1995) is more quantitative, but improves little on Morner.

19. See Anthony Pagden, *European Encounters with the New World from the Renaissance to Romanticism* (New Haven, Conn.: Yale University Press, 1993).

20. The primary subsequent change has been the gradual subdivision of large provinces as populations grew. These subdivisions have added new lines to the map and created new provinces, but almost never have old provinces and local identities been erased. See James Lockhart and Stuart B. Schwartz, *Early Latin America: A History of Colonial Spanish America and Brazil* (Cambridge: Cambridge University Press, 1983).

21. Roderick Barman, *Brazil: The Forging of a Nation, 1798-1852* (Stanford, Calif.: Stanford University Press, 1988).

22. For this reason, curious travelers from France, England, and the United States poured into Latin America soon after independence. Here was another venue for the "production of the foreign." See Mary Louise Pratt, *Imperial Eyes: Travel Writing and Transculturation* (London: Routledge, 1992).

23. Anderson, *Imagined Communities*, 47-65.

24. The island colonies of Cuba and Puerto Rico remained under Spanish control.

25. An excellent overview of Latin America in this period is provided by Tulio Halperín Donghi, *The Contemporary History of Latin America* (Durham, N.C.: Duke University Press, 1993).

26. John Lynch provides the standard English-language synthesis of the independence period. For more on Central America, see Ralph Lee Woodward, *Central America, a Nation Divided* (Oxford: Oxford University Press, 1976). The quite different Brazilian process is well narrated by Barman.

27. Few works bring this phenomenon into clear focus. See John Charles Chasteen, "Cautionary Tale: A Radical Priest, Nativist Agitation, and the Origin of Civil Wars in Nineteenth-Century Brazil" in *The Origins of Civil Wars in Nineteenth-Century Latin America* (London: Institute of Latin American Studies, forthcoming).

28. Guerra, "Identidad y soberanía," 229-231.

29. A famous literary evocation of this baiting is Esteban Echeverría's short story, "The Slaughterhouse," now standard in the Argentine canon for the early nineteenth century. Esteban Echeverría, "El matadero," in *Masterpieces of Spanish American Literature*, Vol. 1, ed. Angel Flores and Helena M. Anderson (New York: Macmillan, 1974), 169-177

30. Pantheons of independence heroes are among the clearly modular aspects of Spanish American nationalism. For a broad interpretation of their importance in world nationalism, see Anthony D. Smith, *The Ethnic Origin of Nations* (New York: Basil Blackwell, 1986).

31. See John Charles Chasteen, "Patriotic Footwork: Social Dance and the Watershed of Independence in Buenos Aires," in *State and Society in Spanish America during the Age of Revolution*, ed. Victor Uribe-Uran (Wilmington, Del.: Scholarly Resources, 2001), 173-192.

32. See Halperín Donghi, *The Contemporary History of Latin America*, 74-114.

33. See Rama, *The Lettered City*, 50-73.

34. E. J. Hobsbawm, *Nations and Nationalism since 1780: Programme, Myth, Reality* (Cambridge: Cambridge University Press, 1990).

35. Tzvetan Todorov, *The Conquest of America: The Question of the Other* (New York: Harper & Row, 1984).

36. Well-founded generalizations regarding these basic, long-term patterns of human life correspond to the macro perspective of "world history." See, for example, William H. McNeill, *The Human Condition: An Ecological and Historical View* (Princeton, N.J.: Princeton University Press, 1980).

37. While Benedict Anderson was not the first to see that nations are fabricated (rather than natural and primordial), his stress on the imaginative challenges of the fabrication has unleashed much productive scholarship on nationalism.

Chapter Eleven

Changing Images and Similar Dynamics: Historical Patterning of Foreignness in the Social Work Profession

Izumi Sakamoto

Introduction

Over a hundred years ago, the field of social work emerged in the United States when wealthy and educated white women began working with those who were considered foreign.[1] How social work defined *foreignness,* and the manner in which those definitions shaped the profession, have shifted over time, reflecting changes in political, societal, cultural, and historical contexts. With such shifts, the particular foreign groups that the profession has chosen to serve have changed as well; and, at the same time, the foreign/native dynamic has reappeared in many new forms. This chapter explores these changes and continuities in the ways that social work, as a profession, has dealt with the foreign "other." I argue that there were—and are—distinctions made between the *similar other* and the *dissimilar other*. My main focus will be on social work efforts from the late nineteenth to the early twentieth century, when the distinctions between the similar other and dissimilar other were conceived along "racial" lines. I will show that the foreigners who were considered sufficiently similar to early social workers were served, while dissimilar ones were not. I will then contrast these early efforts with the work of the profession today. Finally, I will discuss a current example of working with the foreign, drawn from a community organization project with academic migrant families.[2] In this case, I will highlight two forms of foreignness in social work: the foreignness of the clientele and the foreignness of the social worker.

Categories of Foreignness in Social Work

Working with foreign communities has been a consistent theme in the history of social work in the United States since its inception and has reflected struggles of both the profession and the country's social service delivery systems.[3] Moreover, multiple categories of foreignness appear in the field of social work based on the perceived foreignness of the social worker, clients, or both.

The first category is encountered when a client or client system is foreign to a social worker; a primary example is U.S. social workers working with immigrants and refugees—such as the Ethiopians and Eritreans, who were the first large group of voluntary immigrants from Africa and among the most recent arrivals from "less industrialized" countries.[4] Yet many more seasoned immigrant and refugee groups are still considered foreign as well. Over twenty years after the first resettlement began, the Hmong, an ethnic minority mainly from the mountainous areas of Laos, are still perceived as foreign by many.[5] Although definitions vary, the branches of social work that deal explicitly with issues of foreignness in this sense are referred to as multicultural social work or, sometimes, as international social work.[6] Multicultural social work focuses mostly on domestic issues such as working with people of color, women, and other social minorities in the United States, whereas international social work deals with issues that are explicitly international in nature, such as working with non-governmental organizations (NGOs) abroad or with recent immigrants to the United States.[7]

In the second category, emphasized by international social work, a social worker may also travel to a social work context that is foreign. In this case, the social workers themselves are also identified as foreign by the client or client systems. For example, a small number of social workers work with international populations through the United Nations (e.g., the High Commissioner for Refugees or International Children's Education Fund), the U.S. government or government-supported programs (e.g., USAID or PeaceCorp), or social welfare-oriented private voluntary organizations (e.g., Red Cross, Foster Parents Plan, or Catholic Relief).[8] The job in such organizations often includes working in community and social development projects in "less industrialized" countries.[9] Similarly, earlier in this century, many U.S. social work educators went to newly independent countries in Latin America, Africa, and Asia, to spread American models of social work, and some argue that this trend is currently replicated by social work academicians going to postsocialist East European countries.[10] While these educators were (and are) as foreign as they found the host country fellows to be, the meanings of *foreignness* here may vary. For example, the foreignness American social work educators bring in may be perceived as a source of knowledge by some people in a host country, but as a warning sign of possible cultural colonization by others. At the same time, some American social workers may interpret the foreignness that the host context presents as something to "modernize," while other Americans may see it as something from which to learn.[11] In a way, there is a *double foreignness* operating between the social worker and clientele—the environment is foreign to the social worker while the social worker her/himself is foreign to the clients or communities—and the ongoing power negotiation accompanying this process decides the meaning of *foreignness.* Who has the power to name the other *foreign* is both variable and consequential.

Finally, social workers themselves may be foreign to clients or client systems because they themselves are immigrants. This is a peculiar case where foreign social workers may not have as much social power as fellow social workers. On the one hand, they may, as a result, be marginalized by both client systems and the social service delivery systems for which they work. Jansen and Aguilar argue of the foreign social worker that "[b]eing born outside the United States or having lived on the borderlands offers an enduring awareness of being a stranger."[12] On the other hand, this marginalization can lead to greater self-awareness and understanding of power relationships and can afford, as Jansen and Aguilar argue, "understandings of oppressor/oppressed dynamics."[13] Further, the foreign experience of the social worker can also lead to unique contributions to the field, as exemplified by Gisela Konopka, a social worker who emigrated from Germany. She was active in the anti-Nazi movement, interned in a concentration camp, fled from one country to another, and finally arrived in the United States in 1941. Once here, she drew on her past experiences and developed a "social group work" model, which emphasized humanistic values. Her model was translated into many languages and became influential in several countries, including her native Germany.[14]

If there exist multiple layers of foreignness in the social work profession, that foreignness can also be constructed in numerous ways. For example, U.S. citizens who have different religious, racial, ethnic, cultural, class, moral, sexual, and/or gender identifications may also be considered foreign. As Jansen and Aguilar put it:

> Loss of a homeland, far or near, always invites reflections on the political, the personal, and the professional. It is not just national origin that makes the difference: family life, class, gender, sexual orientation, and skin color all inform

the sense of self that is foregrounded by a "foreign" name or status, even when one's passport may show U.S. citizenship.[15]

Thus, although this chapter mainly deals with foreignness conceived in terms of ethnic and cultural differences, there are other domains of difference that create or vary the meaning of foreignness as well.

The Foreign and Social Work: Inherent Dilemma

Working with the foreign other, I would argue, points to a profound contradiction within social work as a helping profession. Social work as a field embodies a fundamental dilemma in that it is constantly defining the foreign—that is, constructing it—while trying to eradicate it by breaking down the inequality between foreigners and natives. If social work helps those who do not somehow meet the standards of the society, it simultaneously reinforces those standards and necessitates a group that does not reach them. It seems that social work needs the foreign to construct itself, but at the same time constructs itself through "correcting" foreignness. Americanization programs and the processes through which Charity Organization Societies (discussed below) determined eligibility of care are examples of correcting foreignness while actively constructing the category of "correctable" foreigners.

Currently, eligibility of care is not determined along as blatantly "racial" lines as it once was.[16] However, terms such as "hard-to-reach" populations and "underutilization of services" often mask discrimination based on perceived eligibility; they soften the tone of discrimination, but, in reality, effect similar categorizations. For example, until recently, training in multicultural social work meant learning about four "ethnic minority" groups, namely, Native Americans, African Americans, Asian Americans, and Hispanic/Latino Americans. While learning about the history and unique communication style of each group is indeed important for effective social work practice, this summary alone has rarely impacted how services are provided. If Asian Americans are reluctant to use mental health services, social workers are supposed to understand that that difficulty is due to cultural values. But this understanding alone does not guarantee that social workers with dominant views will serve Asian Americans more effectively. Alternative approaches to providing counseling might be necessary, such as doing outreach, hiring Asian American social workers, or providing prevention programs through multiservice community agencies.[17] Generating alternative approaches for diverse groups is a skill that is not sufficiently emphasized in social work training. Thus, if minority groups "underutilize" mental health services, this problem is attributed to the minorities themselves—in this case, Asian Americans—for their reluctance in engaging in a dominant way of providing care. If Asian Americans are too foreign to utilize these services, they are more likely than not to be merely left out. This process, in turn, reinforces dominant views of the foreign.

In the following section, I will trace the history of these foreign/native dynamics in the inception of social work in the United States—a history, primarily of affluent American-born Anglos dealing with foreign immigrants, which highlights the first category of foreignness sketched above. I will then, in my final section, move to contemporary social work practice and briefly examine the status of the foreign in it; here, I will focus on the third category outlined above, using a recent case example.

The Historic Role of the Foreign in Social Work

The Inception of Social Work in the United States

When social work was emerging in the late nineteenth century, the political and societal climate was generally hostile toward new immigrants. The influx of Chinese and Japanese immigrants who came into the United States during the mid-1800s and early 1900s was seen as a threat to white miners and farmers—a perceived threat that led to riots throughout the West Coast as well as to evictions and hangings of Chinese immigrants. Many Americans in this era believed that Asians were "sinister and untrustworthy people" and used derogatory expressions such as the "Yellow Peril" to describe them.[18] After the Chinese Exclusion Law of 1882—America's first systematic exclusion of a particular ethnic group from immigration—Japanese immigrants grew in number until a quota was established by the 1907 Gentlemen's Agreement between Japan and the United States. The Immigration Act of 1924, in effect, barred further immigration from China and Japan.[19]

The word *immigrant,* at the turn of the century, however, more often signified Italian, Polish, Russian, Hungarian, or other immigrants from southern and eastern Europe (especially Catholics and Jews) who would be considered "white" today. These white ethnic immigrants who came to the United States mostly between 1885 and 1924 were called "new immigrants" as opposed to the old ones from western and northern Europe.[20] Many of these new immigrants became the industrial labor force in northern and midwestern cities, to the extent that, in 1914, 60 percent of the U.S. industrial labor force was foreign born.[21] Many had to live in dark and crowded slums and in unsanitary conditions.[22]

Even within the same "racial" groups, distinctions were made that identified some as more foreign. Jane Addams documents the treatment received by the "older and most foreign-looking immigrants":

> The Italians whose fruit-carts are upset simply because they are "dagoes," or
> the Russian peddlers who are stoned and sometimes badly injured because it

has become a code of honor in a gang of boys to thus express their derision. The members of a Protective Association of Jewish Peddlers organized at Hull-House, related daily experiences in which old age had been treated with such irreverence, cherished dignity with such disrespect, that a listener caught the passion of Lear in the old texts, as a platitude enunciated by a man who discovers in it his own experience, thrills us as no unfamiliar phrases can possibly do. The Greeks are filled with amazed rage when their very name is flung at them as an opprobrious epithet.[23]

One area in which these varied degrees of foreignness early manifested themselves was housing accommodations. According to Alfreda Iglehart and Rosina Becerra, while poor white immigrants had to endure inadequate housing conditions, "African Americans of all income levels suffered housing problems."[24] In 1913 Chicago, an advocate for African Americans noted, "[w]hile half of the people in the Bohemian, Polish, and Lithuanian districts were paying less than $8.50 for their four room apartments; the steelmill employees less than $9.50, and the Jews in the Ghetto less than $10.50, the Negro, in the midst of extreme dilapidation and crowded into territory adjoining the segregated vice district, pays $12 to $12.50"[25]—and this at a time when African Americans were experiencing chronic unemployment, poverty, and frequent mob lynching.[26] While immigrant families often earned low wages "in the most dangerous and labor-intensive occupations," wage discrimination against African Americans was even worse.[27] Native American communities also suffered the effects of being viewed as foreign; children were taken from their parents and sent to distant boarding schools and the self-help structures of Native American communities were prohibited by law.[28]

Many social initiatives and movements emerged between 1890 and 1920 in response to industrialization and urbanization, often upholding society's problematic assumptions about foreignness.[29] According to social Darwinists, who believed in the "survival of the fittest" and the necessity of competition for resources, "social welfare thwarts nature's plan of evolutionary progress toward higher forms of social life."[30] This intellectualization of conservative ideology offered a "rationale for ignoring the plight of the poor."[31] Other creations of the time included state militias, urban police forces, and urban armories.[32]

However, the turn of the century was also a dynamic era that saw the emergence of many political progressives and social reformers. As numerous social work researchers demonstrate, by the beginning of the twentieth century, social reformers, philanthropists, and many other Americans began adopting environmental explanations for social ills and prevailing poverty—citing, for example, overcrowding, tenements, poor working conditions, exploitation of labor, and defects in the governmental supervision of citizens' welfare—over simple personal explanations such as laziness or "lack of character."[33] Many social reformers saw large corporations, political machines, and corruption to be the real threats to democracy. In addition, they learned that other countries in Europe of-

fered various social programs and regulations for workers and families, which
the United States did not have.[34] This was also the time that many devoted social
reformers, settlement workers, and journalists brought to public attention the
facts about social problems, such as poor working conditions, occupational haz-
ards, and infant mortality, which "bolstered support for reform" by the general
public.[35] Many well-known voluntary sectors were created in this era as well;
both the Salvation Army and American Red Cross were founded in the 1880s.
The African American scholar and social leader W. E. B. Du Bois brought racism to national attention and led the formation, in 1909, of the National Association for the Advancement of Colored People (NAACP). Early social workers
such as Jane Addams, Florence Kelly, and George Edmund Haynes were "galva-
nized" by Du Bois and became active in the formation process of both the
NAACP and the National Urban League on Urban Conditions.[36]

It is in this context, both of hostility toward immigrants and of support for
social reform, that the discipline of social work emerged in the United States. At
its inception, working with new Americans was the core of its practice.[37] When
the first Charity Organization Society (COS) in the United States was established
in 1877, as when Jane Addams and Ellen Gates Starr, in 1889, started working
with poor immigrants in Chicago, foreigners (who manifested concentrated social problems to the public) appeared to be one of the most pressing concerns for
society.[38] While "[t]hroughout the nineteenth century immigrants were also
viewed as contributing disproportionately to social problems like crime,
prostitution, intemperance, and pauperism," the study by the Industrial
Commission of 1901 showed that, in reality, immigrants were no more
represented among convicted criminals or paupers than any other group.[39] One
consequence of this popular (mis)belief was the idea that even impoverished
housing conditions in urban slums were better than what such immigrants had
had in Europe—an explanation that justified the failures of housing reform.[40]

In addition to inadequate housing, immigrants suffered from unemployment,
unsanitary conditions in slums, malnutrition, and other issues stemming from
poverty. There were almost no services available for new Americans from federal and state governments, which for the most part left mutual aid or voluntary
sectors such as settlement houses and COSs to help immigrants "settle down"—
or conform to a particular social order—as quickly and smoothly as possible.[41]
Settlement houses and COSs are commonly viewed as the roots of modern social
work in the United States. The following brief excerpt from a recent social work
textbook captures this standard understanding of the history of the social work
profession:

> Modern social work in the United States arose from two models: the Charity
> Organization Society and the settlement house movement. Begun in England in
> 1869, the Charity Organization Society came to the United States in 1877 and
> set up a relief system based on investigating claims, meeting individual needs,
> and providing minimal relief payment for the truly needy. Workers kept case

records and made regular visits to recipients. In 1887, settlement houses appeared in New York, Boston, and Chicago to help European immigrants newly arrived in America. These community centers offered practical education, recreation, and social cohesion for those in the inner-city ethnic ghettos. Hull-House under Jane Addams exemplified community resources such as a free kindergarten, day nursery, playground, clubs, lectures, library, boardinghouse, and meeting rooms.[42]

Although social work history nearly always identifies COSs and settlement houses as the roots of the profession, it has often overlooked the crucial point of who these organizations served—that is, *foreigners*—and the impact that this clientele had on the formation of the social work profession. While many social welfare researchers have demonstrated that industrialization and urbanization led to urban destitution, which, in turn, led to social unrest, and while many have established that the emergence of social work was one response to these increased social problems, most existing analyses lack explanations of how the massive presence of foreigners and immigrants impacted the development of American social work. Indeed, when compared to the emergence of social work professions in other industrialized countries, this aspect of social work in the United States is revealed as quite unique.

The Impact of the Foreign on U.S. Social Work

While early social work efforts in the United States mostly provided for foreigners, as exemplified in COSs and settlement houses, the same does not hold true for early social work institutions in other industrializing countries. In Japan, for example, while modern social work emerged in an analogous era of industrialization and urbanization, one in which the Japanese experienced increasing poverty and social problems caused by natural and politically-created disasters (famine, the great earthquake, tsunami), by wars (China-Japan, Russia-Japan), and by three economic depressions in two decades (1890-1908), it did not experience the robust impact of immigration that the United States did.[43] The development of social work in early twentieth-century Sweden also bears many similarities to the United States: massive industrialization, urbanization, and economic discrepancy led Swedish female philanthropists, in 1903, to create the social work profession and a national social work organization.[44] But, again, what Sweden did *not* experience was the presence of immigrants in the formative years of social work.[45]

By contrast with both Japan and Sweden, many of the problems that early social workers addressed in the United States—poverty, labor rights, and the protection of women and children, for example—were highlighted by the massive immigration attendant upon U.S. industrialization in the late nineteenth century. Indeed, it was the rapidly increasing manifestation of the foreign in American society that, arguably, conditioned the emergence of social work as a profession. This fact poses the questions, then, of what kind of impact the immigrants had on U.S. social work as it emerged, and of whether there is anything identifiably unique about U.S. social work due to the fact that it was largely conceived as a profession that works with foreigners. One hypothesis is that without the stark dissimilarities presented by foreigners, American social work simply might not have developed as rapidly as it did. But there is little doubt that the impact of foreigners on U.S. social work is deeper and subtler than this:

> The form and ideology governing social services have been evolving since the turn of the century. That evolution only mildly flirted with deviating from its original underpinnings that were derived from the social, political, and economic context of the day. Indeed, social work and social welfare, then and now, are products of the environments from which they emerge. Conservative underpinnings were in the forefront of the formative years of the social work profession when the country was coping with the arrival of diverse, new immigrant populations. These conservative underpinnings were reflected in charity organizations and settlement houses that were derived from the White, Protestant, middle-class segment of U.S. society that sought to assist immigrants in adjusting to American life.[46]

Examining the environments or, rather, the historical and political circumstances that produced the discipline of social work not only improves our understanding of its historical roots, but also bears relevance to current social work practice, since much of what the profession cherishes, thinks, and problematizes today is the legacy of those early days. Stanley Wenocur and Michael Reisch write:

> We recognize that the motivations of social work activists to build a profession were seldom simple and often quite unconscious. We all act in some sense in response to our historical context without being aware of how much that context is shaping our behavior. In fact, this is one of the chief disadvantages of an ahistorical practice that we seek to counter.[47]

It is the argument of this paper that understanding early social workers' involvement with foreigners is a crucial part of the historicized practice that Wenocur and Reisch call for.

The social work field emerged as "charity," evolving around services for poor immigrants.[48] But this presented two problems in the long run. First, while charity was often driven by religious and moral motives, the burgeoning profession wanted itself to be more "scientific"—to be recognized as "objective" and to fit into higher education.[49] Government policies and programs later developed, supplementing voluntary services and sometimes replacing forms of work previously performed as charity. Second, the strong ideology of individualism in American society ran counter to the idea of charity.[50] Identifying the settlement house's successful involvement with foreigners as one of the five reasons why settlements were able to flourish, the late Harry Specht, a leading social welfare scholar, also contends that "the settlements had their greatest success with immigrant communities that had a strong communal orientation and that were upwardly mobile"—that is, that had at least one foot in the culture of individualism. He also argues that "the powerful force of American individualism [still] . . . pervades our thinking about our neighbors," thus making it difficult for social workers in the post-"new immigrant" era to continue on the legacy of earlier settlement houses.[51]

Social work was also shaped by the perceived need to control foreigners. In the early history of the social work profession, one major drive was the moral obligation for citizens to help the disadvantaged. On the one hand, this obligation stemmed from a desire to promote social justice, facilitate community interaction, and empower immigrants:

> The primary settlement house technology used consistently across all houses was that of interaction with and between community residents. . . . The energy flowing from these interactions inspired people to envision change in themselves and their surroundings and then work to achieve those changes. The core technology was the process of human dynamics derived from the interactions occurring in the houses.[52]

The interaction between social workers and community members, which depends on active engagement, could, moreover, be a two-way street. Workers, that is, were also empowered by interactions with and among community residents; in part, by allowing workers the sense of carrying out socially recognized, meaningful work. However, behind this trend arguably lurked a desire for social control driven by xenophobia. Wenocur and Reisch show that immigrants were seen as having vices, lowering the intelligence and morality of society at large, and being a nuisance to the community, and argue that fear drove reform movements as much as moral concern did. It is not difficult to imagine how this fear led to the perceived need to control foreigners. This control was both symbolized and reproduced by a standardized image of the "good American," who possessed, for example, specific religious and ethnic characteristics. This image, write Wenocur and Reisch,

> reflected longstanding anti-urban and anti-European prejudices, particularly against Catholics and Jews, and produced "reform movements" which stemmed as much from fear of political power shifting to the ethnic, non-Protestant masses as they did from moral outrage over the corruption of political machines. . . . Education and religious conversion were two major components of this reform strategy. The development of social services with education or religious overtones was a third.[53]

Many of these tensions between charity and individualism, empowerment and social control, converged on a social problem that was difficult both to ignore and to acknowledge—that is, poverty. America has had a very ambivalent relationship with poverty, and foreigners were—and still are—perceived to be at the center (if not the cause) of this problem. While the United States has always been among the richest countries in the world, its income discrepancy, particularly in the late capitalist state, has also grown to be one of the largest of all nations. Nonetheless, it is often perceived through the myth of the "American dream" as a place of equal opportunity where everyone is supposed to be able, with the right morals and attitude, to "make it." This American myth is threatened by the presence of poverty; it is also frequently invoked in discussions of social welfare, and never fails to surface when the conservative wind is blowing strong. This view, as social welfare researchers Karger and Stoesz summarize, is rooted in a historically strong religious ideal:

> Poverty was seen as a moral failing in the context of orthodox Protestant theology. . . . According to both Luther and Calvin, God-fearing people must work regardless of their wage or type of employment. This Protestant ethic fueled the creation of a work-oriented society and provided a religious foundation for the indifference of the elite classes toward the poor. . . . Some critics have argued that despite the social welfare services provided by the churches, in the final analysis Protestant theology was basically opposed to social welfare.[54]

Social policy, as well as voluntary efforts to eradicate poverty, reflected this ambivalence. On the one hand, at the turn of the century, Social Gospelists, reformers, and progressives were concerned about social ills resulting from industrialization and excessive capitalism, and they counteracted conservative Protestant theology.[55] On the other hand, there was a constant argument against relief and helping the poor because the relief-givers, private and public, feared creating dependency, which was supposed to spoil the work ethic and capitalist principles.

> Relief was still seen as a dangerous expedient since "temporary aid might end in permanent support and . . . the habit of receiving without rendering an equivalent might sap the foundation of that independence of character and one's reliance on one's own resources." Indeed, relief was judged by some observers to be an unfair subsidy to labor in its struggle with capital.[56]

Wenocur and Reisch view this conflict as a "contradiction between capitalist and socialist views of society, the individual and the state," and contend that all forms of American social work reflect this contradiction.[57] Although the causes of poverty were far more complex than, and often had nothing to do with, "lack of character," one way that these dilemmas were resolved was through Americanization projects, which we will look at in greater detail below; these programs made dealing with poverty palatable—and wider support from funders possible—by teaching immigrants a set of values that Americans were supposed to embrace.

Poverty and immigrants both existed before the late nineteenth century, but social work was the first profession to deal with them systematically and in conjunction. Although there are no doubt numerous reasons why exactly social work emerged at the time it did, I would argue that the presence of foreigners in the United States—the great influx of immigrants—played a central role. This prompts us to consider the legacy and limitations of early social work programs, and to assess the meanings of the *foreign* these early social workers delineated.

Settlement Houses and Charity Organization Societies

The settlement house movement originated in London in 1884 at Toynbee Hall and soon spread to the United States. As industrialization proceeded in the United States, and the wealthy grew concerned about poor urban immigrants, settlement houses developed neighborhood-based facilities that brought together people of diverse socioeconomic and cultural backgrounds so that they could share mutually beneficial knowledge and skills. These groups were organized by leaders "as diverse as feminists and Protestant clergymen" and their reasons for engaging with immigrants and the poor also ranged "from benevolence to social control."[58] Private contributions and grants by social philanthropists largely funded settlement houses.[59]

If industrialization was one root of the settlement house movement, another was the presence of college-educated middle- and upper-class women unable to make use of their education and energy.[60] The settlement house movement provided women like Jane Addams and Ellen Gates Starr with the opportunity to act on their social concerns and such women became the major builders of the movement. It was during a trip to Europe, Susan Donner writes of Addams and Starr,

> that they shared with each other their concern with the lack of meaningful options for women, particularly educated women. Although they were influenced by the social and cultural goals of Toynbee Hall in England, the goal of both women in starting Hull-House was to provide for themselves and for other women a new avenue for living independently and giving meaning to life.[61]

Thus, early social work settings were as much about mediating the foreignness of unattached and educated women in their own culture—and particularly in the public sphere—as about caring for foreigners from other cultures.[62] Though a daughter of one of the richest men in northern Illinois, Addams "wrote of the betrayal of educated women by a society that constrained the choices available to them"; thus, settlement house work became "salvation" for her and other women like her.[63] In a way, Addams's work was an example of one kind of foreignness working with another.

By the 1920s and 1930s, the settlement house movement had reached its peak in the United States. The record shows that, by 1936, at least 202 settlement houses were recognized by professional organizations; they were established mostly in the East and Midwest, although some houses existed in California and the South.[64] Although after the 1930s settlement houses as a movement declined, current social work inherited many critical functions from the settlement house movement, including information dissemination, advocacy, social action, policy practice, community and locality development, and social and community planning.[65] Indeed, Addams and Starr's Hull-House is still one of the best known social work agencies in the world. Working primarily with diverse immigrant groups—Irish, Jews, Poles, Greeks, Italians, Germans, Serbs, and, later, some African Americans—settlement houses developed service technologies that still underpin the profession today.[66] These technologies, which sent educators, social reformers, recreational specialists, and social workers-to-be into poor ethnic ghettos, included activities at the personal, communal, and political levels.[67]

Charity Organization Societies (COSs) were also modeled after a British precedent. The first American COS was founded in Buffalo, New York in 1877, and by 1892, ninety-two COSs were established in cities across the United States and Canada.[68] The main focus of COSs was organizing volunteers, called "friendly visitors," who made home-visits to poor families. The key functions of friendly visitors consisted of investigating conditions, registering individuals and families, cooperating with communities, and coordinating care. According to Donald Brieland, "The COSs sought to save cities from the evils of pauperism, reduce the cost of charity, and deal with antagonism created by social-class differences."[69] Emphasis on personal responsibility and the work ethic was intertwined with a religious focus, which viewed poverty as "sin."[70] While criticized by progressive settlement house leaders such as Addams, COSs maintained a moral imperative for determining eligibility of care; "the sturdy beggar, the alcoholic, the womanizer, and the prostitute" were rejected.[71] If some of these dubious COS values are still upheld in family casework agencies today, so too are significant technologies developed by COS workers that became the basis of modern social work, such as careful assessment and accountability as exemplified in the pioneering work of Mary Richmond.[72] Friendly visitors are considered the forerunners of caseworkers and family workers.[73]

COSs and settlement houses, in many ways, contrast with each other to the extent that COSs are often used as an example of bad social work efforts, of bad ideology and methods, while settlement houses are glorified into an example of high ideology, far-reaching vision, and progressive social change.[74] However, some things were similar between these two movements as well. Both movements had religious and educational overtones and both believed in doing investigation at the individual and community levels. Above all, workers in both movements were volunteers who "felt impelled to do something about class divisiveness" and urban conditions and felt obligated, as part of a privileged class, to extend help.[75] There are, however, limitations in both movements that need to be addressed in order to understand their—and the social work profession's—relationship to the foreign other.

Americanization, Cleansing, and Social Control

A further function of settlement houses and the COSs was "Americanization"—domesticating the foreigner.[76] Americanization had both positive and negative aspects. The settlement houses offered English classes, occupational training, and domestic skills that genuinely helped immigrant neighbors advance in the United States. Addams, for example, describes the kinds of practical knowledge such organizations made available to Italian immigrants in urban Chicago:

> [A]n Italian girl who has had lessons in cooking at the public school, will help her mother to connect the entire family with American food and household habits. That the mother has never baked bread in Italy—only mixed it in her own house and then taken it out to the village oven—makes all the more valuable her daughter's understanding of the complicated cooking stove. The same thing is true of the girl who learns to sew in the public school, and more than anything else, perhaps, of the girl who receives the first simple instruction in the care of little children—that skillful care which every tenement-house baby requires if he is to be pulled through his second summer. As a result of this teaching I recall a young girl who carefully explained to her Italian mother that the reason the babies in Italy were so healthy and the babies in Chicago were so sickly, was not, as her mother had firmly insisted, because her babies in Italy had goat's milk and her babies in America had cow's milk, but because the milk in Italy was clean and the milk in Chicago was dirty. She said that when you milked your own goat before the door, you knew that the milk was clean, but when you bought milk from the grocery store after it had been carried for many miles in the country, you couldn't tell whether or not it was fit for the baby to drink until the men from the City Hall who had watched it all the way, said that it was all right.[77]

Addams, an articulate and influential leader of social work and social reform, who documented the conditions of urban slums in an attempt to bring about broad social change, might not have wanted to stress the implications of class differences between her colleagues and the immigrants.[78] But social class was, in effect, used as a tool to Americanize immigrants faster, according to social work and welfare historian, Judith Trolander. She notes the greater willingness on the part of immigrants to be Americanized and acculturated under the well-to-do residents:

Among these institutions, the settlement house was unique in that immigrants of all nationalities were welcome to come together. Furthermore, in the settlement house, immigrants could meet well-to-do settlement house volunteers from other parts of the city along with the college-educated residents. Most immigrants shared the dream of America as the land of opportunity, which was real because of the economic expansion of the times. Within the settlement house, they were, to a certain extent, willing to defer to the well-to-do residents and volunteers in part because they saw an open class system. The settlement house could help them assimilate and move up in American society. The acculturation activities of the early settlement house workers might be regarded as paternalistic, but these activities were eagerly sought by the settlement's clientele. Thus, in an increasingly fragmented city, the settlement house provided a meeting ground for different ethnic groups and for the well-off and the poor to come together, to bridge class differences, and to work together on resolving social problems.[79]

Americanization, however, was also a naive approach that ignored the complexity of cultural adjustment. As Sherraden and Martin put it, "In 'Americanization' programs of the 1920s, it was often assumed that immigrant families replaced their traditional culture with an 'American' culture, but today we know that immigrants do not forget their 'old ways' in a kind of collective amnesia."[80] W. Devore and E. G. Schlesinger echo this sentiment: "The fact that people migrate is not equivalent with rejection of customs, traditions, and approaches to problem solving of the land and culture left behind."[81] While the images of famous settlement houses and their (radically) progressive leaders are well-known (e.g., Jane Addams, Graham Taylor of Chicago Commons, Lillian Wald of the Henry Street Settlement), many settlement house workers "adopted a derogatory view of Americanizing the immigrant with all possible speed."[82] They equated "human betterment with [American] middle class values" and supported "Americanization, voluntarism, and anti-radicalism."[83]

Americanization essentially entailed a cleansing of the newcomers in the early days of social work. For immigrants were often seen as "dirty" upon entrance to the country. Dirtiness was perceived in, for example, their foreign language, appearance, religious practices, and customs. To the public eye, there was something wrong with the immigrants that needed to be fixed, and this view was exacerbated by the economic downturn that began in 1913. For example, before the Civil War, the Irish were thought to bring in diseases, the same stereotype later used against Asian Americans.[84] Many conservative intellectuals of the time bought into the eugenics movement that found its way into the United States in the 1900s, and believed that a number of foreigners had "hereditary mental defects."[85]

To facilitate their acceptance in America, these foreigners at least needed to be "cleaned"—that is, Americanized. These Americanization efforts, mainly undertaken by COS workers, taught new immigrants the "proper" way of living in

American society, and included instruction in everything from what to wear to what to eat, how to clean and decorate the house, how to raise children, and how many children to produce. COS workers thus became the major agents of Americanization; and their job was to domesticate the foreigner through disciplinary and regulatory practices.[86] These Americanization projects clearly reflect the limited view of acculturation and assimilation of the time: Americanization was accepted as an undisputed good. While the work of Du Bois on double consciousness[87] and of more recent scholars on acculturation[88] has explored the possibilities of bicultural experience, at the time, producing hybrid cultures or having multiple identities were not considered to be viable options. Often, immigrants were given binary choices: become Americanized or remain forever foreign.[89]

As these Americanization projects demonstrate, and as Iglehart and Becerra remind us, there is a direct relation between social work and social *control*:

> *Social control* is defined as those practices and policies designed to encourage, persuade, and/or coerce individuals to conform to values and behaviors defined by the larger society. . . . In the United States, there seems to be a dominant or national culture of which capitalism is but a part and this culture reflects the imprint of a dominant ethnic group in the institutions, values, and character of the country. This imprint determines what is truly "American," who is truly "American," as well as social problems, social problem groups, and problem solutions. The cultural imprint of U.S. society has historically made a distinction between racial minority groups and white ethnic groups. . . . The early years of what was to become social work practice dramatically emphasizes this point.[90]

This social control was effected by institutionalizing dominant moral standards that decided who were favorable foreigners (potential "Americans") and eligible for services. Similarly, settlement houses varied in their understandings of the socioeconomic and cultural background of immigrants; the condescension with which some immigrants were treated also functioned as a kind of social discipline—a punishment for foreignness that encouraged Americanization. Social control functions are ingrained in the foundation of social work practice, according to Ann Hartman.[91] She argues that they undergird "the dilemmas inherent in our profession's ideal of self-determination and our use of authority, as well as an appreciation of the limitations and challenges when people are in the relationship under duress."[92] Wenocur and Reisch further the argument by pointing out that social work does not generate income by offering professional services in the usual sense; rather, salaries come from insurance reimbursement, private charity, government social security, and so forth, instead of charging fees directly to clients.[93] Thus, social work historically has been vulnerable to accepting dominant values since it is funded by private, corporate, and governmental authorities who have an interest in sustaining the status quo.

So far we have reviewed the early history of social work and how European immigrants—the foreign other in the United States—were treated through Americanization projects that focused on cleansing and social control. When we look at the boundaries of Americanization, however, it becomes clearer how various foreign groups, foreign-born or indigenous, were treated differently. Such boundaries represented the willingness of the dominant society to absorb certain groups through Americanization and its unwillingness to absorb others. Although the groups that are perceived to be more foreign may change over time, and although the central characteristics that were used in classifying foreign groups were the perceived racial, ethnic, and religious attributes of the time, there nonetheless seems to be a similar underlying mechanism in social work today that determines the degree of an individual's or group's foreignness and which remains one of the limiting legacies of early social work efforts.

Ethnic and Racial Exclusions

Early social work efforts practiced the selective exclusion of certain ethnic groups that were perceived to be too foreign to aid or assimilate. At COSs, priority of service was often given to people who were similar to friendly visitors, as this testimony of a COS worker from 1882 makes clear:

> Until the Italians became numerous, we had at least intelligent means of communication with most of the families we knew . . . [but the Italians] are truly foreign to us. We do not speak a common language; our standards have no meaning to them, and we may well doubt whether they have any applicability.[94]

This view of Italians, and of southern and eastern European immigrants more generally, reflects the attitude that society at large held during this period.[95] Often the COS worker—"a welfare gatekeeper" who believed in "personal rehabilitation of the poor"—determined who could be "Americanized" without any input from the immigrants themselves.[96] Their decisions, furthermore, appear to have been based on their perceptions of the degree of foreignness that attached to the immigrants they encountered. As Iglehart and Becerra suggest, "anti-foreign sentiments were directed against those immigrants with darker coloring and starkly 'foreign' cultures, languages, and practices."[97] Here, entitlement to services was determined by the perceived similarity between the target group and the social workers. Similarities in cultures, languages, and customs probably led COS workers to assume that certain groups held similar moral values; such criteria were then used to determine the eligibility of care. Thus, those who were determined to be sufficiently similar to the workers were included in their services, and those who were perceived as too foreign to be assimilated were not. The former, who I will call the *similar other*, had lighter skin and a similar language and cultural practices, while the latter, the *dissimilar other*, had one or more critical components very different from those of COS workers. While both of these groups were foreign to the COS workers, the degree of perceived foreignness set them apart in their treatment. The kind of foreignness of the similar others allowed early social workers to act as paternalistic Americanization agents, while the greater foreignness of the dissimilar other allowed workers to form a discourse of exclusion that justified lack of services based on a group's purported lack of values, standards, and character.

This tendency to serve *the similar other*, however, did not pass with the era of COSs. Until very recently, contend Iglehart and Becerra, mainstream social work itself, accepted only "the acceptable," that is, only those who ostensibly could be Americanized and become a part of "the melting pot." Who fit in that group and who was excluded changed over time, but the categories of acceptable (the similar other) and unacceptable (the dissimilar other) remained. In the United States today, for example, Muslim Arab Americans may remain very foreign to many service providers. Often practitioners are not aware of the religious customs of Muslims and of the implications of those customs for social work services—for example, the need to provide gender-specific programs for traditional Muslim women. Major social work textbooks, even multiculturally oriented ones, do not touch on (and thus leave many social workers unfamiliar with) this population. Moreover, the diversity among Arab Americans is often not understood well. As long as social workers focus on "the acceptable" or similar other, who can fit themselves into the services that they already provide, social workers may feel little need to expand the services to cater to the needs of the dissimilar other.

An additional result of this focus on "the acceptable" or the similar other was that social workers looked only at the similarities of people they served. Differences or dissimilarities within the client systems of similar others had to be downplayed or ignored by decontexualizing minorities and overlooking differences. Such practices have been justified on the grounds that "people are all the same because we are all human,"[98] which has, in turn, led to the argument that differences among the similar others ought not be focused on because it would have a divisive effect.[99] This view, the "myth of sameness,"[100] assumes that all humans are ultimately the same and thus ignores the needs and strengths of particular populations within the category of similar other, as well as all people within the category of dissimilar other. As a result, social workers have often failed to acknowledge the unique histories, values, cultures, and behaviors of particular populations who fall within the category of the similar other.

One group with which settlement houses maintained an ambivalent relationship was African Americans.[101] African Americans are a prime example of the *dissimilar other* who were completely ignored by most early social work efforts.[102] Karger and Stoesz write, "If the conditions of immigrants were difficult, those of African Americans were even more trying."[103] Even a liberal place like Hull-House could not fully serve the African American community in the same way it did other ethnic groups, and it thus practiced implicit racial segregation.[104]

Elisabeth Lasch-Quinn notes in the introduction to her book, *Black Neighbors: Race and the Limits of Reform in the American Settlement House Movement, 1890-1945,* that "the settlement house movement grew out of an awareness of the severe conditions facing newcomers to the city. While it attempted to address the needs of white immigrants, it largely ignored the parallel situation of African Americans when they began to replace whites in settlement neighborhoods."[105]

Various factors may have kept settlement houses from serving African American residents newly migrated from the South. The institutional racism of the time was, of course, a major cause, what Trolander calls "settlement workers' blind spot on civil rights."[106] After reviewing writings by settlement workers and African American historians, Berman-Rossi and Miller show how settlement workers and social reformers alike were susceptible to "the racial antagonism of the dominant white majority," which led to maintaining "the social segregation of the day."[107] They assert that "the explanation of the difference between the treatment of African American migrants and European immigrants was race and the racism intrinsic to American society."[108] Another factor, which was intertwined with racism, was the difficulty of finding financial support for programs for African Americans.[109] Iglehart and Becerra argue that African Americans posed a challenge for settlement houses because of their different history and status:

> African Americans represented a kind of anomaly to the settlement houses. Many were more "American" than the native-born population who may have had "foreign" stock in their family background. Consequently, African Americans did not need the "Americanization" treatment to which the immigrants were exposed. . . . These Americans did not require proselytizing to direct their faith and souls to Protestantism, for they had already converted years before to American religion. Thus, it seems that the mission and technologies of the settlement houses would have to be modified for these groups to deemphasize Americanization and emphasize social reform.[110]

When we look at the settlement houses' Americanization and assimilation projects, it becomes clearer how African Americans were perceived by whites as the dissimilar other: while they were already Americanized, they were not perceived as assimilable into the mainstream of American culture. This logic justified discounting the needs of African American communities and accorded with the social climate of the time in which "non-whites," and especially African Americans, were perceived as "a separate class of people" who were "the *children* of the human race."[111] Further, as Iglehart and Becerra note:

> Even though they [African Americans] saw themselves as being as "American" as White Americans, they were confronted with a different reality. . . . To many Whites in the northern cities, African Americans were even more undesirable and "foreign" than were the "new" immigrants.[112]

While the foreignness or "dirtiness" of "white" immigrants could be cleansed once they were Americanized, African Americans were rendered foreign not by language, culture, or religion, but by skin color, which could not be "cleansed" or washed away and which developed increasingly charged meanings over time.

The services and social reforms undertaken by settlement houses for African Americans were thus limited, as Lasch-Quinn has shown. Yet it is also debatable whether black communities would have accepted settlement houses if wealthy whites *had* attempted to establish them. Long distrustful of government and the dominant white population, African Americans may well have been resistant to the idea of relying on white social agencies. As Igelehart and Becerra note, "[y]ears of distrust, apathy, neglect, and rebuff cannot, and should not, be minimized."[113] While these circumstances do not, of course, justify the discrimination and segregation practiced by many social workers at the time, they did lead African American communities to develop their own social organizations, usually through churches. Lasch-Quinn, among other authors, elaborates how churches, which had already been centers of social organization for African Americans during slavery, took on even greater force in the era of institutionalized racism.[114] A church reinforced family ties; in turn, the family collective supported and legitimized the church. A church fostered a sense of community among African Americans and encouraged mutual aid through social networking. The function of the black church was very diverse—daycare, welfare, employment counseling, education, entertainment, and social activism—and Lasch-Quinn contends that "such integration of community services and reform resembles the ideal settlement house."[115] Although exclusion of African Americans from private and public social services should not be justified, if African Americans remained foreign to the emerging profession of social work due to racism, it did not mean that African Americans entirely lacked social services; what it did mean is that their social service systems based on mutual help and pooling of resources were neither legitimated by the academic establishment nor funded through the same channels as other social agencies.

The Legacy of Hull-House

While they never served African Americans as fully as other communities, Jane Addams and her colleagues were among the few exceptional social workers who were able to look at the distinctive cultural heritage of each immigrant group as an asset, rather than as a threat or burden to the American mainstream; they were the forerunners of cultural pluralism and multiculturalism.[116] Although in unequal degrees, Hull-House did serve both the similar other and the dissimilar other. It strove to achieve multicultural neighborhoods; this effort included passing on the traditions that first-generation immigrants brought with them to their children. Addams remembers the house's cultural celebrations as "a source of new understanding and companionship with the members of the contiguous foreign colonies not only between them and their American neighbors but between them and their own children."[117] Further, Addams maintained a humble attitude that allowed her to learn from immigrants. After describing the racial slurs and harassment that Hull-House's Italian, Russian, Jewish, and Greek neighbors experienced, Addams praised them as "my cosmopolitan neighbors" for their open attitudes and tolerance toward ethnic differences, which clearly contrasted with other Americans' attitudes:

> Doubtless these difficulties would be much minimized in America, if we faced our own race problem with courage and valuable help. Certainly they are less conscious than the Anglo-Saxon of color distinctions, perhaps because of their traditional familiarity with Carthage and Egypt. They listened with respect and enthusiasm to a scholarly address delivered by Professor Du Bois at Hull-House on Lincoln's Birthday, with apparently no consciousness of that race difference which color seems to accentuate so absurdly, and upon my return from various conferences held in the interest of "the advancement of colored people," I have had many illuminating conversations with my cosmopolitan neighbors.[118]

Addams's practice (especially from 1889 through the 1910s) is thus a good example of early efforts to incorporate pluralistic and multicultural views into social work practice by respecting and helping to preserve the cultural heritage that immigrant groups brought in. While in the 1950s and 1960s the Council on Social Work Education showed examples of culturally sensitive practice—for example, their 1955 casebook included Italian and Puerto Rican families, Czech children, and Orthodox Jewish refugees[119]—many point out how little the field in general has dealt with multiculturalism until very recently. Doman Lum investigated the coverage of multicultural issues in social work journals and textbooks during the period 1970 to 1994; only 8 percent of the articles of the three leading social work journals addressed general or specific multicultural issues, whereas an even smaller proportion (3 percent) of social work practice texts had pages on those topics. Only very recently have textbooks with a multicultural emphasis started to be used widely and the profession as a whole begun to incorporate multicultural visions, like Addams's, in a systematic way. [120]

In sum, while social control and ethnic exclusion lie at the foundation of the discipline, so too does a strong legacy of culturally sensitive social work practices, a tradition that has recently become of central interest to the profession. Social work's relationship to the foreign thus embraces contradictions and inconsistencies, which continue to manifest themselves in the present. In the following section, I turn to the current relationship of the social work profession to the foreign and assess its relation to the profession's history.

The Foreign in Current Contexts

While American society at large has always struggled to incorporate the similar other, it has also continuously reconstructed the dissimilar other, and immigrants are still, generally speaking, seen as a burden to society. In other words, the attributes that make them dissimilar are emphasized over those that identify them as similar. Regulations by the Immigration and Naturalization Service (INS) have been increasingly tightened, and, in the 1990s, the Clinton administration excluded legal immigrants from receiving social security under the "welfare reform" package.[121] Politicians disparage welfare programs for foreign-born residents and the indigenous poor, arguing that it "creates dependency, which is transmitted intergenerationally."[122] Anti-immigrant sentiment has been palpably growing in California, where children of undocumented immigrants have been barred from public schools and denied health care.[123]

These policies and the rhetoric that subtends them, of course, ignore the contribution of immigrants to American society throughout the history of the United States, the way in which immigrants have, for example, supported the American economy by taking on low-wage manual labor: constructing the American railroad system, working in sweatshops in New York, or performing migrant farm labor in the vineyards of California and the strawberry farms in the Midwest. In fact, as Michael Fix and Jeffrey Passel have demonstrated, a well-known study on the costs of immigration, widely cited by the media and politicians, has significant errors in it and overstates "the costs of immigrants by about $9 billion."[124] Fix and Passel also find that "most national studies suggest that immigrants are not an overall fiscal burden on the native population" because the economic contributions of immigrants outweigh the cost of public assistance programs.[125] The political discourse of dependency also overlooks the fact that foreign-born U.S. residents often do not make use of available social services; Yolanda Padilla contends that, "[c]ontrary to popular belief, research shows that immigrants, including those who qualify for services, vastly underutilize government programs in comparison with the U.S. born population."[126]

The erroneous "information" that makes its way into public discourse produces, and is aggravated by, inadequate national policy. Many agree that "[t]he United States is in the midst of the largest wave of immigration in seventy years," yet "little attention has been given to national policy toward immigrants after they arrive."[127] The United States is often characterized as "a welfare state laggard"[128] and has always assumed the desirability of small government. Some argue that this is because U.S. society was founded by runaways, who were escaping from institutions such as government and church and that the society is still unwilling to "look ahead and plan ahead."[129] As a result, the "American system of social welfare is a patchwork quilt of programs and policies" that lacks a systematic plan.[130] State and local agencies must cope with increasing numbers of immigrants, supplementing the minimal services offered by the federal government, although the tax payments of immigrants mainly go to the federal government.[131] This often means that individual social service staff, lacking a national service policy, must play a leading role in meeting the changing needs of newcomers, as Rosenberg notes:

> Sometimes these efforts flow from conscious state or local decisions; sometimes they are a consequence of federal policies; most often they are the result of program staff trying to serve new faces at the counter. Rarely do legislatures debate the issues; comprehensive service strategies are even more rare. Few policy makers or human service administrators recognize the rapid growth in this field.[132]

As a result, the available services for immigrants vary from one locale to another, depending on state and local governments, as well as on voluntary agencies in the area. Thus, the role the social work profession plays in these settings varies greatly according to the availability of state and local support for services. Professional training is also shaped by what public services are offered; the paucity of available public services has led to a paucity of professional training.[133] What is available also has to do with the size of the population of a certain group in a specific area. For example, an Asian immigrant in Michigan will likely have great difficulty locating a social worker who speaks his/her respective language or who understands his/her culture. Moreover, s/he will find that, in this state where general assistance was eliminated in 1991 and more than 80,000 people have been left without public support, immigrants will face difficulty securing any kind of social services at all.[134] By contrast, in the Los Angeles area, services with various cultural and language foci are readily available for Asian immigrants, especially through voluntary agencies, and include subsidized health care, nursing home services, counseling and psychotherapy, substance abuse rehabilitation, domestic violence shelters, and emergency hotlines, to name a few. Social workers in these settings often represent respective cultures within Asia and it is possible to match a client's language and culture with those of a social worker's.[135] This, in turn, affects the kind of training available to, for example, social work students in Michigan as opposed to those in Los Angeles and, subsequently, the cultural competence of their practice.

The meaning of the word *immigrant* has changed with the passage of time. The number of "white" ethnic immigrants has significantly decreased after a peak in the early 1900s, and more recent immigrants have mainly come from Latin America and Asia.[136] Simultaneously, the word *immigrant* has come to represent the dissimilar other, particularly one who comes to the United States from a "less industrialized" or "poor" country, supposedly in order to receive social benefits such as a job and income security.[137] One of the pervasive myths about foreigners in the United States is that "immigrants are heavy users of welfare and that both legal and illegal immigrants are drawn to this country by the lure of the 'welfare magnet.'"[138] This myth has been one rationale behind the tightening of public assistance for immigrants, such as "welfare reform." This is, however, a false notion since only refugees are entitled to receive public assistance from the date of entry, and other types of immigrants are restricted from receiving most forms of welfare.[139] Moreover, in a logic of exclusion similar to that of COSs a hundred years ago, immigrants are often judged to lack the moral standards integral to American society and thus to be undeserving of public social services. While it is a fact that numerous public services exist today that were not available a hundred years ago, it is also a fact that eligibility of care is still established in ways that depend on a judgment about "personal responsibility" or the perceived "moral standards" of foreigners.

Rivera and Erlich's Model: A Solution?

One influential but controversial solution for dealing effectively with the tension between constructing the foreign and working with foreigners has been posed by F. G. Rivera and J. L. Erlich.[140] Their model contends that the role played by a community social worker must be appropriate to his or her relationship to "the community"; the organizer's knowledge of, and identification with, a community determines the level of contact intensity and influence he or she should have. In their view, the *primary contact* role requires that the organizer have a racial, cultural, and linguistic identity congruent with the characteristics of the community. This primary relationship is the role most involved and intimate with the community in which a social worker, foreign within the dominant culture him or herself, will work with a group considered equally foreign (e.g., a Hmong American person working in a Hmong American community). The *secondary contact* role does not necessarily require language identification, and is one step removed from the primary level of involvement. In a secondary contact role, social workers act primarily as liaisons with the outside community and institutions (e.g., a Korean American person working with Vietnamese Americans). The *tertiary contact* role is that of an "outsider" entering a community to work for its agreed-upon goals. At this level, cultural, ethnic, and language identification is not required, and the social worker's role is that of a broker or advocate for the community (e.g., a Caucasian American person working with African Americans). Rivera and Erlich contend, "[a] white outsider, however sensitive and knowledgeable, simply cannot appreciate all that needs to be considered about a fundamentally different nonwhite culture or subculture."[141]

Here, Rivera and Erlich's goal is very clear: empowerment of communities of color from within. Their model could potentially be applied to other groups that are foreign to the dominant culture, such as lesbian, gay, bisexual, and transgender communities, or communities in poverty. In the world of clinical social work and counseling, the necessity of an ethnic and cultural match between therapist and client has often been a point of disagreement,[142] a situation Rivera and Erlich's work also addresses. In social work education, the influence of their model is visible in multiculturally oriented textbooks.[143] Although cultural similarity alone does not guarantee that objectification of foreigners will be eliminated nor that tensions between the "foreigner" and the "native" will be put to an end, Rivera and Erlich's model offers one way to negotiate social work's inherent dilemma.

Their model, nonetheless, is problematic on several accounts. First, it assumes an ethnic community to be homogeneous, and does not address the power differences among the community members, based on, for example, gender, occupational status, education, ability, and age. When they describe "common goals" of the community, how those goals are determined—and by whom— should, I would argue, be of as much concern as the ethnicity of the organizer. The second problem in this model is that it privileges race and ethnicity, which is equated with "culture," over all other social identities. There is no doubt that the historical and present oppression of communities of color led the authors to focus on ethnicity as the most important dimension of the community. However, for some other communities, other dimensions of difference may be more important.[144]

Even with these problems aside, this model remains controversial because it relegates both historic and current social workers to the tertiary level of contact and excludes the majority of social work students from working with communities of color since the typical social work student is a middle-class, young, white female.[145] The theory is also controversial because it calls into question the entire history of social work by, for example, questioning the effectiveness of traditional community organizers, primarily middle-class whites, who have worked closely with a community of color as organizers. Yet despite the opposition by traditional white community organizers, who resent being excluded, many immigrant communities have adopted this model or have been using it in mutual aid work that remains undocumented and unacknowledged in mainstream social work journals.[146]

However, the position that justifies social work by dissimilar and more privileged social workers remains strong. For example, responding to critiques that settlement work has been performed *on*, rather than *with*, the poor, Trolander contends:

> that is precisely the point—settlement house workers have over time either been well-to-do college graduates or professional social workers who, combined with their predominantly well-to-do boards, have brought an outsider's perspective to their focus on low-income neighborhoods. As such, they may be labeled paternalistic and charged with social control, but they also bring a broader vision of society to the neighborhoods along with promoting a greater awareness of their neighborhoods in the rest of the society. It is this mix of outsiders with the neighborhoods that gives settlement houses a certain uniqueness, dynamism, and significance, and also makes them fascinating to study.[147]

Further, with their "well-to-do" background, settlement workers were able to be effective advocates and brought social problems to national attention by providing "a window on poverty for the rest of society."[148]

Whether dissimilar or similar social workers should provide services has not reached consensus.[149] On the one hand, feminists and multiculturalists may support Rivera and Erlich's model, where, in principle, similar social workers should provide services in communities of color because of their sensitivity to the history of oppression and to power differentials. On the other hand, more mainstream social work thinkers may adapt the dissimilar social workers model, where understanding of cultures, the history of oppression, and cultural sensitivity function as an addition to the discipline's main body of knowledge and skills. This may be a more realistic, if not entirely satisfactory, model because it can utilize the mass of social workers who are already in the field. Further, social policies, health insurance systems, and agency realities such as budget, staffing, and other resources also limit the freedom of social workers over who works with whom. There will no doubt be many cases where social workers are mandated to perform as primary organizers although they are very dissimilar to the community in question. Nonetheless, I support Rivera and Erlich's model because it can serve as a starting point for examining the power dynamics operating between social workers and the communities with which they work, and for recognizing workers' limitations in particular communities.

These models of multicultural social work, especially visible in community work, renew those aspects of the profession's history that emphasize social justice and respect diversity. This is a definite strength of the multicultural community organization models to which social work practice models in general need to pay more attention.[150] In the next section, I will describe a case example of a community organization project informed by multicultural community organization models, in which foreign social workers work with a foreign community. In terms of Rivera and Erlich's model, the workers are, in this practice, functioning at the primary or secondary levels of contact.

Community Organization with Academic Migrant Families: A Case Study

The case study to follow highlights a situation where the foreign works with the foreign—the third category of foreignness presented earlier—and where workers are from the same or similar backgrounds as the community of interest: functioning at the primary or secondary level of contact in Rivera and Erlich's model. The example regards a community organization project with spouses and families of international students (or "academic migrant families") on a university campus. This material dates from 1998-1999 when, as an international graduate student, I founded and directed this project.

The globalization of national economies and information services has brought to the United States not only immigrants and refugees who seek economic, social, and/or political security, but also highly educated sojourners who seek academic and business opportunities. One significant migrant population of recent years is comprised of students, visiting scholars, and their families. Indeed, the number of international students enrolled in the United States has tripled in the last twenty years and higher education is one of the American products most purchased by people in other countries. In addition, the advantage of studying in the United States is heightened by the fact that English is increasingly becoming an official language in academia and business throughout the world.[151]

Migration for one's own or a family member's educational or career achievement can be rewarding for many. However, it can also have a negative impact on students themselves or on family members who accompany their spouses to the United States. Culture shock, language difficulties, change of climate and food, lack of friends: these are some of the major challenges faced by the women and men of academic migrant families.[152] However, in most of these academic migrant families, the men are the students or scholars attending the university and the women are in the United States to accompany their husbands. Some of the difficulties experienced by accompanying female spouses can be qualitatively different than their husbands'. This is partly because these women's legal and social status can make them more structurally dependent on their husbands, and partly because they often lack systematic support to integrate themselves into existing communities. Academic institutions, and often husbands too, tend to perceive meeting spouses' needs as secondary. Many of these women no longer possess the jobs, status, or informal support networks they had in a home country. As a result, their mental and physical well-being are rendered more vulnerable.

Being both a foreign national and the spouse of a student augments such women's degree of foreignness, for the academic setting is centered around students and faculty that belong to the university and to dominant cultures. For example, one Korean woman in this situation complained about the lack of opportunity to meet new friends: "rather than having my own friends, my husband's friends become my friends."[153] Being foreign means not only having different customs, but different expectations about people, which may not always prove true in a new context. A Japanese woman expressed much disappointment because her neighbors never asked her over for tea. She and her husband moved into a university family housing apartment, and she expected that Americans would invite newcomers over for tea. After three months had passed, she started wondering if there was something wrong with her.

In addition, neighbors that perceive these academic migrant families as foreign may not be friendly to them and may even be suspicious of them, may, for example, call the police more hastily when they hear a loud noise, a crying child, or a quarrel. The police officers, in turn, may not know how to interact with those who are foreign and do not speak English well. One Korean woman, who accompanied her husband on a postdoctoral fellowship to a U.S. university described her stressful experience of being accused of child abuse a couple of weeks after she had arrived in the United States.

> My daughter was two years old when she came here. . . . I think she was frightened when she first came here. After being separated from her dad, living with him again was a sudden change. Her grandmother was no longer with her, her family members changed, and everything took her by surprise. On top of that, she had a difficult time getting over jet lag. She couldn't sleep at night, and we tried so hard to get her to sleep. . . . It was midnight and too dark to see. And she was crying as if she was going to wake everyone in the neighborhood. . . . Surrounding houses were quiet, and she was crying at the top of her lungs. Her dad yelled at her as he was bringing her out from the house. But the person told the authorities [the police officer] that we put her in the trashcan. . . . My husband (laughs) couldn't speak English off the top of his head. [When the police officer came,] we understood [what he said], but we didn't know what was the appropriate thing to say. In Korea, we would have known how to talk to police officers, but we didn't know how to talk to the officer [in the United States].[154]

This couple spent the next two months trying to clear their names (which they successfully did), but a full year after the incident, this woman, the primary caregiver of the child, still lived with fear and anxiety, worrying about whether her neighbors would report her or her husband again if the child cried. It might have been a very different story if this couple were American and spoke fluent English or, as she said, if this had happened in Korea where language and cultural differences would not be an issue.

The International Families Outreach Project (IFOP) is a community-building project that supports academic migrant families (mainly women spouses) at the University of Michigan. Through a multicultural, multilingual, and empowerment-oriented approach, IFOP's aim is to help activate and strengthen existing resources and networks among academic migrant families so that they can alleviate the inevitably stressful nature of cultural transitions, utilize their unique assets, and help each other to enrich their lives. I initiated this project in 1996 with several faculty and staff mentors. Initially, the university seems to have viewed IFOP as a quite "foreign" project. After all, the university offers services for students, staff, and faculty, but not for families of students and, until we initiated IFOP, there were no systematic services offered for academic migrant families. But the project has recently expanded from a voluntary organization comprised of students, faculty, and staff to a university-sponsored one.

I was, at that time, an international student and functioned as the organizer of the project. While I could be seen as a part of the "community" because I too was an academic migrant, I also stood on the margin of this community because I was not married (as most of the women in this community are), and because I was a woman who had come to the United States to pursue my own studies, not my partner's or spouse's. The mentors involved in this project belonged to the more dominant groups within the university setting (due to their academic positions, native status, or ethnic background), and acted as advisers and consultants, rather than actual organizers, according to the model proposed by Rivera and Erlich. To complement the cultural and language limitations of the staff and advisors, IFOP has had many undergraduate student assistants, many of whom are international students or first generation Americans.

When the funding allowed us in the summer of 1998, IFOP hired two women who are also spouses of international scholars and one immigrant woman who is a spouse of a graduate student. This hiring enabled us to represent our constituency more closely and helped us organize the community from within. These women shared many of the experiences of the academic migrant families IFOP serve. Drawing from multicultural community social work models and from feminist research methods, theory and practice have been integrated in this project using the facilitators who fall into the primary or secondary levels of identification.[155]

We began by listening to group dialogues where one native-speaking facilitator asked five open-ended questions, allowing participants to talk among themselves. This technique, called focus groups, is widely used in psychology, sociology, education, business, and other fields. Nineteen women spouses of academic migrants participated in these focus groups and provided rich narratives that allowed us to assess the needs of this population and plan services to meet those needs. Based on the focus groups, IFOP has, for example, provided services in several areas: information (e.g., orientation, translation of materials); well-being and cultural seminars (e.g., yoga, quilting); volunteer programs (e.g., free newsletters edited by international volunteers); and diversity training and advocacy (e.g., a workshop for university staff regarding Muslim cultures). In addition, IFOP focused on community-based research and on coalition building—networking and building positive relationships with existing university service divisions and community organizations.

IFOP conducted research to assess the assets and the needs of communities, to evaluate our existing services, and to advocate for the academic migrant families. The methods used included a needs assessment survey, focus groups, and semi-structured interviews. The narratives quoted earlier were taken from transcripts of focus groups and interviews. For example, we devised a questionnaire to which 132 residents from other countries responded (eighty-nine were women, twenty-six were men, seventeen did not identify their sex). Respondents were recruited from English conversation classes and events for family housing residents and the survey was carried out in various languages: English (thirty-five respondents), Japanese (forty respondents), Chinese (eighteen respondents), Korean (thirty-four respondents), and Spanish (two respondents). Most female respondents were accompanying their husbands who had come to the United States for jobs or study, while all of the male respondents were either students or visiting scholars themselves. Although random sampling was not possible because we were not able to obtain the list of all international residents, major characteristics of the respondents roughly reflected the characteristics of the target population—academic migrant families on campus. The questionnaire, which was intended to assess the needs of academic migrant families, was partly crafted on the basis of the focus groups findings and partly drawn from an existing "Daily Hassles" scale.[156]

Although the findings cannot be generalized to the entire population, some of the findings pointed to interesting trends. One was the difference between the men (usually students or scholars) and the women (most of them in the United States as spouses). The results of this survey suggested that the nature of men's stress and lives were relatively unchanged from in their home country. The nature of women's stress reported in the survey, however, seemed to have changed greatly. Men were experiencing changes in jobs, studies, and social and family responsibilities. However, the majority of men saw their lives as similar to what they were before they came to the United States. Although the stress that men experience may be intensified by being in a different country, the nature of the daily stress and hassles were similar to what they experienced back home. This may explain why the men did not perceive undue change in their lives.

The women in the survey, by contrast, felt that their lives had changed drastically. Language difficulty was a major source of this life change and, indeed, individuals who had language difficulties tended to experience the life change more keenly. There are several possibilities why women experienced language difficulties more frequently than men did. First, it might be a mere fluency issue; these foreign women who were in the United States as spouses of students or scholars did not need to study English ahead of time, or did not have the structure, opportunity, motivation, or resources to do so—especially when they have young children to take care of, finding time and resources to learn English can be a challenge. A second possibility is that women experience more difficulties with language because the types of vocabulary men and women need for daily life may be different. Since all of the men in this survey were students or scholars, their areas of study were consistent with, and could appropriate vocabulary from, what they had done in their home countries. Therefore, the main daily activities of these men have some consistency with their lives before; although they still face difficult cultural changes, the men are living in a relatively predictable environment where language use is at least somewhat consistent. By contrast, women's role as caretaker of the family often requires them to deal with the society outside the university. This may become a source of stress because interaction, and the kind of language skills needed for it—for example, interacting with neighbors, finding food from one's own culture, deciding which detergent to buy, taking a child to the doctor, or calling the maintenance person—can be unpredictable. Not being able to carry out these "mundane" tasks smoothly may make these women feel inadequate as adults (or as adult "women" in particular), especially when traditional gender roles are assumed in the family unit.

Those women who have language difficulties seemed to have other difficulties in life as well: with, for example, lack of information, dealing with children's schools, not being able to work due to visa status, reading and writing, not understanding the language on television, or planning and preparing meals. Those with reading and writing difficulties also tended to have problems with their spouses, an especially difficult situation for women who identify their husbands as their primary helpers (as did most women participating in the survey). Problems with spouses could mean that these women have difficulty finding an outlet for their problems, especially when language fluency is the issue, and this can amplify their feelings of isolation.

Although there are numerous possible reasons for these differences between male academics and female spouses, a family-based cultural adaptation may well be among the most important. I would argue that family members may share different cultural adaptation tasks on behalf of the entire family (willingly or unwillingly) as they try to adjust to the new cultural context as a family unit, and that women often absorb more changes than men do. IFOP is modifying its services to respond to this cultural adaptation pattern. In addition, we use research findings for further collaboration and advocacy on behalf of these families.

IFOP is an example of the foreign working with the foreign—both clientele and community workers are foreign to the dominant culture—but with the help of dominant allies. To take myself as an example, though a foreign social worker, I may be considered as the similar other by the dominant culture because of my status as a doctoral candidate in an academic institution and my mastery of a dominant academic language. Thus, in my capacity as director and social worker, I act as a broker between the dissimilar other (academic migrant families) and the dominant culture (the university). Difficulty arises when I, too, am considered too foreign to collaborate with, and thus not credible. In my own case, this has been provoked by my relative lack of status as a young, foreign, Asian woman, though long-term commitment to the project has helped increase the credibility of both it and myself. It's been more than three years since the project started, and many are persuaded that we can be trusted.

In addition, some academic migrant families may find me too Americanized, a status marked by fluency in English, the relative lack of subtlety of cultural cues, one's style of interpersonal interaction, or the very fact of being a woman in a leadership position. Although I never heard these complaints voiced, I believe that hiring the new staff members mitigated such potential criticism, particularly since they represent distinctive cultures (Caribbean, Latin American,

European, and Korean) and their perceived foreignness varies. Some others think that the project lacks sufficient attention to Americanization and facilitates nationals clinging to one another, rather than breaking down the barriers between the different nationals. "The [women] should be speaking English and mingling with Americans," is a common refrain by some male staff residents who are academic migrants studying as graduate students or are postdoctoral fellows themselves. This is where the research findings become important for advocacy. We can point to the findings to explain the needs these families have and what kinds of services they request.

As a result, the degree of foreignness that the social worker needs to portray changes context by context; in order to be effective in implementing tasks, s/he must consider who a particular group thinks s/he is and who it thinks s/he should be. Although foreignness cannot be fully manipulated, there is a latitude of change that one can play with. Some fluidity in the degree of performed foreignness helps tune in different audiences.

Conclusion

The complexity of the foreign as constructed by and for social work practices has roots in the Progressive era and has helped shape social work as a profession. However, new forces are emerging to incorporate different ways of working with foreigners as they are defined by dominant cultures. Such work has been undertaken by ethnic organizations as examined in detail by Iglehart and Becerra, Lasch-Quinn, and others. Although it bears some limitations, Erlich and Rivera's model does propose a new paradigm, rejecting inherently paternalistic models of mainstream social work practice with the foreign. It is a very important task for the social work profession to come to terms with the foreign historically ingrained in the field. It means that social work as a field must reexamine the discourse and structure underlying the construction of the foreign. For while the construction of the foreign seems to change on the surface, similar dynamics appear underneath. Understanding these dynamics helps our understanding of the profession as a whole because they are the foundation on which the social work profession has been built.

Notes

1. See Judith Trolander, *Settlement Houses and the Great Depression* (Detroit: Wayne State University Press, 1975); and Howard J. Karger and David Stoesz, *American Social Welfare Policy: A Pluralistic Approach*, 3rd ed. (New York: Longman, 1997).

2. I use the terms "the foreign" and "foreigners" interchangeably in the text. As will become apparent later, I mean more by these terms than just foreign nationals without

permanent visas to the United States. The foreign here is a conceptual category, which might encompass persons who have been U.S. citizens for generations, such as African and Asian Americans, who may still be treated as too dissimilar to become part of the dominant culture.

3. See Margaret S. Sherraden and Judith J. Martin, "Social Work with Immigrants: International Issues in Service Delivery," *International Social Work* 37 (1994): 369-384; and Florence Lieberman, "The Immigrants and Mary Richmond," *Child and Adolescent Social Work* 7, no. 2 (1990): 81-84.

4. A client system is a target of intervention larger than an individual, such as a family, group, community, organization, or state. I use the term "less industrialized" not because this term is problem-free, but because the often-used word "developing" is even more problematic. Although the distinction between "developed" and "developing" has been widely used in public and academic discourse, it implicitly views economic development, as seen in "developed," Western countries, as the ultimate goal of *all* the countries of the world. The characteristics of "developed" countries, such as advanced or late capitalism, urbanization, and industrialization, may not be the ideal of other countries with different historical, political, geographical, ideological, and cultural heritages. This simplistic distinction can also give the false impression that "developed" countries are superior to "developing" countries. On work with Ethiopian and Eritrean refugees, see Tekle M. Woldemikael, "Ethiopians and Eritreans," in *Refugees in America in the 1990s: A Reference Handbook*, ed. David W. Haines (Westport, Conn.: Greenwood Press, 1996), 147-169. On international social work, see James Midgley, "International Social Work: Learning from the Third World," *Social Work* 35 (1990): 295–301; and Ruby C. M. Chau, "The Functions of Negative Aspects of Welfare in Capitalist Societies: A Case Study of Temporary Accommodation for the Homeless in Britain and Housing Policy for Small Households in Hong Kong," *International Social Work* 38 (1995): 87-102.

5. See Timothy Dunnigan, Douglas P. Olney, Miles A. McNall, and Marline A. Spring, "Hmong," in *Refugees in America in the 1990s*, 191-212. The Hmong started arriving in the United States in 1976 from refugee camps in Thailand because of the tragic results of their involvement with the C.I.A. during the Vietnam War. The tendency for seasoned immigrants to be seen as foreigners is not limited to the Hmong; Asian American immigrants and American-born Asian Americans in general are still often perceived as foreigners. Asian American college students, for example, are often keenly aware of this "foreign" stereotype. See R. Ambrosino, J. Heffernan, and G. Shuttlesworth, *Social Work and Social Welfare: An Introduction* (Belmont, Calif.: Wadsworth/Thomson Learning, 2001), 103; and Daphna Oyserman and Izumi Sakamoto, "Being Asian American: Identity, Cultural Constructs, and Stereotype Perception," *The Journal of Applied Behavioral Science* 33, no. 4 (1997): 435-453.

6. Multicultural social work has also been called "multi-ethnic social work" and "ethnic sensitive social work" by W. Devore and E. G. Schlesinger, *Ethnic-Sensitive Social Work Practice* (Boston: Allyn & Bacon, 1996); "culturally competent practice" by Doman Lum, *Culturally Competent Practice: A Framework for Growth and Action* (Pacific Grove, Calif.: Brooks/Cole, 1998); or "cross-cultural practice" by K. V. Harper and J. Lantz, *Cross-cultural Practice: Social Work with Diverse Populations* (Chicago: Lyceum, 1996). See also M. Spencer, E. Lewis, and L. Gutiérrez, "Multicultural Perspectives on Direct Practice in Social Work," in *The Handbook of Social Work Direct Practice*, ed. Paula Allen-Meares and Charles Garvin (Thousand Oaks, Calif.: Sage, 2000), 131-150.

7. Thus, the work of refugee resettlement is considered to straddle both multicultural social work and international social work, but work with "seasoned" immigrants who are already permanent residents of the United States is usually considered a branch of multicultural social work.

8. See Lynne M. Healy, "International Agencies as Social Work Settings: Opportunity, Capability, and Commitment," *Social Work* 32, no. 5 (Sept-Oct 1987): 405-409; and Healy, "International social welfare: Organizations and activities," in *Encyclopedia of Social Work*, 19th ed., vol II (Washington, D.C.: NASW Press, 1995), 1499-1510.

9. See Midgley, "International Social Work"; Healy, "International Social Welfare"; Rosemary Sarri, "International Social Work at the Millennium" in M. Reisch and E. Gambrill, *Social Work in the 21st Century* (Thousand Oaks, Calif.: Pine Forge Press, 1997), 387-395; Doreen Elliott and Nazneen S. Mayadas, "International Perspectives on Social Work Practice," in Allen-Meares and Garvin, *The Handbook of Social Work Direct Practice*, 633-650; and Merl C. Hokenstad, Shanti K. Khinduka, and James K. Midgley, eds., *Profiles in International Social Work* (Washington, D.C.: NASW Press, 1992).

10. On the former, see Katherine A. Kendall, forward to *International Handbook on Social Work Education*, ed. T. D. Watts, D. Elliott, and N. S. Mayadas (Westport, Conn: Greenwood, 1995), xiii-xvii; and Nazneen S. Mayadas and Doreen Elliott, "Lessons from International Social Work: Policies and Practices," in Reisch and Gambrill, *Social Work*, 175-349. On the latter, see Charles Guzetta, "Central and Eastern Europe" in *International Handbook on Social Work Education*, 191-209. Although American or Western models of social work continue to be disseminated across countries, many social workers from "less industrialized" countries, as well as some social work researchers in the United States, question the applicability, and uncritical acceptance, of Western social work theories internationally and even domestically. Thus, they try to complicate social work theory and service delivery systems through attention to historical, political, and cultural contexts. See James Midgley, *Social Welfare in Global Context* (Thousand Oaks, Calif.: Sage, 1997); and Sarri, "International Social Work at the Millennium."

11. See Midgley, "International Social Work"; *Social Welfare in Global Context*; and "Promoting a Development Focus in the Community Organization Curriculum: Relevance of the African Experience," *Journal of Social Work Education* 29, no. 3 (1993): 269-278; and Sarri, "International Social Work at the Millennium."

12. Golie Jansen and Marian Aguilar, "Loss of a Homeland: Insights of 'Strangers' for Teaching and Helping," *Reflections: Narratives of Professional Helping* 3, no. 4 (1997): 7.

13. Jansen and Aguilar, "Loss of a Homeland," 10.

14. See Gisela Konopka, "Human Dignity: All Lives Are Connected to Other Lives," *Reflections: Narratives of Professional Helping* 3, no. 4 (1997): 55-58; T. Kawada, ed., *Guruupu waaku: Shakaiteki igi to jissen [Social Work with Groups: Nature and Practice]*, (Tokyo: Kaiseisha, 1990); and Urania Glassman and Len Kates, *Group Work: A Humanistic Approach* (Newbury Park, Calif.: Sage, 1990).

15. Jansen and Aguilar, "Loss of a Homeland," 10.

16. "Racial" here refers to perceived differences between "whites" and new immigrants. African Americans, Asian Americans, Native Americans, and Hispanics/Latino Americans are often seen as the dissimilar other.

17. For examples of such alternative approaches, see Julian Chaw, "Multiservice Centers in Chinese American Immigrant Communities: Practice, Principles, and Chal-

lenges," *Social Work* 44 (January 1999): 70-81.

18. Bruce Jansson, *The Reluctant Welfare State*, 3rd ed. (Pacific Grove, Calif.: Brooks/Cole, 1997), 132. See also John Higham, *Strangers in the Land: Patterns of American Nativism, 1860-1925,* 2nd ed. (New York: Atheneum, 1988), 165-167.

19. See Doman Lum, *Social Work Practice and People of Color: A Process-stage Approach*, 3rd ed. (Pacific Grove, Calif.: Brooks/Cole, 1996); Roger Daniels, *Asian America: Chinese and Japanese in the United States since 1850* (Seattle: University of Washington Press, 1988); and Sucheng Chan, *Asian Americans: An Interpretive History* (Boston: Twayne, 1991).

20. Jansson, *The Reluctant Welfare State*, 110.

21. Jansson, *The Reluctant Welfare State*, 110.

22. See Jansson, *The Reluctant Welfare State*; David Ward, *Poverty, Ethnicity, and the American City, 1840-1925: Changing Conceptions of the Slum and the Ghetto* (Cambridge: Cambridge University Press, 1989); and Jane Addams, *Twenty Years at Hull-House*, with autobiographical notes (Chicago: The University of Illinois Press, 1990).

23. Addams, *Twenty Years at Hull-House*, 148-149.

24. Alfreda P. Iglehart and Rosina M. Becerra, *Social Services and the Ethnic Community* (Boston: Allyn & Bacon, 1995), 29.

25. Sophonisba Breckinridge, cited in Iglehart and Becerra, *Social Services and the Ethnic Community*, 29. See Breckinridge, "The Color Line in the Housing Problem," *The Survey* (February 1913), 575.

26. See Iglehart and Becerra, *Social Services and the Ethnic Community*; and Lum, *Social Work Practice*.

27. Michael Reisch, "The Sociopolitical Context and Social Work Method, 1890-1950," *Social Service Review* 72, no. 2 (June 1998), 162.

28. See Iglehart and Becerra, *Social Services and the Ethnic Community*; and Lum, *Social Work Practice*.

29. Reisch, "The Sociopolitical Context," 163.

30. Karger and Stoez, *American Social Welfare Policy*, 56.

31. Trolander, *Settlement Houses*, 13. In addition to social Darwinism, Jansson notes two more recent political trends that help the public to ignore poverty and the plight of immigrants: "the political power of corporations, and the national preoccupation with upward mobility." Jansson, *The Reluctant Welfare State*, 113.

32. Reisch, "The Sociopolitical Context," 163.

33. Jansson, *The Reluctant Welfare State*, 116; see also Ward, *Poverty, Ethnicity, and the American City*, 98-100.

34. See Jansson, *The Reluctant Welfare State*, 116-117.

35. See Jansson, *The Reluctant Welfare State*, 118; and Trolander, *Settlement Houses*, 24-25.

36. The formation of the National Urban League on Urban Conditions was mobilized by George Edmund Haynes's study, *The Negro at Work in New York City* (New York: Longmans, Green & Co., 1912). See also Karger and Stoesz, *American Social Welfare Policy*, 60; and Lum, *Social Work Practice*.

37. The National Association of Social Workers (NASW) celebrated its hundred year anniversary in 1998. For recent reviews of the history, see Karen S. Haynes, "The One Hundred-Year Debate: Social Reform versus Individual Treatment," *Social Work* 43, no. 6 (1998): 501-509; F. G. Reamer, "The Evolution of Social Work Ethics," *Social*

Work 43, no. 6 (1998): 488-500; and M. Abramovitz, "Social Work and Social Reform: An Arena of Struggle," *Social Work* 43, no. 6 (1998): 512-526.

38. See Karger and Stoez, *American Social Welfare Policy.*

39. Ward, *Poverty, Ethnicity, and the American City,* 113.

40. See Ward, *Poverty, Ethnicity, and the American City,* 63.

41. See Karger and Stoesz, *American Social Welfare Policy,* 58; and Reisch, "The Sociopolitical Context," 164. Iglehart and Becerra offer a comprehensive survey of ethnic social services from the late nineteenth century. See Iglehart and Bacerra, "Social Work and the Ethnic Agency: A History of Neglect," *Journal of Multicultural Social Work* 4, no. 1 (1996): 1- 20.

42. Lum, *Social Work Practice,* 14.

43. Japan experienced widespread unemployment, homelessness, child abandonment, malnutrition, prostitution (daughters were often sold by families to avoid starvation), alcoholism, and child abuse (especially of adopted children) which, in the early twentieth century, stimulated relief work, charity, correctional and institutional care, and social movements by philanthropists, reformers, feminists, and labor and religious activists. See Kyuuichi Yoshida, *Nihon shakai jigyou no rekishi* [*History of Japanese Social Services*], rev. ed. (Tokyo: Keisoushobou, 1994).

44. The Central Association of Social Work or *Centralforbundet for Socialt Arbete* (CSA). Sweden has long assumed a stronger governmental role in providing social services than has the United States.

45. Indeed, it is only in recent years that postindustrial Sweden has started experiencing increased immigration, which has led the dominant society to express "more signs of intolerance against foreign minority groups, something that may be of concern to social work," and has created "a new form of stress" for social workers. See Hans Berglind and Ulla Pettersson, "Social Work in Sweden: Professional Identity in the Welfare State," in *Profiles in International Social Work,* ed. Merl C. Hokenstad, Shanti K. Khinduka, and James Midgley (Washington, D.C.: NASW Press), 130. The kind of stress that Swedish social workers are experiencing due to increased immigration, is described by ethnologist A. Sjögren: "The newcomers bring with them styles of life from the south of Europe or from the Middle East which are very foreign to the traditional Swedish mentality. The mentality of these Catholic, Orthodox, or Muslim people, often with close ties to the traditional countryside, is far remote from that of the Swedish civil servants who are in charge of their introduction into the host country. The latter are usually middle-class urban people whose lives are permeated with Lutheran and social-democratic traditions." Cited in Willy F. Frick, "Sweden," in *International Handbook on Social Work Education,* 147. This "new form of stress" primarily consists of complaints about the dissimilar "mentality" that these immigrants bring from their various ethnic, religious, political, and cultural backgrounds; these complaints are thus almost identical to what American COS and settlement workers record of their experiences with the "new" immigrants in the early twentieth century.

46. Iglehart and Becerra, *Social Services and the Ethnic Community,* 5.

47. Stanley Wenocur and Michael Reisch, *From Charity to Enterprise* (Chicago: University of Illinois Press, 1989), xi.

48. See Wenocur and Reisch, *From Charity to Enterprise.*

49. See Reisch, "The Sociopolitical Context," 166.

50. See Robert Neelly Bellah, Richard Madsen, William Sullivan, and Steven Tipton, *Habits of the Heart: Individualism and Commitment in American Life* (Berkeley:

University of California Press, 1996); and Charles D. Garvin and John E. Tropman, *Social Work in Contemporary Society* (Needham Heights, Mass.: Allyn and Bacon, 1998).

51. Cited in Karen Haynes, "The One Hundred-Year Debate," 506. In this paper, Karen Haynes debates with the late Harry Specht, former Dean of the School of Social Welfare at the University of California Berkeley. Specht's text, incorporated into Haynes's paper, was taken from the keynote speech he prepared for the National Association of Social Workers conference in 1994.

52. Iglehart and Becerra, *Social Services and the Ethnic Community*, 115.

53. Wenocur and Reisch, *From Charity to Enterprise*, 24.

54. Karger and Stoesz, *American Social Welfare Policy*, 57.

55. See Karger and Stoesz, *American Social Welfare Policy*.

56. Ward, *Poverty, Ethnicity, and the American City*, 54. Ward is citing Boston Overseers of the Poor, *Tenth Annual Report* (1874). For a detailed discussion of the concept of dependency, see N. Fraser and L. Gordon, "A Genealogy of Dependency: Tracing a Keyword of the U.S. Welfare State," *Signs: Journal of Women in Culture and Society* 19, no.2 (1994): 309-336.

57. Wenocur and Reisch, *From Charity to Enterprise*, 74.

58. Wenocur and Reisch, *From Charity to Enterprise*, 25.

59. Progressive settlement houses, which supported diverse social causes, were seen as politically advantageous by many Progressives of the time, which prompted philanthropists and corporate donors to financially support them; this, in turn, helped to "polish [industrialists'] rather tarnished images by supporting worthy causes and groups." Iglehart and Becerra, *Social Services and the Ethnic Community*, 113.

60. James Hurt, introduction to *Twenty Years at Hull-House* by Jane Addams, ix-xix.

61. Susan Donner, "Ellen Gates Starr (1859-1940)" in *Encyclopedia of Social Work*, 19th ed. (Washington, D.C.: NASW Press, 1995), 2612.

62. See D. Brieland, "The Hull-House Tradition and the Contemporary Social Worker: Was Jane Addams really a Social Worker?" *Social Work* 35 (1990): 134-138; Walter L. Tratter, *From Poor Law to Welfare State: A History of Social Welfare in America*, 3rd ed. (New York: Free Press, 1984), 163-164; Wenocur and Reisch, *From Charity to Enterprise*, 26-29; and Iglehart and Becerra, *Social Services and the Ethnic Community*.

63. One view of Jane Addams is to see her settlement house work as "salvation" for herself and other educated women "because through 'social mothering' and 'civic housekeeping' the traditional role of nurturer was preserved." Iglehart and Becerra, *Social Services and the Ethnic Community*, 112. However, James Hurt paints a more complicated picture and evaluates Addams work as "turn-of-the-century feminism." There is no doubt, he argues, she was seen as "a strong, independent woman carrying out the complicated task of administering Hull-House and taking an active role in national public debate." On the other hand, her view of a "liberated woman" was also constrained within "the traditional roles of sacrificial caretakers" and led to her idealization as "Saint Jane" by the public. Hurt, introduction, xviii. Wenocur and Reisch contend of the "peculiar contradiction" early social worker women met with as professionals: "They could move out of their traditional social roles only via those occupations which perpetuated female stereotypes and which were structures to ensure continued male dominance of the occupational hierarchy and the political-economy as a whole." Wenocur and Reisch, *From Charity to Enterprise*, 27.

64. Two registered settlement houses existed in Tennessee, and one each in Texas,

Virginia, Louisiana, and Kentucky. Trolander's estimate cited here only includes professionally recognized houses; see Trolander, *Settlement Houses*, 59. Karger and Stoesz contend that more than 300 houses had been established by 1915.

65. See Addams, *Twenty Years at Hull-House*; and Iglehart and Becerra, *Social Services and the Ethnic Community*.

66. See Karen Haynes, "The One Hundred-Year Debate"; and Abramovitz, "Social Work and Social Reform."

67. Some of the common principles of the settlement house include: (1) acting locally; (2) gathering and promulgating facts; (3) preparing legislation; (4) mobilizing forces for the passage of legislation; (5) securing employment for community members; (6) teaching English, occupational skills, domestic skills, and hygiene; (7) teaching the poor the middle-class values that contribute to success; and (8) stressing the value of self-help. See Iglehart and Becerra, *Social Services and the Ethnic Community*, 114. Not all of the settlement houses, however, focused on social reform; some merely offered social activities. It was only a small number of well-known houses that took on functions of advocacy and social change. Hull-House, Chicago Commons, and University Settlement in New York City, for example, were seen as extremely liberal in their political orientation. See Brieland, "The Hull-House Tradition." Iglehart and Becerra call the trend of equating "the actions of the majority with those of a few reform-minded individuals," a "glorification" in *Social Services and the Ethnic Community*, 5.

68. Donald Brieland, "Social Work Practice: History and Evolution" in *Encyclopedia of Social Work*, 2247-2257.

69. Brieland, "Social Work Practice," 2248.

70. See Brieland "Social Work Practice"; and Karger and Stoesz, *American Social Welfare Policy*.

71. See Brieland, "Social Work Practice," 2248. In one of the most important texts of social work, Mary Richmond lists social diagnosis questions as a guide for COS workers. The first questions on the list inquire whether immigrant families were "thrifty and industrious" and "law abiding," suggesting that these qualities, among other factors, were important in deciding eligibility of care. Mary Richmond, *Social Diagnosis* (New York: Russel Sage Foundation, 1917), 383.

72. See Richmond, *Social Diagnosis*.

73. Iglehart and Becerra offer a comprehensive review of late nineteenth- and early twentieth-century social services, analyze settlement houses, COSs, and various ethnic organizations and examine how these entities formed the basis of social work. See Iglehart and Barcerra, *Social Services and the Ethnic Community*.

74. See Tratter, *From Poor Law to Welfare State*. For recent discussions on the legacy of settlement houses as opposed to COSs, see Karen Haynes, "The One Hundred-Year Debate"; and Abramovitz, "Social Work and Social Reform." On the glorification of settlement houses, see also Toby Berman-Rossi and Irving Miller, "African-Americans and the Settlements during the Late Nineteenth and Early Twentieth Centuries," *Social Work with Groups* 17, no. 3 (1994): 77-95.

75. See Karger and Stoez, *American Social Welfare Policy*; Tratter, *From Poor Law to Welfare State*; and Karen Haynes, "The One Hundred-Year Debate." Class and cultural biases were present in both COSs and settlement houses' Americanization programs. See Reisch, "The Sociopolitical Context," 161-181. For example, Jane Addams's writing and Hull-House's practice upheld the culture of upper and educated middle-class Americans as more desirable than other cultures present in the United States. She warns that

immigrants were "coming in contact with only the most *ignorant Americans* in that city. The more of scholarship, the more of linguistic attainment, the more of beautiful surroundings a Settlement among them can command, the more it can do for them." Jane Addams, "The Objective Value of a Social Settlement," Reprint of 1892 speech (Chicago: The Jane Addams Hull-House Museum at the University of Illinois at Chicago), 10, my emphasis.

Ironically, the emphasis of the social work profession today seems to be on individuals who can afford psychotherapy. While this more "scientific," more legitimized work, perceived as highly professional by society, has a similar reputation to what COS workers possessed one hundred years ago, the class of individuals being served is substantially different. Less interest is expressed in community work, advocacy, and social change because such work is seen as less "specialized," less "legitimated," or less "professional": popular evaluation of this kind of work remains unchanged from the time of the settlement house movement. This may perhaps be the reason why social work academicians reflect on settlement houses in a nostalgic light. See Karen Haynes, "The One Hundred-Year Debate"; Abramovitz, "Social Work and Social Reform"; and Tratter, *From Poor Law to Welfare State*. According to Reisch, casework theories focused only on individual needs and failed to recognize satisfying common human rights, which became the long-standing problem in social work. For recent discussions of how to interpret and combat the current trend in the field, see also Harry Specht and Mark Courtney, *Unfaithful Angels: How Social Work Has Abandoned Its Mission* (New York: Free Press, 1995). Although not all clinical social workers focus on psychotherapy and private practice, the strong preference for this focus is prevalent among current social work students. For example, in recent years, 70 to 80 percent of entering M.S.W. students at the University of Michigan, the top ranked social work program in the country, major in "interpersonal practice," that is, clinical work specializing in counseling and psychotherapy; this field of practice also offers the largest number of job opportunities.

76. See Iglehart and Becerra, *Social Services and the Ethnic Community*; and Elisabeth Lasch-Quinn, *Black Neighbors: Race and the Limits of Reform in the American Settlement House Movement, 1890-1945* (Chapel Hill, N.C.: University of North Carolina Press, 1993).

77. Addams, *Twenty Years at Hull-House*, 147-148.

78. Jansson notes that "Jane Addams was voted the most exemplary American" in the Progressive era. Jansson, *The Reluctant Welfare State*, 117.

79. Judith Trolander, *Professionalism and Social Change: From the Settlement House Movement to Neighborhood Centers, 1886 to the Present* (New York: Columbia University Press, 1987), 10-11.

80. See Sherraden and Martin, "Social work with immigrants."

81. E. G. Schlesinger and W. Devore, "Ethnic-sensitive Social Work Practice" in *Encyclopedia of Social Work*, 48.

82. Raymond Mohl and Neil Betten, cited in Tratter, *From Poor Law to Welfare State*, 159.

83. Tratter, *From Poor Law to Welfare State*, 159.

84. Jansson, *The Reluctant Welfare State*, 137.

85. Higham, *Strangers in the Land*, 151.

86. See Iglehart and Becerra, *Social Services and the Ethnic Community*.

87. W. E. B. Du Bois, *The Souls of Black Folk: Essays and Sketches* (New York: Fawcett, 1961).

88. See Lum, *Social Work Practice*; T. LaFromboise, H. L. K. Coleman, and J. Gerton, "Psychological Impact of Biculturalism: Evidence and Theory," *Psychological Bulletin* 114 (1993): 395-412; and J.W. Berry, "Psychology of Acculturation" in *Nebraska Symposium on Motivation* 37 (Lincoln: University of Nebraska Press, 1989).

89. Even those who were excluded from early social work efforts—those regarded as the "dissimilar other"—went through Americanization in the public education system. In the early 1900s, Asian Americans were, after much controversy and political intervention, allowed to receive public education, though the teachers were all whites. Even in Hawaii, where Asian American teachers were hired, the main focus was on teaching students "Anglo-American values, behavioral patterns, and speech patterns." Chan, *Asian Americans*, 59.

90. Iglehart and Becerra, *Social Services and the Ethnic Community*, 6-7.

91. Ann Hartman, "Social Work Practice" in *The Foundations of Social Work Knowledge*, ed. F. G. Reamer (New York: Columbia University Press, 1994), 13-50.

92. Hartman, "Social Work Practice," 21. Others echo this sentiment; Burghardt states that "every method of social work practice carries with it certain ideologies that serve to reproduce either 'dominant-subordinate' or 'self-determining' social relationships among its participants." Burghardt, "The Future of Community Organization in Social Work: Social Activism and the Politics of Profession Building." *Social Service Review* (March 1986): 2-3. For other critiques of the disciplinary functions of social work, see A. J. Gerald de Montigny, *Social Working: An Ethnography of Front-Line Practice* (Toronto: University of Toronto Press, 1995); and Leslie Margolin, *Under the Cover of Kindness: The Invention of Social Work* (Charlottesville: University Press of Virginia, 1997).

93. See Wenocur and Reisch, *From Charity to Enterprise*, 76.

94. Cited in Jansson, *The Reluctant Welfare State*, 138. Prejudice against Italians was still common in the early twentieth century as documented in the life history of an Italian woman in Chicago, whose husband was rejected from renting an apartment in a primarily German and Norwegian neighborhood. See Marie Hall, "Rosa: The Life of an Italian Immigrant" in *Immigrant Women*, 2nd ed., ed. Maxine Schwartz Seller (Albany, N.Y.: SUNY Press, 1994).

95. Ward, *Poverty, Ethnicity, and the American City*, 55.

96. Brieland, "The Hull-House Tradition," 135; see also Donna Franklin, "Mary Richmond and Jane Addams: From Moral Certainty to Rational Inquiry in Social Work Practice," *Social Service Review* 60, no. 4 (December): 508.

97. Iglehart and Becerra, *Social Services and the Ethnic Community*, 96.

98. Alfred Kadushin, *The Social Work Interview: A Guide for Human Service Professionals*, 3rd ed. (New York: Columbia University Press, 1990).

99. Iglehart and Becerra, *Social Services and the Ethnic Community*, 219.

100. Kadushin, *The Social Work Interview*, 304.

101. See Iglehart and Becerra, *Social Services and the Ethnic Community*, 118-124; Trolander, *Professionalism*, 22, 93-94; Berman-Rossi and Miller, "African-Americans and the Settlements"; and Lasch-Quinn, *Black Neighbors*.

102. Asian Americans were another group that was largely ignored by settlement houses of the time. Asian Americans, however, were mostly concentrated in Hawaii and on the West Coast, where few settlement houses existed—only nine in all of California in 1939 compared to dozens each in Chicago or New York. See Trolander, *Settlement Houses*. It is not clear if there were systematic actions taken to exclude this group.

103. Karger and Stoesz, *American Social Welfare Policy*, 60.

104. Trolander, *Settlement Houses*, 139-140.

105. Lasch-Quinn, *Black Neighbors*, 1; See also Berman-Rossi and Miller, "African-Americans and the Settlements," 84-85.

106. Trolander, *Professionalism*, 94.

107. Berman-Rossi and Miller, "African-Americans and the Settlements," 85-86.

108. Berman-Rossi and Miller, "African-Americans and the Settlements," 82.

109. Trolander, *Professionalism*, 94.

110. Iglehart and Becerra, *Social Services and the Ethnic Community*, 121. Similar points are raised by Berman-Rossi and Miller, "African-Americans and the Settlements," 83.

111. Iglehart and Becerra, *Social Services and the Ethnic Community*, 27. Although not as extensively documented, neither Native Americans nor Asian Americans benefited from settlement houses and COS services.

112. Iglehart and Becerra, *Social Services and the Ethnic Community*, 29. A similar position is taken by Berman-Rossi and Miller: "Europeans were apparently thought to be better able to identify with and be influenced by the cultural and social ideals of the settlements, their leadership, and their 'settlers.'" Berman-Rossi and Miller, "African-Americans and the Settlements," 80.

113. Iglehart and Becerra, *Social Services and the Ethnic Community*, 5.

114. See also Du Bois, *The Souls of Black Folk*; and Edward Franklin Frazier, *The Negro Church in America* (New York: Schocken Books, 1964) and *The Negro Family in the United States* (Chicago: University of Chicago Press, 1939).

115. Lasch-Quinn, *Black Neighbors*, 47. Berman-Rossi and Miller also list a variety of functions organized by African American mutual aid societies, including education, economic assistance, medical care, employment services, and residential programs. See Berman-Rossi and Miller, "African-Americans and the Settlements," 88.

116. See Iglehart and Becerra, *Social Services and the Ethnic Community*; Brieland, "The Hull-House Tradition"; Tratter, *From Poor Law to Welfare State*; and Wenocur and Reisch, *From Charity to Enterprise*.

117. Addams, *Twenty Years at Hull-House*, 149.

118. Addams, *Twenty Years at Hull-House*, 149.

119. Cited in Devore and Schlesinger, *Ethnic-Sensitive Social Work Practice*, 7.

120. See Lum, *Social Work Practice*; Devore and Schlesinger, *Ethnic-Sensitive Social Work Practice*; and James W. Green, *Cultural Awareness in the Human Services: A Multi-ethnic Approach*, 2nd ed. (Boston: Allyn and Bacon, 1995).

121. The Personal Responsibility and Work Opportunity Reconciliation Act of 1996 barred current and future immigrants from receiving Supplemental Security Income (SSI) and food stamps until they become citizens. Karger and Stoesz refer to current welfare reforms as "'welfare behaviorism' that is intended to change the behaviors of the poor." Karger and Stoesz, *American Social Welfare Policy*, 287.

122. Karger and Stoesz, *American Social Welfare Policy*, 267.

123. See Diane Drachman, "Immigration Statuses and Their Influence on Service Provision Access and Use," *Social Work* 40, no. 2 (1995): 188-197.

124. Michael Fix and Jeffrey Passel, "Setting the Record Straight: What are the Costs to the Public?" *Public Welfare* 52, no. 2 (Spring 1994), 12. Fix and Passel are immigration policy specialists at the Urban Institute.

125. Fix and Passel, "Setting the Record Straight," 10.

126. Yolanda C. Padilla, "Immigrant Policy: Issues for Social Work Practice," *Social Work* 42, no. 6 (1997), 604. Along similar lines, Karen M. Sowers-Hoag and Kris Siddharthan report that their immigrant respondents in Florida were reluctant to use health-related social services even when notified of their availability. See Sowers-Hoag and Kris Siddharthan, "Access and Use of Health Related Social Services of Immigrants and Native Born Americans: Implications for Social Intervention," *Journal of Multicultural Social Work* 1, no. 4 (1992): 47-62.

127. David E. Rosenberg, "Serving America's Newcomers: States and Localities are Taking the Lead in the Absence of a Comprehensive National Policy," *Public Welfare* 49, no. 1 (Winter 1991): 28-29. At the time the article was published, the author was Deputy Director of the Commonwealth of Massachusetts Office of Refugees and Immigrants and co-chair of the Subcommittee on Newcomer Services and Impacts of the American Public Welfare Association Task Force on Immigrant Reform.

128. Frances Fox Piven and Richard A. Cloward, "Welfare State Politics in the United States," in *Social Policy in a Changing Europe*, ed. Zsuzsa Ferge and Jon Eivind Kolberg (Germany: Campus Verlag, 1992), 57.

129. Garvin and Tropman, *Social Work in Contemporary Society*, 13.

130. Karger and Stoesz, *American Social Welfare Policy*, 265.

131. Fix and Passel, "Setting the Record Straight," 6.

132. Rosenberg, "Serving America's Newcomers," 28.

133. See Diane Drachman, "Immigration Statuses"; and "A Stage-of-Migration Framework for Service to Immigrant Populations," *Social Work* 37, no.1 (1992): 68-72.

134. General Assistance (GA) refers to a variety of state and local programs which are "the program[s] of last resort for people who fall through the cracks in the federally funded safety net." Karger and Stoesz, *American Social Welfare Policy*, 278.

135. On the desirability of matching the ethnicity of client and social worker, see also Diane de Anda, ed., *Controversial Issues in Multiculturalism* (Boston, Mass.: Allyn and Bacon, 1997).

136. See Fix and Passel, "Setting the Record Straight"; and Drachman, "Immigration Statuses."

137. Gonzalo Santos, "Modern Human Migration and the History of 'Immigration Problems' in California," in *California's Social Problems*, ed. Charles F. Hohm (New York: Longman, 1997).

138. Fix and Passel, "Setting the Record Straight," 9.

139. Fix and Passel, "Setting the Record Straight," 9.

140. F. G. Rivera and J. L. Erlich, *Community Organizing in a Diverse Society*, 3rd ed. (Boston, Mass.: Allyn & Bacon, 1998).

141. Rivera and Erlich, *Community Organizing in a Diverse Society*, 12.

142. See de Anda, *Controversial Issues in Multiculturalism*.

143. A widely read ethnic-sensitive practice model by Devore and Schlesinger (see *Ethnic-Sensitive Social Work*), as well as a multicultural community organization model by Lorraine Gutiérrez (see "Multicultural Community"), directly incorporate Rivera and Erlich's view into their practice.

144. Organizing, for example, with Asian American gay, lesbian, bisexual, and transgendered youths may be difficult due to stigmas prevalent in a particular community. Organizing efforts may be more successful if they go beyond the ethnic community and form a group of GLBT youths of color across ethnic/racial boundaries, where GLBT youths could share common experiences and differences.

145. See Margaret Gibelman and Philip H. Schervish, *Who We Are: A Second Look* (Washington, D.C.: NASW Press, 1997); and Alfred Kadushin and Goldie Kadushin, *The Social Work Interview: A Guide for Human Service Professionals*, 4th ed. (New York: Columbia University Press, 1997).

146. Iglehart and Becerra provide a thorough review of services traditionally provided by and for communities of color, which they describe as "a history of neglect." See Iglehart and Becerra, *Social Services and the Ethnic Community*. Reisch also mentions early self-help efforts among poor Jews, Catholics, African Americans, and Asian Americans. See Reisch, "The Sociopolitical Context," 164.

147. Trolander, *Professionalism*, 1-2.

148. Trolander, *Professionalism*, 5.

149. See de Anda, *Controversial Issues in Multiculturalism*.

150. Because they include community organization, multicultural social work models usually view the community as the target system. Community organization, however, is not limited to the profession of social work and is employed by, for example, urban planning, public health, community medicine, community psychology, education, and various forms of activism from labor, feminist, civil rights, consumer, or environmental groups. See L. Gutiérrez and E. Lewis, "Education, Participation, and Capacity Building in Community Organizing with Women of Color," in *Community Organizing and Community Building for Health*, ed. M. Minkler (New Brunswick, N.J.: Rutgers University Press. 1997).

151. See J. M. Swales, "English as Tyrannosaurus Rex," *World Englishes* 16, no.3 (1997): 73-82.

152. These difficulties have perhaps been experienced by migrant populations throughout history, though the severity of the problems vary across time and by population (e.g., between poor Jewish or Chinese American immigrant families in the early 1900s and professional immigrants today). Today, academic migrant families are among the more privileged in their countries of origin and their economic and social status is more secure in the United States than economic immigrants or political refugees.

153. This (and subsequent) example(s) are drawn from the interviews, focus groups, and surveys described below.

154. This story, shared in Korean at the focus group session for Asian mothers in 1996, was translated by Tae-Hee Hwang.

155. On multicultural models, see Rivera and Erlich, *Community Organizing in a Diverse Society*; and Gutiérrez, "Multicultural Perspectives." On feminist models, see Rivera and Erlich, *Community Organizing in a Diverse Society*; Janice L. Ristock and Joan Pennel, *Community Research as Empowerment: Feminist Links, Postmodern Interruptions* (Toronto: Oxford University Press, 1996); and Lorraine Gutiérrez, "Multicultural Community Organizing," in *Social Work in the 21st Century*, 249-259.

156. The "Daily Hassles Scale" was developed by A. D. Kanner, J. C. Coyne, C. Schaefer, and R. S. Lazarus. See Kanner et. al., "Comparison of Two Modes of Stress Measurement: Daily Hassles, Uplifts, and Major Life Events to Health Status," *Journal of Behavioral Medicine* 4 (1981): 1-39.

Index

abject, the, 6, 16n5, 66n41
Abramovitz, M., 272n37, 274n66, 274n74, 275n75
Abu-Lughod, Lila, 90n41, 113n29
accommodation. *See* adaptation
accommodations. *See* housing
accountability, 12, 188, 249
acculturation, 219n87, 219n97, 250-52. *See also* adaptation, assimilation
adaptation (psychosocial), 10, 26, 27, 173, 186-88, 193, 267. *See also* acculturation, assimilation
Addams, Jane, 12, 26, 29-30, 33n20, 47, 241, 243-44, 248-51, 256-57, 273n63, 275n75, 275n78
aesthetics, 8, 40, 62, 66n41, 67n48, 116, 201, 204, 206
affect (feeling): associated with alien abduction, 23, 30, 166-68, 170; associated with artists' expatriatism, 181, 189, 197, 202, 204, 206, 211-12; associated with nationalism, 23, 228, 230, 232-33; as pathology, 137, 141n14; of power and powerlessness, 17n8, 156, 162, 164, 165, 267
Aflatun, Inji, 105-7
Africa, 33n18, 55, 63n13, 65n29, 84, 94-95, 207-8, 238. *See also* South Africa
Africans, 10, 65n25, 95, 226, 238. *See also* South Africa
African Americans, 15, 21, 42, 94-95, 108, 164, 240, 242-43, 249, 254-56
African National Congress (ANC), 129, 133, 146nn45-46, 147n48, 148n60. *See also* South Africa
Aguilar, Marian. *See* Jansen, Golie
ahl al-kitab [people of the book], 99, 102
Ahmad, Aijaz, 87n13
Ahmed, Leila, 64n20
Ahwal Shakhsiyya. *See* Personal Status Code
alterity. *See* otherness
Akhtar, Salman, 203, 218n77
Al-Bissi, Sana', 108

alien (strange, unfamiliar), the, 7, 11, 32nn8-9, 37, 38, 43, 56, 131, 158-59, 180-81, 184-92, 213; pain as, 61; woman as, 92, 105;
aliens: extraterrestrials, xii, 7, 22-23, 26, 30, 43, 153-74; non-citizens, 59, 100, 147n47
alienation: experience of, 23, 25, 80, 193-94, 195-98, 211, 213n3; relation to allegory, 120, 144n32, 145n44; social processes of, 11, 30, 49n8, 55, 57, 81, 224
alienation effect, 23, 54, 116, 107. *See also* defamiliarization
allegory, 12, 47, 78, 120-21, 123, 127-33, 135, 139, 143n30, 144n32, 144n33, 145n44, 147n50, 149n61, 149n65, 151n69, 194
al-Saadawi, Nawal, 107
al-Sa'id, Amina, 106, 107
Alter, Peter, 32n13
Altorki, Soraya, 111n14
Amaru, Tupac, 229
ambivalence, 40, 166, 182, 214n5, 247
Ambrosino, R., 269n5
Amnesty International, xii, 131, 148n57, 149n63
Americanization, 9, 22, 240, 247, 250-55, 268
Anderson, Benedict, 16n3, 32n11, 32n13, 50, 54, 63, 223, 229, 234n10, 236n37
Anderson, Sarah, John Cavanagh, Chris Harman, and Betsy Leondar-Wright, 65n28
Andrews, George Reid, 234n13
animality, 23, 60, 61, 158
animals, 4, 61, 156, 161, 167, 207, 228
anthropocentrism *See* humanism
anthropology, ix, xi, 14-15, 25, 28, 38-39, 47, 51, 53, 55, 71-90, 114. *See also* ethnography
anxiety, 47-48, 50n34, 82, 94, 156, 204, 215n16, 264. *See also* fear
apartheid, xii, 3-4, 10-11, 20-21, 27, 29, 38, 42, 46-47, 62, 115, 126-39

Notes on Contributors

Margot Badran is a women's studies scholar and historian who specializes in the Middle East and Islam. Currently a Fulbright professor in the Women's Studies Center at San'a' University in Yemen, she has recently taught on feminism and Islam at the University of Chicago. Her most recent book is *Feminists, Islam, and Nation: Gender and the Making of Modern Egypt.* She is the author of numerous articles, the latest of which is "Locating Feminism: The Collapse of Religious and Secular Discourses" (forthcoming).

John Charles Chasteen has taught Latin American history at the University of North Carolina since 1990. An early practitioner of Latin America's new cultural history, he is the author of *Heroes on Horseback: A Life and Times of the Last Gaucho Caudillos* (Albuquerque: University of New Mexico Press, 1995), as well as of articles on machismo, the discourse of insurgency in Latin America, and knife dueling. Chasteen's translations from Spanish and Portuguese have won him wide recognition, as well as an MLA Scaglione Prize in 1997. His current research is on the social history of Latin American popular dance.

Coco Owen most recently worked in the counseling center and as the Assistant Dean of Student Services at Reed College in Portland, Oregon. She also taught psychology at Mt. Hood Community College. Owen received her Ph.D. in clinical psychology, with a specialization in cultural psychology, from the California School of Professional Psychology, San Diego. She also holds an M.A. in comparative literature from UCLA and lived in Paris in the mid-80s.

Peter Redfield is Assistant Professor of Anthropology at the University of North Carolina, Chapel Hill. Trained at Harvard and U.C. Berkeley, he has moved between cultural anthropology and history of science while holding posts at Deep Springs College, UCLA, and Johns Hopkins. He is the author of *Space in the Tropics: From Convicts to Rockets in French Guiana* (University of California Press, 2000), and is currently working on a book about the organization *Médecins Sans Frontières*/Doctors Without Borders.

Izumi Sakamoto recently finished her Ph.D. in Social Work and Social Psychology, and her Culture and Cognition Certificate, at the University of Michigan. Her dissertation was entitled, "Negotiating Multiple Cultural Contexts: Flexibility and Constraint in the Cultural Selfways of Japanese Academic Migrants." As a Fulbright scholar from Japan, she was the founding director of the International Families Outreach Project at the University of Michigan. She has co-authored journal articles on cultural identities, as well as a book chapter on empowering women of color. Sakamoto assumed the post of Assistant Professor of Social Work at the University of Toronto in 2002.

Rebecca Saunders holds a Ph.D. in Comparative Literature from the University of Wisconsin-Madison and currently teaches in the Department of English at Illinois State University. Her work, which focuses on literary and cultural theory, and on late 19th-and 20th century European and African literatures, has appeared in *Cultural Critique, PMLA, Modern Fiction Studies, Novel,* and *Romanic Review.* She is currently completing a book entitled *At God's Funeral: Lamentation and the Culture of Modernity.*

Silvia Tomášková, after emigrating from Czechoslovakia in 1981, received degrees in anthropology and Slavic literature from McGill, Yale, and U.C. Berkeley, and held posts at Deep Springs, Harvard, and the University of Texas at Austin. An archaeologist specializing in the Old World Paleolithic, she is currently Assistant Professor of Anthropology and Women's Studies at the University of North Carolina, Chapel Hill. Her interests include the history and politics of science as well as its practice and her publications include contributions to *Aspekt,* a feminist journal based in Bratislava.

Michael E. Zimmerman is Professor and Chair of the Department of Philosophy, Tulane University. In addition to publishing 80 academic articles, he has authored three books, *Eclipse of the Self: The Development of Heidegger's Concept of Authenticity, Heidegger's Confrontation with Modernity,* and *Contesting Earth's Future: Radical Ecology and Postmodernity.* His research interests include contemporary continental philosophy, environmental philosophy, Asian religions, and paranormal phenomena.